INDIGENOUS HEALING PSYCHOLOGY

"A remarkable culmination of Katz's invaluable life-long work with Indigenous healers, *Indigenous Healing Psychology* is a brilliant, groundbreaking work connecting psychology to its roots so it can more truly become a force for healing and social change. A genuine invitation to a breathtaking journey that is a rare treasure. Just what psychology so desperately needs."

JOAN BORYSENKO, PH.D.,
NEW YORK TIMES BESTSELLING AUTHOR OF
MINDING THE BODY, MENDING THE MIND

"A deeply honest book showing the greatest respect for Indigenous knowledge. You can see how our traditional Anishnabe teachings can offer a path to healing psychology. *Indigenous Healing Psychology* shows how psychology can finally begin to heal our people."

DANNY MUSQUA, ANISHNABE ELDER,
KEESEEKOOSE FIRST NATION

"Katz shares his extraordinary journey through world cultures and methods for inner and community work. Psychology will only be the better for encompassing such powerful Indigenous wisdom. This book is a mind-expanding gift to the reader, a well-researched offering to psychology, and a force for good."

DANIEL GOLEMAN, PH.D., AUTHOR OF
EMOTIONAL INTELLIGENCE

"Katz convincingly argues that the inclusion of Indigenous spiritual worldviews in mental health intervention and treatment will produce better client outcomes and better relationships among people no matter where they live. He offers the reader a profound challenge that is supported with Indigenous ways of knowing and living. His long-awaited book is beautifully crafted, clearly written, convincing, and logically organized—complete with a wealth of thought-provoking material written in a confident, authoritative voice. Anyone who carefully and thoughtfully studies these pages will come out a richer, well-informed person who will view spirit, the sacred, place, and connectedness through a discerning lens."

JOSEPH E. TRIMBLE, PH.D.,
DISTINGUISHED PROFESSOR OF PSYCHOLOGY AT
WESTERN WASHINGTON UNIVERSITY

"*Indigenous Healing Psychology* presents a powerful and inspirational pedagogy into Western and Indigenous healing traditions; it offers valuable guideposts to ways we can all transform ourselves to meet the challenges of our fast-changing world."

HARVEY KNIGHT, INDIGENOUS CULTURAL ADVISOR TO THE
REGIONAL PSYCHIATRIC CENTRE, SASKATOON

"Katz journeys into the heart of what psychology is and what it can be. He exposes the Western myopia that limits the espoused goal of psychology, i.e. understanding the human experience of mind, body, and our relationship to the world. His personal experiences of navigating formal psychology and his subsequent lessons learned from traditional healers point to the ignored facets of spirituality, humanism, culture, and community that cannot be separated from a truly holistic human psychology and healing."

DENNIS NORMAN, ED.D., ABPP, FACULTY CHAIR OF THE
HARVARD UNIVERSITY NATIVE AMERICAN PROGRAM AND
SENIOR PSYCHOLOGIST AT MASSACHUSETTS GENERAL HOSPITAL

"This book is a must-read for all students of indigenous psychology. It teaches all the essentials. Consistent with the experiential focus of the wisdom tradition, Katz does not preach; he tells what he knows experientially. The reader is invited to join him on a personal journey that took him from the lecture halls of Harvard to paths in search of the healing wisdom of the Indigenous peoples. This account of Katz is testimonial to the possibility that doing research in Indigenous psychology is a spiritual journey that can be profoundly fulfilling and transformative for the reader as well."

LOUISE SUNDARARAJAN, PH.D., ED.D., FELLOW OF THE AMERICAN PSYCHOLOGICAL ASSOCIATION, FOUNDER AND CHAIR OF THE TASK FORCE ON INDIGENOUS PSYCHOLOGY

"In this engaging and excellent book, Katz gives the reader a foundation for understanding the quality and depth of Indigenous healing. He has learned from the elders to do it in the best possible way: by telling stories that illuminate complex concepts and make them relatable and usable."

MELINDA A. GARCÍA, PH.D., AUTHOR OF *SOCIETY OF INDIAN PSYCHOLOGISTS' COMMENTARY ON THE AMERICAN PSYCHOLOGICAL ASSOCIATION CODE OF ETHICS*

"*Indigenous Healing Psychology* is a powerful, provocative, and enlivening book that, through Katz's expansive and inspiring voice, offers psychology just what it needs to hear in order to fulfill its promise to be truly healing and equitable. I know from my own work as a psychologist and counselor that people are searching for precisely what *Indigenous Healing Psychology* offers. Celebrating diversity in all its myriad manifestations, this is a bold and exhilarating book."

NITI SETH, ED.D., ACADEMIC COUNSELOR AT THE HARVARD UNIVERSITY BUREAU OF STUDY COUNSEL AND DEAN OF THE GRADUATE SCHOOL OF PSYCHOLOGY AND COUNSELING AT CAMBRIDGE COLLEGE

"*Indigenous Healing Psychology* is a fascinating look at the world of psychology as a discipline in need of healing. Katz traces the evolution of his encounters with some of the giants of psychology at Harvard as well as honored Indigenous healers in other cultures. This book is a major contribution to revisioning mainstream psychology by returning it to its fundamental commitments to diversity, cultural meanings, human potential, and social justice."

STEPHEN MURPHY-SHIGEMATSU,
COFOUNDER OF THE LIFEWORKS PROGRAM
OF INTEGRATIVE LEARNING AT
STANFORD UNIVERSITY

INDIGENOUS HEALING PSYCHOLOGY

Honoring the Wisdom of the First Peoples

RICHARD KATZ, PH.D.

Healing Arts Press

Rochester, Vermont • Toronto, Canada

Healing Arts Press
One Park Street
Rochester, Vermont 05767
www.HealingArtsPress.com

Text stock is SFI certified

Healing Arts Press is a division of Inner Traditions International

Note to the reader: *This book is intended as an informational guide. The remedies, approaches, and techniques described herein are meant to supplement, and not to be a substitute for, professional medical care or treatment. They should not be used to treat a serious ailment without prior consultation with a qualified health care professional.*

Library of Congress Cataloging-in-Publication Data
Names: Katz, Richard, 1937– author.
Title: Indigenous healing psychology : honoring the wisdom of the first peoples / Richard Katz.
Description: Rochester, Vermont : Healing Arts Press, 2017. | Includes bibliographical references and index.
Identifiers: LCCN 2017038629 (print) | LCCN 2017012046 (e-book) | ISBN 9781620552674 (paperback) | ISBN 9781620552681 (e-book)
Subjects: LCSH: Ethnopsychology. | Spiritual healing. | BISAC: PSYCHOLOGY / Ethnopsychology. | BODY, MIND & SPIRIT / Healing / Prayer & Spiritual. | SOCIAL SCIENCE / Anthropology / Cultural.
Classification: LCC GN502 (print) | LCC GN502 .K37 2017 (e-book) | DDC 155.8/2—dc23
LC record available at https://lccn.loc.gov/2017012046

Printed and bound in the United States by Lake Book Manufacturing, Inc. The text stock is SFI certified. The Sustainable Forestry Initiative® program promotes sustainable forest management.

10   9   8   7   6   5   4   3

Text design by Virginia Scott Bowman and layout by Priscilla Baker
This book was typeset in Garamond Premier Pro with Hypatia Sans, Gill Sans, and Avenir used as display typefaces

To send correspondence to the author of this book, mail a first-class letter to the author c/o Inner Traditions • Bear & Company, One Park Street, Rochester, VT 05767, and we will forward the communication, or contact the author directly at **rkatz@firstnationsuniversity.ca**.

*To the Indigenous elders and healers who entrust me
with the responsibility of offering their teachings as a
path toward healing psychology; and to those who, in
reading this book, will hopefully feel a
healing psychology in their lives.*

Contents

— ☙ —

PART TWO

THE WORKINGS OF PSYCHOLOGY

PART THREE

A FUTURE OF PSYCHOLOGIES

A NOTE ON TOPICS COVERED

Indigenous Healing Psychology offers a pathway to an enhanced perspective and a call to action; it is not a textbook. Therefore, rather than providing comprehensive coverage of all the major topics in mainstream psychology—the task of a text—*Indigenous Healing Psychology* seeks a decolonization of mainstream psychology, seeking ways it can expand beyond its Western intellectual and cultural borders to better serve all people, especially those denied access to its empowering resources.

A central element of the Indigenous perspectives presented in this book is the extensive reciprocal interpenetrations and merging among areas of knowledge. As Danny Musqua, an Anishnabe elder, says: "All ways of knowing, all teachings are connected. One thing leads to another, making it more clear." Therefore, from an Indigenous perspective, the topics in mainstream psychology, even the chapters in this book, are arbitrary, artificial, and ultimately unnecessary divisions of a knowledge-creating whole. Also, though similar terms may be used in the mainstream and Indigenous approaches to psychology, they typically can have very different meanings, emerging as they do from their very different cultural contexts. For example, the term *self* within a mainstream perspective emphasizes an individually based experience with clearly felt boundaries, while *self* within an Indigenous perspective emphasizes a communally and spiritually infused experience with permeable boundaries that still maintains ultimate respect for an individual's integrity. And finally, *Indigenous Healing Psychology* introduces important new dimensions into the study of psychology that cut across and go beyond any particular mainstream topic; for example, the critical importance of culture, consciousness transformations, and spirituality; the need to recognize and honor diversity; and the cultivation of healing and the commitment to social justice. These dimensions are just now beginning to be discussed in mainstream texts, though still superficially.

While introducing new viewpoints, *Indigenous Healing Psychology* seeks to reshape the landscape of mainstream psychology into less rigid, separate, and separating categories in order to expand the discipline's potential for growth. Still, it can be helpful to see how chapters in this book have particular relevance to topics historically and more recently addressed in mainstream psychology. The list below suggests some of these connections, mentioning some mainstream psychology topics relevant to each chapter.

Chapter One—what is psychology
Chapter Two—research; learning; states of consciousness
Chapter Three—states of consciousness; personality; psychology of religion
Chapter Four—research
Chapter Five—development over the life span; motivation; intelligence
Chapter Six—therapy and counseling; psychological disorders; emotions, stress, and health
Chapter Seven—behavior in social contexts
Chapter Eight—what is psychology

Acknowledgments

I wish to thank the many, many people who've contributed to making this book happen. But I know I can't possibly get it totally right—there will be both omissions and inaccurate characterizations. So first I ask forgiveness if I offend anyone: those omissions and inaccuracies are my responsibility and not meant as a sign of disrespect.

The inspiration as well as the foundation for this book takes shape well before its particular birth. Beginning in 1968, there are several Indigenous communities where I live and work; that's where the seed for this book is planted and its growth nourished. I'm taught by elders and healers about spiritual health and social justice and charged by them with the task of trying to bring a healing influence to psychology and thereby increase that field's service to all. Through years of clinical work and community consultations, teaching, and writing—culminating in *Indigenous Healing Psychology*—I'm attempting to fulfill that responsibility.

There are so many wonderful, caring, and helpful people in the villages where I live and work, people who bring my family and me "home," so many that I can't mention all of their individual names. This is not a sign of disrespect but of pragmatics, for it is those people who feed and nurture this book. To them a warm and grateful thanks. When I do name a few of them, such as those with the most explicit responsibility for teaching me, perhaps they can help represent the many.

Here are those places and their teachers as well as those who help me connect with those teachers. A deep gratitude to all. I am honored to be part of your lives. In the Kalahari Desert: Kinachau, Kxao Tjimburu, =Oma Djo, =Oma !'Homg!ausi, Tshao Matze, and !Xam n!a'an and his family; Megan Biesele, Richard Lee, and Lorna Marshall; Kxao Jonah /O/Oo, Tshao Xumi, and /Ukxa; and the people of /Kae/kae. On the Sicangu Lakota Rosebud Reservation: Joe Eagle Elk and Stanley Redbird; Vickie Eagle Elk and Jerry and Robbie Mohatt; and the people of Rosebud. In Fiji: Sevuloni Bose, Ratu Civo, and Saimoni Vatu; John Lum On, Fred Lyons, Ifereimi and Sereana Naivota, Asesela Ravuvu, Chris and Vula Saumaiwai, and Suliana Siwatibau; and the people of Naqara. In Alaska: Rachel Craig, Angayuqaq Oscar Kawagley, and Howard Luke. And in Saskatchewan: Mary Lee, Walter and Maria Linklater, Danny and Thelma Musqua, Tony and Emma Sand, Sid Fiddler, and Harvey Knight.

I know I don't fully appreciate all the riches offered to me. For the ways in which this book demonstrates that I'm not always a good learner, I take full responsibility.

The concrete shaping of *Indigenous Healing Psychology* is a long time coming! In 1994, Sid Fiddler, then dean at the Saskatchewan Indian Federated College (SIFC), Saskatoon Campus, where I'm a faculty member, asks me to develop a new, culturally respectful introductory psychology class for our students. "You know the present situation," he says, "they're now taking a course that doesn't connect to their lives—and too often they fail it." Yes, I know that. Almost all our students are Indigenous, but with psychology being taught to them by others from a conventional, routinely unexamined Western perspective, our students feel alienated—unrecognized, unappreciated, erased, and thus oppressed. Psychology becomes just another instance of the long-standing and still-continuing process of colonization they and their families are resisting.

What a gift—an opportunity to do something that matters! I develop an introductory psychology course for our SIFC students, bringing in Indigenous perspectives so psychology becomes more a way of thinking, being, and doing they can see as their own—and they talk about being empowered through that connection. The power psychology exerts, often over them, can be transformed into an affirming and respectful power they can exercise in their own lives and the lives of others—to bring about more health and well-being. One student seems to say it all: "Now this is a psychology course I can understand—it speaks to me . . . and with me!"

Subsequently, that Indigenous-infused introductory psychology course grows as I continue teaching it at SIFC (which later becomes the First Nations University of Canada), and then in 2005 I begin offering it at the University of Saskatchewan to Indigenous students enrolled in what is now called the Aboriginal Student Achievement Program. Starting in 1998, I also work with selected materials from the course while teaching a seminar on culture and healing to University of Saskatchewan clinical psychology doctoral students.

The perspectives and materials in the course are also enhanced through my presentations at a number of conferences and gatherings. Two of the most important venues are also two of the most recent ones, gatherings where I'm encouraged to tell my story as a non-Indigenous psychologist working with and within Indigenous communities. The first is at Western Washington University—thanks to Joe Trimble and Jeff King for that invitation; the second is at the annual meeting of the Society for Indian Psychologists, and I'm grateful to Carolyn Barcus and Joe Trimble for that invitation and especially to Melinda García, whose loving persistence seals the deal, convincing me I have something to say to a group of Indigenous psychologists. Louise Sundararajan is also a guiding presence.

To all the students who are my teachers over the years, including Harvard College undergraduates; undergraduate and graduate students in the Department of Psychology at Brandeis University; master's degree students in the Community Psychology Program at the University of Alaska Fairbanks; and especially master's and doctoral students in the Counseling and Consulting Program at the Harvard Graduate School of Education and students I work with in Saskatchewan at both First Nations University of Canada and the University of Saskatchewan; and to all those who listen intently and openly during my talks—my gratitude. Again, there are so many bright and brightening faces, so many deeply thoughtful and intensively feeling exchanges—too many to mention individually but none thereby passed over. I'm inspired being with you. I feel teaching involves lots of energy—I give a lot, and a lot more comes back in return!

Insightful advice about the *Indigenous Healing Psychology* manuscript comes at differing stages of its completion, often encouraging me to turn a corner, or even restart the writing. I really appreciate the generous help of Marie Cantlon, Allan Casey, Melinda García, Tanya LaFontaine, Margot Lasher, Stephen Murphy-Shigematsu, Danny Musqua, Valerie Naquin, Mario Núñez-Molina, Tara Turner, and especially Niti Seth, whose dedication is only eclipsed by her incisive reflections. I'm lucky to work with the people at Inner Traditions, a publishing house that still has a commitment to make their books better; in particular thanks to those with whom I interact most directly: Jennie Marx, Erica Robinson, Patricia Rydle, and, in the close background, Jeanie Levitan, a most talented editor and loyal supporter. I treasure that my kids contribute creatively and generously to the book: Laurel, responsible for the map presentations, Alex for logistical support, and Hannah for her inspirational painting of the butterfly, which serves as a guiding beacon.

It seems ironic that I leave for the last what is really the most important support for this book's coming into existence—my family. Perhaps it's because their influence is so pervasive and therefore hard to pin down, even describe. And I'm aware that what I say may seem trite, even considered platitudes, since every other author seems to say similarly glowing things about her or his family in the acknowledgments. But I think that's because they can actually mean what they say, as families support authors in profound ways. For me a platitude is a truth either misunderstood or misapplied or overused—but still in its essence a truth.

There are two families: my ex-wife Mary Maxwell West and our kids, Laurel and her spouse, John, and Alex and his spouse, Barbara; and my ex-wife Verna St. Denis and our kids, now deceased Adam and Hannah. And the grandchildren: Ruby, Abel, and Jayden. Yes, the next generations are concrete, joyful, and expanding futures.

Family is the rhythm beneath and within this book, enabling and encouraging the learnings that fuel it. For example, living in a small Fijian village with my first family is living fully, and our substance and joys rest on all of our commitments to being there.

I'm a big ocean guy, and I joyfully engage in the waves and the tides. The ocean heals, and as it heals, it teaches: there is a time and space for every thing. When the tide is in, certain things are possible; when it's out, other things become possible. The ocean shows us the rhythms in the universe that holds and cares for us all.

I hope that *Indigenous Healing Psychology,* traveling through these various places of opportunity and promise, being shaped and reshaped by so many listening and teaching spaces, is now ready for a wider audience. Ready, I hope, for you, the reader, to realize the potential of psychology to serve the well-being of all and thus encourage social justice. Informed by Indigenous perspectives, psychology can now become a more effective model of best practices—for all.

Author royalties from the sale of Indigenous Healing Psychology *are given to the Indigenous people who make this book possible.*

NAMES AND NAMING:
EXPRESSIONS OF CULTURE AND IDENTITY

The names of Indigenous places, people, and experiences used in *Indigenous Healing Psychology* emerge from a fundamental respect of a people's right and privilege to construct and choose their own names. The process of self-identification can be empowering, an important part of decolonization process. I only use names that are used by the Indigenous people I live and work with, and considered as appropriate and respectful by them; not, for example, names generated by colonial intrusions and now rejected by the people themselves.

Sometimes these names are in a people's own Indigenous language, and sometimes they are translated into English—and then only to facilitate readability and to reflect common and respected usage. Often there are various spellings of names and places, especially with English translations and transcriptions of Indigenous words. I use spellings as preferred by the specific Indigenous elders who speak in this book.

Historically, the naming process—central to culture and identity—is also entangled with politics. Names of Indigenous places and people most typically accepted in the West are fraught with the distortions of oppression and racism. There is the shameful history of Indigenous people being named by their colonizers, without the colonizers acknowledging that naming act as a racist means of control. The naming process typically devolves into an act of labeling or pinning people down into limited characteristics, often accompanied by dehumanizing connotations.

The process of naming can also be fluid, reflecting changes in historical understandings and cultural priorities. All the while, Indigenous names and naming ceremonies persist and provide strength within the culture.

To facilitate a more correct pronunciations of certain frequently used words from the Indigenous cultures central to *Indigenous Healing Psychology*, the following guide is offered; approximate pronunciation appears in [ ].

Ju/'hoan [Zhun-twa]   Fiji [Feejee]
Ju/'hoansi [Zhun-twasi]   mana [mahna]
/Kae/kae [Xai-xai]   Naqara [Nangara]
n/om [num]   Ratu Civo [Ratu Theevo]
=Oma Djo [Toma Zho]   yaqona [yahngona]
!aia [kia]

"Things of Power"

Releasing the Healing Potentials of Psychology

It's 1968, my first trip to the Kalahari Desert in northwest Botswana. I'm interviewing =Oma Djo, an experienced and respected healer from the hunting-gathering Ju/'hoansi. His village of /Kae/kae, with nearly one hundred people, is defined by small grass-thatched dwellings set deep within the sandy, bush-scattered expanse of the Kalahari. =Oma Djo is my friend and guide into Ju/'hoan healing and community. As is the custom for field research, I have my tape recorder running during our interviews; its external microphone, extended on its cord lying in the sand, is facing him. I don't want to miss a word.

There is no electricity or other tools or signs of the so-called modern world of technology and communication among the /Kae/kae Ju/'hoansi at this time. What we now consider dated modes of communication, such as my tape recorder with its external mic, are not in =Oma Djo's world. He has rarely seen any kind of tape recorder before the one I bring.

I have the music from several Ju/'hoan healing dances, their central ritual of healing and community development. Today, I'm playing back some of those recorded healing dance sounds for =Oma Djo—and at his request, playing those sounds over and over. The very idea of a tape recorder, which, as =Oma Djo says, "captures our voices inside a little box, so we can hear them over and over again," deeply impresses him: "Now this is something definitely powerful," he says. And now, jolted by =Oma Djo's fresh vision, as I think in a manner less encumbered by habitual but superficial patterns of understanding, seeing as if never before what this machine *actually* makes happen, it also becomes for me "something definitely powerful."

=Oma Djo's hunting-gathering world contains very special, and extremely valuable, wisdom experiences and teachings. We as humans have lived 99 percent of our history as hunter-gatherers. As a member of a group that provides a contemporary window into that lifestyle, =Oma Djo offers glimpses into understandings and insights that occupy a central place in our evolution and, therefore, potentially a central role in guiding our future development. In short, I believe it makes more than sense that we listen to =Oma Djo—it is imperative.

Suddenly, in the middle of the interview, =Oma Djo leans forward, a deep curiosity furrowing his brow. He begins to question me about the tape recorder, first remarking on the true wonder of this machine whose functioning I take for granted. With his perplexed look, sharpened by the sincerity of his questions and softened by the joking current of his teasing, =Oma Djo brings me to a new awareness about "things of power" and that particular thing of power—this tape recorder that in replaying the healing dance releases anew its potential to bring about healing and community development.

"There are times," he says, "when I sit looking at this," pointing to the tape recorder, "and I forget it's a box. . . . I imagine seeing the people whose voices are singing right in front of me. You know, if you look at it, it's just a piece of metal. *That* is certainly not anything that's going to throw back your voices at you. I wonder how it works?"

I labor to explain and start simply. "What happens is, when you make sound, this little part," I point to the microphone, "picks up . . ."

=Oma Djo interrupts, not impatiently but eagerly. "Look," he comments, "I know about that, I know about the part the voice goes in. It goes in here," he says, pointing to the microphone, "and then it goes up that line," pointing to the microphone wire, "and then it goes into that main box," nodding toward the tape recorder, "and the voice is collected there. But what I suspect is that this thing," pointing directly and sharply to the microphone, "this thing is not really hearing. This big box it goes into is the one that's got the real power in it. This little thing," now touching the mic almost dismissively, "is just a pickup; it's like an extension. The sound goes through and then *really* gets caught up in the main box."

All I can say is, "That's it."

=Oma Djo smiles and pushes on. "You should be telling us about things like this because what I still want to know is, how does it work? How do its insides work?"

Retreating to my only resource, a form of popular and for me still "fuzzy" physics, I begin talking about energy waves and sound waves—concepts I'm actually not very familiar with.

"We already know those things," =Oma Djo assures me, without being condescending, "but what I really want to know is, how does it work?"

I have to admit that while there are people back home who make the tape recorder and therefore know how it works, I'm not one of them.

=Oma Djo looks at me with great sadness. "That's too bad, Dick. For whenever we're given a thing of power by our ancestors—and surely this thing that captures our voices is powerful—we're always told how it works and how to use it."

When =Oma Djo speaks of a "thing of power," he means literally things imbued with *n/om,* the spiritual energy that permeates Ju/'hoan life, making healing and community development possible. But he's talking more profoundly about all things of spiritually infused power; all things that motivate, mystify, and inspire us; all things that help unfold the complexities of our lives. =Oma Djo is cautioning against releasing a thing of power without knowing about its workings, without knowing how to use it for healing and the common good. In his world, there is never a *full* understanding of these things of power—

true mysteries remain and are respected as such—but there is always an attempt to release a thing of power within a context of the best understanding then available. =Oma Djo's teaching shapes my life, and it has guided my use of that contemporary thing of power, the discipline of psychology.

The power of psychology, too often expressed in sociopolitical terms, and subverted for purposes of control, rather than in spiritually infused terms for purposes of healing, is affirmed throughout our lives in so many ways—positively, negatively, and typically a mixture of both. I know this intimately because as a Ph.D. in clinical psychology, I am both a provider and, like many of us, a recipient of psychological services. There are psychological assessments that open doors for persons to pursue previously unknown dreams. At the same time, there are psychological tests that reinforce, even create stereotypes that consign people to paths of lost opportunities. Also, there are psychotherapies that offer understanding and relief from deeply troubling anxieties and depressions, at times opening up possibilities for embarking on a healthier life path. At the same time, there are psychotherapies that overrely on diagnostic categories that can function more as moral or political labels than expressions of psychological insight, thereby not only predetermining but also limiting therapeutic outcomes. And there are community development projects that encourage enhanced participation and social justice. At the same time, there are community development projects that maintain an oppressive status quo being wielded by those in positions of power, prestige, and privilege.

Psychology pervades our lives but unfortunately not always for the good. How can we encourage psychology to return to its healing roots, where the welfare of all is the commitment and social justice the aim? Put another way, how can we break one common sociopolitical expression of psychology's power; namely, its stranglehold over health and therapeutic services? This stranglehold too often undermines our personal responsibility to develop our full potential by insisting that psychological professionals, studying us from the outside, are the experts in telling us who we are—thereby ignoring that vast wealth of intimate self-knowledge that we, as residents in our lives, possess. And this stranglehold too often targets those who are already marginalized—in part through that very stranglehold. That is when and how psychology as a professional discipline and institution becomes a vehicle of and for colonialism. When racism and oppression and their consequent diminution of others infects mainstream psychology, its power becomes overpowering, denying diverse nonmainstream groups their rightful access to healing resources and social justice. These resources then become the concealed or hoarded riches of psychology.*

=Oma Djo is opening a door to what in the West remains a relatively unexamined but essential source of knowledge about psychology; namely, the collective wisdom of our *first psychologists*—Indigenous healers and elders, like =Oma Djo, who are from communities who are the original inhabitants of lands throughout the world. In this book, we meet and learn from these elders and healers who welcome me into their homes; people whose wisdom I deeply respect; people I wish to honor and support with this book. For nearly fifty years now, I spend varying periods of time living and working with those elders and healers from among the Ju/'hoansi in the Kalahari Desert, the Fijians from the South Pacific, the Sicangu Lakota people from the Rosebud Reservation, and the Cree and Anishnabe First Nations people from Saskatchewan, as well as the Athabascan and Inuit peoples in Alaska. Though only the Ju/'hoansi still live primarily as hunter-gatherers, the original human mode of adaptation, all Indigenous people speaking in this book retain strong social, cultural, and spiritual links to their respective ancient

---

*The grip of colonialism is pervasive and dangerously surreptitious. I grow up as an outsider to mainstream Anglo-Saxon Christian (Western) culture, and I am taught to question assumptions and arbitrary authority. I try from an early age to fight against inequities, especially those fueled by racist attitudes. *Indigenous Healing Psychology* is one attempt to resist that colonial structure. But as I still function within an overarching Western structure, I benefit from colonialism's rewards and privileges, which are fed by resources expropriated from those denied power.

ancestors and have strong ties to their ancestral lands, which function as both a source for and anchor to their traditional teachings.

Indigenous Healing Psychology only *suggests* emphases central to Indigenous approaches that enhance Western approaches, to highlight certain themes that are healing; this book is not prescriptive, with no offering of a detailed or complete picture of how that enhanced psychology looks. And most important, *Indigenous Healing Psychology* emphasizes *principles* rather than *discrete practices,* acknowledging that practices exist within a worldview and to assimilate them without taking their worldview context into consideration is appropriation, an expression of colonization.

We look beyond the limits of mainstream psychology toward these first psychologists. As we reconnect with these evolutionary roots of psychology, we reapproach original meanings, derived from ancient Greek, of the word and world of "psychology"; namely, the study (logos) of the soul or spirit or enlivening breath (psyche). We can then better journey toward envisioning a healing psychology.

PART ONE

PREPARATIONS

CHAPTER ONE

"If We Can't Measure It, Is It Real?"

Entering the Profession of Psychology

THE HARVARD EXPERIENCE

Seeking a professional path toward working, in a helpful way, with those unjustly denied access to health and healing resources, I enroll in the clinical psychology doctoral program at Harvard University in 1961. For someone feeling as I do, an outsider who questions the assumed and often unspoken principles of the mainstream and realizes there is something very important, something spiritual beyond and within what is accepted as "reality," it is, I find out, a strange place to land.

At Harvard, clinical psychology, which functions as part of the program in personality psychology, sits within the Department of Social Relations, where it is joined and enriched by programs in developmental psychology, social psychology, sociology, and social anthropology. This cross-disciplinary milieu, powered in its origins by an openness to explore and deal with a full range of human experience, is a rich and challenging environment. When I'm in the clinical psychology program, a consideration of "grand" theories of personality still prevails, offering a wholistic perspective, while emphasizing a full range of functions, attributes, and motivations. As a result, there is some respite in my graduate training from the prevailing and more limited focus on psychopathology that characterizes clinical psychology in general.

But the Department of Social Relations is increasingly under siege,* especially by the experimental psychologists, who historically and fervently maintain their work as the "real" scientific approach and who seek to be exemplars of mainstream psychology. These experimental psychologists, so named because they are committed to a tightly controlled laboratory-influenced or experimental research methodology, now constitute the Department of Psychology. Separated off from social relations in its own building, featuring closed-door experimental laboratories, the Department of Psychology is newly empowered by the behavioristic model championed by the emerging Harvard superstar, B. F. Skinner.

MAINSTREAM PSYCHOLOGY

I use the terms *mainstream* or *conventional* psychology in a primarily practical sense. I draw on material covered in standard psychology texts, as well as my own years of experience being defined as outside the mainstream, to generate a description of this conventional approach. But this description is only a practical approximation, not a definition, and clearly not definitive.

I occasionally use some synonyms for mainstream or conventional, each touching on a particular and more theoretical definitional aspect of this prevailing psychology. For example, the terms *Western* and *Eurocentric psychology* refer to mainstream psychology's roots in the work of European and North American psychologists and identify a psychology that dominates not only in the geographic west but in those areas throughout the world that are influenced by Western culture and thinking. The irony is that some of the more philosophically rigorous

---

*Founded in 1946, the Social Relations program as an independent entity formally ends in 1972, with the establishment of the Department of Psychology and Social Relations, and then it's further buried into the mainstream, as in 1985 it's incorporated back into a department now simply called the Department of Psychology.

and humanistic psychological theorizing originates among European psychologists—but this countercurrent to the mainstream is typically and incorrectly dismissed by the mainstream as "only" philosophical and therefore not belonging in psychology, which is a "scientific" discipline. The adjective *positivistic*—as in positivistic psychology—highlights mainstream psychology's experimental, behaviorally oriented epistemology and research methodology, in contrast to a more humanistic perspective. Finally, the adjective *biomedical* is employed to signify mainstream psychology's commitment to biological (including neurological and genetic) dimensions of human nature as most fundamental and predictive, instead of social or cultural dimensions.

Yielding under the influence of the self-proclaimed scientific rigor of these behaviorists, social relations begins to wilt in its more humanistic commitments. For example, I soon discover that clinical psychology's actual commitment is to do research showing why psychotherapies *don't* work rather than to train people to do effective therapy. And instead of working to change the system, so that those unfairly underserved are treated with dignity and equity, the program is more committed to maintaining, even justifying, the status quo. Those commitments are especially dangerous because they are typically subtle and implicit. They are even more dangerous within the context of Harvard because they carry the imprimatur of the university and its arrogantly held standards, which falsely signal to the world that Harvard is not only a bastion of enlightened thinking, but it's also the "court of highest approval and last resort."

Mainstream or conventional psychology is increasingly in the hands of those who are trying to fortify psychology's control over people, claiming a special expertise over issues of identity and development, even to the point of telling people not only who they are but who they should become. It's in this regard that mainstream psychology can be seen as an instrument and institution of colonialism. For example, the mainstream typically proposes as *the* model of human nature what is in fact a Western model, and then, considering that Western model as *the* standard of excellence, it labels other non-Western models as "lacking" or "less developed"—shorthand for "inferior"—rather than considering them as valid and valuable contributions in their own uniqueness. This abusive, racist-fueled labeling not only erases personal identity and dignity but also denies rightful access to sociopolitical and economic resources.

COLONIALISM

Colonialism is a term often, and especially historically, associated with militarily powerful nation-states invading the territories of less militarily powerful peoples, imposing oppressive conditions on the conquered, and unjustly extracting material benefits from them. Colonialism's socioeconomic plundering relies on a strong cultural and value component, highlighted by the colonists' racist assumptions of the inferiority of the conquered and the presumed need for them to be "saved" by the colonists' "superior," even "more godly" way of life.

While Indigenous lands and resources are still being stolen today, colonialism now often emphasizes its subtler though no less dangerous and abusive forms. Without formal or extended military interventions—though instances of this still occur!—and instead leading with processes of cultural invasion or imperialism, this form of colonialism contains classic racist ideologies and their accompanying economic and political oppressions. Though it can be masked or falsely softened within this process of cultural imperialism, the colonialism remains deeply oppressive. When an Indigenous person feels, or is even told, his culture, history, identity is "inferior," even "worthless," damage is done to who one is, and, more poignantly, to who one becomes.

Colonialism is fed by *white privilege* that allows for pervasive, unacknowledged, and unmerited access to resources and benefits for people because of white skin color. White privilege is devastating, all the more so because it is stealthy, at times "excused" by the white person with phrases such as "but I didn't intend that to happen." Though there may not be identified invading nation-states, those oppressed by this colonialism are still being invaded with constant attacks on the intertwined resources of socioeconomic security and personal and cultural dignity. When racism fuels poverty, there is terrible suffering. When racism erases personal dignity, ignoring a person's basic humanity through demeaning and dismissive judgments, there is terrible injury.

And this contemporary colonialism, with its economic and personal integrity invasions, which are always linked together, is promoted obviously by multinational corporations in their greedy grasp for resources, as well as more secretively by powerful professions like psychology in their desire to define and control, telling us "who we are." It is this more subtle contemporary form of colonialism that can describe aspects of mainstream psychology's relationship to Indigenous cultures and psychologies. See *Decolonizing Methodologies* written by Maori scholar Linda Tuhiwai Smith (1999) for an eloquent discussion and searing indictment of how colonialism corrupts social science research.

But why use such a strong word as *colonialism* to describe mainstream psychology? That's a legitimate question. Strong words seem needed to highlight hidden purposes. *Indigenous Healing Psychology* seeks to offer data that colonialism *does* accurately describe certain processes, strategies, and structures within mainstream psychology. Documenting the many ways this contemporary colonialism of mainstream psychology robs Indigenous people, and other groups outside of the "mainstream," of their rights and resources, *Indigenous Healing Psychology* offers leverage for the acceptance of alternatives to the mainstream, alternatives that can now promote work toward healing and social justice.

Behind this mainstream effort at control is the fascination, even obsession, with measuring and categorizing people according to their scores on various measuring instruments—most of which implicitly express Western conceptions and standards of human nature. With this reductionist process of translating human complexity into numerical categories of culturally bounded and biased behavior, only traces of humanity remain.

I'm talking with a friend, Carol Phelps; we're both new doctoral students at Harvard, though she's enrolled in the experimental track in the Department of Psychology. We're discussing human motivation, in particular our need to understand things beyond the five senses. Under the sway of Skinner, Carol is already dedicated to translating the ambiguous, shifting characteristics of human nature into the manageable realm of measurement, preferably measuring human characteristics with a number—though she proudly calls her approach experimental, rejecting the term *reductionistic* as inaccurate and pejorative. "It's hard to measure what you're calling a 'motivation to explore the unseen,'" she comments. Then, only half jokingly, she adds, "And if we can't measure it, is it real?" "Do you mean 'does it matter'?" I suggest. "Well, if that's how *you want* to put it," she says, as she conveys more resignation than agreement.

In one sweep of the experimental paradigm, any motivation toward what is transcendent can be banished from psychology's purview. Like Skinner, Carol doesn't dismiss that motivation to explore the unseen as nonexistent but insists that, until it can be measured, it is just like being nonexistent, or at least "nonreal." And like Skinner, she's vastly optimistic about what "good" (i.e., experimental) research can do. "But if we work at it," she concludes, "we could eventually develop an experimental way of measuring even that motivation."

The Skinner-energized experimental paradigm follows inexorably down a fateful path. Once measured, or tested, people are ranked and on that basis excluded or included in various groups and privileges. IQ (intelligence quotient) testing is a paradigmatic enterprise, as people are earmarked for privileges or schools or jobs *if* they get high scores. And predictably, since the IQ tests are flawed, reflecting the values and skills of their white, male, middle-class inventors, historically marginalized groups (such as cultural and ethnic minorities) score poorly, "confirming" their exclusion from the affirmations and rewards they deserve and merit.

But at Harvard I find mentors, like psychologists Erik Erikson and Henry Murray, who are fighting mainstream psychology's reductionism (trying to reduce life's intrinsic complexities into manageable but limiting measurements) and imperialism (seeking to force the diversity of unfolding and intrinsically influenced paths of people and events into a false Western universalism). These mentors, appreciating the richness of human nature, accept that many of the most important aspects of life, such as spiritual development, cannot—and should not—be measured. Those aspects can remain a respected mystery and retain an unquestioned reality.

Erik Erikson

Within his imposing wood-lined, tall-ceilinged office, far removed from the other discipline-related faculty, Erik Erikson establishes a zone of intimacy for our talks. Warm shafts of sunlight pierce through the darkened but soft cave-like space we inhabit. Time often stands still, or at least flows most carefully, when I visit—highly unusual in the ultracompetitive, time-conscious Harvard milieu. This subdued, secluded atmosphere is almost a necessity, as Erikson speaks in a gentle, soft voice.

Though esteemed in psychology for his work in ego psychology and especially his incorporation of the entire life cycle into his widely quoted eight stages of human development, Erikson is not accepted by the Harvard establishment. "After all, he doesn't even have a Ph.D." is what I often hear—and at Harvard, that's a cardinal sin! In fact, Erikson, though officially a Harvard professor, doesn't even have a B.A.—but that amazing fact is lost in the institution's Ph.D. obsession.

Yes, Erikson has no Ph.D. in psychology; his Ph.D. is in understanding human behavior, through his intensive and sensitive clinical work, his background as an artist, and his own fluid identity experiences.* How many psychologists can have as part of their emerging understandings of human nature a psychoanalysis by Anna Freud? But as was his character, Erikson rarely mentions that gift, never attempting to gain credibility or authority from it. Harvard students flock to his courses that transcend the typical boundaries of psychology. Undergraduates fill a large classroom to hear his lectures, offering enthusiastic, even glowing course evaluations, which at Harvard is often cynically seen as a sign the course is too easy or not up to academic standards.†

I like the way Erikson frames his stages of development, stressing human potential. Though each stage represents a crisis, he suggests that crisis, once met, engaged, and even embraced, can be an opportunity for movement forward, rather than merely a time of being overwhelmed, and therefore to pass through as quickly and painlessly as possible. I'm also especially intrigued by Erikson's discussion of wisdom, which involves spiritual understanding, as the primary task of our later years.‡ He dares talk about and indeed emphasize, even cherish, something that defies psychology's conventional measurement procedures and yet remains essential to being fully human.§ Though Erikson stays

---

*An at times ambiguously acknowledged Jewish ancestry underlays his early years, raising basic identity dilemmas.

†As if to celebrate his path beyond the boundaries of mainstream psychology, Erikson's most popular course is offered as part of the General Education curriculum, a transdisciplinary, humanistically oriented, inquiry-based series of undergraduate courses.

‡These Eriksonian interpretations of stages of development can be seen as drawing inspiration from his time spent with the Oglala Sioux to Yurok people.

§Erikson's groundbreaking eight-stage developmental model finds an early formulation in his *Childhood and Society* (Erikson 1950). In this book, he also offers descriptions of his visits to two Native American communities, the Oglala Lakota of Pine Ridge reservation and the Yurok people in northwestern California. These descriptions focus on child-rearing, forefronting the critical importance of what he sees and learns in those two communities and the formulation of his stage-based developmental model, with its sequence of challenges and potentials. Yet Erikson's underlying theorizing remains within a Western, and particularly psychoanalytic perspective, and thus fails to acknowledge fully the valid depth and breadth of that Indigenous influence. See King et al. 2016 for a discussion of Erikson's connections to these sources of Indigenous knowledge.

true to shis psychoanalytic roots, by always considering the neurotic, even pathological aspect of human functioning as well as the positive promise of human potential, his gifts of understanding and compassion, lived through his actions, bring a special balance and equanimity to his work—for example, neuroticism is not reduced simply to human weakness or inadequacy but is also seen as a potential precursor to creativity and a fullness in development.

Henry Murray

Henry Murray works in an old, elegant two-story Cambridge dwelling, a home more than a psychology office or lab.* But in that building, supported by a series of creative and brilliant psychology doctoral students and young professors,† Murray develops essential elements of psychology, such as fundamental concepts of personality theory,‡ and research methods to unlock hidden elements of personhood, including the Thematic Apperception Test (TAT), a widely used clinical/research assessment instrument. Working out of a separate space suits Murray just fine, as he has a critical, almost conspiratorial attitude toward other psychologists, especially those in the experimental branch. "We don't have to take in their messages," he says to me, with a distinct twinkle and a strong half smile.

The separate and separated setting of Murray's work fosters an especially conducive atmosphere for creativity, exploring and daring to transcend conventional boundaries in psychology. But the very isolation that

---

*The Harvard Psychological Clinic, which Murray headed, is housed in Morton Prince House.

†Some of these students and coworkers include Robert White, Donald MacKinnon, Nevitt Sanford, Jerome Frank, and Erik Erikson. "Now that makes sense," I say to myself, when I learn about this connection between Murray and Erikson.

‡Published in 1938, *Explorations in Personality* is Murray's groundbreaking contribution to personality theory; in that book he articulates his approach, called personology, which emphasizes whole person research. As a mark of his respect for the team that carries out the research providing the data for that book, Murray lists authorship as "by the workers at the Harvard Psychological Clinic," followed by his own name, and then the names of twenty-seven other researchers, listed in a somewhat smaller font.

supports this creativity also isolates Murray's work from the everyday realities of those not existing in the refined atmosphere of a university and the even rarer atmosphere of Harvard—those, for example, in the nearby poverty-stricken areas of Boston. The deeper he goes inside, to mythic lands of history and consciousness, the more he travels in inner framed realms of experience. Murray is not alone in this disconnect, but the cloistered nature of his workplace highlights its distance from the streets. It's rare for any psychologist at that time, especially if teaching within the protective and protected walls of Harvard, to work in marginalized neighborhoods and deal with issues endemic to those poverty and racism-dominated sites, such as substance abuse and family violence.

He is a fatherly presence for me, and I am part of Murray's family, spending time not only in his office but also his home. While being sharply insightful, he's also calmly confident and forgiving—in spite of the many slights and insults Harvard sends his way over the years. He creates a welcoming presence for careful understanding. As his last gift to me, he takes me into the library in his office to a special section in his bookshelves. "Here, take whatever books you would like," he says. Classics line the shelf, some first editions. I take a few—and they all have intimate greetings from the authors, including glowing praise for Murray's work. Without pretense, even comment, he's giving me parts of his self.

Influenced by Freud and Jung, his psychoanalyst, Murray makes a profound journey into Jung's archetypical realms.* He is a student of literature, in particular Melville's novel *Moby Dick,* and seeks to draw inspiration from mythic transformations to inform his research on

---

*Jung, even more than Freud, is generally anathema in psychology at Harvard. While both psychodynamic psychologists are dismissed because of their "scientifically" unproven clinical concepts, such as the unconscious, Jung is further targeted because of his support of mythological, even spiritual realities in human consciousness, earning him further denigration as dabbling in dangerously unprofessional mystical experiences. Jung is a prolific writer, but a helpful entrée into his work can be found in his autobiography *Memories, Dreams, Reflections* (Jung 1965).

personality. Moby Dick, the great white whale, can be a symbol of the elemental and mysterious forces of the world; Captain Ahab, who pursues the whale, a symbol of humanity's search for understanding, which can devolve into a need to control (killing the whale). Various sculptures of the great white whale adorn the shelves of Murray's office, attesting to his humanistic expansion of psychology, sculptures that colleagues at Harvard treat mainly with humorous disregard. Yet I find the search for the great white whale an exciting entrée into psychological thinking.

At the same time, Murray is attuned to and knowledgeable about the biological realm of human nature. He draws upon his M.D. and a Ph.D. in biochemistry to bring neurological and instinctive dimensions into play. What a wonderful training in the respectful interplay of all dimensions of human experience. Crossing disciplinary boundaries in our work together, drawing upon literature, philosophy, history, and mythology to enrich psychological discourse, Murray helps me be at ease with allowing curiosity and exploration to guide my training as a psychologist.* And as a committed researcher, he demonstrates that research, infused with humanistic values, can discover.† Ambitiously pursing new major research projects, whether it be a new study of personality or a substantial literary biography of Melville, Murray leaves most unfinished—and a sense of potential failure lingers. But it is more an engaging with reality than failure as Murray, while reaching for the elusive brightness of the stars, remains connected to the shadows cast in

---

*As one of the founders of the social relations program at Harvard, Murray expresses his interdisciplinary commitment in one of the earliest explicitly and deeply interdisciplinary approaches to personality by publishing a book with Clyde Kluckhohn, his anthropologist colleague in social relations (Kluckhohn et al. 1953)

†Murray seeks to forge a new humanistically valued approach to psychological research, as he feels that the psychodynamic approach focuses on the right questions but employs inadequate methods, while academic psychology employs more rigorous scientific methods but focuses on trivial questions. He characterizes the contemporary Harvard laboratory-based research into sensation and perception, at that time a dominant force in the experimental psychology faculty, as "eye, ear, nose and throat psychology" (Murray and Shneidman 1981, 339).

his underground worlds. I can only admire what he accomplishes, and all with passion and balance.*

Murray is continually kept at the margins, though treated with respect. When the new William James Hall is constructed to house all the psychologists in one place, Murray is given a special penthouse office, acknowledging his prior independently productive lodgings. In what is a little journey of reflections, I honor his new lodgings by walking up the fifteen flights to the penthouse as we continue our visits.

Skinner and Radical Behaviorism

B. F. Skinner walks confidently but unassumedly, hands behind his back, slightly slumped with rounded shoulders, to and from his lab in the basement of the imposing Memorial Hall, whose large-stoned construction dwarfs passerbys. That's the home of the Department of Psychology, now dominated by experimental psychologists. Skinner is already being hailed as the father of radical behaviorism, the latest incarnation of the behaviorally oriented research being hailed as an exemplar of psychology *as science*. Though still in the beginning stages of his career as one of the giants of mainstream psychology, Skinner fits the mold of the classic Harvard professor—an acknowledged leader in his field, an embodiment of success, and unafraid to offer his views to others as truths—and with Skinner, this can occur with a disarmingly quiet, almost polite arrogance.†

Arguing that a topic's ability to *predict* behavior is the key to

---

*An area of his work that we never discuss is his involvement during World War II with the Office of Strategic Services (the precursor of the CIA). He helps devise assessment procedures to select effective counterespionage workers. I think he feels this work, so involved in political intrigue to make much of its essence off-limits and so focused on adaptation rather than potential, is not central to our joint explorations.

†The Harvard environment is a common culprit in this capricious aggrandizement of self. Faculty recruits to Harvard can come with good intentions, some even with humility—though they are necessarily already leaders in their field. But once at Harvard, for all but the principled and self-accepting few, a certain arrogance becomes necessary for promotion, if not survival.

determining whether psychology should study it, Skinner therefore dismisses inner states and experiences as proper topics since they are subjective phenomenon: eluding objective measurement, they therefore remain useless for prediction. He thus defines psychology in limited and limiting terms: psychology should focus on what is materially observable—namely, behaviors—and therefore what can be measured *so that* we can see what those behaviors can or cannot *predict*. Skinner concedes that inner states, such as free will and consciousness, intentions and attitudes, exist, but they are of no use since they have no predictive value. For example, until we discover the *actual* behaviors that cause things we now *attribute* to free will, free will remains only a concept, a convenient place marker for something that shows our ignorance—it is, says Skinner, merely an "explanatory fiction" ready to evaporate when the *actual* causal behavior is discovered. I have to admit—explanatory fiction is a very elegant, even disarming concept.

While seeking to fully understand Skinner's theory and practice, Erikson and Murray resist his dismissal of what they see as the often unfathomable yet essential heart of human experience—and so do I. "What's free will," I wonder, "if it's not—at its core—*beyond* the concrete definitional characteristics of behaviors and actions?" I know the *feelings,* the *experience* of freely choosing paths, and I believe, those choices make a difference—and can even help me predict outcomes. But I'm not sure I can describe the details or mechanics of that predictive process. Also I'm not immune to external pressures, so I may be exaggerating to say *freely* choosing, but doesn't the *desire* or *effort* to choose freely count for something? I know Skinnerians will say to me: "Yeah, you think you know free will exists and predicts, but do you have the research to back up that assumption—and not just your wishes or aspirations, which are basically just your *own personal* experiences?"

Skinner's research is also propelling him into clinical work, so impressive are his findings on modifying specific behaviors. For example, he and his students are invited into the back wards of the local mental hospital to introduce their programs of conditioned learning with some of the most severely withdrawn noncommunicative patients, for whom all other treatments are failing. Using M&M's candies as the reward, Skinner's team gets some of these patients to move, ever so slightly, toward connecting with the worlds outside themselves—a major therapeutic accomplishment. If a patient makes even the slightest gesture toward communication—for example, a quick shift of the eyes or slight turn of the body toward the member of Skinner's team—that behavior is immediately rewarded. The rewards continue, so that not only does the frequency of that initial gesture increase, but also it sometimes leads to even more communicative behaviors, such as a brief though stammering conversation—all of which are also rewarded. This progressively connecting communication process doesn't occur with all patients, and the final stages still are meager, as most patients remain hospitalized. But some change, at least for a time, at least enough to become noteworthy, does occur.

I'm not the only one who's skeptical, even critical, while still, mostly silently, amazed: "He's getting those patients to come outside of themselves . . . and just to eat some M&M's?!" Though I believe the Skinnerian approach ignores deeper wellsprings of behavior, I have to acknowledge its ability to get results. M&M's! Yes, they can reward and so directly, especially within the deprived setting of a hospital back ward. And then in honesty, I ask myself: "How much of *my* life is characterized even dictated by habit, unthinking arrivals of behaviors? How little does it take for me to be rewarded so I change—without even knowing I'm changing?"*

Skinner's radical behaviorism provides fresh and compelling evidence to support strict behavioral approaches to therapy. With the acceptance of cognitive and emotional factors as crucial aspects of

---

*Later, I more fully explore this disturbing yet revealing question of the dictating force of habit in our lives though my connection with the Gurdjieff meditation work and especially the Gurdjieff teaching that we are all, most of the time, "asleep." The crucial act of "waking up," or becoming aware, is the key ingredient necessary for our growth.

human functioning, this strict approach morphs into the more inclusive and flexible cognitive behavioral therapy, or CBT—today's dominant psychotherapeutic approach.

Analytical Theory and Therapy

Attending Harvard's clinical psychology program means I learn about analytically oriented psychotherapy, in particular Freudian theory and practice.* Harvard as an institution keeps a respectable distance; generally uncomfortable with *any* clinical versions of psychology, it is especially critical of psychoanalysis, seeing it as too speculative and therefore insufficiently academic. But my clinical training occurs outside the pristine nonapplied walls of Harvard, in a series of Harvard-affiliated hospital settings. And the general Boston area is a hotbed of psychoanalytical work; it prevails as the therapeutic game in town.† Behavioral approaches, including CBT, are not emerging as a viable local alternative, humanistic orientations have only a few scattered practitioners, and psychopharmacological interventions remain in their infancy.‡

---

*I use the terms *analytical* or *analytically oriented work* to include Freudian or Jungian approaches. The terms *psychoanalytical* and *Freudian* refer more specifically to approaches developed by Freud.

†One measure of the pervasive dominance of the Freudian psychoanalytic approach is the number of psychologists who start out their careers attracted to and trying to work with Freudian ideas—and then give up that orientation to form another contrasting approach. Two of the important founders of CBT, Aaron Beck and Albert Ellis, are cases in point; though both begin their careers within the psychoanalytic model, each gives up that orientation.

‡In 1962, Elvin Semrad, a renowned Harvard psychiatrist, delivers a classic indictment of that nascent pharmaceutical approach: "When I see my colleagues prescribe drugs for their patients, I say that's a sign of their therapeutic failures." For Semrad, the still dominant analytically oriented therapy, which he practices with rare skill, are the only "real" psychotherapy. Since the time of this Semrad quote, the number of available psychopharmacological interventions has radically increased, as does research on their effects. Yet Semrad still has a valid point; not only are these interventions being overprescribed, but also the role of psychiatrist is frequently reduced primarily to prescribing medications, with verbal therapeutic interactions becoming a little-used skill.

Though I have an introduction to analytic thinking through both Erikson and Murray, theirs is a flexible, exploratory approach, drawing insights from analytic work, without being strictly beholden to it. But I find a more dogmatic approach among many of the psychoanalytically oriented practitioners who are now in charge of my clinical education. Powered by a sense of elitism and entitlement, these practitioners assume that only specially trained experts can make judgments about people's mental health—and being an expert means being formally certified as a psychologist or psychiatrist and, informally at least, a psychoanalytically oriented one. As the arbitrators of mental health, these experts are charged with the task of placing people into mental illness categories, which though meant to suggest appropriate treatments too often create boxes that can limit peoples' own power and capacity to engage in journeys of self-discovery. The *Diagnostic Statistical Manual* (DSM), first published in 1952, is the primary vehicle for and repository of these diagnoses, and it has extensive shortcomings and biases.

I learn enough about psychoanalysis to understand its implications for practice but, sensing some important limitations, don't become a psychoanalytically oriented therapist. While the Freudian approach has a wonderful appreciation of a client's depth of being, there's also a failure to appreciate the full range of being. For example, I'm attracted to Freud's discussion of the unconscious. It is, he claims, a storehouse of painful and conflict-ridden memories of early childhood anxieties that, as a result of unexamined defense mechanisms that function to dampen or ignore the pain, remain unresolved. And though those unresolved anxiety-ridden memories are now largely inaccessible to current, adult awareness, they continue to influence, in hidden and often neurotic ways, our present lives. And I find that dreams, which Freud calls the "royal road to the unconscious," are an excellent pathway toward unlocking unrecognized potentials of meaning.

But I believe Freud, with his stance against the validity and value of spirituality, places unrealistic and limiting boundaries on the nature of the unconscious. For me, the unconscious is but one phase of a larger picture of consciousness with its often spiritually powered transformations. Ironically, this more fluid and expanding understanding of consciousness is vividly understood by William James, one of Harvard's own iconic pioneering psychologists. But at the time of my entering graduate school, James is still being judged by many as too vague and speculative, even too spiritual, and so is often discreetly hidden from public discourse within the Harvard psychology community.

Also, I find Freud's concept of anxiety as the primary stimulant for the formation of unconscious material to be unnecessarily narrow. Rather than focusing as he does on anxieties that come from neurotic processes of socialization, I feel there must be a place for existential anxiety, for the organic and unavoidable stresses, challenges, and opportunities of being human—the anxieties of living life fully.* And finally, with its undue focus on psychopathology, I miss in psychoanalytic therapies an appreciation for the full complexity of mental illness, including its reservoirs of strength. If the focus is on illness and how to fix that disability, then it becomes hard to value the voices of clients who, since they are *actually experiencing* those terrible anxieties and terrors, can potentially give some expert advice on their own treatment.

The Wisdom of Patients

And so I seek another, less accredited or reputable source of wisdom while at Harvard—the patients I meet as part of my clinical internship. I listen to the painfully earned knowing that comes from those called "patients," an establishment label that marginalizes them. The term *patient*—more a pejorative label than an accurate descriptor—highlights the power structure that puts doctors and therapists in charge, not only of the patients but also of all the knowledge that might lead to their recovery—in essence of knowledge generation itself. But for me that psychiatric power structure turns inside out. It becomes my

---

*I appreciate the conversations I have with Professor Mario Núñez-Molina about existential anxiety and Freud.

privilege to learn from patients—and even though as a student I'm still in a low-status position in the hierarchical clinical world, I insist that these patients are "clients" and feel we are co-journeyers on the path of sickness and health.

During my clinical practicum at Massachusetts Mental Health Center,* I'm placed on the back ward and instructed to learn about psychosis by *observing* the patients. Unable to just observe, I'm drawn into conversations, interactions, and, at times, unknown spaces. An older woman, with saliva dripping from both corners of her mouth, her clothes torn open, exposing one lacerated breast, races toward me with a menacing look. "Whoa! Do I want to be run over?" I rapid-think, as slight shivers of fear take over. "This is out of control!" And in the immediate next split second, I catch myself falling into retreat. "Wait, hold on," I tell myself, "it's only a person in need; she needs something."

I can't turn away. Sounds spit out of her mouth, projectiles meant to back me away—and still I can't turn away. That's what she's expecting me to do—everyone else on the ward does. But I stand, waiting, listening, until she stops in front of me. Grunts, moans, partial words keep sputtering out. She relaxes a bit; the spitting stops, though saliva still drools from the right side of her mouth. And then, with a renewed, almost supreme effort, she begins to speak; she's barely articulate, but I can understand most of her words. "It's terrible . . . just terrible . . . just terrible this pain . . . this pain all the time . . . this pain inside, right here . . . ," as she points to her heart. I think I understood that even before her spitting sounds became recognizable words. And now she wants to embrace me—and we hug. I'm touched to my core, shaken but in balance. And quietly she walks away.

I don't describe this encounter to my supervisor later that day—

---

*The center used to be called Boston Psychopathic Hospital. It's one of those manipulations of words that is supposed to signal a new and enlightened understanding (from "psychopathic hospital" to "mental health center"), but as is too often the case, actual changes on the ground are less dramatic and real than the name change suggests.

probably a good idea, as the supervisor begins by reminding me that we psychologists in training are supposed to be cultivating our *professional distance* as we *observe*—without becoming involved—the manifestations of *psychosis* in the patients. All these labels are meant to help socialize me in being a professional—a person without the true heart for healing. How can I explain that I have just met another human being who is teaching me about pain and healing?

My clinical internship is at Judge Baker Guidance Clinic. I'm doing therapy with Frank,* a twelve-year-old boy, and like many twelve-year-old boys, he's physically active. The concept of therapy at Judge Baker is based on the classic fifty-minute hour of talk therapy derived from the psychoanalytical model. So here's Frank, sitting in his chair, me sitting in my chair, and we're supposed to talk. And Frank is fidgeting, endlessly fidgeting, his body calling for movement, his face sullen, his tongue silenced—and we're supposed to do talk therapy, for fifty minutes no less.

After two sessions of what must be real discomfort for Frank—it certainly is for me, so much so that I cut our second session short—I ask him at the beginning of our third meeting if he wants to take a walk. He literally leaps at the offer, and before I can suggest where we might go, he's out of the office, out of the building, walking briskly and bouncily down the street—away from the clinic. We walk and walk and walk—and I begin to talk a bit. And Frank begins to talk a bit. He has lots of "things that bother me." In the next three weeks, we do a lot of walking, occasionally shooting a few hoops—and Frank begins to talk about those "things that bother" him, including a physically abusive father and being bullied at school. "This kid is going through a lot," I think to myself. "It must be hard for him to talk about it." I feel we've engaged in our therapeutic work.

In my supervision meeting, I receive a different message. After

---

*Frank is a pseudonym used to respect that young boy's privacy. Throughout this book, pseudonyms are used when talking about clients unless they specifically request otherwise.

describing our walks and games, my supervisor, in classic psychoanalytic fashion, says: "You're doing good work. You've established a therapeutic alliance with him. Now the *real* therapy can begin. When you get back into the office, you can have him really talk about his problems." That's strange, I think. It seems to me that Frank and I are reaching out to *each other,* creating *between us* a "therapeutic alliance": our walk and play is not just the *context* for the therapy but the therapy itself. How cleverly classical Western models of therapy, in this case psychoanalytically oriented therapy, can sometimes overlook healing.

The Best of the Rest

Harvard, in its search for "the best," also offers a quality introduction to a variety of important mainstream psychological approaches. In addition to being invited into the grand theorizing phase of personality psychology, being birth-side to Skinner's radical behaviorism and being immersed in psychoanalytically oriented clinical work, I take graduate courses from other professors who are leaders in their fields or leaders to be; outstanding figures, such as personality theorist Gordon Allport and cognitive psychologist Jerome Bruner offer a rich diet of theory and research.* My thesis on experimenter bias, supervised by Professor Robert Rosenthal, a young, talented, and energetic experimental social psychologist, employs a quantitative research methodology, with a heavy reliance on statistical analyses. As a graduate student, I establish this strong foundation and fluency in the contours and content of large areas of mainstream psychology, so I'm now in a position to explore more fully and honestly alternative views to and in psychology.

---

*Among my other teachers are Talcott Parsons on sociological theory; David Riesman on sociology and popular culture; David McClelland on motivation; John and Bea Whiting on cultural anthropology; Elliot Aronson on social psychology; and Ken Gergen on social psychology and constructivist theories. The influence of the then burgeoning field of cognitive psychology is also felt in my program of studies, as George Miller joins Jerome Bruner in stating strong empirical and theoretical positions in the Harvard social sciences.

EXPERIENCES BEYOND
THE HARVARD PROGRAM

Abe Maslow and Humanistic Openings

But Harvard is not my only source of academic psychological training. Abe Maslow is teaching at neighboring Brandeis University, and he's emerging as one of the key founders of humanistic psychology. He's working to create what he calls a third force in psychology, a vital but still distinctly minority position in psychology, emphasizing a wide and deep range of human potentials that can create harmonious and fulfilling relationships and institutions. This third force counteracts what he perceives as the limitations of the two prevailing approaches to psychology: the psychoanalytic, with its deterministic philosophy and undue emphasis on pathology and negative emotions; and the behavioristic, with its mechanistic and reductionistic approach to understanding human behavior.*

Abe is another of my mentors, and we are colleagues and friends as well, especially as I take my first job in his Brandeis psychology department.†

---

*Two of Maslow's earliest books remain among his most influential: *Motivation and Personality* (1954) and *Toward a Psychology of Being* (1962).

†I first meet Abe Maslow in the mid-1960s, eventually joining him in the Brandeis Department of Psychology in 1971. In talking about him, I discuss his work and personality more extensively, and include more critical comments, than I do with other mentors such as Erikson or Murray. I think this is more a function of the fact that I know Abe more intimately and over a longer period than either of the other two, rather than there being something particularly negative or inadequate about Abe and his work. Abe is more of a friend and colleague in addition to being a mentor, as indicated by my talking often about him as I would a friend—he is to me, Abe.

I don't know anyone who is not multisided and, in *being human,* living out both positive and negative aspects and aspirations. For example, there are those who feel there are serious questions about Jung's personal views. This fact of human complexity and frailty also holds true, of course, for the Indigenous elders who offer their teachings in this book. They, too, are human beings first and foremost, not saints or gurus, and their humanity, with its positives and negatives, lows and highs, is ever present.

If sometimes a description of one of the people in this book, elder or psychologist, seems particularly one-sided, even, at times, suggesting saintliness, that description isn't meant as a full portrait. But I emphasize the positive struggles of people rather than focus too much detail on the foibles and deficiencies they are often struggling to overcome.

Abe is a true and brave trailblazer, standing up for the humanistic and wholistic values I seek during those years at Harvard, as he withstands frequent criticism, cynicism, and even mocking from the psychology establishment, negative feedback that always seems to outweigh in his mind the support and appreciation he gets from the emerging humanistic psychology movement.* Though he is elected president of the American Psychological Association, a very public and prestigious recognition, he's profoundly anxious about his upcoming presidential acceptance address—way beyond the normal nervousness preceding such events. "I feel so unsure about this presidency," he tells me. "What will I say in my acceptance speech? Will they just dismiss me as a romantic dreamer? Not a *real* psychologist? Even a fraud?"

A beacon illuminating spirituality as critical to full or self-actualized development, Abe presents psychology as a discipline wherein moral values, such as honesty and altruism, are encouraged and human courage and discovery nurtured. Because of his overwhelmingly positive orientation, he is criticized as being unrealistic, a misleading Pollyanna, a "dangerous dreamer," and, what hurts Abe especially, not a "real" psychologist. But Abe tells me, "If I'm a dreamer, at least I'm talking about essential dreams!"—dreams supported by research and dealing with actual and necessary potentials.†

And yet Abe is not easily cowed. "What do those guys really know about the world, about how to be a good person?" he says,

---

*Though clearly Abe is not the first psychologist to highlight the innate human potential for positive spiritually infused human development, he is one of the first to champion that potential with enduring commitment and integrity and with an enthusiasm that encourages him to apply that humanistic perspective to a wide range of individual, social, and cultural contexts.

†Abe is constantly demanding rigor in thinking and empirically based conclusions. His training in experimental psychology, working as a graduate student researching dominance behavior in monkeys in Harry Harlow's lab, seems to be an enduring, though rarely discussed influence. It is not that he espouses the experimental method per se but more the need for rigor and careful observation. Famous for his exhaustive lists, such as the many characteristics of self-actualizing people, Abe feels he is only being inclusive of what he actually observes.

naming a behaviorist or two who are among his most vocal critics. Abe's confidence is bolstered by his belief that he is writing for the ages, trying to connect with a community of famous thinkers, most long since deceased. "My real audience," he tells me, "is people like Plato and Aristotle . . . I want to engage them in dialogue." Yes, Abe is a bit dismissive and arrogant. Or is he trying to defend himself from contemporary critics since he's not especially thick skinned?*

Abe is a dear friend and loyal supporter. I spend many evenings at his house, at times as part of the academic soirees he holds, usually stimulated by some visiting scholar. Abe is very famous at the time, and many visitors to his house are overfilled with adulation for him. He's not entirely comfortable with this but not sure how to control it. His wife, Bertha, isn't at a loss for words or actions. One evening, Bertha enters a roomful of essentially adoring students gathered around Abe to offer them a plate of cookies and is clearly heard to chirp, "Peek, peek, peek . . . peek, peek, peek!" Her birdlike iteration of a concept central to Abe's theory—namely, peak experiences, the spiritually oriented sources of insight that energize the further reaches of human development—momentarily silences the strongly animated strings of conversation. Bertha's "peeks" throw Abe off balance and temporarily irk him, deflating the seriousness of the ongoing conversation. But he recovers quickly, as he too realizes the need for a grounding in the ordinary, if effective conversations are to evolve within that visiting group. "After all," he later tells me, "I have to keep remembering—I'm not such a big deal."

Deeply ensconced in his American academic context, Abe is not fully open to the wisdom of Indigenous peoples.† His earlier contacts

---

*Within the confines of his friends and family, Abe can express a cutting and righteous (even self-righteous) temper as he dismisses some of his harshest critics.

†Working from within a cultural context far removed from Indigenous peoples is a characteristic of North American psychologists of that time who typically are living a Eurocentric upper middle class lifestyle.

with Indigenous cultures seem to have faded into the background.*
Working honestly within his own middle-class Eurocentric world
space, Abe is taking risks, seeking truths. Though he experiences difficult economic conditions and anti-Semitism growing up, he is functioning, as a psychologist, primarily within urbane, academic settings.
His agenda for social change, while offered as revolutionary, lacks
the substance of being anchored in the daily crushing realities of the
oppressed and marginalized. But Abe is not alone in this disconnect
between his theories and the realities of lives oppressed by poverty

---

*At the suggestion of the eminent anthropologist Ruth Benedict, who is one of Abe's early
mentors, he visits the Siksika Blackfoot Reserve outside Calgary, Alberta, in 1938. But Abe
never talks to me about this visit, even though he knows of my rapidly emerging research
with Indigenous peoples. Only after Abe's death do I learn more about Abe's visit to the
Blackfoot people—first in his posthumously published diary, then in the joint presentations
of Blackfoot elder Narcisse Blood and educator Ryan Heavy Head (e.g., Heavy Head and
Blood, 2011), and finally through the research of Blackfoot scholar Sidney Stone Brown
(2014), who reproduces two of Maslow's unpublished papers on his Blackfoot research that
are stored in his official archives. What emerges is a picture of the extensive influence that
visit to the Siksika reserve has on Maslow, but more unfortunately, the degree to which
he seems to either overlook, misunderstand, or ignore essential aspects of the teachings he
receives from Blackfoot elders who work with him.

For example, Blood and Heavy Head point out that self-actualization is seen in
Blackfoot culture more as simply actualization, a process within each individual that
is *supported by and expressed within community,* as each person strives *to be of service to
others.* In contrast, Abe's concept of self-actualization is more individualistic, keeping an
emphasis on the "self"; and even though he says that altruism is one of the characteristics
of the self-actualized person, it is the *individual* who seeks to find her or his own sense
of meaning and purpose in his or her own life. The Blackfoot concept of actualization
describes a process that is *open to all people* and *at all times*; spirituality and its attendant
transcendence are seen as the gift to and responsibility of all. In contrast is Abe's more
elitist conception where self-actualization is reserved for the very few and comes as an
end point of development.

If only Abe had allowed the full meanings of the Blackfoot teachings to enter into
his theorizing, it could have been far richer and more fully developed—as it could have
expanded beyond its Western assumptions. Crucial to that respectful openness to the
Blackfoot teachings would have been an attempt by Abe to get actual feedback on the
accuracy of what he learns from the Siksika elders who offer him their teachings, and, as
a sign of respect for that traditional Blackfoot knowledge, a more public acknowledgment
of its impact on him.

and racism; psychologists of all persuasions, including mentors like Erikson and Murray, are generally not actively engaged in issues of social justice. There is a historically honored tradition in the social sciences, such as sociology, of being an instrument of social justice, but not until the emergence of community psychology in the mid-1960s is mainstream psychology forcefully called to task from within for not facing these issues.

Abe is an admirable psychologist. But I'm disappointed that he doesn't see how spirituality is possible at all levels and how the physical and spiritual are often merged in healing work, so that, for example, physical sacrifice can be a simultaneous pathway in and toward spiritual understanding.* When he offers visits to art galleries to see great works of art as one example of a peak experience, his way of describing moments of transcendence, Abe is betraying not only his cultural blinders but also his elitism. This elitism is reinforced through his central concept of self-actualization, which for him is the highest and most fully realized stage of development but remains a stage reserved for the very few.†

Abe also puts great faith in the highly educated, the intellectuals, to become enlightened leaders, further expressing his elitist notions. This often implies a distrust of experiential learning when it remains unexamined. The personal growth movement, which draws inspiration from Abe's writings but pushes experiential learning to

---

*There are numerous examples in the Indigenous world, in addition to the Ju/'hoan healing dance, where physical struggle and sacrifice become vehicles for spiritual experiences and that are, in themselves, spiritual activities. In this book, we discuss, for example, the Lakota sweat lodge and vision quest and fasting rituals in general. Fasting is also an example of a physically influenced path for spiritual understanding in the Western world as well.

†In his late work, including the posthumously published *The Farther Reaches of Human Nature* (1971) and in particular with later concepts such as "plateau experiences," which are extensions and elaborations of peak experiences, Abe moves beyond the selectivity of self-actualization toward a more inclusive and constantly striving state of actualization. This theoretical development reflects more accurately the teachings he receives from the Blackfoot people.

some limits,* tests his acceptance—and patience—in this regard.

Esalen Institute, founded in 1962, is a leader in that personal growth movement. In the mid-1960s, I give a workshop there on education as healing. The early morning of the second day of my workshop, I walk by one of the Esalen workshop rooms to pick up Alex, my fifteen-year-old son, who has come with me to Esalen and falls asleep in that room that night. As the first few people file quietly into the room for an early morning meditation session, Alex is just getting up from his sleep, stretching his arms and rubbing his eyes. The newly arrived people sit quietly, respectfully, eyes fastened on my son—and offer their devotional attention to him whom they perceive as this young "guru"! Fitting neatly into their yearnings for spiritual guidance, my sleep-arising son is a young Buddha for them. He has no idea what is going on, and as he quietly leaves the room, others touch him gently, affirming the spiritual transmission they so desperately seek. It's probably best my son has no inkling of what is transpiring. Yes, he's now awake—but not awake in the *spiritually awakened* state. In any case, Abe would have smiled knowingly. "See," he might have said, "you need to understand what your experience means if it is to mean something!" There is, of course, also some very serious and dedicated work occurring at Esalen, and experiential learning that is truly educational.

The Yeasts of Consciousness

During the years of my Harvard graduate school training, two powerful paths of consciousness emerge in my life: psychedelic research and meditation. They provide yeast to my developing insights about the limitations of mainstream psychology and, even more importantly, about what exists beyond that culturally delimited framework.

---

*The sometimes casual experiential ethos that occurs in some of these personal growth centers earns them the caricature of being places for "touchy-feely" people and experiences.

CAUTIONS ABOUT THE
HARVARD PSYCHEDELIC RESEARCH GROUP

Before even discussing my involvement with the Harvard psychedelic research group, including my own use of psychedelic substances as a participant in the research, I want to mention several important points. At that time all the psychedelic substances that are used in our research are legal—including psilocybin, mescaline, and LSD. Also those psychedelic substances, which induce strong, even life-changing alterations of consciousness, are taken within a guided and controlled context. With the psychedelics coming directly from a world-renowned pharmaceutical company as part of our research program, I know the substance I'm taking, including the actual amount.

Equally important, I take these psychedelic substances within a supportive environment, guided by principles and structures derived from spiritually based ceremonies. For example, our group turns often to Buddhist teachings, especially Tibetan and Zen Buddhism, as well as the ceremonial structures of Indigenous Mazatec *curanderismo* work with their naturally sourced psychedelic sacred mushroom, in order to guide our transformations of consciousness toward the experience of ego death and beyond.

We don't have the opportunity to actually work with elders from the cultures that create those ceremonies, so that information about these ancient pathways toward transforming consciousness is often filtered through Western eyes. That is a definite limitation, and sometimes we are just struggling along, doing the best we can. But we are at least trying to follow one ancient Indigenous teaching; namely, that strong consciousness altering substances are sacred, taken in the context of ceremony for healing and spiritual development not used for recreation or pleasure seeking or escape—which is considered an abuse.

While the above description details the intentions, aims, and ideals of the Harvard psychedelic research group, as expected, actualities don't always meet up with ideals. At times, for example, a hedonistic path overwhelms the search for spiritual understandings. It's this kind of degradation of sincere spiritual explorations that leads the Indigenous Mazatec healer Maria Sabina to be disillusioned and highly critical of the many pleasure-seeking Westerners that begin flocking to her traditional mushroom ceremonies. She feels deeply disappointed by the personal agenda of the Western visitors, even though the aim is to "know God." As she says: "Before nobody took the children [the mushrooms] simply to find God. They were always taken to cure the sick." The mushroom ceremony is sacred, and as is typical with Indigenous use of psychedelic substances, eating the mushrooms is directed toward the good of the community, in this case healing the sick. It is through service that knowing or understanding God becomes concrete and actual, for it is a higher power that heals.

But my experience with *psychedelics* is clearly different from and totally opposed to the use of *drugs*, especially addictive and destructive substances such as cocaine, crystal meth, and the host of opioid-related drugs like heroin, prescription painkillers, and synthetic opioids like fentanyl—which often, taken in adulterated form, become lethal. These highly addictive drugs are not only illegal but are also often linked to criminal activities to support the drug habit. Especially among marginalized and oppressed communities, such drug usage becomes a vehicle of colonization, destroying will and dignity, reinforcing despair and deterioration.

Therefore, in no way is my following discussion about psychedelics taken as part of the Harvard research group a support for or in any way condoning the use of addictive drugs, which are both dangerous and destructive. But since a too quick judgment could lead to a confusion between two very distinct substances—psychedelics and addictive drugs—I still remain somewhat conflicted in talking about my psychedelic research experiences at Harvard.

One thing is for sure: spiritual journeys are at the heart of a healing psychology. And under careful, sensitive, and knowledgeable guidance, within profoundly growth-supportive and culturally wise settings, psychedelics can encourage intense, spiritually oriented explorations of consciousness. Instances among Indigenous peoples exist. And more recently, instances are developing in the West. Recent United States FDA government-approved research studies are, once again, suggesting the therapeutic potential of carefully administered psychedelically initiated experiences of transcendence and self-discovery for a range of conditions, such as anxiety, depression, and cancer-induced end-of-life transitions. This new line of research is rediscovering and reaffirming many of the principles and processes used in the therapeutic interventions of the Harvard group.*

"Now that's *some way* to get through graduate school," I'm often told when I describe my being part of the Harvard psychedelic research group, spearheaded by Harvard faculty Tim Leary and Dick Alpert and drawing mainly on graduate students from the personality and clinical psychology programs.† There's so much more of substance and innovative discovery occurring within that group than is suggested by the

---

*See for example, Griffiths and Grob 2010; Griffiths et al. 2011; and Ross et al. 2016.

†Though I meet Leary and Alpert at Harvard as a graduate student and do most of my psychedelic work while still enrolled at Harvard, that work has an intensely anti-Harvard ethos. Leary and Alpert enlist the often radicalizing support of those outside the academy to avoid Harvard regulations, turning Harvard into the "enemy" to be actively resisted, and soon the psychedelic research is functioning within relatively independent niches within the wider university community. This conflict with Harvard becomes more severe and ultimate than that experienced by professors like Murray and Erikson. Not only does so much of that psychedelic work occur outside the physical, intellectual, and ideological boundaries of Harvard, but with the firing of Leary and Alpert, a rare and extremely serious event, Harvard puts its official stamp of disapproval on that work. That's why I see the psychedelic research project as essentially existing outside Harvard, rather than serving as an example of how Harvard can support a wide variety of paths toward knowledge, even those seen as radically disruptive.

media frenzy, which focuses selectively and in an exaggerated manner on the "irresponsible" and "out-of-control" behaviors of Leary and Alpert (aka Ram Dass), who are eventually fired from Harvard for their unprofessional conduct.

A charming, often fun-loving, brilliant antiestablishment man of ideas and ideals, Leary is a public figure and most willing to be recognized as the leader of the group. He cares about my education and models ways to explore new and hidden pathways toward a more revolutionary psychology. An equally charming but more serious and careful critic of the mainstream, Alpert, also a public figure, is willing to be second in command. He's more personally committed to supporting me as I navigate my way through the Ph.D. program, now carrying within me psychedelic insights. And then there are the two psychedelic community houses, one where Leary, Alpert, one graduate student, and other associates and their families live; the second where I live with several other Harvard graduate students and our families. These homes, in continual interaction, are centers of discourse and experience, places of respite and struggle—including what to make of psychology and how to remake it.

Yes, graduate school is more exciting because of that psychedelic research. Psychedelic sessions can release discoveries into the nature of reality, fueled by shifts in perception and understanding. Sometimes these discoveries seem similar to psychotherapeutic insights, though often more profoundly felt. For example, in one session I realize for the first time, with fresh and lasting power, that my feeling of inner hollowness is a yearning not just for some personal fulfillment but for spiritual fulfillment. Sometimes these discoveries come with dramatic narratives that reveal fundamental understandings. In one session my body outlines melt into a felt fire, my sense of solid being dissolving into sparks that rise and vanish into the night air. "Really . . . I mean *really* we're here on the earth only briefly," I affirm without fear, "and then . . . and then . . . we return into the Great Mystery where it all began— and begins again." The impermanence of our lives within the sacred permanence of our spiritual universe becomes real for me in that moment.*

But our psychedelic experiences are not only nor purely blissful or beautiful. Fears are common and not always easily confronted or accepted. Visions of hellish pain and anguish are part of many sessions, offering a more realistic picture of the heavens and hells of reality. These "bad" sessions require special processing, especially after the physiological effects of the psychedelics end, as we realize that acceptance of the negative forces can affirm the reality of the positive.

To many outside our group, any drug-induced experience is not valued or even considered real, and the more dramatic psychedelic narratives are further dismissed as illusions or even delusions. But as one of the mentors for our group, Aldous Huxley, says, the doors of perception are certainly opening with psychedelics and most often into new realities. We take comfort in the fact that similar extraordinary experiential reports of spiritual journeys or spirit travels, at times induced by psychedelic substances, appear in many Indigenous spiritual traditions, especially among Indigenous healers. And we are affirmed in knowing that the frequent psychiatric labeling of these Indigenous healers as "psychotics" arises mainly from a lack of understanding and an attempt to diminish and control what is not understood and therefore seen as a threat to Western professional identities.

And yet, all is neither profound nor profoundly spiritual. More than once a person emerges from a psychedelic session looking both wondrous and perplexed. "In that session I saw right into the nature of the universe . . . it was really powerful!" says one young man in hushed awed tones. "But I forget what I saw," he laments, his feet now firmly planted on the earth.

The translation from psychedelic experiences into professional discussions within the psychology department, or even among our net-

---

*As my life unfolds after those early psychedelic experiences, I see both the utter wisdom of such a realization *and* the near utter impossibility of living that wisdom in daily life. Living each day as if it is to be your last is, for sure, not easy to do.

work of friends, is not easy. We wade through layers of disbelief and dismissal, attempting to approach core experiences of seeing into the nature of reality. We are energized by the fluidity of consciousness and our glimpses of spiritual transformation released in those psychedelic sessions and gather more data to add to the ongoing construction of a psychology of deep human potential.

Focusing on a variety of purposes and situations, including therapeutic and spiritual explorations, the Harvard group studies psychedelic substances within an experiential and collaborative research paradigm, stressing respect for persons taking the substances by establishing a supportive and caring environment within which the research occurs. There is, for example, Wally Pahnke's Good Friday Experiment (Pahnke 1963), demonstrating the power of psychedelics to deepen spiritual commitment among a group of divinity students,* and the Concord Prison Experiment (Leary et al. 1965), whose outcomes encourage the use of psychedelics coupled with psychotherapy to build a more positive identity among inmates, which in turn can affect recidivism. As researchers, we all take psychedelics and, at times, take those substances with the participants during certain specially designed research projects, though there is always a researcher in the "control tower" who is not taking the substance and maintains a sensitive monitoring and research presence. The primary data collected are self-reports, supplemented by standard outcome measures. Both the privileging of self-reports of experience and the shared, collaborative relationship between researcher and research participant are key learnings for me.

---

*Wally is a good friend of mine; he's a special, dedicated, and wonderful seeker of truths. His attempt to work with psychedelics within the skeptical, even cynical institution of a divinity school is admirable. Several years after that Good Friday research, Wally, Carl Salzman, and I do a similar piece of research within the "heart of the beast." We conduct psychedelic sessions—for divinity students in two rooms at Massachusetts Mental Health Center, where Carl is working. Before each session we move the furniture into the hallways and bring in a relaxing décor, including comfortable homelike furnishings. At the end of the sessions, late in the night, we return the rooms to their institutional clarity. We feel like undercover psychological freedom fighters.

But the visionary thrust of this psychedelic research program suffers from an idealism that blinds us to important realities of spiritual transformation. If the transformational paths of Indigenous peoples are more fully understood, we might see that their spiritual journeys represent not only deeply culturally grounded and cultivated communal journeys, but also psychic struggles as necessities, helping them to counteract the oppressive sociopolitical contexts they exist in.* In most parts of the world, these Indigenous paths are carved out from within conditions of oppression and deprivation, adding layers of challenging realities that we are divorced from. Reading about Indigenous paths, as we do with a passion, is not the same as living in and within the actual context of those paths. Thus an element of romanticism colors our spiritual journeys, accompanied by a failure to respect the origins of the teachings that guide our explorations and, most importantly,

---

*Two of our guiding resources are the writings of D. T. Suzuki on Zen Buddhism (e.g., Suzuki 1948) and the teachings of the *curandera* Maria Sabina, an Indigenous Mazatec healer from southern Mexico, on her ceremonial work with the sacred mushroom, the natural source of psilocybin (e.g., Estrada 1981). Other examples of writings about ancient pathways, now filtered through Western perspectives, focus on Buddhism and include books by Alan Watts on Zen (e.g., Watts 1957); the German writer Hermann Hesse's *Siddhartha,* an inspiring novel about the quest for enlightenment drawing heavily on Buddhist teachings; and, most importantly, Evans-Wentz's interpretation of *The Tibetan Book of the Dead,* a Tibetan Buddhist text about the spiritual passage to death, psychic as well as physical (Evans-Wentz 1927). The Evans-Wentz book serves as a guide for structuring and processing our psychedelic sessions; in fact, our group writes a concrete and detailed psychedelic session guidebook based on that Evans-Wentz translation (Leary, Metzner, and Alpert 1964).

Yet the Evans-Wentz translation draws heavily on his own involvement with theosophy, so the Evans-Wentz version of this critical passage of consciousness clearly goes through Western filters of interpretation. But in most cases, these Western-influenced discussions of ancient, non-Western teachings are, *to our knowledge at that time,* valid and valuable sources—we aren't looking specifically for more authentic, local sources, a measure of our own ethnocentrism.

Also, eminent Western thinkers who also take psychedelics, such as Aldous Huxley, offer guidance into a realms of expanding consciousness; Huxley's *The Doors of Perception,* discussing his spiritual experiences with psychedelics, is very popular with our group (Huxley 1954).

to give back to those from whom the teachings emerge. Our failures to deal with how psychedelics relate to on-the-ground issues of racism and poverty is part of a larger failure of our not attending sufficiently to the application of psychedelic insights into everyday life.

The work of the Harvard research group has an element of chaos that comes from being at the cutting edge of discovery but also invites the dangerous possibility of unintended negative consequences. Sometimes the desire to spread the word about psychedelic potentials overreaches the ability to maintain the necessary care and caution. We all struggle to find a balance that feeds the insights and avoids potential harm.

All the while my solid learning about psychology, including mainstream approaches, continues. Rather than undermining my studies of the mainstream, the psychedelic research expands my understanding, sharpening and deepening my insights into and critique of mainstream psychology. Both Leary and Alpert come into the program as respected psychologists and while at Harvard still retain their identity as psychologists, though more and more as critics of and mavericks in the field.*

---

*For example, Leary arrives at Harvard as a respected theoretician of personality, offering a valuable interpersonal perspective. One doesn't get hired at Harvard without substantial academic credentials. Toward the end of my graduate studies, and especially after they are fired from Harvard, Leary and Alpert's commitment to working within psychology weakens, and after my graduation, both move further and further away from their professional identities as psychologists into their more widely known work. Leary is a forceful and influential advocate for psychedelic visions and social change (see e.g., Leary 1998, 1999); while Alpert (now known as Ram Dass) is a teacher about the spiritual journey, with his book *Be Here Now* serving as an early beacon to seekers in the West (Dass 1971). *Be Here Now* is first available in pamphlet form, artistically decorated and beautifully printed on large-size pages hand-bound with twine. We feel that it's a wonderfully informal collection of teachings, meant just for the small number of us who are associated with Ram Dass at that time; its morphing into "best seller" book status is not even conceived.

Meditative Journeys

In the midst of our psychedelic explorations, a number of us in the group realize that though psychedelics open the door to expanded consciousness, more is needed to sustain and develop the awareness that is given to us. It's the recurring issue of how do these psychedelic insights make a difference in our daily lives.* To learn more about a practical application of enhanced consciousness, I turn to the teachings of G. I. Gurdjieff, who stresses meditation *in daily life* in a practice he calls "the work."†

Gurdjieff draws upon teachings from the Middle East, including Buddhist and Sufi spiritual traditions, and creates a system of practice speaking to the abilities and needs of seekers in the Western world. He suggests we are "asleep"—unaware, robot-like automatons—during most of our waking hours. We need to "wake up"—become aware of who we really are, what our place in the universe is, and how to evolve spiritually. That process is initiated by meditative practices *while engaged in our day-to-day existence.* I really like the practicality of Gurdjieff's approach, as it goes beyond the cloistered setting of many meditation approaches. I become an active member of a group guided by Willem Nyland, who is one of Gurdjieff's trusted students, and to this day Nyland's group seeks to keep Gurdjieff's teachings

---

*The general issue of how to apply insights from spiritual journeys so that they serve others and enhance daily life is at the core of Indigenous approaches to transforming consciousness.

†There are many references dealing with the Gurdjieff work. I list just three core writings by Gurdjieff in the bibliography. The teachings offered in these books, especially *Beelzebub's Tales to His Grandson,* are not easily accessible—on purpose; Gurdjieff means them for serious students wishing to put his ideas into practice and therefore willing to make the required effort to read and understand his writings. These three books represent a trilogy under the general title of *All and Everything.* Though I include publishing information in the bibliography, I don't specifically recommend a particular publisher for these Gurdjieff books because most of the earliest versions I'm familiar with are now out of print and some of their titles have changed: for example, when I initially read Gurdjieff's first book in the mid-1960s, its title was *All and Everything: Beelzebub's Tales to His Grandson, First Edition.*

alive.* I build on principles of the Gurdjieff work through various yoga and meditative practices, which all help to ground and expand some of my earlier insights about transformational possibilities.†

I come to Harvard to enter a profession that can work in helpful ways with others and, over time, increasingly to learn about healing and spirituality. Without a doubt, for most of my Harvard education, I'm in the wrong place. Can psychologists be educated to heal? Certainly not with the official blessing of Harvard!

MAINSTREAM PSYCHOLOGY

The Dominant and Dominating Perspective

The shape and contours of mainstream psychology, etched so dramatically during my Harvard training years through the actions and reactions of leading Freudian, behavioral, and humanistic psychologists,

---

*Mr. Nyland intentionally does not have any publicly available published works; he stresses the importance of Gurdjieff's teachings being given directly to those who are seriously interested, such as those already involved in the Gurdjieff practice.

†A problem with my involvement with these various meditative practices is that many meditation groups are disconnected from the challenges of sociopolitical change. Related to that disconnect is a pervasive arrogance in many of those groups, stemming from the misguided belief that the group is the *only one* doing the right thing. If the group follows a particular path, such as hatha yoga, then only hatha yoga is the right way.

One expression of this self-assumed importance and almost self-righteous claim of knowing the truth is a rigid insistence on a *particular* way the practice *must be* carried out. This is dramatically the case when I am involved with macrobiotics: I work briefly with Michio Kushi, when he first comes to the United States, and I meet and eat with George Ohsawa and his wife on a visit to Japan. A macrobiotic mantra is "you are what you eat." When macrobiotics is first introduced to the United States, that mantra takes a particularly rigid form, with brown rice taking not only a primary but also sometimes an exclusive role in the diet. But the macrobiotic approach is meant to be sensitive to the natural environment in which it is practiced, respecting the foods available locally; therefore, there is relative flexibility in what constitutes macrobiotic *eating*—which is more important than macrobiotic *food*.

Fortunately, the meditation and yoga groups I engage in most intensively bypass that tempting arrogance and offer their teachings in a more flexible manner—as just one possible alternative, without sacrificing either the intensity or validity of that teaching.

as well as the emergence of cognitive psychology, remain today—though some of the raw vigor of the disagreements among those approaches, for example, between Skinner and Maslow, is gone. This mainstream approach can be characterized by certain perspectives and actions and rests upon a set of overlapping fundamental assumptions by which it seeks to dominate the dialogue about what is psychology, thereby validating its own approach and devaluing alternative perspectives.* Though these fundamental assumptions initially draw heavily from the psychology that prevails during my Harvard graduate training, they remain psychology's guiding assumptions today. Major dimensions are articulated during my time in graduate school by major figures in psychology; contemporary psychologists still carry out those assumptions, though they may rename them.

While these assumptions can be guiding *principles,* they don't describe the full range of *actual* work done in mainstream psychology because within its boundaries there are always elements seeking to avoid being bound. I discuss examples of these *Western* critiques of the mainstream under the section "Countercurrents within the Mainstream."

HIGHLIGHTING THE DISTINCTIVENESS
OF THE DIFFERING APPROACHES
TO PSYCHOLOGY

Indigenous Healing Psychology attempts to create a vehicle for constructive comparisons between mainstream psychology and countercurrents within that mainstream and Indigenous approaches to psychology. I'm trying to offer stimulating *paradigms* of these approaches, focusing on distinctive core elements, to create jumping

---

*See Katz (2012a), for another relevant discussion about mainstream psychology's dominating stance.

off points that highlight distinctive differences rather than painting *caricatures* that undercut fruitful inquiry. Sparks of understanding can emerge from such an examination of differences, which if considered openly can highlight avenues of similarity, and nurture collaborative pathways toward enhancement.

But this is not a clear-cut, firmly bounded inquiry. These approaches to psychology are dimensions, not dichotomous categories. The boundaries of each approach are more fluid than static, and there is overlap between the approaches. For example, what is a countercurrent within the mainstream at one point in time can be part of the mainstream at another time. The strongly emerging influence of women, as well as an explicitly feminist perspective, in mainstream psychology is but one example. But the examples I've selected to illustrate countercurrents are meant to represent perspectives or principles that exist largely outside of and are critical toward the mainstream.

Yet there are distinctions that remain important, and these need to be highlighted. For example, though often countercurrents *seem* similar to Indigenous approaches, there are typically crucial differences, differences whose subtlety can mask their reality. This doesn't imply that the countercurrents are of no value; they make valuable contributions to enhancing mainstream psychology even though those enhancements may be less profound or far reaching than enhancements offered by Indigenous approaches.

Working with paradigmatic examples of the approaches to psychology can encourage the lively and enlivening analyses and reflections that can support a healing of psychology, and a healing psychology.

Psychology as a Universal Framework

Mainstream psychology presents itself as a *science* of human behavior, generating universal truths about human nature; yet in reality, it is the characteristically unacknowledged expression of one cultural context: Western or what I'm calling mainstream culture. What is a legitimate expression of a particular historical period in a particular culture is exported throughout the world. This particular Western view of psychology dominates the shape and function of psychology because the cultural context from which it emerges is the seat of political, economic, and technological power—not because that particular form of psychology is superior. Western psychology promotes itself as the standard for psychology or more subtly simply as "psychology." It buttresses this claim of exclusive validity with authoritative statements such as "psychology demonstrates that individuals are most motivated by individual rewards," as if that statement represents what is the case for people throughout the non-Western world where what is often most motivating is working with and serving the *community,* rather than just representing the case for most people in the West, from whom the data is typically drawn. Mainstream psychology is an expression of *false* universalism, *a* form of psychology indigenous to *a particular* setting.*

Psychology, or more accurately Western psychology, is said to officially begin in the late nineteenth-century German laboratories of Wilhelm Wundt, who is hailed as the first "real" psychologist. He's considered the first scientific researcher because he establishes the first laboratory-based or *experimental* research center. Laboratory research is the gold standard of research; behavior measured in the controlled and isolated setting of the laboratory is considered the measure of naturally occurring everyday behavior.

Introductory psychology textbooks suggest there are psychological *preludes* to Wundt's "real" psychology; for example, Greek philosophers like Plato or Aristotle display psychological *thinking.* But

---

*I'm not calling mainstream psychology an Indigenous psychology, reserving that term in this book for psychologies developed by Indigenous peoples. But mainstream psychology can be considered a psychology *indigenous* to a particular cultural/historical setting—i.e., growing out of a particular setting.

the texts are clear that these philosophers are not really psychologists; their psychological thinking is typically dismissed as either uninformed or ill formed and sadly primitive. Some texts might broaden their historical net and include a Chinese philosopher like Confucius as an example of psychological thinking, but until recently, Indigenous peoples are not included in the psychology family, even peripherally.

Psychology is a set of theories and data, initially growing out of, and still dominated by, a Western mind-set, with a bias toward white, middle-class, male perspectives. This characterization of psychology is perversely logical. Most of its research findings are derived from observations about white, middle-class North American male behavior, for it is those males who historically populate colleges and take introductory psychology classes in droves—and a typical requirement of these introductory classes is that students become subjects in a research project.* The professors and researchers are themselves typically an older version of that same subset of people (white, male, middle class), so they see nothing wrong with their limited subject pool, too easily seeing reflections of themselves as accurate representations of "what is," which further solidifies this Western bias. The *founders* of psychology easily morph into the *fathers* of psychology, as face after face of influential psychologists portrayed in standard texts are white males.

But most perniciously, this double layer of Eurocentrism in psychology remains largely unexamined, often unrecognized. Data from a biased sample of human behaviors dangerously morphs into a "universally" appropriate description and explanation for who *all of us* are and who *all of us* might become. The idea that "middle-class white, framed through a male perspective" represents a distinct

---

*Currently, because of ethical concerns, participation in research is not required in introductory psychology classes, but there are strong inducements, such as extra grade points, for participating.

cultural phenomenon is not discussed, remaining implicit or, at worst, considered nonexistent, but that particular cultural framework continues to be offered calmly as a description of what is "natural" or "normal"—of the way it is, or most dangerously, the way it should be. This is a powerful underpinning for mainstream psychology acting as a colonizing force. The very idea of psycholog*ies* is not acknowledged; the contributions of Indigenous approaches to psychology are rarely even conceptualized.

The Pursuit of Science

A preoccupation irreverently called "physics envy" lurks over the shoulder of mainstream psychology, steering the discipline toward what is perceived, incorrectly, as the scientific purity and power of physics. "Science" for psychology is an enterprise of seeking logical, causal relationships through the controlled study and measurement of laboratory-isolated variables, which can result in a series of scientific laws.* And with this emphasis on this *particular* form of science comes the assumption that it is *only* through such a form of science that valid knowledge in general is produced.

Skinner's work exemplifies this physics-driven perception of science. He's not satisfied with correlations, which characterize much of psychological research but only indicate a relationship or connection between variables, but seeks causal relationships, in which one variable is shown to *cause* the other. And he develops sophisticated, yet simple measures to tell us how much or how little there is of whatever

---

*The irony is that, at the time of my graduate work, the discipline of physics, spearheaded by some of its brightest practitioners, such as David Bohm, and their work on quantum physics, is already moving beyond the conception of physics emulated by psychologists with its emphasis on materialistic, clean-cut causal relationships, and toward a new conception that stresses shifting and extensive interconnections, probabilities, and unpredictability. Even consciousness, in all its fluidity, is given a fundamental reality (see e.g., Bohm 1980). The supposed firm and solid foundation that psychology is seeking in the "pure" science of physics is transforming into a fluid, creative base.

he is studying. It becomes a hallmark of psychological validity that any concept becomes valid only after you develop a scientific way of measuring it, and the more elegantly and directly number-based that measurement is, the better.

One result of this focus on concrete and simple measurement, symbolized by an almost obsessive pursuit of numbers, counting, and categorizing as vehicles for knowing, is that psychology is increasingly reductive. It chooses measurement accuracy over the meanings of what is being measured, resulting in an increasing focus on more limited, even trivial variables. Preferring to analyze problems into a minimum number of separate, and increasingly more manageable units, psychology forgoes what is a more natural quality of human behavior—the interconnectedness of variables that suggests a wholistic as opposed to this segmented or fragmented approach. So, for example, intelligence is what the intelligence test measures—discrete responses to a series of separate, focused questions with standardized criteria for measurement, rather than a more intuitive search for the complexities of thought and understanding, which allows intelligence to include the critical dimensions of wisdom.

Carrying this objectifying notion of science one step further, Skinner says the important thing is not only measuring accurately but also *predicting* outcomes and then, almost logically, *controlling* them. In contrast, the aim of the more humanistic psychologists like Murray, Maslow, and Erikson is *understanding* human behavior, recognizing that, with a deep enough understanding, accurate predictions and effective interventions result, though they are transitional, always remaining subject to the evolving complexity of life itself.

Materialism as the Ultimate Criterion of What Is Real

In an effort to be scientific, psychology emphasizes the material—that which is observable either to the human senses or the senses aided by machines that record physical responses, such as brain waves or galvanic skin responses.* Psychology assumes that if we can see or touch something, it's real or real enough to merit being researched. Positivism is a label for psychology's almost peculiar search for truths, where some biological explanation is passionately pursued, as if it were a magic bullet capable of solving all problems.

In this surge toward materialism, psychology is striving to distance itself from its conceptual roots in religion and philosophy, the two fields that historically deal with issues of human nature and behavior that psychology now claims as its domain. But, it's stated, since those two fields deal with those issues in a way they can't be concretely measured, their conclusions fall outside the purview of psychology. The major wedge used to create this historical separation is the new discipline's commitment to a strictly controlled scientific method, as opposed to what is considered the more speculative and personal ways of knowing that currently characterized religious and philosophical discourse and knowing.

This effort at intellectual cleansing not only cuts psychology off from its roots, it also leaves off a major part of its definitional task. Psychology comes from the Greek word *psyche,* meaning "life force," "breath," "mind," "spirit or soul," all of which are immersed in spiritual implications. Topics such as healing and spiritual transformation— indeed anything considered beyond ordinary human behavior—are

---

*After dealing with introductory topics such as "what is psychology?" and "how do psychologists do research?" mainstream psychology texts typically start out their discussion of more content-oriented topics by presenting chapters dealing with genes, the brain and the nervous system, and sensation and perception. All these subjects are heavily based in a materialistic paradigm, and by putting them in the opening chapters, these psychology texts promote their foundational importance. Also, within the remaining chapters, which deal with topics such as thinking and intelligence, motivation and human development, the discussion typically begins with a focus on the genetic, physiological, or neurological approaches to the topic, as if to say again that the biological perspective remains the foundational approach. For example, explanations for and even roots of intelligence are sought in genetic and neuropsychological functioning, as opposed to differences in the way social-political environments support the development of intelligence. Other perspectives, such as the sociocultural, become secondary, even ephemeral representations of a biological base and unnecessary.

therefore not considered capable (even worthy) of scientific investigation.

Mainstream or Western psychology rarely discusses the fact that most non-Western cultures place topics of spirituality and healing at the center of their reflections on human nature, at the center of their psychology; and when this fact is discussed, it is often interpreted as a sign of the primitive and superstitious nature of these cultures. This same process of discrediting and belittling is applied to the fact that Indigenous peoples typically do not make clear distinctions between the material and spiritual, thus giving spirituality a firm and recognizable place in the material flow of ordinary life, acknowledging that the beyond is also within us.

Problems to Be Fixed Rather Than Potentials to Be Fulfilled

Mainstream psychology focuses on human and social problems and pathologies and how to fix them or, in a more positive vein, how to make things better. The clinical fields are psychology's most popular professional pathways, exerting a large influence on what is researched and studied, and their primary clinical expertise is in dealing with neuroses and psychoses rather than growth and actualization. The *Diagnostic Statistical Manual* (DSM)—the so-called bible of clinicians—focuses on these neuroses and psychoses and details the available categories for establishing mental illnesses and serves as the blueprint for both the creation of research programs and the confirmation of their success, while establishing proper procedures for clinical work. With the pressure from insurance companies to reimburse only identified illnesses, the DSM's illness categories provide fuel for that commodification of health and healing. In the process, prevention efforts—healing at the level of root causes—are minimized or ignored.

But there are three important consequences of psychology's emphasis on problems and pathologies. First, psychology is committed to finding something that is broken in order to fix it or make it better; personal neuroses and social dysfunctions are targeted. In the effort to find worthy subjects to work on, there is a second consequence: medicalization.

Ordinary life issues and challenges are labeled as medical problems or mental illnesses and therefore must be fixed *and* fixed by the appropriate professional—namely, a psychologist or other mental health worker. For example, grief over the loss of a significant loved one, which is an inevitable life challenge deserving a wide variety of responses, is too easily medicalized into a mental illness when the DSM states time and feeling limitations to what can be considered the proper or healthy experience of grief. What may be an existentially appropriate *process* of grieving can be too easily labeled as clinically unacceptable grief; in short, a mental illness problem. A third consequence of this focus on problems and pathologies is that psychology overlooks enormous areas of human potential. Certainly dealing with life's challenges, including those severe enough to become mental illnesses, is a necessary element of such growth and development. But when psychology emphasizes fixing problems, the creative potential in human development can become an afterthought.

Psychology as an Ahistorical, Apolitical Approach

The worldwide forces of colonialism, fueled by racism, are undeniable. Tragically, through its naïve and inaccurate claims of universalism, coupled with its culturally biased focus on what it perceives as normative and subsequent efforts at fixing what it determines is wrong, which often amounts to processes of assimilation to the status quo, mainstream psychology too easily becomes another vehicle of colonialism. Freud's influence remains strong within mainstream psychology, even when theoretically dismissed, and thus his claim that forces within the individual are the engines that determine change. So though psychology does work toward change—certainly Freud seeks to improve his clients' mental health—those efforts focus on the individual and especially what is within the individual.* Therefore, the variety of powerful

---

Indigenous approaches to psychology place the long sweep of one's cultural history, including historical and continuing struggles stemming from that context, at the core of any understanding of human nature.

socioeconomic and political forces that lead to oppression, such as systemic, institutionalized racism, are not prioritized and at times ignored, with the consequence that psychology becomes apolitical. Though psychology can claim that social change is the province of other disciplines, like sociology, it's hard to conceive of the individual as immune to the effects and challenges of surrounding sociopolitical forces. This disclaimer might defend the apolitical stance but ignores the reality of actual living situations where external sociopolitical forces and internal motivational forces are interwoven and *both* contribute to change. A further argument mounted in defense of this apolitical stance is psychology's embrace of the concept of science as a neutral and therefore objective pursuit—ignoring the increasing evidence about the interactive and intersecting nature of the researcher and researched and the need for those in positions of authority and power, such as psychologists, to take necessary political stances.

With its particular brand of ahistoricity, psychology does not deal with the many instances in which history affects contemporary human thoughts and actions. Historical facts of racism, as displayed, for example, in the enforced and abusive residential school systems for Indigenous people,* leave enduring, often indelible scars, on individuals, communities, and cultures, cutting into human dignity and limiting efforts toward releasing full human potential. Mainstream psychology is unwilling and unprepared to deal with such historical tragedies, even when it's clear they persist, feeding into and maintaining poverty and oppression.†

This occurs in spite of the fact that by the 1960s poverty and racism

---

*See for example, Assembly of First Nations, 1994, for one of the earliest reports of the way the Canadian residential school system abuses, dehumanizes, and colonizes Indigenous children; and the terrible costs of those abuses on their children and future generations— "intergenerational trauma" or "the cycle of abuse."

†As a graduate student, I don't receive any training in issues of drug use and addiction or domestic violence or sexual and emotional abuse, all consequences of the stresses, desperations, and psychic wounds of institutional racism, along with the continuing and debilitating forces of poverty and oppression. "Those issues of addiction and abuse," I'm told, "are the concerns of social workers, not us psychologists."

are already acknowledged as causes of mental distress and illness—which psychology does claim within its province. William Ryan's concept of blaming the victim* exposes this individual, indeed individualistic, apolitical approach of mainstream psychology. Ryan describes how someone who is poor, unemployed, or marginalized is too often blamed for his condition, rather than seeing the causes of poverty in institutional forces, such as racism and oppression, forces typically beyond the control of individuals. Something "wrong" with the way the person acts and thinks is unfairly considered the primary reason for his being poor.

Psychology as a Colonizing Force

With its Eurocentrism intact, unchallenged because of its subtle and deeply embedded implicitness, mainstream psychology is able to offer, even demand, its version of reality and human nature as *the* version— a universal framework and description of the way things really are. Those who differ from this universal version are seen not just as different but also as lacking or even inferior; they are often labeled pejoratively, using the cover of a professional assessment, as having a psychological problem, sometimes even pathology. The only path toward "progress," toward becoming *more* rather than *less than,* is to be more like the *version* of human behavior portrayed by mainstream psychology as *the* standard of human behavior—a goal ultimately unachievable (and indeed unacceptable) for vast numbers of people living in non-Western milieus. Rather than following an agenda of social justice, mainstream psychology is a proponent of the status quo—in the process leaving aside a commitment to psychological health *for all people.*

Behind mainstream psychology's unacknowledged colonial agenda is the increasingly overwhelming power of psychology as an institution. The psychological testing industry is one case in point. Almost all people, especially in the West, are tested, scored, and ranked, whether it be

---

*Though formally trained as a sociologist, Ryan's work deeply influences psychologists concerned with social welfare and justice (see e.g., Ryan 1971).

for intelligence, personality traits, or social skills. Because tests are commonly given to school-age children, their results help determine the life paths open to people, as the scores compare individuals with each other, focusing more on whom to exclude from opportunities. These psychological tests help define and support the power structure of psychology, as they can be administered and interpreted only by psychological experts—formally trained and licensed (legitimized) psychologists—and those experts typically come from the West.

The results are tragic. Mainstream psychology is a vehicle of colonialism in large areas of the world, evaluating and categorizing peoples as failing to meet standards or, even more pernicious, as "needing our help," which means "needing (help) to become like us."* It works most ashamedly with groups it helps to marginalize, including minority groups with their own culture and the vast numbers of people throughout the non-Western world. Rather than opening psychological services up to the people, psychology too often helps the helpers to become more entitled, more in control of psychological resources. Psychology not only supports the status quo but also embellishes it, bringing a psychological dimension to the exercise of political and economic power over others.

Countercurrents within the Mainstream

As this dominant and dominating version of psychology is articulated and gaining strength, there are still movements within the discipline of psychology that are resisting, offering instead a series of more humanistic, wholistic, value-centered, and culturally and spiritually sensitive alternatives. Even as Wundt is hailed as the "father of modern psychology" because of his experimental laboratory, William James, almost in spite of his wide-ranging acceptance of enhanced states of consciousness as well as ordinary motivations, is

---

*My good friend, Jeff King, a psychologist who is a registered member of the Muscogee Creek Nation, puts it this way: "Why do we have to become more White to become better?"

also venerated by some in mainstream psychology as one of its earliest and most insightful theoreticians.*

There are many interconnected and overlapping streams in these alternative approaches. There is, for example, humanistic psychology. Characterized by the work of Maslow and his concept of self-actualization and Carl Rogers† with his person-centered counseling and its identification of empathy, unconditional positive regard, and authenticity as keys to being an effective therapist, humanistic psychology offers a wholistic view of human nature, with a focus on potentialities for growth.‡ Humanistic psychology evolves into another alternative approach—transpersonal psychology. Transpersonal psychologists discuss concepts like altered states of consciousness and out-of-body experiences; express the influence of Eastern religions and philosophies, especially Zen Buddhism and Buddhist insight meditation; and insist on the need for spirituality to enter into the counseling relationship. And the at times romantic and oversimplified concept of human potential espoused by these humanistic approaches gets a dose of hard reali-

---

*And James does not eschew research. One of his contributions is to suggest that enhanced states of consciousness can be studied, if the methods used are appropriately sensitive, respectful, and innovative.

†*Client-Centered Therapy* (1951) is Rogers's classic work describing his approach; he later changes the name of his approach from client-centered to person-centered counseling, reflecting his evolving embrace of more thoroughly humanistic values.

‡The personal growth workshops at the Esalen Institute in Big Sur, California, help initiate the increasingly popular movement of offering personal growth workshops that implement humanistic values and goals. There's a strong experiential emphasis in these workshops, and Fritz Perls, one of the founders of Gestalt therapy, is a leader in this experiential learning. One day Abe Maslow is giving a talk to a small group at Esalen, and Perls is attending. In the middle of Abe's talk, Perls drops to the ground and crawls up to Abe, assuming the physical posture of an adoring disciple. He is trying to make a point: "we have no experts or gurus here, so let's have a dialogue rather than a lecture." But Abe is mortified; this is too experiential for him. As the personal growth movement is more expressed in these experiential workshops, Abe is more and more disenchanted with what he sees as the "sloppy thinking," and "irresponsible excesses" of those workshops. This debate between intellectual rigor and experiential authenticity persists in the fields of humanistic and transpersonal psychology.

ties with the emergence of an existential psychology, influenced by European existentialists like Sartre and their discussion of the need to face, and accept, inevitable anxieties and crises, which are intrinsic to living life fully.*

Mainstream approaches to psychoanalysis are enhanced by alternatives like ego psychology. For example, Erikson, resisting classical psychoanalysis's preoccupation with inner states and pathology, stresses opportunities for growth as well as obstacles and considers social and cultural contributions to development as respected realities. Meanwhile, Jungian archetypical psychology, with its focus on balance, mythic functioning, and the search for meaning, continues to provide a more wholistic, spiritual, and less pathology-oriented alternative to the psychoanalytic orthodoxy.

Mainstream psychology's ahistorical, apolitical stance, which dilutes and deflects a concern with sociopolitical change and equity, is dramatically challenged by a particularly vibrant alternative; namely, feminist psychology. Symbolized by the concept of "reclaiming" the voice of women, and by extension all those who are historically silenced by psychology, and spearheaded by psychologists such as Nancy Chodorow and Carol Gilligan, feminist psychology seeks to go beyond a simple critique of the current male-oriented definition of psychology and instead offers a new vision of psychology itself (see e.g., the early work of Chodorow 1978 and Gilligan 1982). Insisting on the centrality of underappreciated

---

*My dear friend and long-time colleague Stan Krippner exemplifies, through his prolific writings, this emerging and then expanding humanistic countercurrent (see e.g., Krippner et al. 2014). From his early research on hypnosis, dream analysis, and parapsychology, into his active and lively series of studies about spiritual journeys and cultural contexts, and then into his work on post-traumatic stress syndrome, Stan shows how a commitment to study enhanced consciousness can not only embrace dedicated research but also must include ways in which that enhanced consciousness functions within a cultural context having deep implications for practical issues of clinical health and social justice. And Stan remains a teacher, sharing his enthusiasm for knowledge; he still conducts early morning dream workshops for his students, offering them an exciting venue for psychic explorations.

concepts such as caring and sensitivity to the relational world, feminist psychology also states that social change must be in the forefront of psychology's definition and practice. This emphasis on social change is also championed by the emerging field of critical psychology, with its trenchant critique of the moral and political failures in psychology, including to some extent community psychology, the very field within psychology that has apparently emerged specifically to deal with these sociopolitical issues.*

There are also some important countercurrents within mainstream psychology that draw heavily from other disciplines, such as cultural and medical anthropology. This anthropologically inspired countercurrent, with its emphasis on ethnography as a whole culture methodology, brings a new level of appreciation of natural settings and cultural context rather than isolating what is studied in the artificially bounded laboratory setting. This anthropological perspective also brings a renewed appreciation of the interconnections among phenomenon, including the individual, group, family, community, and culture, rather than separating what is studied into smaller and smaller disconnected units. The fields of psychological anthropology and multicultural counseling are born.

Underlying, as well as ingrained in these alternative approaches to psychology is a set of emerging alternative methodologies, conceptions of research as a way of qualitative knowing rather than quantitative measuring. These qualitative methodologies emphasize respect for all participants in the research process; understanding rather than prediction; the valuing of human complexity in contrast to reductive categorizing; and goals of social change and liberation. Based on the assumption that there is more than one ("official") way of doing science, these alternative methodologies are nurtured within fields like phenom-

---

*Fox, Prilleltensky, and Austin (2009) present a summary of the foci of critical psychology. This emphasis on social change is a hallmark of sociology, one of psychology's sister disciplines.

enology, life history research, feminist research, and community-based participatory research.

Though these various countercurrents from within psychology are vibrant in their challenging of the dominance of the mainstream approach, they remain by and large marginalized, dismissed, and devalued by the psychology establishment. As I work as a psychologist in various settings throughout my career, I find support in these countercurrents, but predictably, because of their very "counter" nature, I feel marginalized because of that support. It's from this position of being an insider with an outsider's perspective that my psychology career unfolds.

PROFESSIONAL PATHWAYS AFTER HARVARD: BECOMING AND BEING A PSYCHOLOGIST

After obtaining my Ph.D. in clinical psychology from Harvard in 1965, I engage in interrelated work in teaching, clinical practice, research, and writing. In my various jobs in psychology, I continue balancing these four foci and increasingly direct my energies toward working with diverse cultural groups and groups that are often marginalized through racism and oppression.

Teaching is always an immediate and dynamic commitment, and I get continual feedback from students that I'm "doing a good job."* My clinical work is never done as part of a private practice. As part of my various jobs, whether it be teaching or community development

---

*Besides strong positive student evaluations, there are numerous teaching awards. I'm most proud of the award for teaching a special introductory psychology section for Indigenous students at the University of Saskatchewan. I'm nominated for the award by those Indigenous students, and I take pride not in my performance but in the fact that those Indigenous students are able to master the *implicit* rules and roles of success in the university, an environment new to them all. They now know one way to express *their voice* about what kind of teaching they value.

work, I respond to a variety of counseling and therapy requests from individuals, families, and communities but never charge any fees.*

Finally, I find that my research and writing flows from and feeds back into both the teaching and clinical work. The four foci energize each other. For example, I tell my students that before each class I'm nervous and excited—I often wonder "What will I say?" or "Do I have enough material?" or "Will students connect to the material?" And then I tell them: "Being nervous in that way is good. I can't be complacent and just do what I did before. Each class has to be fresh. I'm nervous because I feel vulnerable, knowing I have to be there, really be there in class—come what may. And you can and should expect your professors to be vulnerable in that way so new learning can happen."

I continue and expand on the directions offered by mentors such as Erikson, Murray, and Maslow and by the various humanistic, transpersonal, existential, and social justice countercurrents emerging within psychology. But I always feel there is something very basic lacking in these influences, something entailed in the limited worldview within which these influences function.

What ignites the defining spark that shapes my work as a psychologist is my first opportunity to live and work with Indigenous elders and healers (see map #1, page 85). These elders and healers are wisdomkeepers, persons respected for their knowledge about traditional spiritually based teachings and their commitment to nurture those teachings and share them, in the interest of service, with their communities. They are also our "first psychologists." I generally use the term *elders* to refer to those Indigenous people whose gifts of teachings are the central thread

---

*I've never had to tie my financial earnings into variables like number of clients seen or clients' ability to pay. I've been fortunate to work in employment settings where my counseling can be seen as part of the job, a valued extra commitment, or even "something you want to do but it's on your own time." But I appreciate the difficulty psychologists in private practice face in trying to balance a desire to be helpful with a need to earn a living. I really support the establishment of a sliding fee scale, including pro bono work whenever possible, and am pained whenever I hear about therapists compromising their desire to be therapeutic by overloading their schedule with full-fee-paying clients.

throughout this book; they are also healers, which enhances and intensifies their understanding.

INDIGENOUS PEOPLES

The term *Indigenous* as referring to the first peoples to inhabit the various parts of the globe is a richly complex term. Since Indigenous peoples' teachings are so central to the intentions of *Indigenous Healing Psychology*, it can be helpful to explore some of the meanings of that term. Chapter 2 also presents more material about the sources and actual practice of these Indigenous teachings.

There is, for example, the formal, bureaucratic, and intentionally neutralized discussion of Indigenous by the United Nations. Though the United Nations' perspective does not convey much of the lived experience of being Indigenous, it does offer a powerful mainstream perspective—and thus one that determines the boundaries and even the outcome of many debates about Indigenous people.

Here's an extract from UN discussions* of Indigenous cultures and peoples:

> Considering the diversity of indigenous peoples, an official definition of "indigenous" has not been adopted by any UN-system body. Instead the system has developed a modern understanding of this term based on the following:
>
> • Self-identification as indigenous peoples at the individual level and accepted by the community as their member.
> • Historical continuity with pre-colonial and/or pre-settler societies
> • Strong link to territories and surrounding natural resources
> • Distinct social, economic or political systems
> • Distinct language, culture and beliefs

*For the full document, please see the United Nations Permanent Forum on Indigenous Issues (Indigenous Peoples, Indigenous Voices/Fact Sheet), available at www.un.org /esa/socdev/unpfii/documents/5session_factsheet1.pdf.

• Form non-dominant groups of society

• Resolve to maintain and reproduce their ancestral environments and systems as distinctive peoples and communities.

For a more pointed perspective, dealing more with the actual struggles and potentials of Indigenous movements in the face of continuing colonization, Indigenous Maori scholar Linda Tuhiwai Smith's discussion (Smith 1999, 7) is helpful, especially as she gives prominence to the principle of self-determination, which includes the right of self-identification:

> The final "s" in "indigenous peoples" has been argued for quite vigorously by indigenous activists because of the right of people to self-determination . . . [The] world's indigenous populations . . . share experiences as peoples who have been subjected to the colonization of their lands and cultures, and the denial of their sovereignty, by a colonizing force that has come to dominate and determine the shape and quality of their lives, even after it has formally pulled out.

Finally, emphasizing the importance of lived, grounded experience in understanding the term *Indigenous*, rather than conceptual elegance, as well as the evolving potentials for empowerment in Indigenous movements that draw energy from their histories, =Oma Djo offers a simple and profound perspective on his ancestral home: "This land feeds us . . . it always has. It's where we live . . . it gives us life. It's not an easy life, but it's our life. And this is where we can keep being Ju/'hoansi [real people]." And their ancestral land—in both the literal and symbolic senses—continues to generate identities and therefore meanings and power for Indigenous peoples.

One editorial note: I capitalize the word *Indigenous* out of respect for the struggles of Indigenous people to assert and develop their inherent rights. The capitalization also helps distinguish that usage from the word *indigenous*, which is meant to describe a wide range of phenomena local to place, including plants.

In 1968, living with the hunting-gathering Ju/'hoansi, Indigenous people in the Kalahari Desert (see map #2, page 86), I experience spiritually based community healing. At the Ju/'hoan community healing dance, I'm wrapped in a wave of calm and balance, created by the combined efforts of all, and moving through all—and that enveloping wave can touch all corners of daily life, whether it be gathering root foods, sharing wild meat, or constructing village sites.* I carry on the work begun in the Kalahari, interspersed throughout and woven into my career as a psychologist, nurturing that initial spark, living with and learning from a wide range of Indigenous healers and elders. Early in my career, these journeys to Indigenous cultures are rarely understood, almost never appreciated.† But it's these learning experiences, as well as my attempts to apply these Indigenous knowledges and healings within North American psychology, that inform this book.

As a freshly minted clinical psychologist, I move more firmly into two directions newly emerging within and critical of mainstream psychology: community psychology and cultural healing and development. The 1960s are a time of sociopolitical turmoil, with increasingly powerful cries for social justice. Working within mainstream

---

*As with all people, the Ju/'hoansi experience a range of emotions and attitudes. Though the healing dance evokes a sense of connectedness and balance, there are conflicts and difficulties throughout Ju/'hoan life—as with all communities I've ever heard about. But their healing tradition does offer them a relatively strong sense of community and connectedness, balance and well-being. See Lee (2012) for a discussion of conflict among the Ju/'hoansi.

†When I inform the head of Massachusetts Mental Health Center, a Harvard teaching hospital where I'm in charge of the program in Community Mental Health, that I am leaving to do research on community healing in the Fiji Islands, he is truly perplexed—while instantly leaping into a negative stereotype. "You're leaving the valuable work you're doing here at the hospital? You're leaving Harvard? Harvard! To go where?" he says. "Fiji? Isn't that the place where they do nothing because they know nothing?" "Wow," I think to myself, "that's just what the colonizers of Fiji and many other parts of the world state to justify their oppression: we must take over running this country because the people are primitive and lazy, do nothing and know nothing." This judgment typically precedes the colonists' bringing in oppressed people from other lands to "really" work the colonized lands, such as developing the local sugarcane industry.

psychology's primarily ahistorical and apolitical framework, clinical psychologists are sitting in their offices, doing one-on-one psychotherapy. But when they look out their windows, they can see that all the real action for change is occurring on the streets. A few of them decide things must change: they move out of the quiet of their cloistered offices and join communities and the action on the streets, lending whatever expertise they can, including joining in these community efforts. I am part of this social action thrust of psychology. This movement of clinical psychologists dissatisfied with the limited effectiveness, even irrelevance of their one-on-one psychotherapy model, is how the discipline of community psychology is born.* Likewise, there are disciplinary options, both within and outside psychology, for me to express my commitment to cultural healing and development. But the institutional frameworks for each of these two commitments soon fails me: community psychology becomes itself more institutionalized and assimilated into a positivistic research model, and the disciplines dealing with cultural healing never fully appreciate either the depth or distinctiveness of non-Western cultural approaches.† Soon I'm left where I often seem to be—trying to find the path as I walk it.

On the recommendation of Abe Maslow, I'm hired for my first job in the psychology department at Brandeis University in 1967. Abe, a

---

*In 1965, a conference is held in Swampscott, Massachusetts, bringing together these clinical psychologists wishing to move from community mental health, the focus of the day, toward working with the community as a whole on a range of psychological, economic, and political issues and to transform psychologists from one-on-one therapists more into agents of social change. The Swampscott conference marks an "official" birth of community psychology (see e.g., Rickel 1987). The field of community psychology in its early years is most receptive to my early work on Indigenous approaches to community well-being; Julian Rappaport, a key figure in the shaping of community psychology, accepts one of my first published articles on that Indigenous approach (Katz 1983–1984).

†While various fields attempt to recognize the contributions of non-Western cultures, such as cross-cultural psychology and medical and psychological anthropology, they still fall short of a deep appreciation of these other cultures and a substantially radical critique of Western assumptions and values. Therefore I resist being identified as being in one or another of these disciplines.

key figure in the department, is my colleague and friend. Inspired by his commitment to open up education to permit deeper learning, I decide to teach my classes in a circle so that all of us, teacher and students, can have equal footing in and responsibility to the learning process and so that dialogue, or at least interaction, is encouraged. But this is not how classes are then taught—at Brandeis, or at most any other university. Though students thrive in that interacting pedagogical approach, the university is not pleased. Higher learning is still supposed to be situated within classrooms with desks clearly and cleanly in rows, and the teacher remains in charge, especially since he—not many women faculty at the time—possesses the knowledge, which he then imparts.*

It's not long before there's the official repercussion of my circle teaching. I'm told that at a university-wide meeting of the Brandeis faculty, the dean publicly censures a faculty member for his "unacceptable, countereducational behavior." In a serious tone, the dean laments that "*that* faculty member disrupted the classroom by moving the chairs from their straight rows into a circle!" Today, I still teach primarily in a circle, and of course, so do many others. The circle encourages equal access to knowledge, a foundation for social justice.†

My next job is out in the community, running a drop-in center, hoping to give youth who are becoming drug addicted an alternative place to be safe and sober. One night a group of young men, self-proclaimed "enemies" of the center, storms our building, starting to fight with those

---

*The analysis of Paulo Freire (e.g. 1968) is very relevant here as he distinguishes between the "banking" method of learning, where the teacher deposits knowledge into the student, and "dialogue," where the teacher and student create knowledge together—more likely within a circle of learning. My later meeting with Freire joyfully confirms the beauty and truths of his knowledge creation model.

†My teaching-learning in the circle expresses some of the principles of a then emerging field—experiential education—and leads to my first book *Preludes to Growth: An Experiential Approach*. Published in 1973, when experiential education is still in its early development, many unknowingly recategorize the book, fitting it more neatly into mainstream psychology, telling me how much they enjoyed reading *Preludes to Growth: An **Experimental** Approach*.

of us inside. I quickly realize nothing in my training as a psychologist prepares me for this random street violence. Without thinking, I and another staff member, joined by several young people attending the center, begin what could be called an amoeba response: we hope to end the violence by getting as many nonviolent people as possible to surround and in effect smother the swinging fists. It works that night, and though I can't say that technique is always effective, it does bring me further out of the protected boundaries of academic psychology.

Continuing that community work, in 1973 I become the director of Community Mental Health at the Massachusetts Mental Health Center, a Harvard teaching hospital. Returning to Harvard?! And to a main site of my clinical training? Haven't I already decided that university is not a place of or for healing? Yes . . . but. I still believe I can stand on Harvard's powerful institutional platform to speak more clearly and effectively about the changes I now know are needed in psychology. In fact, as my career in psychology unfolds, I find the name, and more importantly the symbol, of Harvard is a valuable asset for social change—when I speak for such change as a *Harvard psychologist* people pay extra, even more respectful attention. I'm not against using the Harvard platform to generate authority, but I'm always careful to resist the assumption by others that I am that authority and thereby deserve personal compliments, even rewards. The Harvard mystique is particularly effective in gaining access to government officials and institutional leaders when I'm suggesting changes in mainstream health policies toward still unacceptable community-based healing principles. And I come to Massachusetts Mental Health Center for another very pragmatic reason—we are established as a family in the locale of the center, with our two young school-age children cementing that physical connection.

As director of Community Mental Health, I expand the job focus to community health and development and learn what is obvious but is not part of my academic training: in order to work in community health and development, one has to *be in and work in* the community. During the time of intense community protests from the Black community in inner city Roxbury—disempowered with the racist code-word label "race riots"—I have to decide about whether to continue my work with a group of activist Black women who are trying to strengthen the local Roxbury health center or wait until "things settle down," as the media coins that dismissive phrase. Maybe with some combination of commitment to my work and the need for social justice—and I'm sure a healthy dose of naïveté along with a little bit of courage—I walk into the Roxbury community to work with those women. Predictably, I'm the only white person visible anywhere. And I do feel afraid, but more importantly, I know that I'm in the right place at the right time. We have some productive meetings, those women and I, and they soon take the lead in documenting the plan for improving local mental health services.

I learn something else at Massachusetts Mental Health Center—an effective way mainstream institutions can undercut, or co-opt community movements, which typically have a different, more politically aware agenda, is to offer community leaders a job in the institution! For a community activist to be a community liaison worker for the prestigious (at least among mental health professionals) Massachusetts Mental Health Center is hard to resist: there's the salary, when the activist typically has no steady income stream and, more devious, the promise that "you can do so much more for your community when you work from the inside." I plead with the institutional hiring authorities to resist conventional institutional-based employment offers and instead to support community workers with jobs that keep them *in the community,* working on ground-level issues. But to no avail: two potent community activist women are hired to be regular staff members to supposedly "represent the voice of the community." Sadly, pressured into complying with the very institutional agenda they are fighting to change, their voices are muted, even to the point of participating in case conferences where staff wonders, "How can we help *those people* out there in the community?" The almost unconscious desire to fit into the institution's agenda—typically at odds with the community's agenda—is powerful, seeking to overwhelm us, so we're not just working for the institution but also speaking on behalf of it. Some of us resist, but then our tenure at the institution ends.

In 1979, after a two-year period of research and work on community healing in the Fiji Islands, I am an associate professor in Harvard's graduate school level Program in Counseling and Consulting Psychology, now housed in the School of Education.* Didn't I just raise that question, "What, Harvard again?" Well, again there are compelling reasons: a special teaching-learning-research opportunity is waiting to be realized in that Harvard counseling and consulting psychology program, and that job allows me to continue living in Cambridge, Harvard's home, where my family, with our two kids, continues to be firmly embedded. Teaching in that Harvard program I am connected with a bright, vibrant, deeply knowledgeable, and politically aware community of graduate students, animated by the perspectives of those from Latin and Native American communities† as well from non-Western countries across the globe. Together, we make cultural diversity a reality and a foundation from which scholarship and clinical work can grow and be recognized.

Research projects emerge, culminating in a series of engaging and seminal doctoral theses. These focus on a variety of cultural and community healing and development themes, including Olivia Cheever on how Western psychiatrists can be more effective if they are educated more

---

*Several years after I graduate from the clinical psychology program at Harvard, it is disbanded. This Program in Counseling and Consulting Psychology is the present iteration of a clinical psychology program at Harvard and features Chris Argyris as the faculty representing the "consulting" theme, while the rest of the faculty, though we are all clinical psychologists, represent the "counseling" theme. A new Clinical Psychology program gets reestablished shortly into the twenty-first century.

†The official U.S. government term for such students is *ethnic minorities,* but it is a terribly inaccurate term, steeped in a racist perspective. For example, the Latina students, including Chicanas and Puerto Ricans, are only minorities in the context of their oppressed living conditions within the United States, not in terms of their fundamental cultural identities and communities. As well, students, for example, from India, while considered minorities, are from an enormous and vibrant home country and are minorities only by their enforced marginalization in a majority Western culture.

like Indigenous healers (Cheever 1995); Virginia Gonzales on the mental health challenges facing Mexican women during processes of migration (Gonzales 1988); Ada Gonzalez Ortega on the collaborative sharing of knowledge within a classroom taught by a Puerto Rican teacher (Gonzalez Ortega 1991); Eber Hampton on the transformational aspects of Native American perspectives on education and development (Hampton 1988); Al Meza on the enhancement of Chicano identity within a mainstream Caucasian educational context (Meza 1988); Steve Murphy-Shigematsu on ways in which a biracial Japanese American identity can be a source of strength and knowledge rather than being reduced to a vehicle for racial discrimination (Murphy-Shigematsu 1986); Mario Núñez-Molina on the community service and spiritual development emphases in the training of traditional Puerto Rican healers (*espiritistas*) (Núñez-Molina 1987); Becka Reichmann on community empowerment among *tricicleros* (bicycle street vendors) in Brazil (Reichmann 1985); Niti Seth on empowerment and healing among village women in India (Seth 1987); and Fernaz Sayal Shah on the ways that transformational effects of synergy are differentially expressed in American and Pakistani versions of a residential mental health program (Shah 1987). These research efforts also develop new approaches to qualitative, narrative, and community-based research. And most important, as we strive to meet standards of the highest quality, their research seeks to be rigorously thoughtful and sensitive, not settling for casual or poorly conceived critiques of the mainstream that exist *merely because* they are presenting *culturally diverse perspectives*—the new "can do no wrong" buzz phrase.*

---

*One expression of the body of work emerging from this group of intellectually talented, community-engaged, and culturally diverse students is a project initiated by one of them, Ada Gonzales. Ada suggests we honor our time together by publishing a volume describing the various research projects we have worked on together, including both student doctoral research and some of the research I'm engaged in. Through many permutations, including four different starts, stops, and restarts, Ada's original idea, helped along the way especially by Niti Seth, Mario Núñez-Molina, Val Naquin, and Steve Murphy-Shigematsu, takes the form of a published book (Katz and Murphy-Shigematsu 2012a), *Synergy, Healing, and Empowerment: Insights from Cultural Diversity.*

Yet Harvard, still implicitly encased in its Eurocentric worldview, struggles to understand this culturally diverse line of research. My school of education dean asks me: "I know your work is highly respected, and I know the students really connect with your teaching . . . but . . . but how does your work on the education of healers in Africa relate to education?"* The dean is asking a simple but severely narrow question: How does my research on healer education, which articulates a model of "education as transformation," fit into your ordinary *Western/American school curriculum*? She's not able to grasp the generic importance of the *principle* of transformation throughout education nor the importance of education that occurs outside the classroom, exemplified by the fundamental teachings that occur in many cultures of the world yet to establish the primacy of widespread formal classroom settings.†

There are also bright spots for me among the faculty during those later Harvard years. Carol Gilligan and I are mutually supportive colleagues; I'm attracted to her emerging narrative research methods and feminist commitment to social justice—and her commitment to teaching. We create and coteach a research course—"Methods of Inquiry"—presenting the range and variety of qualitative approaches.‡ And then there is my dear friend and colleague, Kiyo Morimoto, the director of the Harvard Bureau of Study Counsel, the place where student counseling occurs. Kiyo says simply: "Our job as counselors is to

---

*The dean is referring to my 1968 research on Ju/'hoan community healing in the Kalahari Desert, which is first reported in Katz, 1981, 1982a.

†The dean maintains her limited view of education despite the fact I am a lecturer at Harvard Medical School for a number of years, working on curricula issues, bringing the insights from Indigenous healers' focus on "education as transformation" into the academy. For example, we stress the importance of vulnerability in the education of doctors; though typically ignored in the classic medical school curriculum of the time, which is dominated by an emphasis on competence, vulnerability is today recognized as a necessary ingredient in their education (see e.g., Katz and Murphy-Shigematsu 2012b: chapter 7, "The Experience of Vulnerability: A Key to the Education of Health Professionals").

‡I think the graduate school agrees to making our course a requirement in part because Carol and I each have, by a very wide margin, the largest number of graduate students working with us.

listen. First listen to our clients—and resist the urge to right away offer advice, to fix their problems." Kiyo has no interest in mainstream psychology's commitment to fixing problems.* He also insists that the individual is the expert on his or her experience. Kiyo is a brother-in-arms.

And there is a small, still almost beleaguered group of scholars and researchers I regularly meet with who are exploring enhanced states of consciousness and spiritual healing and development, including Harvey Cox in the Harvard Divinity School and his studies of religion and spiritual and social change† and Joan Borysenko, a skilled researcher who is a member of Herb Benson's medical school project, which is beginning investigations of the relaxation response.‡

But my Harvard sojourns establish the same conclusion: I'm not meant to work from the inside of an institution that is so fundamentally conservative. Better to find institutions that in themselves are committed to exploration and therefore offer support for my intentions. As I mature in my profession, it is more important to do actual work toward the common good—whether it is recognized or not with the Harvard-type stamp of approval.

From Harvard, I move in 1986 to the University of Alaska in Fairbanks to head the community psychology master's program. The program focuses on community mental health, with an emphasis on rural villages—and that means an emphasis on Indigenous mental

---

*Kiyo writes a wonderful article on counseling, "Notes on the Context for Learning" (Morimoto 1973). It puts into words his enormous insights into counseling, but as is Harvard's way, he's continually disrespected and discounted, not only because he has no Ph.D. and doesn't publish widely, even though his work is brilliant, but also because as a second-generation Japanese American does not fit the Ivy League mold—even though he serves the country of the Ivy League and all other leagues with great distinction and heroism in World War II. This reprehensible treatment of Kiyo, which I speak out against to our faculty, is one of the saddest chapters in my various associations with Harvard.

†When we are meeting, Harvey is gaining considerable recognition, which began from his early work, *The Secular City* (Cox 1965).

‡Joan grows out of the limiting experimental orthodoxies of the Benson project, becoming a leader in the application of spiritually infused practices for the promotion of health and well-being.

health, as Alaskan villages are by and large Indigenous communities.* But there are very few Indigenous students in the master's program; for most, Fairbanks is too far and inaccessible from their villages so a commute is impossible, and a residence in Fairbanks is both too expensive and unreasonable, as prospective students typically have large families to look after. As a result, our program lacks a reality-based commitment to community development and healing.

I see an easy, almost logical solution: move out of the university's isolated and isolating ivory tower and transform our residence-based graduate program increasingly into what is then a relatively new and untested model—distance-delivered education. And we do that: enrollment of Native students goes from 5 to 35 percent in one year and maintains that percentage, as those students can continue much of their learning in their home communities. These Indigenous students bring their real concerns to the program's discourse, issues troubling their communities, such as alcoholism, drug abuse, and family violence. We are more honestly a *community* psychology program, while disproving the dire predictions that there is a "lowering of academic standards." Thesis research occurs more and more frequently in village settings, suggesting practical Indigenous-based strategies to make the Alaskan mental health system more responsive and thus effective with Indigenous Alaskans, and in that process develop a model of best practices.

My present job, which I begin in 1989, is teaching in the Indigenous social work program at the First Nations University of Canada (formerly called the Saskatchewan Indian Federated College, or SIFC). Here my work in Indigenous health and healing is firmly grounded in an Indigenous† institution of higher learning that is built on and energized by the traditional teachings of Indigenous elders and healers

---

*At the time of my work in Alaska, the preferred terms for Indigenous people are *Native* or *Native Alaskans.*

†*Aboriginal* is the official governmental word at the time used to describe Canada's three Indigenous groups—First Nations, Metis, and Inuit people.

and focuses on educating Indigenous students. Elders are central to the curriculum, and their traditional spiritual ceremonies form an ongoing thread in the work of the college. In line with these teachings, students are encouraged to engage in their own healing journeys; spirituality is understood to underlie knowledge, which then becomes shared and renewable; classic subject areas are taught within an Indigenous perspective; and students are trained to better serve their home communities and thus promote social justice in their communities, which can be considered marginalized and oppressed nations within Canada.

To further develop the curriculum at First Nations University, I help create a Master of Indigenous Social Work Program,* which graduates respected Indigenous students who now go back into the community with a stronger skill set and deeper commitment to Indigenous healing methods. I'm also asked to develop an introductory psychology course with an Indigenous perspective. The course highlights the limitations and colonial assumptions of mainstream psychology while also offering ways to enhance that psychology through Indigenous understandings of psychology, in particular through listening to Indigenous elders and healers, who I believe are our first psychologists. As an adjunct professor in the Department of Psychology at the University of Saskatchewan, I also teach a version of this course to Indigenous students who are part of a special cohort in the Aboriginal Student Achievement Program. Material from that Indigenous perspective on psychology is as well a part of my department seminar with doctoral students in clinical psychology, entitled "Culture and Healing."

Now, with the strong supportive context of my Saskatchewan families and First Nations University and primarily through living and

---

*First Nations elder Danny Musqua and First Nations political leader and social worker Sid Fiddler are the other two driving forces behind creating the master's program; and Jon Sealy, a respected social worker originally from Barbados and current department chair, provides the essential administrative support. See Katz, Musqua, Lafontaine (2012) for a more detailed description of the Master of Indigenous Social Work Program at that university.

learning with elder Danny Musqua, I turn more intensively and practically to the healing paths and gifts I receive in my various work with Indigenous elders and healers. A network of local Indigenous elders and medicine people are a welcoming and effective workspace. Models and strategies of cultural and community healing develop, stressing collaboration based on respect for each other's ways. The challenges of this collaborative work are more fully understood because I am working within communities in the place that I now live.

And it's here in Saskatchewan that I once again meet students who care deeply about their learning, about cultural integrity and respect, and about social justice. Typically first-generation students, often coming from backgrounds of poverty and oppression, they struggle to overcome many obstacles and yet remain curious and committed. A student sends a frantic text the day before a final paper is due: two drunk guys, spillover from a drinking party in town, have forced their way into her house, knocking things over, smashing her computer to the floor, and threatening her physical safety. She's now in a safe place and wants to complete her final paper, lost in that mangled heap of her computer. "Of course you can have time to complete your work . . . but your safety, your health must come first," I respond, and then we talk about ways toward safety and protection. Her dedication and courage are profound. Another student, a single mom, carries her crying two-year-old daughter to the doorway outside the final exam room because her babysitter is sick. And Mom is also crying, almost hysterically. She sees "no way out." "I guess it's over for me . . ." she sinks into resignation, "but . . . but. . ." *"But,"* I say immediately, "But we can work it out!" She's a good student, is serious, and works hard; she's earned my trust. She deserves to take the final and deserves a chance to complete the course. "Here, take the exam, and find a quiet place to work, and do it," I tell her. "And you *can* do it," I assure her. And she delivers. Working quietly in a student study room, with others there to help look after her baby, she writes her exam—and passes with ease! I tell her how proud her little girl will be when she learns about her mom's university degree.

Traveling the treacherous pathways of healing from the terrible effects of colonization, with its attendant racism and poverty, these Indigenous students often face daunting issues, such as alcohol and drug addiction, family violence, and adolescent suicide. Mainstream psychology does not prepare me to teach, to work with, and to learn from such students. I feel privileged to be part of their journeys.

HOW CAN WE EVOLVE INTO A HEALING PSYCHOLOGY?

The Increasing Bifurcation in Psychology

The general shape and contours of mainstream psychology when I was a graduate student remain today. A biological, materialistic approach continues to dominate, promoted as "superior," that is, as more clearly and cleanly scientific; and neuropsychologists now sit close to the head of the class in mainstream psychology departments. This biological approach is also attractive as a possible source of the silver bullet—an identifiable, measurable answer to a pressing problem, as in a genetic link to explain schizophrenia.* The irony is that—with few exceptions—neither the explanatory variable (genetic markers) nor the variable being explained (a mental illness) is typically either simply identifiable or measurable. We now know that isolating genetic markers is a very complex task, involving groups of interacting genes, and that something like schizophrenia is really schizophrenia*s* and is itself a complex and shifting condition.

At the same time there is a growth and deepening of humanistic and transpersonal approaches, which offer a contrasting path to this biological orientation. For example, the understanding of mainstream psychological topics such as motivation, human development, psychotherapy,

---

*One mainstream introductory psychology text (Wade et al. 2017), discussing research focusing on genetic phenomena, heralds the promise of genetic research with a dramatic section title: "Unlocking the Secrets of Genes," thereby promoting the field as a likely source of this silver bullet.

and consciousness, including the dream state, are now being more explicitly, comprehensively, and knowledgeably influenced by Buddhist spiritual teachings and practices. Buddhist-influenced insight meditation programs are almost commonplace, appearing in schools to facilitate learning, hospitals to facilitate healing, and businesses to facilitate profits. The rapid emergence of positive psychology is also helping to energize the humanistic side of psychology.

But something is still lacking in psychology's attempt to be more of a healing force. For example, though the insight meditation programs are offered in a wide variety of everyday, mainstream settings, the programs are often offered in a diluted form, stressing more ordinary attention than deep meditation. The meditation programs focus more on allowing people to be better at what they are already doing—such as learning faster or earning more profits—than engaging in life-changing processes of balance and compassion, the basic tenets of the Buddhist approach. Also, positive psychology remains bounded by its Western cultural framework. For example, when positive psychology proposes that an individual's personal happiness is critical to full human potential, researchers from non-Western countries are dubious. They see that kind of happiness as one more Western expression of a self-focus, even self-indulgence, and demonstrate instead that engaging in life's challenges and serving others are people's priorities—and yield a happiness of their own kind.

There is also an increasing number of collaborative efforts between these two main directions of the biological/genetic and the humanistic/spiritual; for example, there are laboratory studies, exemplified by the work of Richie Davidson,* that focus on the neurophysiology of meditation. Davidson stresses the concept of *neuroplasticity,* or the ability of

---

*I first connect with Davidson when I'm teaching at Harvard and he is finishing up his Ph.D. there. Now his colleague, I admire how he turns to his own meditation practice to inform his research and seeks continual guidance from the teachings of the Dalai Lama about Tibetan Buddhism. See, for example, Davidson and Harrington 2001; Davidson 2004; Davidson and Lutz 2008; and Davidson and Begley 2012.

the structure and function of the brain, even the adult brain, to change with new learning. He suggests that insight meditative practices stimulate neurological supports for the development of compassion, a key component of that meditative practice.

Today's mainstream psychology, through countercurrents from within, is also progressing along another healing direction for psychology—a better understanding of the depth of cultural diversity. There is an increasing realization that the heralded "cross-cultural" counseling movement is itself culturally biased, originated primarily to "sensitize" *white* clinicians to the different cultural worlds of their *nonwhite* or "minority"* clients, worlds that are often stereotyped for ease of understanding, limiting ways of being more effective to a focus on relatively superficial traits and values. For example, therapists are advised not to look their Native American clients directly and steadily in the eyes, as it would be felt not as being "direct" and "straightforward" but as being "intrusive," even "dominating." Such direct looking *is* disrespectful in Native American culture, but it's the *value* of respect for another's space, even identity that's the critical issue, not the *behaviors* that express that value. And it takes someone like Joe Trimble, one of the founders of multicultural psychology, to deal with this more essential level of cultural values and identity.

Joe Trimble is a respected and productive Native American psychologist, honored both within mainstream psychology and among those dedicated to Indigenous approaches. He makes a deep cultural sensitivity—dealing with values, identity, and spiritual teaching—a legitimate, even necessary part of psychology. While authoring numerous foundational texts and articles about cultural dimensions of

---

*The term *minority* is a formal U.S. government designation of the following groups: African American, Asian American, Latino, and Native American. But these groups are minority primarily based on their racialized separation from their rightful access to resources and basic human dignities. Psychotherapy and counseling is one of those resources that can lead to dignity, whereas in its contemporary form, that counseling typically further solidifies racially based misunderstandings and subsequent degradations.

counseling, consulting, and community development (see e.g. Pedersen et. al., 2015; Trimble et. al., 2014), Joe also speaks from the heart, sharing the spiritual teachings of his Indigenous world, opening up about his own spiritual journey and discoveries (see e.g. Trimble, 2010).* What a wonderful teacher—others listen to him because he offers but doesn't lecture.†

Yet mainstream psychology finds it hard to accept the radical implications of this new field. For example, psychology remains wedded to the culture-specific Western concept of self as a bounded, even isolated engine of achievement, ignoring the common non-Western concept of self as a dynamic experience intertwined with and inseparable from community/culture and the universe at large, functioning to establish a sense of belonging and being rather than achievement. Non-Western cultures are often victims of psychology's reductionistic preoccupation, being portrayed only at a surface level, characterizing, indeed caricaturing Indigenous peoples by emphasizing their traditional cultural dress or food, ignoring the more complex and subtle realities of their interacting concept of self-in-community. This superficial "beads and feathers" approach masks the real experiences of painful struggle felt and resisted.

And so mainstream psychology continues to be more of a colonizing than liberating force for the vast majority of the peoples of the world—the worldview of one small but economically powerful people is making its way across the globe, telling people who and why they are. The Americanization of mental illness, exemplified by the global

---

*Joe Trimble's body of work has inspired a lineage of attempts to examine and critique mainstream psychology from an Indigenous perspective (see e.g. King 2012).

†*Indigenous Healing Psychology* is just one of many efforts to bring Indigenous perspectives into mainstream psychology. Among the more recent examples are contributions from Indigenous psychologists like Professor Patricia Dungeon, Melinda Garcia, Ph.D., and Professor Gayle Morse, as well as from groups such as the Society for Indian Psychologists and the Indigenous Psychology Special Interest Group in the American Psychological Association. The contributions from these two groups are discussed more fully in chapter 8; by then special contributions *Indigenous Healing Psychology* is seeking to make are clearer.

adherence to the Western-sourced *Diagnostic Statistical Manual* (DSM) as *the* definitional authority for what is mental illness, is but one example of the continued exportation of a false universalism. Where before cultural differences were largely ignored, and typically misunderstood, there is now a desire to "help" others: "we must be more sensitive to the needs of others different from ourselves" is a common mantra. But this stated desire to help is often a cover for a desire to define and control, for exporting instructions on the "correct" way to be.

Turning to Our First Psychologists for Guidance about Future Directions

How can mainstream psychology welcome its responsibility for encouraging social change and respecting real cultural diversity? How can mainstream psychology overcome its present momentum toward a bifurcation between the biomedical and the humanistic approaches, with the former dominating, and instead work toward creating a balance, appreciative of both sides? In short, how can mainstream psychology be more of a healing psychology?

In this book, we turn to a new, underappreciated source for guidance, the Indigenous peoples themselves, and privilege their voices, voices that are tragically ignored within mainstream psychology—and all other institutions of power in the Western world. The first or Indigenous peoples of the world, the original human inhabitants in their respective lands, are the original ones to gather in groups and grapple with the basic issues of psychology. They thus are our "first psychologists." They ponder questions we still struggle with: Who are we? How do we develop? How do the individual and community interrelate? How do we fit into the larger universe? What are the meanings of our lives? Over the centuries of trial and error, they evolve effective, often liberating, responses to these questions. These Indigenous cultures ponder and work on issues that mainstream psychology is ignoring at its peril, such as how social justice is the right of all people and how an appreciation of the significance of spirituality in everyday life opens doors to a fuller and deeper understanding of human nature and potential. Our first psychologists, now represented by contemporary Indigenous elders and healers, have something to teach us.*

Indigenous Healing Psychology offers Indigenous perspectives as a way to critique, illuminate, and hopefully enhance mainstream psychology, but it isn't a book on the Indigenous perspective. There is no unitary Indigenous perspective or set of agreed-upon perspectives; furthermore, respecting a fundamental Indigenous teaching I receive, I present only my personal experiences in several Indigenous cultures and my understandings from their teachings. As Ratu Civo, my Fijian spiritual teacher says, after my nearly three-year healing apprenticeship with him: "Tell only what you know . . . no more . . . no less." And so I'm seeking not a *comprehensive* discussion of either mainstream psychology or Indigenous perspectives on psychology but an *accurate* presentation of core features of each approach that can *highlight* differences and similarities. I look forward to *Indigenous Healing Psychology* being placed within a fuller, more understanding context that includes other books written by Indigenous psychologists, as well as Indigenous elders.

In this effort to highlight differences and similarities, there's the temptation to romanticize and essentialize. For example, it's too easy to portray Indigenous approaches as pure and perfect and mainstream psychology as misguided and flawed, all the while exaggerating the homogeneity within each approach and the separations, even dichotomies,

---

*Indigenous approaches to psychology are not the only sources for enhancing mainstream psychology. There are the many invigorating influences that come into psychology from other social science disciplines. For example, systems theory, which is an innovative perspective in understanding group, family, and community dynamics, originates from a number of nonpsychological disciplines, including physics, economics, and game theory. The methodology of community-based participatory research, enabling research to more directly and intensively bring about social change, gains its creative impetus from sociology and applied anthropology. But I focus on Indigenous approaches to psychology, not only because they are what illuminates my path as a psychologist, but also, more importantly, because their incredibly valuable and unique perspective, existing within a whole, evolutionary-basic cultural context, is largely ignored by the mainstream.

between them. I know this temptation well, and I try to guard against a too superficial path of pitting the "good" against the "bad," which points me toward more nuanced, complex, and interrelational realities. All ways have contributions to make, and none are free from drawbacks—at least as far as I know!

One can argue that comparing mainstream psychology with Indigenous approaches is unfair and unrealistic—the former is an institutionalized profession, the latter a way of living. But that is precisely one of the points. To be more healing, mainstream psychology needs to be more respectful of and connected to the ongoing web of daily life from which it too often distances itself, claiming "objectivity" as a higher necessity. Within Indigenous perspectives, what can be considered psychology—though it is rarely labeled as such—is one aspect of and way to understand real challenges and opportunities from inside lived truths. Indigenous perspectives on psychological thinking and practice are whole culture perspectives.*

As *Indigenous Healing Psychology* continues its journey through mainstream psychology, offering ways to enhance that psychology, it might seem like those suggestions all center around the phenomenon of healing. Considering that my own background is shaped by clinical psychology and that the Indigenous elders I work with most intensively are also healers, that assumption *can* seem likely. Yes, the book is about healing, but healing understood broadly and inclusively. It's not merely about more limited and institutionally framed instances of healing, such as psychotherapy, though it does deal with them. Instead, the book is about healing as a generic life process of understanding and growth—healing that is the movement to and from meaning, balance, wholeness, and connectedness. And this generic conception of healing is what Indigenous elders teach and what they

---

*Chapter 8 discusses more fully the potential synergistic relationship between Western and Indigenous approaches to psychology. The former, though still a professional-based discipline, is enhanced by insights from Indigenous approaches, showing how, as a result, services to *all* people can be encouraged.

tell me Western psychology needs to become to more truly serve the people.

Indigenous teachings offer guidance about how the still incipient healing directions *within* mainstream psychology can be encouraged. I discuss these intrinsic emerging directions in successive chapters under the subsection "Countercurrents within the Mainstream," focusing on those countercurrents *pointing in the direction* of those Indigenous teachings.* But though these Indigenous approaches seem similar to some of these humanistic countercurrents, often using similar descriptive terminology, there are important and fundamental differences.

The wisdom of Indigenous psychologies is more than a continuation or fulfillment of these humanistic countercurrents; these Indigenous psychologies offer a new type of guidance as well. So that though these countercurrents offer positive and hopeful directions, they still are missing essential ingredients contained in Indigenous approaches. For example, phenomena such as respect, exchange, balance, and spirituality exist within and are shaped by mostly implicit and fundamental worldviews, which construct qualities of life and living. But Indigenous and mainstream psychological worldviews are quite different. One result is that such phenomena typically involve more depth and commitment when experienced within Indigenous cultures. So there is respect as discussed within these humanistic perspectives, and respect as discussed within Indigenous perspectives; and we need to resist the temptation to too quickly cast the sometimes disturbingly unfamiliar into the comfortable familiar. Respect from an Indigenous perspective entails more of an unquestioned connection to and acceptance of others that goes more directly and simply to the core of being human, and this respect is

---

*There are many countercurrents within mainstream psychology attempting to reshape and enhance the field. Ones that point in directions other than Indigenous perspectives can also be useful and effective. For example, the increasing precision of diagnostic technologies for studying brain functioning, one focus in neuropsychology, clearly provides valuable new information, but a question would still remain about how that information is applied in the service of health for all—a central Indigenous commitment.

accorded to all parts of the universe, erasing the Western labels of animate and inanimate. As Indigenous elder Danny Musqua says, "We're all part of the creation and therefore we all . . . and I mean 'all'—plants, animals, wind, and rocks—all are deserving of unquestioned and ultimate respect *as part of life*—though that respect can be tested through our actions."

These Indigenous teachings also suggest ways the present divisiveness within psychology is resolved at a higher level of acceptance, even harmony,* as well as preparing the terrain for an appreciation for psycholog*ies,* including Indigenous as well as Western forms, where the whole of available psychological resources is greater than the sum of its parts. And most important, Indigenous perspectives can offer a way of doing psychology so that it can begin to function outside the matrix of colonization. These futures of possible collaborations between Indigenous and mainstream psychology are explored in the "Future Collaborations" section.

In the next chapter, we meet the Indigenous elders whose teachings animate this book, learn about the cultural contexts in which they thrive, and hear about the ways in which I strive to connect with them—the actual and concrete discipline of spending the necessary time, energy, and commitment to deserve these teachings. In *Indigenous Healing Psychology,* I focus on those elders I work with most closely,† those who take me on as an apprentice: =Oma Djo (Ju/'hoan), Ratu Civo (Fijian),

---

*This higher level of acceptance, even harmony, wherein the whole becomes greater than the sum of its parts, occurs when synergy is released. Synergy emerges as a central concept in *Indigenous Healing Psychology.*

†My singling out particular elders in this way reflects only *one aspect* of the teaching-learning relationships that occur throughout the cultures I live and work in. There are countless, often unnoticed learnings occurring within daily life. As well, singling out individuals is not what is valued in the community-oriented cultures I work in; the knowledge shared in this book is in essence knowledge of a people and culture and certainly not owned by any individual. But for purposes of clarity in communication, I keep this focus on the few elders with whom I have the most intimate relationships and whose relationships are the most explicitly directed toward teaching me about healing and living the good life.

Joe Eagle Elk (Lakota), and Danny Musqua (Anishnabe). All of these elders are also healers, respected in both domains; the two functions overlap and reciprocally support their meanings, creating exponential power and understanding. They are each dedicated to teach, to share their knowledge and experience, and, especially, to reach out beyond their own communities to others.

The process by which these teachings are heard and learned is an essential part of the teaching. These teachings don't exist in isolation: the cultural context, the experiential atmosphere in which these teachings emerge and thrive, is their nurturing soil; the context is the story. They are not abstract or theoretical; they are guiding principles for action and potential in our everyday lives. *Indigenous Healing Psychology* is not a cookbook of therapeutic techniques or spiritual ceremonies but an inviting hand toward actual change—and the elders, through their stories, offer embodied forms of their teachings.* Therefore, we need to learn how to listen and hear these Indigenous teachings, intuitively as much as cognitively. And to hear effectively, we need to respect the value of those teachings, which emerge through generations of struggle and hard times endured by Indigenous peoples. We also need a commitment to offer something of equal value in return for these teachings. A beginning can be for mainstream psychology to let go of its carefully guarded position of being in control. Though Indigenous knowledge is offered as a gift, it is a gift that must be earned.

---

*The thrust toward commodification of all and everything in mainstream Western culture seeks to put these dynamic Indigenous teachings into limiting containers, the more easily to establish units of teaching, and then establish appropriate market prices. It is truly absurd—like trying to capture smoke in a cheesecloth.

Maps

MAP #1*
Sources of Indigenous Wisdom
within *Indigenous Healing Psychology*

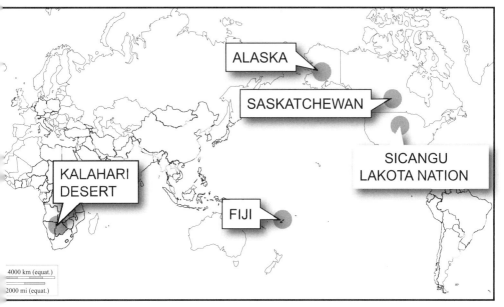

Base map from d-maps.com

---

*The world map (Map #1) used in *Indigenous Healing Psychology* is based on the contemporary conventional Mercator map, originally designed to focus on navigation along European colonial trade routes. Hence it's a Eurocentric and therefore misleading portrayal of the world. The *relative size* of various continents in this conventional format become systematically either exaggerated or minimized—sending a not-so-subtle and incorrect message about the relative importance and significance of Europe as compared to large areas of the developing world.

More accurate representations of relative area sizes in the world are available in less Eurocentric formats like the Gall-Peters Projection; viewing such a map version is an enlightening experience (www.npr.org/sections/thetwo-way/2017/03/21/520938221 /boston-students-get-a-glimpse-of-a-whole-new-world-with-different-maps). Unfortunately the Gall-Peters map version is not available for use in the editorial revisions necessary for this book.

MAP #2
/Kae/kae, Kalahari Desert, southern Africa

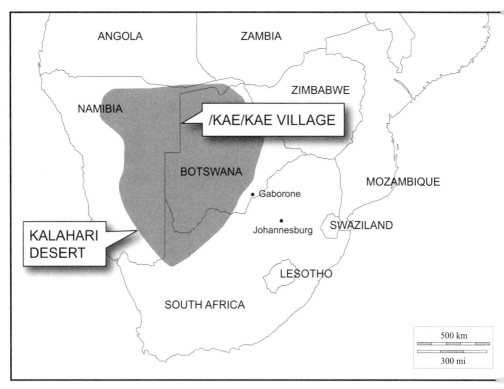

Base map from d-maps.com

MAP #3
Fiji, southern Pacific Ocean

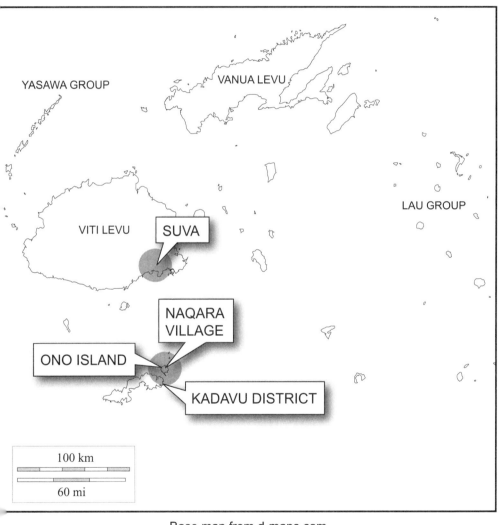

YASAWA GROUP

VANUA LEVU

VITI LEVU

SUVA

LAU GROUP

NAQARA VILLAGE

ONO ISLAND

KADAVU DISTRICT

100 km

60 mi

Base map from d-maps.com

MAP #4
Alaska, USA

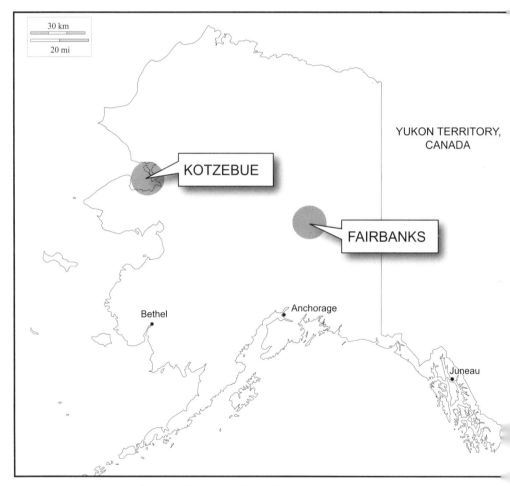

Base map from d-maps.com

MAP #5
Southern part of Saskatchewan, Canada

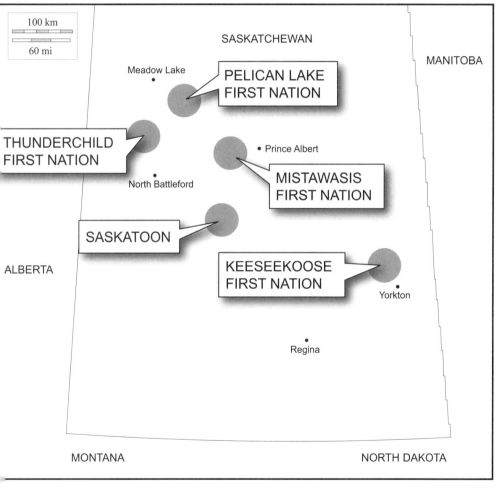

Base map from d-maps.com

MAP #6
Sicangu Lakota Nation, South Dakota, USA

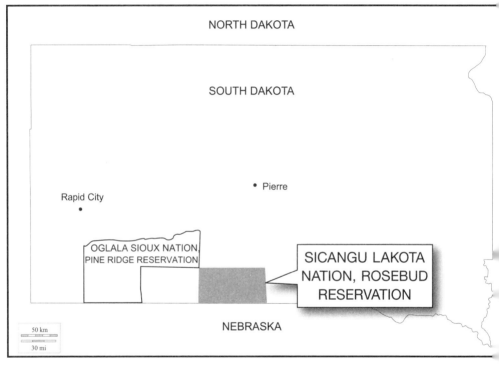

Base map from d-maps.com

CHAPTER TWO

"We Try to Understand Our World—That's Just What We Do"

Indigenous Elders as Our First Psychologists

INTO THE KALAHARI DESERT

It's 1968 in the Kalahari Desert, and we're heading for /Kae/kae, a permanent waterhole surrounded by four Ju/'hoan camps, situated on the far northwestern edge of Botswana, Africa.

My only thoughts are about the sun. It's now piercing brightly into the sand, the heat ramping up its influence. Sitting on top of our four-wheel-drive truck, I'm first amazed, then secretly proud that I'm not sweating like my companions. "Must be that I'm in good shape," I muse.

A short time later, it hits me—a direct and terrifying realization. I'm in an enormous oven, baking beyond anything in my experience, with no release into cool. Nowhere in this open, arid land, with its tall walk-through grasses, scrubby bushes, and scattered trees covering the flat, sandy ground, nowhere is the cool I naïvely assume is there for me, somewhere. Shade, yes; shade enough. But the sun heat lingers on, only slightly diminished under shade branches.

The land is a cauldron—a test pit with no way out. Terror is of breathing space.

In an instant—sooner even than the "next" instant—I accept the oven I'm in. I have no choice. I don't want a choice. Before I can decide, I've decided. I'm here, and that is where I am. Soon, I release into the land, and my body shows its wisdom, as I start to sweat along with the other proper inhabitants of the Kalahari. I begin living more fully in the Kalahari, allowing me to be more fully with the Ju/'hoansi.

The summer temperatures remain high, sometimes reaching 110 degrees Fahrenheit during the midday. And there is no air-conditioning, or even fans, which in itself is an absurd statement to make, as there is no electricity or running water in /Kae/kae!

The roughly one hundred Ju/'hoansi living at /Kae/kae still engage primarily in hunting and gathering for subsistence.* They live in simple, grass-thatched homes with branches as the framing structure, all made from the materials at hand in the surrounding land. Possessions are not accumulated and emphasize the essentials— survival tools like hunting bows and arrows, digging sticks for gathering edible roots, sharpening stones, a cooking pot and food preparation implements—and then other items that serve not only a more decorative function but are also valuable items to exchange, helping maintain crucial Ju/'hoan social networks, such as ostrich-egg necklaces, beadwork headbands, and the small handheld thumb piano that provides casual, relaxing listening, especially in the firelit softness of evenings. This living style supports their periodic moves, necessary to follow migrating game and ripening food resources. When what is left behind, like your house, can be easily reconstructed, it's *easy* to leave it behind, and you aren't weighed down by too many unnecessary possessions.

---

*In the 1960s, in Botswana, Namibia, and southern Angola, there are about fifty thousand San people (which includes Ju/'hoansi), of whom about five thousand live primarily as hunter-gatherers. As is the case with so many current Indigenous peoples, their present homeland often displays the most demanding features of their original homelands, being forced to live in the less environmentally friendly regions of that original home territory by the pressures of colonization.

In written material on the hunting-gathering Ju/'hoansi, their dwellings are often referred to as "huts." I choose not to use that term because of its racist connotation implying a lack of civilized living. On the contrary, these thatched dwellings serve the people well in the desert heat, providing shade and allowing whatever breeze may be present to circulate throughout the interior. And though heavy rains will soak in and through the dwelling, new homes or repairs to old ones are rarely a problem.

They share resources, circulating food throughout the camps so no one is hungry when some have more than enough, and allow neighboring groups to access resources in their territories through a reciprocal access: one group gathers and hunts in a neighboring group's land when game and roots are plentiful there, and in return, that group does the same when these food resources are more plentiful in the former's territory. As well, egalitarianism is the guiding principle for social and economic organization, where each person is valued as worthy of support and connection. Community exists and is continually re-created and reenergized because it is the key to survival in a land that yields stingily to individual efforts at sustenance.

It is in /Kae/kae that I begin to learn about Ju/'hoan community healing, intensely expressed in their primary cultural ritual—their powerful spiritually oriented healing dance.* Those dances reinforce the importance of *everyday context,* as the healing comes from and permeates back into the community. As these dances express the cultural values of sharing, reciprocity, and egalitarianism, I see how synergy is released in the dance, making healing a renewable resource, which as it expands becomes available to all, creating a healing community. This valued resource of healing, rather than being a scarce commodity people must compete for—the too typical situation in the West—instead is a continuously accessible resource all can share, and paradoxically, even

---

*My research on the Ju/'hoan community healing is discussed more fully in Katz, 1982a and Katz et. al., 1997.

remarkably, the more healing is expressed and utilized, the more it is available.*

I'm privileged to be part of an *ongoing* way of life of sharing and healing, reaffirming and making experientially robust what I've only seen glimpses of. The Ju/'hoan approach to community healing imparts a reality to an ideal, the more powerfully so, since as primarily hunter-gatherers—the way we live for 99 percent of our human history (Lee and DeVore 1968)—the Ju/'hoansi offer an evolutionary window into our earliest patterns of adaptation as a species. Therefore, their ways of living and being suggest what can be foundational principles of our functioning as human beings, principles that can continue to inform our contemporary existence. And just as Ju/'hoan teachings can offer a window into the earliest evolutionary dimensions of our human existence so, too, can they offer a window into the fundamental origins of psychology, a way of knowing and being central to that existence and its survival.

SIGNIFICANCE OF THE JU/'HOANSI TO OUR HUNTING-GATHERING ORIGINS

In 1968, when I do my initial fieldwork among the Ju/'hoansi of /Kae/kae in the northwestern Kalahari Desert in Botswana, they are living *primarily* as hunter-gatherers by foraging on the wild produce in their areas. That mode of adaptation is rare today. It is generally agreed that the basic dimensions of human nature are forged during that huge 99 percent span of human history when people live as hunter-gatherers. Therefore, a consideration of Ju/'hoan community healing has the potential to generate crucial evolutionary insights into the basic nature of the human community and its healing and empowerment resources.

---

*Synergy is a concept that is central to *Indigenous Healing Psychology;* see also Katz and Murphy-Shigematsu (2012a), and Katz and Seth (2012) for a fuller presentation of the concept and its functioning.

There is some debate among anthropologists about how accurately those /Kae/kae Ju/'hoansi "represent" a hunting-gathering way of life, or more specifically, how much they have already been in contact with and affected by neighboring pastoralists (see e.g. Soloway and Lee 1990). In this debate I follow the lead of my mentor in my Ju/'hoan research, Richard Lee, who, though he acknowledges that outside influence, still says that those Ju/'hoansi historically display the independence and self-sufficiency to retain the social traits and organization that make hunting-gathering possible.

But another issue becomes relevant. Who "decides" the outcome to this "debate" and even whether it's a "debate," or a *worthy* debate? The search for "essentialism," for a "pure" or "essential" example of a people or way of adaptation is full of dangerous stereotypes, and eventual the denial of actual integrities. Cultures are always changing, and, as Lee so rightly points out, who is a Ju/'hoan is an ever-changing dynamic. To try to rigidly categorize the Ju/'hoansi, or any other cultural group, is not only impossible but also an act of disrespect. And most important, the Ju/'hoan's own voice in this "debate" has too often been muted, at times ignored. And thus a vital source of information about who they are and how they had been and are adapting is lost.

Indigenous Healing Psychology chooses to especially honor the Ju/'hoansi's own narrative of origins and history—a series of lived truths that resist being captured by any one "objective" truth. As =Oma Djo says: "We've always been here, doing what we do." And for us today, that can be enough. Knowing what those /Kae/kae Ju/'hoansi "do" can be a significant insight into what we once all did as hunter-gatherers, and thus a promising guide for our shaping more healing and equitable futures.

It is here in /Kae/kae that my life changes, committing me now to pursue the realities of what are only ideals, and as part of that, my life as a psychologist changes as well. Indigenous teachings are a crucial aspect of my learning and growth. And as the Ju/'hoan approach to community healing is so crucial for a healing psychology, it is also here in /Kae/kae that the seeds are sown for this book.

Every week or so, depending on when there is a need for healing, the community gathers to create a healing dance, typically beginning at dusk and often ending at dawn the next day.* As the healers dance around the women, who encircle the fire as they sing the healing songs, a spiritual energy (*n/om*) heats up: it becomes boiling n/om and is released throughout the dance, while most concentrated in the healers. Boiling n/om activates an enhanced consciousness (*!aia*), which makes healing possible.† This n/om expands as it is released and is renewable, thereby more accessible to all at the dance. The valuable resource of healing thereby is a renewable, expanding, accessible resource for the community.‡

As the n/om boils, it can overpower the inexperienced healers, forcing them, writhing in pain, to the ground, and even challenge the experienced ones, as their sweat, a sacred substance, pours over their bodies. N/om is powerful and dangerous if not understood. Kinachau, an older, experienced, and respected Ju/'hoan healer, describes his first experience of n/om to me: "N/om got into my stomach. It was hot and painful . . . like fire. I was surprised and I cried." But once n/om encourages the experience of !aia, the consequences are critically important, as !aia allows the healing energy to touch all at the dance.

---

*A more detailed description of the healing dance, including the experiences of n/om and !aia, is found in chapter 7. For more comprehensive discussions of the dance, see, for example, Katz 1982a, Katz, Biesele, and St. Denis 1997; Lee 1967; and Marshall 1969.

†This n/om, though it can exist most intensely at the healing dance, in the base of the healers' spine, as well as the dance fire and the healing songs, also occurs in other phenomena in the Ju/'hoan world, expressing their power (see e.g., Marshall 1969 for a further discussion of n/om and its functions and settings).

‡This expanding, renewable n/om lies at the heart of an experience of synergy.

Yes, this n/om is a fearful thing, for sure something not to be approached casually. But I have a different, more immediate, and less profound challenge. Since I'm not a night person, it soon becomes clear I can't easily stay up all night for the dances. At first, in an effort merely to stay awake, I start to dance. This makes total sense to me, since I quickly confirm the importance of participant observation as a research methodology—learning about a phenomenon by participating in it.* Then, without really thinking it through, I begin dancing like other young Ju/'hoansi, most of whom are already seeking to learn to heal. And there are lots of dances occurring, sometimes two or three a week. I go to them all, dancing seriously, ever more seriously. The Ju/'hoansi affectionately call me "the healing man," even though they also give me a proper Ju/'hoan name (!Xam) when they adopt me into the village.†

Being the "healing man" fits. Like other young Ju/'hoansi seeking to experience n/om and eventually be a healer, I need to be focused, even passionate, and dedicated to the learning process. Being here in the Kalahari without my family, I can devote my time to this pursuit, devotion even more necessary since my time in the Kalahari is limited. But this focus feeds something of a tunnel vision, as my participation in the dances keeps me at times from participating in the context, indeed the soil from which the dance grows—the ordinary texture of daily life.‡ After a full night into the dawn hours of dancing, it is almost

---

*Participant observation, though at the time an accepted methodology in anthropology, is rarely employed to study healing, especially when there is an intense altered state of consciousness involved.

†Typically, as I'm adopted into the kinship network that guides the Indigenous places in which I live and work, I'm given an Indigenous name that signifies my place in that network. For example, in the Kalahari, I'm named !Xam, after my adopted father. But for ease of understanding, as I receive different names in each of the places I work, I'll just use my English nickname—Dick—when referring to myself during dialogues with my Indigenous teachers.

‡It is this very context that is primary during my second trip to the Kalahari.

impossible not to sleep the next day—sometimes a necessity since there is another dance the very next night.*

It's to =Oma Djo, an experienced and respected though at times unconventional healer, that I turn to in order to learn *about* healing— and now, it seems, to learn *how* to heal. We very quickly become friends, and he is my best friend among the Ju/'hoansi. He eagerly takes on the role of instructing me about the healing dance, but this is not a straightforward matter. =Oma Djo has a mischievous side,

---

*This first trip to the Kalahari occurs for three months in 1968, from September through November. The intensity of my experience with the Ju/'hoansi is suggested by the fact that during that time I participate in eighteen dances and conduct more than twenty in-depth interviews with healers and other Ju/'hoansi. I'm not equating the number of dances I attend or interviews I conduct as some precise measure of my understanding of Ju/'hoan healing; I mention these facts only as an indication of my commitment to that understanding and involvement with their healing approach as one avenue toward understanding. See Katz 1982a, for a presentation of the research from my initial 1968 work in the Kalahari.

But it is the larger context of my research that makes it all possible. I'm part of the Harvard Kalahari Research Group (HKRG), which is composed of a number of anthropologists and other social scientists who are working extensively with the Ju/'hoansi in a variety of areas, such as subsistence activities, child rearing, and population biology (see e.g., Lee and DeVore 1976, for an early collection of these research efforts). There is a constant exchange of ideas and understandings among members of the HKRG, and I benefit enormously from the generous sharings of this dedicated group of researchers. Especially helpful are Richard Lee and Megan Biesele, experienced and highly respected researchers with the Ju/'hoansi, who both then offer intensive feedback on my Ju/'hoan understandings and writings (for just a few examples of their extensive work, including their commitment to pressing issues of social change and justice, see Lee 1979, 2012; Biesele 1993; and Biesele and Hitchcock 2011).

The HKRG champions the need for an engaged scholarship, committed to social action and social change. In 1973, it helps found the Kalahari Peoples Fund (KPF) whose mission statement says that social scientists need to have their research make a positive difference in the lives of the people they work with, stressing collaboration with those people and being advocates on their behalf. See the website for KPF for a current description of activities (www.kalaharipeoples.org).

For my 1968 Kalahari research, Richard Lee, a remarkable intellect and scholar who is a longtime researcher with the Ju/'hoansi and fluent in their language, is with me for the entire three months. Richard helps make my first trip to the Kalahari not only productive but also simply possible. He counsels and advises me upon my return, serving as a collaborating sounding board for my attempts to write up that data.

which means simple, direct conversations are a bit too boring for him.

Though nearing sixty, and already with many family responsibilities, =Oma Djo remains youthful in his enthusiasm and playful in his demeanor. He continually leavens his teachings with teasings and gentle tweakings to be sure I don't take myself too seriously. And that's helpful, though at first I'm taken aback—I the "serious" researcher am learning to relax in order to learn. =Oma Djo is a good teacher not only because he knows much about Ju/'hoan healing but also because he's testing the boundaries of that tradition. For example, being more withholding than the Ju/'hoan norm about teaching young people to heal, he insists he only wants to work with "those who really want to drink n/om" (meaning those who are very committed to the difficult learning process).

Early in my stay in the Kalahari, I'm interviewing =Oma Djo about the healing dance; my questions keep dealing specifically with the dance, his responses keep dealing generally with his life and the life of his community. "Could you tell me how people decide when to have a dance," I ask. "Let me tell you about where my family originally comes from," he says, "and then how we ended up where we are now, here in /Kae/kae."

Eventually, =Oma Djo does talk about how dances are started, but now that information has a real-life context. If I want to learn about the Ju/'hoan healing dance, I must first understand what it means to be a Ju/'hoan, and *then* a Ju/'hoan who participates in the healing dance.

Not only is there this need for cultural context but also a need to understand more deeply the profound transformation of consciousness entailed in "drinking n/om."* I may have already experienced intense

---

*To say the expression *drinking n/om* is only a metaphor is to miss an essential point. From within the Ju/'hoan perspective, to drink n/om is to engage with n/om as it boils or becomes active, to engage it so that you take it within yourself in its active and activating form and thereby make it possible to enhance your consciousness (to experience !aia) so as to make healing possible. But the "drinking" is an actual experience of consciousness transformation, and the "boiling" n/om is a process during which n/om is activated and can be active or effective within the healer. Boiling n/om is experienced as hot, often intensely so as healing becomes imminent, and is therefore painful. Drinking n/om is more than a metaphor in the Western sense; it's a graphic description of a transformational process.

transformations before coming to the Kalahari, but now and here, in the Kalahari, it's a new challenge. The dynamics and shape of that transformation may eventually become more familiar, but in order to participate in the release of n/om, I have to be there as new and open, living those transformations as if for the first time.

"But this n/om must boil before we can heal," =Oma Djo warns, "and that's painful. As the n/om boils within us, we explode like a ripe seedpod bursting open." The ultimate part of the pain comes from facing one's own death. To heal, one must die and be reborn into an enhanced state of consciousness (the experience of !aia). "As we Ju/'hoansi enter !aia, we fear death. We fear we may die and not come back!" =Oma Djo cautions. Within the relaxing context of his characteristic whimsy, he wants to be sure I hear him clearly: "What would people say if they heard I was putting boiling n/om into teaching this guy from another land and teaching him to heal. 'How could you do that?' they would ask."

I can't take refuge in the fact I'm from another land, nor hide behind my knowledge that I know about metaphors for transformations, including metaphorical expressions of dying. This is no allegorical rite of passage but a terror-filled experience of death. If I have any hope of gaining even a little understanding of the Ju/'hoan approach to healing, I have to appreciate the true depth of this dying. And with this acceptance of the reality of the dance, I realize the precarious nature of my search to learn about healing. It's not something I can readily, even easily learn; it's something that only comes with intense struggle, facing fears and wishing intensely for the health of the community. Within this struggle is the key—letting go, being willing to accept or drink the boiling n/om, going through the fires of doubt and fear. What is apparently a most *dramatic* change in consciousness becomes a most *simple* process of accepting what is in the moment.

For twenty years, after I leave the Kalahari, I wish to return. Being within, the Ju/'hoan healing environment remains deeply felt. In 1989,

I'm able to return to /Kae/kae.* But as I actually approach /Kae/kae again, I'm really nervous. I'm with my two coresearchers, my then-wife Verna St. Denis, an expert in antiracist education, and Megan Biesele, a highly respected researcher in Ju/'hoan culture and our translator. "Will anyone remember me?" I wonder. "My initial visit could not be as important to /Kae/kae people as it has been to me." Then I recognize an older Ju/'hoan woman, relaxing in the sand outside her grass home. We really don't know each other in 1968, but her major overbite makes her easy to identify. "You remember Dick here, don't you?" Megan asks. The old woman looks warily up toward me and with exquisite kindness says: "If I could see better—you know I'm old now—I'm sure I could recognize him." My heart falls.

But not for long, because the message has gone out to =Oma Djo that "Dick has returned!" And very soon, a now older =Oma Djo, with noticeably more white hair, comes running, almost bouncing toward me and me toward him. We embrace—a warm, deep hug. Who knows whether it's what the Ju/'hoan do on such a reunion, but clearly, it's what we do. I'm back.

Back . . . and with a big difference. On this second trip, my knowledge of Ju/'hoan healing deepens as my engagement in a more modest and grounded life in the Kalahari grows. Verna and I set up a living space that becomes our home.† As a family we can become more connected to /Kae/kae village life. Verna begins establishing relationships with many of

---

*This second time in the Kalahari I'm once again part of a larger research network. My then-wife Verna St. Denis and I receive valuable support from Megan Biesele prior to and during our time in /Kae/kae. Especially important is the ongoing research team in /Kae/kae, which plans directions and the daily logistics necessary to carry out the research. The team consists of the Ju/'hoan healers =Oma Djo, Kxao Tjimburu, =Oma !'Homg!ausi, and Tshao Matze, as well as three young Ju/'hoansi who serve as translators—Kxao Jonah /O/Oo, /Ukxa, and Tshao Xumi. See Katz, Biesele, and St. Denis (1997) for a fuller description of the work accomplished during this second trip to the Kalahari.

†During my first time in the Kalahari, I stayed with Richard Lee and his then-wife Nancy Howell in a little camp next to the Ju/'hoansi camps. It was a home but more "their" home.

the Ju/'hoan women, bringing a natural fullness to our stay in /Kae/kae. This fullness brings me more intimately into the flow of daily life there, which enriches and expands our research. For example, she prepares morning bowls of porridge so, around the welcoming warmth of the cooking fire, we can eat breakfast together with members of what has become our informal research team, planning the day's schedule of interviews and other events. Most important, as an Indigenous woman and antiracist scholar and activist, Verna continually points out the realities of oppression and opportunity manifesting in /Kae/kae.

During this second trip, I seek to make a more realistic contribution to the healing work of /Kae/kae. I no longer seek to have n/om boil inside me so I can become a healer in the Ju/'hoan way: given the time limitations of my stay, there's not enough space and time to be a real Ju/'hoan healer, and even then, I can't devote my life to being in their healing circle. Now I am more part of the ongoing needs of village life, giving myself over to the practice of helping other Ju/'hoansi at the dance, as they seek to become effective healers. No longer the "healing guy," I am a helper in the healing way. This role of helping is readily available to me, and with commitment and calm in the face of boiling n/om, I can fulfill it well. And as a result, my understanding of Ju/'hoan healing deepens, generating enriching opportunities for eventual applications within psychology.

Both my commitment and calm are challenged when a young Ju/'hoan, still learning to release and modulate his boiling n/om, is overwhelmed with pain, falling to the ground, body twitching and writhing. Immediately, without asking, I do what's expected of Ju/'hoansi at the dance—help someone in such distress. I'm joined by three other Ju/'hoan men, yet the four of us barely are able to restrain, let alone calm down, the tortured, twisted body. There is amazing strength in these spiritual states, even when they are being short-circuited. Eventually we bring a relative calm into the young man's body and spirit, helping him cool down the boiling n/om to better prepare him to work with it for the purpose of healing. Through this intimate contact with the boiling n/om within another, the n/om enters me—and healing moves through yet another body in the community, the better to reach all.

Most important, during this second stay in /Kae/kae, new understandings emerge about the oppressive claws of colonialism that grip the Ju/'hoansi. Since my first visit, /Kae/kae now has a Western-oriented health clinic and school and the regular availability of alcohol. Each of these phenomena are actually controlled by the increasing presence of the Tswana and Herero people who live in /Kae/kae; the terrible irony is that the Tswana and Herero are acting, often unwittingly, as frontline deliverers of the larger scenario of Western colonialism in southern Africa, a process in which they themselves are caught as well. More than ever the Ju/'hoansi are dominated by these colonial pressures, since they are now remaining more or less permanently in /Kae/kae without access to resources that would prevent their growing dependence—this enforced sedentization itself a result of that very colonization process.

Ju/'hoan efforts at subsistence are increasingly being compromised. Their historical hunting options are decreasing as more restrictions flow from governmental licensing policies and the Herero-dominated cattle herds eat up more and more land for grazing. "We've lost our land so we can't feed ourselves properly," says =Oma Djo. But as they attempt to build economies of the future by entering the cattle and farming activities that increasingly dominate /Kae/kae, they are often thwarted by their lack of necessary capital and the unwelcoming barriers established by the local Tswana and Herero, who, backed by the central government, now control those activities.*

These new central government "services" of the school and clinic are clearly a mixed blessing. For example, the school, while definitely providing options for some of its more outstanding students, is

---

*See, for example, Hitchcock et al. 2006 for a description of the powerful contemporary colonizing pressures on the Ju/'hoansi, as well as processes and institutions of Ju/'hoan empowerment that are supporting their resistance to these pressures and building possible pathways toward self-determination amidst social, political, and economic development aspirations.

characterized by a central government curriculum that typically ignores Ju/'hoan culture or, in treating it as unimportant or filled with super- stitions, diminishes that culture and cuts into Ju/'hoan students' self- confidence and sense of self.

And most terribly, the central government has a new "enlightened" policy for Ju/'hoan education. "We must take them from their families who are only holding them back and send them to a residential school, far away, so they can really become able to look after themselves," pro- claims the Ministry of Education and Skills Development spokesperson for rural schooling. Now that I'm living in Canada, I can hardly believe my ears. The disastrous effects of the Canadian residential schools for Indigenous peoples are already firmly established; those schools' com- mitment to eradicate the students' culture leads to a terrible destruction of students' identity and self-esteem, which too often leads to abuses and addictions in later life.* I share some of that research with him. And he says with assurance, "But we will be different." I can't convince him otherwise.

The /Kae/kae clinic relies almost exclusively on distributing peni- cillin as a cure-all for a variety of ailments, thereby compromising effec- tiveness of the drug. The nurse who runs the clinic is a Western-trained Tswana woman, who treats her Ju/'hoan clients in a disrespectful, often demeaning manner, as if they were malingerers. She also sees the Ju/'hoan healing dance as mostly superstition and an obstacle to a pro- ductive life. "The dance keeps kids up at night so they can't go to school the next day," she laments.

Most painfully, because its destruction is so clearly visible and imme- diate, there is a daily trail of Ju/'hoansi, including many women, to the two sites serving Herero or Tswana home brew. It's terrible to watch a broken and wavering trail of drunk Ju/'hoansi coming back from these home-brew sites. This regular alcohol use, still new, is already showing

---

*See, for example, the various publications of the Aboriginal Healing Foundation (www .ahf.ca), and the groundbreaking Assembly of First Nation's book *Breaking the Silence* (1994).

its terrible aftermath, with increasing arguments and fighting among families and a lessening of energy toward survival activities. "We seem to be fighting more," says =Oma Djo, "and that's not our way."

Yet within all these cages of colonization, there remains resistance and empowerment of purpose—and those too are growing. =Oma Djo expresses this resistance in terms of the enduring experience of healing and community: "N/om is just the same as long ago, even though it keeps changing." It's during their healing dance—what is their most important cultural ceremony—that n/om is the strongest.

Addressing a more explicitly political dimension, Tshao Matze, an active community leader and healer, says, "We Ju/'hoansi need to speak more and more, louder and louder to the government—we want to help ourselves as we always have." Presently, the Ju/'hoansi are faced with loss of resources essential to their survival as the central governments that control their fate consistently ignore their requests for support and seek to destroy their independence so they can get better access to the valuable resources on the Ju/'hoan land. Without a voice in the government, the Ju/'hoansi feel, and often are, powerless. "You are paper people," says Tshao Matze. "You can write papers to those in government who control our fate and help them hear our voices." Tshao Matze has not yet learned to write; the ability to write, and especially to write documents that can successfully negotiate the government bureaucracy, does not yet exist in the village of /Kae/kae—though it is in the future.*

Tshao Matze emphasizes a job we researchers can do to assist their cause, a job Megan Biesele and others in the Kalahari Peoples Fund are already committed to. Looking at Megan, Verna, and myself, Tshao Matze speaks forcefully, yet respectfully: "You know about papers. You write on them. That's how you can help us. Send a letter to those government people. Tell them about how we're no longer a people. And tell them that we need our land back to become a people able to feed

---

*See, for example, the website for Kalahari Peoples Fund (www.kalaharipeoples.org) for a description of some ongoing Ju/'hoan literacy and other empowerment projects.

ourselves." As "paper people" we can use our good fortune of master-ing that *particular* form of communication called the *written* word—not to be conflated with any special abilities we have with language, or thought, or knowledge—to possibly influence those in power to respect what is rightfully and historically Ju/'hoan. Paper is practical, a weapon for change. Megan is taking a lead here with the Ju/'hoansi—including empowering people via their own literacy skills.* As a book-writing paper person, I seek to direct my writings, including this book, toward this liberatory aim by presenting accurate and empowering Indigenous-directed stories of community healing—though I know my contribu-tions remain tiny. These letters by outsiders supporting the Ju/'hoan cause are only a temporary step in the real process of change, now unfolding—the change *from within* the Ju/'hoan community.

The Persisting Oppressions of Colonization

This story of colonization and resistance among the Ju/'hoansi is not unique, though there is a searing quality in witnessing the actual intro-

---

*Megan Biesele, Richard Lee, Bob Hitchcock, and others have a long history of writing these letters, documents, and petitions, all bringing Ju/'hoan concerns to the people in power, the government. But as Megan emphasizes, she is not speaking for the Ju/'hoansi. She understands that she can take away the people's power by being too helpful.

The Ju/'hoansi always have their own voice. Increasingly, through Ju/'hoan literacy programs and experiences with government bureaucracies, their voice is now also being expressed in contemporary political forms, appreciating the necessary power residing in words and bargaining strategies. This reshaping of voice among Indigenous peoples so it can better be a potent force for liberation in contemporary global politics is a worldwide phenomenon among Indigenous peoples. Verna St. Denis, for example, brings this understanding and respect for voice powerfully into her work in antiracist and Aboriginal education in Canada.

But as documented in Hitchcock et al. (2006), the processes of Ju/'hoan empowerment goes far beyond the sparks provided by literacy. As so clearly demonstrated by the work of Paulo Freire (e.g., 1968), words can create change, or as he puts it, literacy is an act of "reading worlds," of understanding how the power structures of the world work, including how they work to dominate and oppress, and how those who are oppressed can use that knowledge to better understand how to analyze and then resist that domination. And so it is with the Ju/'hoansi; their liberatory movements seek to create vehicles built from whole community sociopolitical strengths.

duction of some of the classic vehicles of colonization, such as the loss of land-based survival resources, the introduction of Westernized schools and clinics, and the creeping devastation of alcohol. The exact forms and processes of colonization may vary, but the processes of colonization, fueled by racism and oppression, work to undercut a sense of identity and will; an experience of wholeness, well-being, and value; and a dignity and power that creates liberatory opportunities.

At the same time as these forces of colonization are demanding subservience, there are forces resisting this colonization, processes of affirmation and empowerment that are also central to the lives of all the Indigenous peoples who speak in this book. These journeys toward self-empowerment, expressed through individuals nestled within communities, must be respected and supported, as the focus shifts in Indigenous communities from an enforced identification with victimhood to a created identification with empowerment.*

Whatever it is that Indigenous peoples are willing to teach us, we always have to remember this colonial context and their breaking down and through that context toward locally initiated renewal. Indigenous peoples are sharing from an environment in which they are being denied their rights and dominated against their will; their teachings, originally earned through struggle and sacrifice, are nurtured through more devastating and externally imposed struggle and sacrifice. These teachings are gifts, willingly shared, in the first instance for the people of their own communities and then to others. As =Oma Djo says, "What I'm teaching you is for your people too." Building on our evolutionary sources enhances our present coping; drawing on our deep past reveals new insights.

But these Indigenous teachings are gifts to be earned, not simply taken. To honor these gifts and be worthy of hearing them, we too must struggle and sacrifice—though we typically can't match the intensity

---

*As they increasingly identify with Indigenous peoples' movements globally, the Ju/'hoansi also are increasingly nourishing their own cultural pride.

of the Indigenous life narratives. But we must do whatever we can to create a fair exchange, giving in return for getting—even better, giving *before* getting. We do what it is we can do, and then seek to do more—including working actively with the Indigenous teachings in this book, which are offered as a healing for that still dangerously subtle vehicle of colonization, psychology.

MEETING THE STRAIGHT PATH

To the Western-steeped eye, it certainly looks like a paradise. My family and I sail through a break in the barrier reef and enter into the gentle bay of Naqara, a rural village of approximately one hundred Indigenous Fijians, on Ono, a small, remote island in the southern Kadava region of the island nation of Fiji (see map #3, page 87).* From January 1977 until December 1978, I live with my then-wife Mary Maxwell West and our two kids, Alex, aged six, and Laurel, aged nine, in Naqara.

A sterling white beach pencils in the curved shore of the village, while coconut trees line the shore and dot the village, whose thatched homes, some with tin roofs, are neatly laid out along footpaths criss-crossing lush expanses of grass. Subsisting on their fishing and root crop farming activities,† with the only direct daily contact with the larger world being through the often unreliable radiotelephone. Though there is some back and forth with the urban center of Suva, Naqara people live what is called a "village life," existing in connection to and support of each other within the context of an everyday spiritually infused net-

---

*There are many written sources about Fiji and Fijian culture; I find the books by Indigenous Fijians to be especially helpful; for example, Nayacakalou (1975, 1978) and Ravuvu (1983, 1987). I have many conversations with and helpful guidance from my dear friend Asesela Ravuvu, whose knowledge he summarizes in his two books.

†Fish of various sizes are almost always available, whether through the women's net fishing or the men's fishing in the bay; farming focuses on growing root crops, such as *dalo* and cassava (source of tapioca). During ceremonies, special foods are often prepared, including roasted pig for especially important occasions. A few pigs are raised, and wild boars are also hunted.

work of traditions. Though the beaches and ocean waters of Naqara are crystal clean, and the land lush and bountiful, they aren't felt by Naqara people as expressions of a "tropical paradise"; instead the land and its surrounding ocean is "our place," with its beauty appreciated but also respected as it is not always a gentle beauty. The ocean, with its abundant fish, is primarily a place for the at times demanding subsistence activities, while the beach can be a defenseless boundary against a sea whipped into whitecaps by an oncoming storm. The yearly hurricane season can bring wicked destruction to homes and crops.*

We're welcomed into village life, with meaning-filled ceremonies and unpretentious generosity. As is the tradition in Fijian culture, we perform a *sevu-sevu* ceremony, asking permission to enter the village and live there, and our request is accepted. The sevu-sevu ceremony, performed with great respect and graceful dignity, celebrates the foundational Fijian principle of exchange. In Fiji, respect is highly valued, so the intense respect entailed in the sevu-sevu ceremony is always appreciated. The ceremony is also performed at the beginning of all other ceremonies, including the healing ceremony, as a way of respectfully asking for the blessings of the spirits or gods.

In this initial ceremony and throughout our stay in Fiji, we're helped by Ifereimi Naivota, a local *mata ni vanua* ("herald or spokesperson for the chief," also translated as "face or ambassador of the land or people"), who becomes our close family friend, as well as guide and translator. His wife, Sereana, the local Western-trained Fijian nurse, offers essential support and also becomes part of our family.

I'm here in Fiji to learn about traditional Fijian healing, a resource widely and effectively utilized in the predominantly rural Fiji but lacking formal governmental approval, even recognition. Ironically, this healing system is also used by many government officials in urban areas, though typically they personally deny such usage. Perhaps my research

---

*The year after we leave, a hurricane devastates the island, causing a cinder block church in a neighboring village to collapse, killing ten people out of the less than fifty people living there.

can provide some data to help document the effectiveness of this healing system, even encouraging government support.*

My family and I establish a home in Naqara, living in a smaller version of a typical village dwelling, with thatched sleeping quarter and a separate little thatched cooking area, where our wood-burning fire helps us prepare our meals. My then-wife Mary is studying child rearing practices, and her work provides valuable contextual and developmental insights, her active and engaging presence among the Naqara women an essential part of being a Naqara family. As with other Fijian women, she is the center of the home, creating a welcoming space.

Our kids add a special yeast to our growing village connections. Alex and Laurel attend the village school and learn very soon about Fijian values. When the teacher asks a question, both of them quickly raise their hands to answer. Because they are educated in "good" U.S. schools, their school knowledge exceeds that of the local village kids, and they are trained to answer questions eagerly and competitively, drawing attention to themselves. But after a few of these excited hand raisings, Laurel realizes where they are. She sees that before any Fijian classmate raises her or his hand to answer a question, even when the student clearly knows the answer, the student first waits, reading nonverbal cues. After determining that most of the students in the class know the answer, then and only then—but now along with nearly the entire class—the student raises his or her hand. Many hands shoot up at once. In that way one student doesn't stand out but supports the group and is supported by the group.

Seeing this Fijian expression of communal support and respect in the classroom, Laurel "becomes" Fijian, no longer enthusiastically raising her hand—and she passes that learning on to Alex. Our kids are happy, knowing they are both being recognized for their understanding and are welcomed into the community. Communal support and

---

*For example, I know that the Fijian Medical School, which sets the tone for health care policy in the entire country, is perhaps open to such documentation, though presently traditional healing systems are not discussed and are therefore, by implication, denigrated.

interconnections provide a calming context for individual achievement and recognition. It's no longer critical to be the *first* with an answer or solution as much as *collaborating* in developing an answer—now better utilized by the group for the benefit of all.

We participate increasingly in village life, learning how to be productive members of the subsistence activities that shape existence. My then-wife and I become contributing members respectively to the women's net fishing or the men's fishing from the boat out toward the barrier reef, and the kids add their tasty kids-sourced foods as they become proficient in collecting shellfish along the shoreline and spearing small fish in the bay.* The tides become more than our clock—an inevitable and at times rude reminder of how to live carefully and adapt effectively. If you happily take advantage of an early morning low tide and bring the boat very close to the shore after a cold night of fishing so that you can go right to bed, you may pay the price the next day: if the tide is out, the boat, now stuck in the sand, becomes a very heavy weight to lug until it can once again sit in the water.†

Our daily visiting and participation in cultural events and ceremonies allows us to move toward being like just another village family.‡ Our kids, especially at the start, enter into spaces with their own innocent desires to reach out to playmates, frequently opening paths of relationship with families we might have taken too long to establish because of our shyness or not knowing how to be Fijian. "Hey, Dad,"

---

*Almost all subsistence activities, as well as most social gatherings, are gender segregated. Large and formal ceremonial gatherings and intimate family times, including eating, are not—though the ceremonies typically prescribe separate locations for men and women.
†Yes, it can be "cold to the bone" on this tropical island, especially in the winter and after a night on the sea in an open boat. Winter, accompanied by rains, makes the village a damp, chilly environment. Without any indoor heating, people suffer from this deep chill, aggravated by various rain-induced fungi, which make personal cleanliness more difficult. Yes, it's all relative! A wet 60 degrees Fahrenheit can feel cold in Naqara, where summer temperatures can reach into the 90s.
‡Our participation in these traditional spiritual ceremonies gains an extra dimension because of my work with the elders and healers who often exercise positions of ceremonial leadership.

says little Alex or Laurel, "you should meet my new friend here." And then the next step, we meet that friend's family, and our two families, still powered by the direct intensity of children just playing with each other, become closer than we ever might have been without that young relational yeast to start us off. Naqara is now our home, and family becomes a central aspect of all my future work in the area of healing.

Throughout my stay in Naqara, I make numerous trips to Suva, the capital city of Fiji. I'm an active participant in healing ceremonies there and have many extended interviews with healers and elders. Saimoni Vatu, an elder living in Suva who is part of the chiefly lineage in Naqara village and who invites our family to work in his village, tells me: "There's one Fijian healer I think you should see—Ratu Civo. He's very good. Very respected. A real healer . . . and a real elder. And he lives right here in town."*

But it's not easy to make that connection with Ratu Civo—he's actually hard to find. Saimoni Vatu tells me, "Ratu Civo keeps a low profile. Doesn't show others his true [healing] work." Eventually, with many twists and turns, I do find him, and he immediately takes me in—on the condition that I learn to *do* the healing work under his guidance. I've come to Fiji naively thinking I'll just learn *about* traditional Indigenous Fijian healing, but as with my experience with =Oma Djo in /Kae/kae, I soon discover I must learn *how* to heal. "We can't just talk about healing," Ratu Civo insists. "We must heal."

Tough minded yet softly compassionate, Ratu Civo, a man now in his early sixties, carries his humility with dignity. Not only is he a respected healer—even more so because he doesn't advertise his prowess—but he is also a respected member of an important chiefly lineage, which in the still chiefly driven Fijian culture places him in a position of very high standing. Yet he prefers to speak and act calmly, drawing upon his knowledge rather than resting within his powerful cultural or traditional positions.

---

*The word *Ratu* when used before a man's personal name signifies that he is of chiefly rank; the word *Adi* fulfills the same function for women.

Taking me on as his student, Ratu Civo has strong guidelines, expecting me, as would any Fijian seeking that healing knowledge, to work hard and with commitment. "You do the *best* you can," he says, "*always* as best you can." During my first visit to his house, I sit on the floor with him for our discussions, as is the custom in Fijian culture.* "Oh, why don't you give Dick a seat in our chair here," his wife almost pleads. There are very few chairs in the homes of traditional Fijians, and they are typically reserved for guests, especially guests of honor. "That's enough," Ratu Civo interjects. "If Dick is going to learn about our healing, he will learn about it the way we do . . . on the floor and as one of us . . . not as someone special." His tone is sharp but more definitive than critical.

Over many nights, well into the mornings, of long discussions and sharing of knowledge, I sit with Ratu Civo in his small house. He offers his teachings always woven into the intimate fabric of our own life situations, the very nature of a serious and honest teacher-student relationship in the healing arts. As we talk, we drink together the sacred *yaqona*, a plant that can open the connection with the gods, whose dried roots are pounded into a powder, infused with water, and served out of a ceremonial bowl (*tanoa*).

Talking about the *vu,* the traditional Fijian gods, and the *mana,* the

---

*There are times when, as an American-trained university professor, I am considered by some Fijians as a person of special honor in the status-oriented social structure of Fijian village life. Even at times I'm addressed as Ratu Rusiate—Ratu being an honorific, chiefly label, and Rusiate being my given Fijian name.

But I firmly but gently seek to establish myself in what I feel is a more proper middle-ground social status; namely, one determined by my age, my experience in Fijian culture and life, and my own felt humility. In this I'm in tune with Fijian culture, where humility is very highly valued, often overriding considerations of status. For example, though persons of high status are seated at the "top" or front of a ceremony, and those seen as deserving of that position if not already there are asked to *toso ecake* (or "move up to the top"), whenever I'm asked, I gently demur, saying I'm fine where I am—which is usually in the middle level of the ceremony, or if it is a very important and formal ceremony, I attempt to sit more toward the lower end or back, even near the rear door, a place more befitting to my age group. Yet I seek to remain sensitive to the wishes of the local community, not wishing to impose my own criteria of what constitutes a deserving social status on to their own local criteria.

spiritual energy emanating from the gods and creating sacred power in the world, Ratu Civo emphasizes the straight path* that describes how we honor these phenomena in our daily lives. The straight path expresses a way we are meant to live, seeking to craft a journey imbued with honesty, respect, and humility, a journey neither easy nor comfortable but essential.

Ratu Civo is a *dauvaqunu,* which translates as "one who is a master or expert at drinking (using) the yaqona." The dauvaqunu uses yaqona as a central ingredient in his healing ceremonies—the yaqona serves as a conduit between the healer and the spirits. The dauvaqunu is one of a number of traditional Fijian healers who draw their powers from a spiritual source, including the *dauveibo* ("one who is a master at giving a healing massage") and the *dausoliwai* ("one who is a master at giving medicines" or "herbalist"). But it is during the dauvaqunu's ceremony that the spirits are especially active, entering into the ceremony in order to make healing happen; as well, the dauvaqunu typically also offers prescriptions for healing herbs and can give a healing message. Thus the dauvaqunu assumes a healing role of special importance in Fijian culture.

The yaqona helps create the sacred space we often inhabit, elevating our teaching and learning into commitment—and practice. Living in Naqara, I'm offered that opportunity for practice. Sevuloni, a longtime student of my new mentor Ratu Civo, lives in Naqara, and at Ratu Civo's request, I begin to support Sevuloni while he runs his weekly healing sessions—conducted under the ongoing spiritual guidance of Ratu Civo. Gradually, still continuing my direct apprenticeship with Ratu Civo, I am more able to contribute to that Naqara-based healing process. Energized through this healing relationship, Sevuloni's family and mine are deeply connected—our kids are often seen forming their own free-ranging play group.

"I'm teaching you about healing," Ratu Civo says, "and you'll show your knowledge through your own practice. Your practice here in Fiji

---

*The straight path is discussed in more detail in chapter 5. This word *straight* in the context of Fijian culture refers to a moral and ethical developmental process and quality of life, not a particular sexual orientation.

. . . and then your practice back in your own home." My learning to heal invites me into even deeper, more protected dimensions of Fijian life and culture.

When we leave Fiji on that first visit, our small boat motoring out to the larger ship waiting in the harbor to take us back to Suva, people from Naqara line the beach for a traditional leave-taking. Waving their hands, sometimes holding small cloths that catch the slight wind, they call out, accented with occasional earth-grabbing wails: *Isa! . . . isalei! . . . isa! Isalei* is a lament, a cry of sorrow, now expressing a deep sadness at our leaving and a fervent wish for our return, our quick return. We are all now waving, back and forth—and crying, not hiding the tears. And the Naqara people keep waving until they can no longer see us—and we likewise until we can no longer see them. That is the Fijian way.*

Seven years later I return to Fiji—and I'm both excited and nervous†—excited to be in one of my homes and explicitly nervous about whether I can still speak Fijian: Will I have to tumble through barely understood communications? But I'm also implicitly nervous about being, in fact, able to come home again. I arrive in the main Fijian airport early in the morning. It's fairly empty—two men over in a far corner and a group of four Fijian women, who work on the airport

---

*To this day, I honor this traditional leave-taking whenever possible; for example, while watching a plane or car leave with my friends or family, I wave—though usually discreetly so as not to make a scene—and I keep waving until the car turns a corner or the plane is out of sight. This leave-taking seems to give depth to our relationship.

†In June 1985, I return to Fiji, staying in the Suva area in order to work again with Ratu Civo. I'm bringing a draft of my book *The Straight Path of the Spirit* that has been written under the guidance of his teachings and describes my Fijian research project and its cultural underpinnings. Fulfilling his request, I'm seeking further teachings and, in particular, feedback on the book. Really, approval. And Ratu Civo teaches once again: "That book is your area . . . you're the writer. I'm teaching you, and I believe you've learned well. So just carry on."

In that earlier book, Ratu Civo, per his request at that time, is identified by the pseudonym Rt. Noa—a request for anonymity that he now no longer desires, so a fuller appreciation and honoring of his knowledge can occur in this current book. The same is the case for the other Fijians I mention in *Indigenous Healing Psychology* who appeared in that earlier book.

cleaning staff, sitting at a table within earshot of me, as I sit alone at another table. The women are looking me over, ever so discreetly, but their conversation is anything but: "Now that's a good chunk of man," one says. "What do you say we go over and get him and have some fun." Another chimes in, with a playful laughing voice, "Yes, that's a choice piece for us girls. We could use a guy like that." Their sexual undertones are overtones. And that banter goes on for another minute or so. Then I have to leave to catch my bus. As I pass by the women's table, I say, in Fijian and with a definite smile of enjoyment: "Well, thank you, ladies for all your compliments. You've made me feel really good today." "Oh, you," they say almost in unison, clapping their hands above their heads with enthusiasm and wagging their fingers at me in mock disapproval. "Why didn't you tell us you speak Fijian?!" We all enjoy the good fun of the teasing, such a fine example of Fijian joking. Yes, I can still speak Fijian. Now I'm not nervous at all.

But once again, we have to speak of the global colonial narrative, and its grip on Indigenous peoples. For example, the British colonizers of Fiji bring people from India—already a British colony—over to Fiji to work the local sugar cane crop. The colonizers' justification, as erroneous as it is common among colonizers, is that Indigenous Fijians are "too lazy" to work the fields. In fact, Fijians are hardworking, though their work rhythms respect communal values more than the more individualistically oriented and regimented British approach. As a result, there is ongoing social, political, economic, and cultural conflict between these two groups, sometimes expressed through aggressive, even violent actions.* For example, Indigenous Fijians, as the first people to inhabit the land, have long-standing traditional rights and privileges in terms of cultural power and integrity, including historical claims over land ownership. They point to the fact that sometimes those who emigrate from India unfairly take control of the nation's economic resources,

---

*These conflicts are expressed in and exacerbated by a series of coups in Fiji between 1987 and 2006, and continuing tensions resulting in constitutional uncertainties.

which historically belong to them as Indigenous peoples. And those who originally come from India (sometimes called "Indo-Fijians") believe it is their right, as Fijian citizens, to work hard and thereby accumulate economic resources. But the divisions between Indigenous Fijians and those who migrate from India are only part of the picture. Some of the most valuable real estate, including resort hotels, and important economic and financial institutions in Fiji are controlled by *kai vulagi* or white people and their corporations from the neighboring countries of Australia and New Zealand.

OUR FIRST PSYCHOLOGISTS*

We all have our roots in Indigenous peoples or the first peoples to inhabit the different parts of the earth—we all come originally from a place first inhabited by our distant ancestors, who live primarily as hunter-gatherers. As these first people gather together, they engage in the human concerns of community building, interpersonal relations, and spiritual understanding. Being human means to ponder the meaning of their lives and the lives of others. Without that self-reflection and delving into the meaning of their existence, survival is not possible. These first people of the various lands engage in the defining concerns of psychology. As such they are our first psychologists. Within Indigenous cultures, these first psychologists are more accurately considered healers or elders. *Psychology* and *psychologists* are terms emanating largely from a particular historical and Western-cultural context and are thereby connected to a particular set of roles and functions. Indigenous healers and elders perform roles and functions that overlap sufficiently with that particular Western-oriented set to also be considered as psychologists, but most important, since elders' and healers' roles

---

*Material in this section is complex, with conflicting views both inside and outside Indigenous communities. I try to have Indigenous peoples' *own* definitions and conclusions guide my statements and conclusions. For example, in this section, I support Indigenous principles of self-definition and control over issues of cultural identity.

and functions go beyond those of the conventional psychologists, they can offer insights into enhancing that conventional approach.* These Indigenous knowledgekeepers are not psychologists as defined by some contemporary professional accrediting body, but psychologists as validated by the tasks and challenges of living well.

As we ponder our history as a species, it makes ultimate sense to listen to and learn from the teachings of these first psychologists, who lay the evolutionary foundations for principles and processes of human adaptation and transformation. We are fortunate, indeed gifted, that there are today existing connections to these ancient first psychologists among their direct descendants; namely, *contemporary* Indigenous peoples. And it is especially through their elders and healers that the ancient teachings of those historically first psychologists are most treasured and accessible. Though typically not labeled as psychologists, these Indigenous elders and healers are living and doing psychology. As Ratu Civo put it, ever so simply: "We try to understand our world— that's just what we do." These Indigenous elders and healers, whose voices are ignored or degraded within mainstream psychology, can offer a key to our search for ways toward healing psychology, toward what can be a healing psychology.

In presenting teachings of these Indigenous elders, as they ask me to do, I'm humbled by that responsibility, which remains a continuing aspiration. "Take my teachings to the people of your land, and to others

---

*The term "Indigenous psychologist" has its own set of complexities. Here is one possible example. There are Indigenous people, who are taught well by their elders and who also train in a Western-oriented psychology program. When such a person is formally recognized as a psychologist, she can be called an Indigenous psychologist. But she is different from those Indigenous elders and healers who do not receive formal Western psychological training. As she acts *as a psychologist,* her Indigenous teachings and understandings—indeed her Indigenous worldview—are in dialogue with the lens and filters of a Eurocentric psychological worldview and methodology. Numerous Indigenous peoples who train and now practice as psychologists are wrestling with this very dilemma and craft creative and honest personal and professional narratives to honor both their Indigenous teachings and their Western professional training. In succeeding chapters, some of these people are highlighted.

like yourself who are trying to straighten out people's minds," Ratu Civo states. All of the words spoken in this book by Indigenous elders appear here with their explicit permission.

But I'm not presenting a complete or organized view of these teachings, not an "official" version, as there is none. Realizing I'm working with teachings given honestly and truthfully, I write seeking to honor those two guiding words.

Yes, =Oma Djo and Ratu Civo, Indigenous elders who also do the healing work, already share with us much of value in this search for a healing psychology. But finding such persons is not so easy. Questions, even challenges abound—some cynical and even mean-spirited, some heartfelt, springing from honest confusion—and come mostly but not exclusively from outside the respective Indigenous community. "How can you tell she's an elder, especially since she seems so young?" "Can I rely on the stories of a healer's patients to know if his healing actually works?" "How do I tell when I find a 'real' elder?" Quite often such questions and challenges can't be dealt with definitively. There are many factors, such as an elder's community reputation or documented cases of a healer's work that come into play, and they sometimes offer conflicting evidence.

INDIGENOUS ELDERS AND HEALERS: RICHLY COMPLEX EXPERIENCES

The criteria for determining who is a real or genuine Indigenous elder or healer are relatively clear, creating an *ideal* portrait; what remains often contested is whether a particular person, *in practice,* meets those criteria. Being first and continuously human beings—who are elders or, better, are seeking to be elders—they rarely, nor should they, fulfill this ideal portrait. "You know that saying that 'even medicine men put their pants on one leg at a time'? Well . . . I can tell you this . . . it's true," Joe Eagle Elk, a powerful Lakota medicine man, announces with a serious smile.

Ideally, Indigenous elders are not self-selected but earn that status as a result of being acknowledged by their communities as persons who live a long life and are now able to *reflect on* their life to generate valued meanings and understandings. Simple age is not enough, as there are some older people who don't seem to learn much from their journey— or at least are not able to share the knowledge they gain.

The life journeys of Indigenous elders can be filled with even more than the usual twists and turns of life, as many, for example, under the duress of colonization, deal with the ravages of addictions and abuse. "How can I claim I'm better than anyone else . . . just look at my life and the troubles I've been through," says Ratu Civo. He's making a statement of fact, not a confession.

Elders are also considered sources of traditional, spiritually infused cultural teachings and are considered worthy teachers of that traditional knowledge, including the ability to perform important ceremonies. In practice, the functioning of Indigenous elders often defies neat boundaries. Cree culture can illustrate this point. For example, elders who are primarily teachers or advisers, offering life advice to others, are not necessarily active in performing major ceremonies like the sweat lodge, and vice versa. Most but not all elders are asked to say prayers to open meetings or at special gatherings, like funerals, and those prayers are themselves a ceremony. There are also a series of more specialized meanings attached to elders and their functions, which offer yet another layer of meaning. For example, there are elders who are identified as traditional storytellers, persons entrusted with remembering and telling the old stories and their teachings; or as medicine people, those who carry sacred healing teachings performed in their healing ceremonies. These more specialized functions can be combined with each other and with the other more general elder functions. The function of traditional counseling, a source of many of the teachings in this book, is also practiced only by certain elders. Today, with many young Indigenous people seeking Indigenous counseling, given the crushing oppressions they currently face and the availability of addictive temptations, those traditional counselors who communicate well with young people offer an especially valued resource. Attention is paid to the effects an elder's talk or ceremony has on others, but rarely is someone asked not to be an elder because he or she is not producing positive results.*

Elders are not paid for their knowledge or ceremonies, though the person requesting such knowledge typically offers a gift of gratitude. Most important, Indigenous elders are respected as persons *seeking* to live a good life, always working toward being honest, trustworthy, generous, and truth loving—rather than claiming already to be that way. "I'm still learning," Ratu Civo tells me. "I'm just like all of us—still learning." Humility is an essential ingredient in becoming and being an elder.†

Ideally, Indigenous healers share many similarities with Indigenous elders, including community respect and living a good life. These healers, however, are not necessarily older, as the gift and power of healing—which typically comes from a spiritual source and is often transmitted by an older healer who is a mentor—can appear in younger persons as well. Their respect and support comes not only from their knowledge of cultural traditions but also, and more importantly, from their knowledge of their particular healing ceremony, which is often encased in cultural traditions. Ratu Civo performs his healing work within a yaqona ceremony that is a Fijian ceremony, adapted in slight ways to the particulars of his approach.‡

---

*There are exceptions to this general principle. For example, if an elder is engaging in behaviors that violate fundamental human norms and cultural teachings, he or she is at the very least shunned and often confronted to cease performing the functions of an elder.
†Sometimes there is such a thirst for traditional Indigenous knowledge that Indigenous elders allow themselves to be placed on a pedestal by these seekers and even begin to believe that they *do know* rather than that they *know things and are still learning.* This lack of humility doesn't necessarily imply the elder is too proud or too ego inflated; at times the hunger after knowledge and the human need for approval merely play out to an extreme. All of the elders and healers who speak in this book come from traditions where humility and being human are emphasized; there is no belief that they merit reverent and devotional attitudes from their followers or that, as in certain spiritual traditions, they may be gods incarnate.
‡There's often an assumption that Indigenous healers from a particular cultural tradition should all practice similar healing ceremonies. But the particular ceremony a healer performs typically comes from a particular source, such as his or her own vision or ceremonial lineage, and so there is variation in both the conduct of a particular ceremonies and in the range of ceremonies performed, even within one community.

As with Indigenous elders, Indigenous healers are not supposed to request or even accept payment for their work: there can be no fee for services. Instead, they can accept expressions of gratitude voluntarily offered by clients. In contrast with elders, healers are often judged by the effectiveness of their healing; if clients don't recover, and especially if they tend to get worse, healers can be encouraged to cease their work or at least suspend it for a period of time—maybe to allow them to seek more training or to bring more moral character to their lives.

Indigenous elders living in urban settings face particular challenges in their pursuit of those ideal characteristics discussed above. As connections with their typically rural home communities are weakened, they can miss the critical component of a stable home community's approval and support. Community context and support are essential aspects in the process of becoming an elder. It's one's own community that can know one best and who you, in turn, can know best, based on long-term and intimate knowledge.* Drawing more on shifting urban sources for their identification as elders, including very often non-Indigenous service agencies seeking elder participation in programming, it can be harder to make a reliable and accurate judgment about an elder's authenticity and validity. The opportunities for persons to incorrectly offer themselves as an elder increases, as do instances of self-promotion.

The role and function of money symbolizes the contemporary complexity of Indigenous elder authenticity, especially in urban settings. Historically, there is always an exchange with the elder, whereby a gift is given in gratitude for services given. The gifts help the elder or healer to meet her or his subsistence needs, given that he has to take time off from meeting those needs in order to offer his counseling and ceremonial services. For example, historically among the First Nations people of the prairies, wild food is often given, or on special occasions, for example with an intense and extended healing ceremony, a blanket or a

---

*There's also, however, the element of family favoritism that can be a factor, compromising the accuracy of a community's judgment about a particular elder, depending on whether he or she is a relative.

gun or even a horse. Today, as the money economy increasingly dominates all, in rural as well as urban Indigenous communities, money is the primary avenue toward meeting subsistence needs. A gift of money, though it is still *literally* money, can still be used to express gratitude for help received; it need not be a payment or a fee for services.

Urban elders and healers are essential, as the number of Indigenous people now living in cities dramatically increases, along with the number of non-Indigenous peoples needing their help. There are many elders and healers practicing in urban areas, struggling with great challenges and temptations to offer important, valuable, and respectful work.

One major source of disagreement and complexity about who is and who is not an Indigenous elder or healer revolves around the issue of authenticity*: Are the elder's teachings or the healer's ceremony "real"

---

*The very word *authentic* is problematic, as elders can be devalued not on valid criteria but on sometimes superficial criteria of "looking" or "acting" the part—a matter of appearance that *may not always* reflect inner knowledge.

The existence of "plastic medicine men" highlights the special and intense challenges of authenticity. The term *plastic medicine man* is used among Indigenous people of North America to discredit people improperly seizing the role of Indigenous spiritual and healing leaders—those who assume sacred roles without the proper training and, more important, the necessary moral character. These plastic medicine men are most frequently found among non-Indigenous peoples. There are, for example, non-Indigenous people who claim to be an "Indian in a prior life" or the "latest link in the chain of great Indigenous healers"; and on the basis of such self-proclaimed validity, they justify offering a makeshift sweat lodge, disconnected from its traditional roots, even at times selling admission to that now bogus ceremony. This rape of sacred cultural knowledge is further dishonored by the admission charge as the traditional sweat lodge is open, *without* any payment, to all who are seriously seeking healing. Unfortunately, fraudulent offering of traditional services can also occur among Indigenous peoples, especially those with weak links to their ancestral communities and families.

Kxau Chimburu, the Ju/'hoan healer, offers a counterexample of this plastic medicine phenomenon. "Do you sometimes find yourself at a healing dance," I ask him, "and the n/om is not boiling; it's not even getting hot?" Immediately, I feel bad to have asked such a private, perhaps invasive question. But I'm wrong. Kxau Chimburu is disarmingly direct and ready to respond. "Yes, that does happen," he says. Now affirmed, I continue: "So what do you do?" "I just do the best I can . . . the best I can even though the n/om is not boiling for me . . . I just try to be helpful." Kxau Chimburu is a real healer, not a plastic one—and in reality, the healing power is not always available, at least in its strongest form.

or "valid"? To determine if the teachings and ceremonies are authentic, it is common to first establish if they are traditional, meaning that they are accurately drawn from and based on ancient spiritually infused and time-affirmed teachings from within the culture. At times, issues of confirmed lineage with such teachings are used to bolster or discredit claims of authenticity.

But what is tradition and what makes something traditional? =Oma Djo helps us understand tradition with his succinct comment: "N/om is just the same as long ago, even though it keeps changing." To remain alive and enlivening, a tradition is always growing, responding to changing times while retaining its essential and guiding core. So to be traditional or to convey traditional knowledge is never a rigid identification but one that sensitively balances validity and relevance. Just by saying something is "traditional" does not in itself either tell us what is actually being taught nor whether it is accurate. "Knowledge from our elders can't be tampered with," says Ratu Civo. "But what good is that knowledge if we can't communicate it to others in a way they can actually put it into practice?" Indigenous elders are often distinguished by their particular skills or talents; for example, some are especially known by their ability to work well with young people—they have kept up with the times and terms of contemporary life, including the language of the streets. Though the knowledge base of a related group of elders can be the same, their specific ways of working into and through that knowledge can differ.

There is a current running through the work of Indigenous elders that can identify a particular period of time or cultural context as *the* source of tradition. Typically, it is a time that is envisioned prior to colonization, though the exact boundaries of that period can vary. "Yes, we do our healing," says Ratu Civo, "but it's too bad you weren't here to see my grandfather. Now he was a real healer!" And then Ratu Civo's son says basically the same thing—now about *his* grandfather! The "time of our grandparents" identifies a fluid period in which tradition is felt to be strongest. There are also constant refrains about the loss of elders with their passing, meaning the loss of traditional knowledge: "Soon the elders will be gone, and the people will be lost." The emergence of new elders from the natural progression of age is not emphasized, implying that the knowledge of the older elders, being more "pure," is more valuable.

But clearly the process of colonization has unleashed a devastating effect on the clarity and purity of those traditional teachings. The concept of tradition can be invoked to justify or authenticate activities or behaviors that are actually the result of the colonizing process rather than expressions of Indigenous teachings.

"We have what we have," says Ratu Civo. "We have what has survived, and that's enough. It's our teachings." Though the wounding of colonization continues, the honest and truthful teachings that survive continue to serve—especially for contemporary Indigenous people and, through their generosity, to the wider non-Indigenous community—even as those teachings are continually exposed to compromise and dilutions.

Lineage can be used to help solve this problem of authenticity, but the Indigenous elders who speak in this book don't come from cultures where lineage is the primary criterion for authenticity.* The focus is more on the spiritual source of the teachings and whether they are offered truthfully by a respected and respectful teacher.† Truthfulness

---

*In contrast, there is a stronger and more detailed emphasis on lineage as an indicator of authenticity in other spiritually based teachings, including authenticity as a most recent incarnation of the Divine (e.g., most Hindu practices).

†Mr. Nyland, the Gurdjieff teacher I work with closely for a number of years, makes this point clearly. One of the aspects of the Gurdjieff meditation approach is the practice of sacred dances—opportunities to experience meditation in action. I'm pretty committed to these dances, and they're important to my meditation practice. I'm about to leave for Fiji and wonder how I can continue my practice. "What will I do, when I get to Fiji," I ask Mr. Nyland. "There'll be no one there to practice the dances with." As I think about it now, what a naïve question! But Mr. Nyland's response is simple and honors my desire for continued growth: "Don't worry, Dick. Just go to Fiji . . . and really meet the people. Listen . . . and learn. You'll find Fijians who have never heard of those sacred dances, who've never heard of Gurdjieff! But they will know more about what Gurdjieff was trying to teach about the spiritual path than you've yet heard." Yes. That's just what happened.

and validity outweigh *particular* and *particularly detailed and lengthy* paths of lineage. Rather than determining if a ceremony is done *exactly* how it is done historically, the criterion is that the ceremony is done the *right* way. Considering how time makes some parts of the original ceremony, including certain ceremonial paraphernalia, impossible to repeat, the ability to do the ceremony in the full spirit of the original remains.

And so I'm trusting that the elders whose teachings form the heart of this book are for you what they are for me—honest sources of wisdom and guidance on the path toward healing, health, and a just and balanced life. And the elders with the primary teaching responsibility—=Oma Djo, Ratu Civo, Joe Eagle Elk and Danny Musqua—also share certain other characteristics.* They are either based in their home rural settings or maintain close ties to those settings so they are in essence practicing traditional village-based principles and practices. Emerging from that intimate connection to their ancestral lands, they draw their fundamental power from a knowledge and practice of spiritually inspired time-affirmed traditions; as well, they all have their Indigenous language as their first and for several only language.†

Clearly, this intimate connection these elders have to their ancestral land and language deepens their traditional knowledge base and practice and underlies the clarity and truthfulness of their teachings. But I'm sensitive to the unnecessarily restrictive judgments of what is called the "culture police," who in their desire to establish who is real or authentic employ *superficial* criteria of authenticity—including the

---

*Other Indigenous elders who share their teachings, such as Mary Lee, also share these additional characteristics.

†Because speaking in their Indigenous language can bring elders in some ways closer to their traditional teachings, translating their teachings into English can be problematic. In all cases my translators, who are my colleagues in the field, are fluent in both their Indigenous language and English, as well as knowledgeable about their own Indigenous spiritual teachings and healing practices. In this way, I get the best translation possible.

apparently valid criteria of how many ceremonies a person may or may not attend.*

I try to minimize this ongoing debate about authenticity by spending time to feel and sense who or what is valid and valuable, drawing heavily on the advice and guidance of persons of knowledge in the community, as questions of authenticity seem overly influenced by who is making the judgment, with personal and political positions often clouding those judgments. I also choose to value deeply felt self-identifications, especially those set within a context of humility, honesty, and experience. Certainly, humility is an important component, but it's not a narrowly defined trait. =Oma Djo's exuberant and playful teasing and bravado betray any superficial expression of humility, and yet, especially in his later years, he's intent on promoting what he believes is true and valuable knowledge and wants his fellow Ju/'hoansi to respect that knowledge more than him as the individual expressing it. It's this emphasis on knowledge, being a knowledge-keeper, that expresses his humility.

Each of these four elders with primary teaching responsibilities adopts me into a teaching relationship with the appropriate ceremonial process; and each charges me with the responsibility of carrying their words into my worlds and applying what I know to improving the health and well-being of others. These four are my culturally sensitive mentors in living a good life. It's a way of life that thrives on selflessness, a way of life that compels commitment. I rely on community judgments, especially from their home communities,† and the

---

*There are Indigenous elders fluent in their language, living in their ancestral homes, who are not specially trained in spiritual ceremonies and teachings. They *are* obviously knowledgeable in those areas, but that's not their special area of expertise or practice. Also with the rapid and tragic demise of many Indigenous languages—in spite of many vigorous Indigenous language retention programs—emerging elders, who may possess spiritual knowledge, may not have fluency in their Indigenous language.

†These community judgments are, however, not simple nor straightforward. They are based on intimate knowledge, but they can also be influenced by familial ties and even petty community jealousies.

assessments of other elders, healers, and clients, triangulating these assessments, to arrive at a decision on whom I work with. Finally, each of these elders explores potentials and possibilities, following the spiritual path as it winds through contemporary challenges, rather than rigidly adhering to what is always done in the name of traditional purity. They are creating traditional wisdom as they live out their traditional teachings.*

The elders who are my primary mentors are all men. There is a simple reason for that. Their cultures, the context in which their teaching occurs, are typically gender segregated. In most daily subsistence and social activities, men and women typically fulfill different, often separate but equally valued roles. During spiritual ceremonies and teaching situations, including healing practices, this division of function also exists, with even stronger taboos against crossing sexually based designations. The assignment of differing tasks and responsibilities to women and men doesn't prevent men and women from working together for the good of the larger community. In fact, their specializations of function promote intense bonding within sexes and more effective outcomes for the community at large, which now rests on skilled performance of tasks.

It is culturally inappropriate, even unnatural for me to work extensively and intensively with a woman elder or healer as my personal mentor in those cultures, especially in culturally intimate and sensitive areas such as healing, and especially considering that competent and respected male elders are available and accessible.

Nonetheless, several Indigenous female elders whom I work with

---

*As I reflect about these elders, I wonder how we work so closely together. Clearly, there is a reciprocal and reciprocating commitment to teach and learn, honestly and respectfully, as well as other characteristics they share, such as their exploration of spiritual paths. But I can't dismiss that certain personality characteristics make our connections feasible in the beginning and productive, even inspiring, as the relationship unfolds. I enjoy working with each of these elders, a deep enjoyment that transforms into joy and appreciation. I like them as people—and I can say without boasting that these feelings are mutual. How important is it that our personalities mesh or even attract?

in *specific* living and healing contexts do offer their teachings in the book. There is, for example, Mary Lee, a Cree elder from Pelican Lake First Nation in Saskatchewan (see map #5, page 89). Drawing on her teachings about the Medicine Wheel, she shares her understanding of traditional Indigenous counseling, wherein listening *is* the counseling, in contrast to mainstream approaches where listening is typically posited as an ingredient, even an essential ingredient *in* counseling. Also, in urban areas, where the gender-segregated structures tend to break down, female healers are more directly and widely accessible. For example, in Suva, the largest city in Fiji, many of the healers are women.

As well, I am part of a most significant form of learning while being in the presence of female Indigenous elders and healers: careful and sensitive observation of their work, careful and sensitive listening to the teachings they might offer in settings with other people around.* You can learn so much by this process of absorption, fueled by an open and respectful attitude. And the permission to listen and learn is given, so it's a teaching experience with true exchange. These teachings, which are part of the flow of living, are obviously not expressed only by the women, but the opportunity to learn by just being there and being open to my surrounds invites me into what can be an inaccessible source of teaching.

I still remember one of those powerful female teachings by absorption that occurs in Fiji while living in our home village of Naqara. It's October, and the night, with its sharp-edged stars, sparkles. It's peacefully quiet as insect sounds surround the sleeping village. My family and I are wrapped within the nearly impenetrable folds of our dream worlds. Then a piercing shaft of sound breaks into our soothing night blanket. Not yet recognizable, it's clearly disturbing. The sounds yank at us, forcing us to hear, like a pack of wolves calling into the night air. But there are no wolves here, I realize, as we drowsily arise from

---

*Thank you, Melinda García, for guiding me toward highlighting this form of teaching and learning.

our deep sleep. Louder and louder come cries—no, wails or howls. The sounds are not clear, but their meaning is getting clearer. It's the almost beastly cry of total grief.

There's been a death in Naqara, and the women are wailing, shrieks muffled within weeping and moaning. As we enter the room where the newly draped corpse lies, we feel the pulsating cover of the women's elemental expressions of grief. As a somber and very sacred yaqona ceremony is now underway, the women are crying for and to the spirits for guidance and healing. The women, in their deep emotional presence, are showing the importance of expressing our profound feelings within a spiritually healing context. The women are showing us that grief is purified when spiritually expressed—and that energizes the transformation of that grief into a healing experience. Yes, it's the women's role to do this intensely public grieving in Fijian culture, but they are acknowledging, honoring, and transforming all of our grieving and, in that process, embracing and enhancing the more silent sorrow typically felt by the men.

This segregation of the sexes, and the consequent highlighting of male elders as my mentors, does not, however, imply that there is a differential valuation of men's and women's activities and their teachings; in fact an actual separate-but-equal ethos is the tradition. Within many Indigenous settings in Saskatchewan, there is a contemporary devaluation of women, but the source of this devaluation can be traced to the European colonizers' worldview. Despite the influence of colonization, a stance championed by the Catholic Church, that equality, though often submerged, still prevails. Anishnabe elder Danny Musqua strongly sets the record straight: "The word 'fire' in Saulteaux is defined as a 'woman's heart.' They say that the love of a woman is so great, so powerful that it caused creation to take place. . . . We survive because our women are strong. The day we begin to recognize this is the day we will begin to become great again" (Knight 2001, 36).

The Ju/'hoansi offer yet another illustration. From a Western colonized perspective, it might seem like Ju/'hoan men, who dance and heal dramatically heal, often collapsing to the ground, are more important than the Ju/'hoan women, who typically heal more quietly while sitting in their singing circle. But for the Ju/'hoan, the n/om of women and men is basically the same and equal, and the n/om, not how it is generated, is the essential condition. Discussing the n/om experienced by the men and the women, =Oma Djo explains, as if it should be obvious, "It's one n/om." //Uce N!a'an, an experienced woman healer, sums it up without hesitation: "There is only one n/om," she says, "the n/om that heals." No dichotomy or hierarchy here, even though both characteristics frequently influence mainstream psychology's approach

Most important, in this book, I am only talking about *general principles* in the elders' teachings, and those principles, which apply sacred and time-tested teachings to *all human beings,* are the same whether taught by female or male elders; for example, the importance of respect in relationships and living a good life. More *specialized* and *technical* teachings—for example, the details of performing any ceremony or the intimate particularities of ceremonies marking special developmental passages for boys and girls, women and men—are not discussed because of their privileged and protected status within the culture.* I'm always seeking to focus on general *truths* within Indigenous teachings, not specialized and closely guarded *secrets.*

I'm still amazed and grateful for the enormous commitment Ratu Civo makes to teach me about healing and the life of healing, and to work patiently through my initial limited understanding of Fijian culture. I never ask him directly about his commitment, but he seems to sense my silent questioning. After a particularly long teaching session, he says to me, "Maybe you're wondering about our work together. Why am I doing this?" Ratu Civo has grasped my attention in a new way. "I'm teaching you," he continues, "because I want you to take what you have learned to make your psychology work more powerful

---

*"It's our respect for women that prevents us from talking about their special ceremonies," says Anishnabe male elder Danny Musqua. "I really don't know about women . . . that talk is for them to do." I follow Danny's path.

so that others can be helped more. This knowledge is not just for the Fijian people. It comes from the Creator, and we're all children of the Creator. As you bring my teachings into your practice, you bring back to me what I value . . . helping others. That's the exchange."

The question of exchange in regard to the healers and elders I've worked with is both complex and straightforward. Straightforward because there is always an exchange that from both our respective perspectives must be seen as equitable and respectful. Complex because the actual materials or processes of exchange can vary not only across various cultural contexts but also across healers from within a particular culture. I never pay any of the healers we meet in the book for their teachings, whether in cash or goods. Yet I always exchange something of value as an expression of gratitude and respect for the teachings; and money can sometimes be this expression of gratitude, not a fee for service.*

My commitment follows one of the central principles of elders' teachings. "Our sacred teachings are never for sale," cautions Ratu Civo, "though I've met people from outside Fiji who've made such an offer!" If I do meet someone who seeks payment for his teachings, I avoid him.

---

*The role of money in the work of Indigenous elders is in rapid flux at this time. When money is given as a *gift of appreciation* (not a *fee for service*) it carries on a traditional process of exchange. Saskatchewan Indigenous communities offer some examples of a general phenomenon. Before money gains its prominence, Indigenous elders and healers are looked after by their community. The community helps meet elders' and healers' needs by providing resources, including food, that they might not be able to secure themselves because of the time and energy spent in their sacred duties and responsibilities. Today, most elders still need this kind of support, and money is the contemporary medium needed to secure those resources.

But things get a bit more complicated. For example, in Saskatchewan there are now persons hired on a salary basis as elders for institutions—working in the prisons or hospitals or at the university. The need for them is great; the terribly high percentage of incarcerated Indigenous inmates, many in need of traditional spiritual counseling, is but one case in point. The elders will offer traditional elder services, including smudging ceremonies and sweat lodges. The challenge for these elders then is offering their services in exchange for the salary now accepted *as if it is a gift.* The services are then offered with traditional integrity, even if the hiring institution doesn't fully understand this traditional principle of exchange.

"These teachings I give you aren't free," Ratu Civo advises more than cautions. "Freely given . . . yes. But not free. You do pay for these teachings. You pay in your struggle to understand them and even more in your struggle to apply them in your life."

Other dimensions of the necessary exchange have their own special significance. There's the exchange of a sacred substance, given to the healer when requesting he share his teachings. Accepting that substance opens the door to sacred knowledge, allowing the healer to share his teachings—though acceptance is neither guaranteed nor required. In Fiji, it's the yaqona that is given as a means to unlock the doors to sacred knowledge; in Saskatchewan, a sacred offering of tobacco serves that purpose.* Also, each of the healers I work with is aware that my work with them can help open doors to a more respectful appreciation from those who possess power over them, in particular the government authorities, leading hopefully to more equitable treatment.† The way these elders teach confirms the dynamics of the exchange. They are not pouring knowledge into me as if I were an empty container but offering teachings that I can take or leave—and I take them in my actions of applying them.‡

---

*I talk more about the dynamics of this exchange in chapter 6, which deals with the process of healing, where exchange is a critical element. These sacred substances are a necessary part of any interactions with a specific question in mind or an extended conversation; the teachings that come more as part of spending informal time together, traveling and being on the land, are covered by the more formal offerings or are accompanied by a more informal but still sacred offering.

†The specific knowledge of how this influence on outside powers might work, through vehicles such as my research presentations and writings, is understood to different degrees. For =Oma Djo, who has never seen a book, it's a concept that I can write messages to "make the government change"; with someone like Ratu Civo, who understands the written world, it's a potential for influence that he entrusts me to fulfill, partly in the writing of this book.

‡I'm inspired by the way Paulo Freire (1968) discusses this distinction between the student as an empty vessel into which knowledge is deposited, even stuffed (the banking model of learning), in contrast to the true teaching-learning process featuring dialogue, application, and eventually *conscientization*. Part of this inspiration comes from my spending time with Freire and our sharing the realities of those concepts.

I also always bring various gifts to the healers I work with, and to their families and communities, to express my gratitude but never given as a quid pro quo payment for teachings. With =Oma Djo, for example, there is more of a continuous giving of items helpful to his survival and—since he passes them on to his family, his camp, and others—helpful for the survival of the Ju/'hoan community of /Kae/kae. As I live close to him, it becomes clear when certain items are scarce, such as food to supplement times of difficulty with hunting activities. These gifts then meet survival needs more directly, but there is never a quid pro quo for the information about healing he shares. I try never to underestimate the importance of material exchanges, especially considering that I'm invariably, because of my home situation, in a better economic position than the Indigenous elders I work with.

Though I hear some Fijians speak of their traditions as being for Fijians only, Ratu Civo is, through his spirit and the spirituality of his Fijian culture, a person of the world, of the universe—as are the other healers and elders who live in this book. They are all dedicated to sharing, not withholding or accumulating, their teachings, but always sharing because it's deserved. Perhaps reading this book, coming in contact with Indigenous teachings, can create for each of us a responsibility for an exchange. And if so, and it's up to each of us to determine what we give back in return. For me, putting those teachings into practice to make a difference in people's lives is one key element of the exchange.

"There is no one way, only right ways." That's a teaching of Anishnabe elder Danny Musqua, from Saskatchewan. Danny is my close friend and enduring teacher. I can't find better words to describe how I decide which Indigenous elders and healers to work with, seeking the strength that comes from tolerance and acceptance to remain open to honest teachings in all their forms.

COMING TO A HOME IN
SASKATCHEWAN

Over a three-year period, from 1986 to 1989, I live in Fairbanks, Alaska, with my then-wife, Verna St. Denis. We are both connected with the University of Alaska Fairbanks, she completing her master's in community development, I heading the community psychology program. We're actively involved with the Indigenous community in and around Fairbanks, as well as making trips to Indigenous villages spread out throughout the Alaskan land, such as Nikolai, which is Athabascan, and Kotzebue, which is Inupiat (see map #4, page 88). I feel very fortunate to be able to work with some elders from three of the main Indigenous groups in Alaska; they are all dear friends: Howard Luke from the Athabascan people, Rachel Craig from the Inupiat people, and Oscar Kawagley from the Yup'ik people.*

Indigenous people in Alaska are committed to continuing the enlivening energy of their cultural traditions and making that energy part of their resistance to the insidious historical and contemporary inroads of colonization. These days, those oppressive inroads are primarily engineered by the U.S. federal and state governments as they enable multinational companies to voraciously extract oil from the often pristine Alaska lands that are the ancestral homes of the Indigenous people. Through their insistence on "owning" rights to resources below the surface, like oil, the federal and state governments force Indigenous people off their inherent resources. Then government officials seek to convince these Indigenous peoples that these unfair oil extraction deals, are "in their best interests."

Though I have no ongoing apprenticeship relationship with them, each of these elders offers me teachings; Howard's teachings emerge at

---

*It's during my stay in Alaska that I become close to Athabascan elder Howard Luke, helping with his daily life tasks and making numerous visit to his Tanana River fish camp, which I detail in chapter 8. His teachings are extensive, though always set within an informal context, occurring as we might be checking his salmon nets or bringing in firewood for his woodstove.

his fish camp and within our therapeutic work with young Indigenous men labeled schizophrenic, Rachel's as she bridges the traditional Indigenous and Western-university worlds of knowledge, and Oscar's while elucidating the principles and facts of Indigenous science. Oscar captures the challenges for Indigenous people today: "Our land is our life . . . it expresses the spirit of our lives . . . and when we treat it with respect, it feeds us. We care for it and it cares for us. But now our lands are being ripped apart. No respect. No honoring of the spirit of the land. Just take . . . take . . . take. Our traditional ways can help us resist this destruction of land . . . and resist we must."

Alaska is cold in the long winters, but don't forget, it's also brilliantly warm and sunny during the long summer days, highlighted by nearly twenty-four hours of daylight as June 21 approaches. That kind of extreme weather makes one extra sensitive to the rhythms of the environment, and especially the limiting parameters of its temperature extremes. People accept their climate; as Oscar says, "It is what it is." No one enjoys being cold, and people complain about aberrations—when it gets exceptionally hot or cold or rainy or snowy—but they make the best of it. That "best" can, for outsiders, seem like the "worst"—as when an early snowfall that highlights animal tracks, giving hunting and trapping an unexpected boost, brings complaints from the city folk about "it's snowing already?!" There's a magnificent beauty and clean feeling in the land: Alaska is home to its Indigenous people. I learn from that land; I learn even more from those people. And as I continue my journey in the north to Saskatchewan, my time in Alaska is helpful preparation.

In 1989 there's a job opening at the Saskatchewan Indian Federated College (SIFC), Verna tells me, as she goes on to describe the college's Indigenous educational focus and institutional structure. And she's sure this is a good place for me to work. So we move to Saskatchewan (see map #5, page 89) and with that fulfill her long-term and unwavering commitment to come home after completing her master's degree in Alaska. She is a First Nations/Metis woman, and Saskatchewan is her place of birth—that's where her family and friends live. I start teaching

that year at SIFC—now called First Nations University of Canada*—
and I continue teaching there to this day.[†]

Founded on and still guided by traditional First Nations spiritually based teachings and ceremonies, First Nations University develops
a full range of courses with Indigenous perspectives and highlights its
teaching functions with the active participation of Indigenous elders,
who offer opportunities for students, who are almost all Indigenous,[‡]
to participate in ceremonies like smudging, pipe ceremonies, and sweat
lodges, all of which initiate intense contacts with the spiritual world.

As an opening to important gatherings or meetings, or as part of
Indigenous counseling practices, as well as to initiate traditional ceremonies like the sweat lodge, there is a smudging ceremony. Sweetgrass
or sage is burned in a small container and passed around so that
each person can have the smoke move around him or her, cleansing
and preparing him or her. The pipe ceremony often has four elders,
each with his or her own sacred pipe, preparing their pipes and then
sharing the smoking with those in attendance, the smoke rising up,
taking prayers to the Creator. Finally, the sweat lodge refers in the
first instance to an actual lodge, constructed from willow branches
and covered with tarps to make the shape of a dome, but the sweat
lodge ceremony extends far beyond that physical manifestation. Hot

---

*To reduce possible confusion and in the interest of simplicity, I use only this new name,
First Nations University, to refer to the college. I talk more about this Indigenous educational institution and in particular its Master of Indigenous Social Work Program in
chapter 8. First Nations University is a worthy example of how multiple psychologies,
including Indigenous psychologies, can productively collaborate.

†I also begin teaching as an adjunct professor in the Department of Psychology at the
University of Saskatchewan. I work with Indigenous undergraduate students in a special
cohort introductory psychology class that introduces Indigenous perspectives, as well as
with clinical psychology doctoral students, presenting material to help raise their awareness of the colonizing and racist pressures that can create mental health problems for
Indigenous peoples and how they, as clinicians, might be of some help.

‡Yet the school's commitment is to accept all students as it emphasizes the Indigenous
principle that all people are to be respected, and therefore all are welcomed to apply to
the school.

rocks are brought into the darkened lodge, causing intense heat and consequent sweating. As the suffering from the heat releases the potential for intense prayer the sweat lodge offers healing and guidance for a good life.

I become more at home, especially developing relationships with the Indigenous elders working at First Nations University. I often work with students who are the first in their family to attend university. These caring and idealistic students, who overcome a range of difficult and at times overwhelming life circumstances, inspire me. I re-realize how important teaching can be as a healing and empowering communication for *both* students and teachers.

It's in Saskatoon, an urban center of approximately two hundred thousand people, where Verna and I raise our two children, and within a strong and extensive family context, connections to the people and land become stronger. Everyone knows Verna: "Oh, so you're the guy she's with," is a constant refrain at first. Verna brings me into the Saskatchewan worlds, Indigenous and non-Indigenous, with her extensive relational network, nurtured by a highly respected professional life as a teacher and researcher. She is, for example, a worldrenowned antiracist educator; her work brings into sharp relief the way psychology, with its individualistic focus, ignores root causes of racism within ongoing and powerful institutional structures (see e.g., St. Denis 2004, 2011). Seeing racism more as an individual trait or motivation, psychology can too easily slip into a blame-the-victim mentality; for example, positing Indigenous peoples' personal inadequacies as a justification for the emergence of racism, and their incorrectly perceived failure to resist.

For me, living in Saskatchewan is different from my other experiences in Indigenous lands. This has now become my home, as much by adoption as by an accumulation of experiences, and the realities of family life bring my family and me into extended and extensive interactions with the local Indigenous and non-Indigenous communities. These connections are not necessarily stronger than with other places, but the continuity of living there, not having my stay bounded by time, gives the Saskatchewan experience a different nature. The everyday rhythms of *just* living are interspersed with marking occasions. Alongside ordinary birthday parties for our kids, there are special traditional First Nations' naming ceremonies for them performed by Tony Sand and Danny Musqua, Indigenous elders who have brought us strongly into their families. Tony traditionally adopts me as his younger brother and Danny as his son, bonding our families. There are many sweat lodge and vision quest or fasting ceremonies* to participate in, as becoming part of Tony and Danny's family also means becoming part of their ceremonial sweat families.†

As my eyes open, the Saskatchewan prairies express their rare beauty, carried by the wind and exposed through a 360-degree vision to sky; and the Saskatchewan winters yield their uniquely clear and clean pleasures—but those brief, fierce stretches of minus 40 degree Fahrenheit require an acceptance my body, at least, comes to acknowledge. There's a Saskatchewan saying: "There are four seasons in Saskatchewan: almost winter, winter, still winter, and road construction." (Work on improving roads is commonly done during what others call summer, as the Saskatchewan snow and ice melts, clearing room for road repairs.) For a city boy, used to the conventional four seasons of the temperate zone, the climate and the easy access to the bush signals the intensity of the changes in store for me.

---

*These vision quests (in Lakota *hanbleciya,* meaning "crying for a vision") are typically known as fasts or fasting ceremonies in Saskatchewan.
†It would be a mistake to assume that my connections with the Indigenous communities are either easily made or comfortably maintained. For example, in attending sweat lodges and other ceremonies, I'm often the only white person there. At certain sweats, I can feel the questioning attitude of some of the younger Indigenous men in attendance. Though they never express it openly, they say with their body language, "What's this white guy doing here at our sweat?" I respect this feeling, coming from young men actively seeking their own Indigenous identities, but always defer to the elder in charge of the sweat—it's his ceremony, and he's the one who invited me to attend.

Indigenous people in Saskatchewan* are primarily from one of five groups of First Nations people: Cree, Saulteaux (as the Anishnabe people are known locally), Nakota, Dakota, and Dene, as well as numerous Metis or people with a mixture of First Nations and European heritage. After contact with the colonizers, First Nations people are forced to live on reservations or reserves, where their subsistence on wild game is severely limited and their freedoms of movement and cultural, political, and economic growth are cruelly restricted.[†] Living in Saskatoon, we are connected to and visit primarily with the Cree and Saulteaux peoples who live in their home reserve community and with a wider variety of Indigenous peoples in the city of Saskatoon. Some people living on the reserves are surviving with strong cultural values, often fueled by continuing access to some wild foods through hunting, trapping, and gathering and their participation in traditional ceremonies.

Yet throughout Saskatchewan, Indigenous communities, in both rural and urban settings, experience a pervasive oppression, where their economic opportunities are limited, their internal political processes undercut, resulting in a burgeoning of social and psychological difficulties and abuses. And this situation is replicated with Indigenous peoples throughout Canada and the world. The process of colonization

---

*Indigenous peoples in Canada are typically referred to in mainstream settings, such as government documents, as Aboriginal people, but to emphasize the strong links between Canadian Indigenous peoples and other Indigenous people throughout the world, I use the term *Indigenous* in the Canadian context. It's also a term preferred by many Indigenous peoples in Canada.

†In Canada, the government-appointed Indian agent had strict control over the lives of those on the reserve, especially in regard to any movements or activities off the reserve, which are very limited and require a pass. Many Indian agents exercise that control in arbitrary and dictatorial ways. These reserve-type colonizing conditions are forced on Indigenous peoples throughout North America and, in varying forms, throughout the world.

Though the *formalized* oppressions of that earlier era of the Canadian reserve system, such as the pass system, no longer exist, there is continuing oppression, fueled by ongoing racism that forces and binds Indigenous peoples into basic health and housing situations that are woefully and inexcusably substandard. And again, this movement from formal agents of oppression to insidiously more informal agents, occurs worldwide for Indigenous peoples.

lives on, fueled by racism and powered by economic greed. Statistics of this unacceptable and devastating situation are compelling, especially knowing that each statistic is not an empty number but a human life, overwhelmed with pain and hurt and sadness. Indigenous people in Saskatchewan are tragically and dramatically overrepresented in a variety of interrelated measures, such as unemployment, poor health care, lack of educational opportunities, and substandard housing, as well as in rates of incarceration—and these rates are not falling! Statistics Canada, in its bureaucratic, almost soulless voice, spews forth statistics that portray the real hurt and devastation that exists: while Indigenous children represent 25 percent of the population in Saskatchewan, 85 percent of the children in foster care are Indigenous; while only 9 percent of dwellings of non-Indigenous people require major repairs, 54 percent of the dwellings of Indigenous people on reserves do; while Indigenous adults represent only 10 percent of the Saskatchewan population, 57 percent of the prison population is Indigenous; and suicide among First Nations and Inuit people is eleven times higher than among non-Aboriginal people. And "suicide," someone taking her or his life out of despair, is not just a word! On and on, one tragic statistic feeding on the other. Here in Saskatchewan, the term *cultural genocide,* used to describe the systemic and institutional destructiveness of colonialism for Indigenous people, highlighted by the too recent tragedies of the residential school period, seems totally and painfully accurate.

And at the same time, there is resistance and intrinsic empowerment within Indigenous communities, as sparks of light and power merge into fires, bringing confidence and hope to those communities. Out of pain comes strength; out of tragedy, resilience; and out of hopelessness, life-changing energy. It is critical to see this hopefulness and concrete self-empowerment as a thriving force, rising to redress insults and injuries, claiming a path of justice and development for Indigenous people. The specific manifestations of this path are numerous and expanding, including access programs for Indigenous students to increase success in higher education and training in the trades to increase employment opportunities;* changes in school curriculum and the provision of health care to bring a sensitivity to and appreciation of Indigenous cultures, with the hope of improving education and health care;† and vigorous and courageous demands for rightful participation, according to treaty rights, in the fair sharing of the economic fruits of resource extraction (such as oil and minerals) on traditional Indigenous lands, lands beyond the colonial markings of the restricted reservations.‡

Idle No More, a most promising grassroots movement that deals explicitly with socioeconomic and political justice and challenges the abuses of mainstream governmental power in its disregard of Indigenous rights and aspirations, is one exciting new movement of resistance and empowerment. It's a spontaneously organized gather-

---

*In addition to institutions of higher education specifically focused on Aboriginal education, such as the First Nations University of Canada and the Saskatchewan Indian Institute of Technology, mainstream universities are providing programs to provide special support for Indigenous students, such as the Indian Teacher Education Program (ITEP) and Aboriginal Student Achievement Program at the University of Saskatchewan. Using the term "indigenizing" to describe these mainstream efforts makes the efforts seem more true to Indigenous values, and more committed to full-scale institutional change than they actually are; much, much more remains to be done.

As well, the schools are now being required to teach about the treaty process, showing that treaties between Indigenous people and the Canadian government involve a two-way process and are meant to be honored, stressing what Indigenous people actually *intend* by signing the treaties rather than the surface, and misconstrued meanings of their words; for example, the settlers are granted *use* (not ownership) of the land. Emphasizing that "we're all treaty people," treaties are shown to involve commitments by the colonizers to support Indigenous peoples, so the treaties are binding for those who promise support as much as for those who are demanding the support they are promised.

†For example, Saskatoon hospitals now have a traditional Indigenous elder as part of their religious or spiritual counseling team, available for counseling and support of Indigenous patients, as well as facilities for sacred Indigenous ceremonies such as smudging and pipe ceremonies.

‡There are ongoing struggles by Indigenous peoples for their rightful share of the economic benefits from resource extractions, now unfairly siphoned off by multinational corporations. This Indigenous resistance is energized by an insistence on the sacredness of the lands and that are their ancestral grounds of being.

ing of people in different places and structures, demanding a more respected and equitable treatment of Indigenous peoples by the Canadian government (see e.g., Kino-nda-niimi Collective 2014). The Idle No More movement shows the power of Indigenous-focused political action, fueled by contemporary and traditional Indigenous teachings, and the commitment to join with non-Indigenous allies to work toward good for all people.

A source of strength for many in these movements toward empowerment is the invigorated return of Indigenous spirituality as a way of strength, ethics, and being. That spirituality can be energized through ceremonies like the sweat lodge, which previously is outlawed by oppressive government policies, reinforced by the churches, and therefore driven underground. But throughout these efforts toward change, the challenge will always remain: How to avoid changes that can be temporarily assuaging "window dressings" and to initiate real change, substantive and enduring restructuring?

The cornerstone of my work with Indigenous people in Saskatchewan is my relationship with Danny Musqua, a respected Anishnabe* elder from Keeseekoose Reserve, who is also a traditional storyteller and ceremonialist.† A large man, in size and presence, he's highly sought after as an elder for his special blend of deep and extensive traditional knowledge coupled with a keen appreciation of and expertise in contemporary issues. For example, he's especially knowledgeable about issues of Indigenous treaty rights, articulating the importance of respecting the historical meanings of treaties with the colonizers, and the rights that thus inhere in those treaties in relationship to contemporary economic and political issues—as opposed to the current climate of governments

---

*Though people from the Anishnabe First Nation who have settled in southwestern Saskatchewan are often referred to locally as Saulteaux people, Danny prefers to be identified as Anishnabe.

†Danny is unusual for a Saskatchewan elder in that some of his teachings have been presented in written form (see e.g., Knight 2001; and Stonechild 2016). This can cause some jealousy among his peers.

ignoring the treaties or intentionally misinterpreting them at the expense of Indigenous people. With his historical knowledge of culture, he's able to articulate the actual intention of the original Indigenous treaty signers, demonstrating their expectations for equity and sharing, intentions that can be ignored if one only looks at the literal words used in the treaties. Danny is frequently asked by institutions and people for guidance and ceremonies, especially in Saskatoon, where he has spent the majority of the past twenty-five years. Here's a true intellectual. Though prevented from pursuing his wish for a full formal education, he's truly educated—an avid reader and questioner of "what is."*

You might think all of this recognition from the community would go to his head—and we joke about that. "You know, your head is already big. Can it get any bigger?" I tease him. Danny is a large, handsome man, and his head, with its full head of hair, is impressively large. "Well, it depends on whether I've just gotten a haircut or not," he replies, feigning seriousness. It's his humor that makes Danny most human and most thoughtfully humble. We joke a lot. At a gathering of traditional Indigenous storytellers, one old man, who is blind, gets up to speak. He gestures strongly to make his points, in the traditional manner. Very impressive. There's only one problem. He has gotten up and, unbeknownst to him, is facing in the wrong direction, so he's gesturing dramatically to the wall rather than the audience. He's gently turned around. Danny and I can only enjoy the moment because it's a human offering of lightness.

The central cultural-spiritual experience for me in the Indigenous world of Saskatchewan comes with and through Danny. To fulfill the task he's been given by his teachers, he formally adopts me and three other men as his spiritual sons, thereby bringing us into his Bear Clan, and passes on to us his clan teaching, including the permission to perform many of his ceremonies. Members of the Bear Clan have

---

*The obstacles of racism undercut his opportunities, limiting him to a 10th grade education and denying him the formal chance to become the Ph.D. scholar he already is.

three traditional responsibilities in serving the rest of the clans in the Anishnabe community: healing, protection, and learning the teachings and ceremonies of all the other clans, so that in case a particular clan loses some of its traditional teachings the Bear Clan can help reintroduce them. I immediately realize the harmonies between my life path and the first two Bear Clan responsibilities, as I already have my long-term commitment to the study and practice of healing and to looking after and taking care of family and friends. But then I see the harmonies in my life with the third responsibility; namely, learning the teachings of other clans. It all makes sense considering my continuing efforts to learn about spiritual teachings from Indigenous peoples around the world. As I use my skills with writings, lecturing, and community collaborations to present material about such teachings, thereby fulfilling responsibilities given to me by Indigenous elders, perhaps non-Indigenous peoples can become more understanding of these Indigenous cultures, and thereby more supportive of their movements toward empowerment from within.

Within an extensive and intensive ceremonial context over the years, including fasting, Danny offers his teachings to the four of us he has adopted as sons—and whenever we can offer our sacrifice and commitment, we attempt to learn. In our first fasting ceremonies, we go four days without food and water, and to make what is difficult almost impossible, we have a sweat lodge each day. Only our prayers can give us sustenance, begging for the Creator to be with us. For me, ordinary worries and concerns—"I'm really hungry," I think, or "Only two more days," I obsess—often crowd out the prayers. But as the ceremonies continue over the years, the prayers gain strength.

We four, each in our way, work closely with Danny over the years, helping him, practicing with him.* It's a deep and enduring relationship;

---

*Through Danny's keen interest in my work with Indigenous healers in other parts of the world, and especially their ways of teaching me about healing and permission to practice that healing, he encourages me to renew my commitment to the healing work in Saskatchewan. Danny and I, in our collaborations, are able to bring together different healing traditions and practices into a respectful, synergistic whole.

family and ceremony are linked as I also gain another new group of brothers and sisters, as Danny already has a large family.

Danny and I also are best of friends, like brothers. We share, joke, tease, and spend time together, eating, traveling, visiting—and we talk about all and everything; our personal difficulties and our searching for spiritual understandings, the mundane and the sacred are all part of our web of exchange. Often tears of laughter fill our eyes, and we're not above raucous fits of joy, even as we're eating in our favorite diner.

Before entering a sweat lodge on one of our group fasts, Danny realizes he hasn't brought a pair of shorts to wear in the lodge; that's the way men typically dress to participate in the sweat, taking along only a towel. "Oh . . . no shorts," he says with a mischievous smile. "Well . . . I guess I'll just do it the old way." And he grabs a piece of canvas lying near the lodge, rips it up, and quickly and skillfully makes what he calls a breechcloth. But the way he's constructed it, it's more than a breechcloth. To all of us it is a comical field diaper, and now Danny has become a big bear of a man outfitted in his baby diaper. Danny himself is one of the loudest in our collective laughter at this strange and wonderful sight. And then we go into the sweat lodge, and seamlessly, the ceremony, in spiritual earnest, begins.

Yes, Danny and I have lots of fun together. It seems we're able to joke about almost everything, and typically the laughter is interwoven within our unquestionably serious exchanges about spiritual teaching. Danny remains my spiritual father, and the respect that's essential to that relationship transcends the familiarity and intimacy of friendship and brotherly companionship, while not diminishing the latter. Taking leave of each other, we often say, "You're my best friend," or simply, "I love you." And that says it all.

It always remains important to identify the continuing colonization of Indigenous peoples, though at times it comes in deviously subtle forms; for that oppression colors the realities of much of what occurs every day. One especially painful, and tragically dramatic, example for Indigenous peoples in Canada is the only recently ended devastating experience of the residential schools.* As children, Indigenous little ones are forced to attend residential schools, too often run by mean-spirited, even terrorizing priests and nuns, where emotional, spiritual, and physical abuse are rampant. These kids are routinely dehumanized and brutalized by a pervasive attempt to "take the Indian out of them" and force them into a white Christian mode of living. Most lose their cultural knowledge and pride, and in the process a sense of self-worth and positive identity. "Being forced to go to the residential school," says Danny Musqua, "was a sin against humanity. They tried to take away my culture. If I spoke my own Anishnabe language, they beat me. But I felt good speaking my own language. It was me being who I really was. And I was only a little guy, and they made me feel ashamed and dirty and worthless. Imagine . . . I was only a little guy. What harm could I do? Why was the school so brutal?"

Lives after the schools are too often devastated with substance abuse and violence feeding and fed by enforced poverty. Because these people are denied access to their traditional learning experiences, they never learn what it means to be a good parent, so a "legacy of abuse" is passed on to the following generations.

The Canadian government finally owns—but not fully—its role in setting up these residential schools, which it farms out to the churches to run. The government offers an apology and establishes a mechanism for compensation. To get more than the standard minimum compensation, residential school survivors have to detail the particular abuses they suffered. There's an official scale of compensation: the more serious the abuse, such as sexual abuse, the more the compensation. For acts that can't be described in a written document, survivors can detail abuses in oral hearings with government officials.

But what on the surface seems like a constructive move on the part of the government is, ironically, another form of abuse. Survivors must present as devastating a portrait as possible if they wish to get full and

---

*See publications by the Aboriginal Healing Foundation (http://ahf2.ca) for some painful descriptions of these residential school experiences and some empowering examples of resilience and liberation.

deserved compensation, emphasizing the difficulties they *still* suffer, such as nightmares or substance abuse. For someone like Danny, who has been sober for years and years and has achieved stability, success, and wide respect, his present situation will actually detract from his compensation package. I'm with Danny at his compensation hearing, and we both realized that he has to paint a picture that emphasizes his struggles, not his strengths—and that is humiliating, a retraumatizing experience, a new form of abuse. Rather than being what he is—a justly proud elder—Danny has to reenact the past degradations he has overcome. He has to show he is now a broken-down man, a grown-up form of that humiliated, abused schoolchild. But Danny can't play that game, despite the financial losses. "Look at me now," he says. "I can look at myself in the mirror and be proud, proud as an Anishnabe man, proud to be on a path of well-being, proud of my family. I can't be that old broken self again . . . It's not me."

The works of resistance and empowerment that are spreading vigorously throughout Indigenous communities give voice to insights and wisdom available from ancient teachings made new for today's world. They guide us toward listening to Indigenous elders and healers with more care and concern—listening so we might hear, and hearing so we might act.

DYNAMICS OF TEACHING AND LEARNING

Listening In Order To Hear, Applying In Order To Understand

Listening to the teachings of Indigenous elders is only a first step, a very small one, in fact. The challenge is to listen in order to actually hear. And the further challenge is to hear with enough depth of understanding that we can apply that knowledge in our lives.

Danny Musqua often finds that people, especially young people, who are too much in awe of him as an elder will listen to his teachings too naïvely. They believe too much of what he says based on their inexperienced faith or, even worse, habits of obedience disguised as respect. But just as he says his teaching creates a responsibility in himself to be honest and humble, he also insists that listening creates a responsibility in the others to forge their understanding through the risks of practice. The listener must work to make traditional teachings a part of his or her life.

"Take whatever you find valuable from my teachings, and then see if it's actually true, for you," Danny says. "Apply that teaching in your life," he continues. Then, pausing for emphasis, he quietly asks: "Does the teaching work for you? Does it make sense for you? Only after working with it can you begin to understand the teaching; only then does the teaching have a truth for you, telling you how you can begin to live a good and respectful life." "You show respect for my teachings," Danny concludes, "by applying those that make sense to you. As you struggle to live those teachings, you show you've been really hearing, not just listening."

Knowing Danny as I do, I understand his caution about an unexamined acceptance of his teachings. Danny, like all respected elders, is an ordinary man with extraordinary traditional knowledge. And as an ordinary man he, like all of us, still struggles to make sense of his life, still struggles to achieve balance and understanding. As we listen to the teachings of elders and healers in this book, it might help to have this respectful self-reflective yet questioning attitude that Danny so values.

But other obstacles to understanding these Indigenous teachings remain, and they are both fundamental and to some degree inherent. Simply put, who is doing the listening? Here I am, a white middle-class psychologist, trying to understand teachings from Indigenous cultures, teachings that emerge from environments very different from those I grow up in. That presents an inherent and at times insurmountable obstacle to understanding. And this is true despite spending many years and moments engaged in Indigenous ceremonies, teachings, and families, and despite the fact that for many years I practice spiritual and meditative disciplines that occupy similar territories of experience as Indigenous teachings. I can't know certain things at the deepest lived level, such as living a life of pervasive sharing, existing throughout times of piercing scarcity.

And so I am the filter through which the teachings pass—my coming into and evolution within psychology is just one characteristic of that filter. But since we can't fully remove our filters, I can try to describe mine as fully as possible so that we all have an idea about the transformations, even distortions, that Indigenous knowledge undergoes as it passes through that filter. That's what the preceding chapter has attempted. In the end, I trust that my filter is not too deeply flawed with biases.

Now I'd like to add another layer of relevance: how I approach the challenge of learning to hear Indigenous teachings. At times, that learning occurs within contexts that are unfamiliar, being in another cultural setting—such as the Kalahari; at times, it occurs within contexts that can seem familiar because they are part of my home setting—such as in Saskatchewan. But the challenges can be the same in both instances. Maybe some of the ways in which I try to move from listening to hearing to applying are relevant to your attempts to make a similar journey with and through the teachings presented in this book. Maybe, your relationship to psychology is affected, hopefully enhanced. In the end, we must *do* the best we can—not settle too easily or comfortably for "I *try* to do the best I can."

Expecting the Unexpected

It's tempting, even reassuring, to compare something we experience as unfamiliar with something we know as familiar. This process of making the unfamiliar familiar can become almost routine in situations that we consider to be in our home or our own place. It's almost as if the security of being home lulls us into missing what can actually be there; but what seems like the same old thing may hold hidden treasures.

I can overassume I know what I'm confronting, to presume I know something before I have a chance to really see it. I'm good at being a lazy listener. For example, Indigenous elders often have a limited repertoire of stories. When I spend many different occasions hearing an elder tell her stories, she seems to repeat the same story, over and over again. It's so easy to turn off and glide through the listening. But Danny Musqua sets the record straight: "Even though it seems like you've heard the story before, it's really a new story. It's being told now in a different time, in a different context, and the elder and you are new—neither of you are in the same place as when you heard it before. So appreciate the story as new and really listen—and hopefully you'll learn something new." That advice works!

Danny and I have many talks, and the intersections and even similarities between our experiences *seem* ripe. For example, Danny describes how living for the winter months on the trapline allows him to get to know the animals of the boreal forest: how you and the bear that lives nearby learn to respect each other's boundaries, how the beaver you trap must be respected if it's to yield its fur to you, and how these relationships with animals, who live more closely within nature, can teach humans about the need for balance and resiliency.

I can hear Danny's stories and relate them to my walks in the bush with my dog, where we see coyote and deer and, on one occasion, a wolf. I can feel the animals' teachings—how, for example, the deer judges the distance between itself and my dog and runs just in time to avoid the charge of my dog, thereby conserving energy and ensuring survival. Now that's a good teaching, having the calm and confidence to use our energy both sparingly and effectively.

By focusing on similarities between Danny's and my connections with the animals, I can fool myself into thinking I know what he's talking about. There's comfort in this conclusion of similarity. But if I'm careful and honest, I know that Danny's stories about the animals are set within a context of serious survival: trapping is for income, and one must know how to keep warm and safe in the bush. On the other hand, walking in the bush on an afternoon with my dog is a leisure activity. I'm still learning things from the animals, but it's not within a context of concrete physical survival, so my learning process is not as deep or nuanced. I need to unlearn assumptions in order to relearn knowledge.

When listening to Indigenous elders, assuming we are not living in their world, it's best to resist attempts to make their teachings too familiar too soon, to eschew the comfort and comforting of the familiar. It's helpful to let the vulnerability that can arise from uncertainty and confusion in the face of the unfamiliar be a companion—frightening though it may be, especially at first. Even if we think we're in familiar territory, this openness to being vulnerable remains a precious ally, allowing us to hear as if for the first time something we assume we already know.

As we acknowledge the spiritual dimension of Indigenous elders' and healers' work, we can appreciate the inevitability of the unfamiliar, as the spiritual dimension by its very nature brings the unexpected into our lives. Best I think to let something we don't quite understand disturb us a bit, confuse and surprise us. Through the mysteries of not understanding, a deeper understanding can emerge. Living with this edge of unfamiliarity allows us to moderate mainstream psychology's drive toward universalizing, which can suck the reality out of distinctive realities.

I hear from certain Saskatchewan First Nations elders who are exposed to Catholicism that the traditional First Nations' sweetgrass smudging ceremony, meant to purify one's thoughts, feelings, body, and spirit, is like the burning of incense in the Catholic Church. Other First Nations elders disagree, insisting that the smudging and incense are each their own thing. They say that to respect what each ceremony does, we must see them as different paths toward the same end, to pray to and connect with the Creator.

Several years ago, I'm in a coastal Yu'pik village in Alaska, doing a community-based process evaluation on a traditional healing program meant for dealing with youth alcohol and drug abuse. The head of the local church community tells me, with open pride, that his church has become "enlightened" because it now displays traditional Yu'pik spiritual symbols on its walls. Later that day, after relating this conversation to a Yu'pik elder, I hear a different story. The elder says, "I respect the church and what it does. And I respect our traditional ways and what they do. Best to keep our traditional symbols where they belong, in our homes, in our community gatherings. That's where they live and breathe." The paths are different, and in their difference is strength.

The eagerness to see similarities between different approaches, to see how one can fit into the other, to even welcome the other approach, can lead to the assimilation and consequent diminution of a less socio-politically powerful approach by a more dominant and dominating approach. As we remain open to the unexpected, we can better appreciate there are many paths toward understanding, and that diversity deepens the understanding.

Immersion within Experience

In the beginning of our stay in the Fijian village of Naqara, my grasp of the Fijian language is limited. I'm constantly interacting, at first haltingly, with villagers who speak no or little English. For example, I spend hour after hour after hour many nights a week, well past midnight, with the men who gather together to drink yaqona and visit. And at the start, I hardly understand a word that's spoken. I'm just there, soaking it all in, calling upon patience to guide me. Eventually, I am fluent enough in Fijian, able to engage intelligently in everyday conversations and to conduct interviews with healers on my own, though formal, oratorical Fijian and clearly written Fijian still elude me.

Learning a language also means you have to be open to being the source of, and even a target for, jokes. Your language mistakes are another person's greatest amusements. I provide many such opportunities for laughter, the key being I avoid hastily made assumption that I'm being picked on, disrespected, or ridiculed. In the beginning, there are two closely sounding Fijian words I constantly confuse: *kama,* which means "fire," and *kaba,* which means "to climb." There were times I would ask if "we could fire up the stairs to get into the house," or whether "climbing would send out too many sparks." What's not funny about that!

Knowing the language of the Indigenous teachings is essential to understanding them, but that knowing can take various forms. The verbal form of the teachings is a core ingredient. In addition to the various degrees to which I learn the Indigenous languages, I always have the gift of skilled and sensitive interpreters, who come from the same community as the elders and are grounded in the cultural context of the teachings.* At times it can be as if we are speaking in one voice. And this is an important protection against my unwarranted abstractions, such as bringing my own concepts in to summarize Indigenous teachings. While seeking to stay close to, if not within, the words and meanings of the elders I work with, I seek to have any concepts I use that are not explicitly in their language speak as much as possible to the experienced realities already within their teachings.†

Among the elders I work with most closely, all are totally fluent in their own language, including a knowledge of that ancient form of the language that contains the deepest spiritual teachings and is often lost in contemporary speakers. But their command of English varies: =Oma Djo speaks no English, Ratu Civo only a rudimentary form, and Joe Eagle Elk a basic English, while Danny Musqua is fluent in English.‡

But some form of immersion, some form of patient commitment to sacrifice comfort for uncertainty, seems necessary as well. Not only can it enrich the verbal understanding but also it brings in the many contributions of the varied and subtle nonverbal languages. Nonverbal

---

*When the interpreter is also especially knowledgeable on the subject, such as traditional healing, it adds another dimension of value. Ifereimi Naivota, my Fijian friend and interpreter, is an example of this unique contribution.

†One example of this conceptualizing dilemma is with the concept of synergy. Though that actual or specific word is not part of the Indigenous languages I work with, the *meaning* of synergy is. "Yes, we know that synergy idea," says Danny. "We know that's the way our universe works. Synergy is just a modern word to describe what's in our ancient knowledge." I also keep in mind that accurate conceptualizing is part of my job as a writer: "You're the one who has to make our teachings relevant to your people," Ratu Civo reminds me. "It's what you're trained to do."

‡Some of the intimacy that Danny and I share is certainly facilitated by his bilingual fluency.

communication has always been my preferred mode, and I've had lots of practice in it.

I know I'm in clear communication with my fellow Naqara villagers one night, as we sit around drinking yaqona and talking, despite the fact that most of the Fijian words still float above my understanding. As I get up to leave, my Fijian friend sitting next to me attempts to pull off my *sulu,* the traditional Fijian cloth that one wraps around the waist. Without words, he's telling me: "Now you know that you're one of us because I've just shown you how we Fijians tease each other." Fortunately, I'm wearing a pair of shorts under my sulu, as I still need that protection to preserve my dignity while I continue to master how to keep the sulu in place—despite these friendly efforts to expose what's underneath.

I'm reminded of a saying I hear often from First Nations people in Saskatchewan and elsewhere: "We have two eyes, two ears, two nostrils, but only one mouth. We have to patiently take in many things before we speak so when we speak it can be closer to the heart and the truth." A patient taking-in is critical for effective immersion, for transforming mere submersion into creative immersion. Immersion takes us into corners of understanding hidden from a more casual presence. It is an exchange: in order to deserve a teaching, we must give, even give up, something in return.

While immersion in the community of the elders I work with yields rewards of connection, community, and understanding, it also opens me to threats and dangers. I can't choose to experience only the good and ignore the bad, since both are part of the natural flow of life. Living in the beautiful Fijian village of Naqara is many times a beautiful experience but not always easy. There are struggles and challenges, disappointments and fears. While we are living in the village, there are three deaths. Because there is no obvious physical cause or ailment, witchcraft is suspected. As newcomers to the village, my family might be natural, almost logical, suspects. And on our part, as outsiders (*kai vulagi*), it can be easy for us to distance ourselves from the presumed threat of witchcraft and assume a mantle of invincibility. "This witchcraft stuff is something *they* believe," I can think to myself, "but not me, not me the psychologist/ anthropologist that has read about this witchcraft stuff and knows how much it can be fueled by superstitions and social tensions rather than facts of spiritual danger."

But being immersed reduces the ability to choose what you will or will not experience, and more importantly what will or will not affect you. I realize that if I am part of the village, living in the village as I participate in its healing life, then I, like others in the village, am vulnerable to this witchcraft. It isn't really a decision I can make because our immersion is so pervasive and intense that I, like others in the village, already feel the need to deal with this witchcraft. I seek the help of the village healer, who does a ceremony of protection for our family and tells me, "We Fijians don't go after the person suspected of witchcraft. Instead we build a protective wall (*vira ni bai*) around ourselves through our own healing ceremonies." Others in the village do the same. Immersion makes us vulnerable, but being vulnerable opens the gates to deeper understanding.

There are limits and conditions to this process of immersion. I sometimes go a bit overboard in my efforts to connect with the groups I'm living with, motivated by a combination of respect for the local people, my own enthusiasm, and often a leavening of naïveté. In retrospect, it is almost ridiculous that I volunteer to walk back to the village with three young Ju/'hoan men while others work on fixing the gas line in our truck in which we all have been riding. It is a long, long trek in the blazing Kalahari sun, punctuated by the roar of nearby lions. After nearly succumbing to heat prostration on our arrival in the village, I've gained the admiration of others: "He walks just like a Ju/'hoan" becomes a repeated phrase. Yes, but just like a nearly heat-defeated "Ju/'hoan," I think.

Also, in places where I'm not living as a permanent resident (as I am in Saskatchewan), there is a certain level of awareness that I'm not permanently part of the situation I'm in. This knowledge is typically buried so deeply during times of intense immersion, as in the Fijian web of witchcraft, that *it is not present,* and during my daily routine, it's a faraway rarely remembered thought. But I can and do (eventually) leave. I have the privilege of a workable level of choice.

HOME IS WHERE YOUR HEART IS

A big part of the process of immersion is family and community; being part of a family highlights the facts of immersion. Saskatchewan is where I now live, where a big part of my family lives, where I'm part of two other Indigenous families through spiritual adoption. When I work with Saskatchewan healers and elders, immersion is rarely an issue; I am, without question and planning, working at home.

But I can wonder at times, especially with all my traveling, with my various residences, with my two sets of kids in different places, dramatizing the different phases of my life course: Where do I belong? Where is my land? Where are my people? Joe Eagle Elk, a highly respected Sicangu Lakota medicine man from Rosebud Reservation in South Dakota, helps me with those questions.

Soon after my return from my first visit to the Kalahari, I make my first trip to Rosebud (see map #6, page 90). It's 1969, and I am invited by my friend Jerry Mohatt, a trained psychologist, who I later help supervise in his doctoral work at Harvard. A faculty member and later president of Sinte Gleska—the Indigenous college on Rosebud—Jerry has lived on Rosebud for many years, is fluent in Lakota, and is deeply involved with the medicine men who practice there and on the neighboring and closely related reserve of Pine Ridge. He brings me to Rosebud and introduces me to his Lakota medicine men friends. The doors to my continuing work at Rosebud are opening, and the medicine men invite me in.

As part of a gathering of these medicine men to talk about possible ways they can support each other, I'm asked to give a little talk on the healing approach among the Ju/'hoansi. I'm so naïve! I so underestimate the power and knowledge that lives in those medicine men. Yet they don't underestimate me or at least the *me* who is the "one who tells the story of these wonderful healers on the other side of the world"—that's how Stanley Red Bird, a close associate of Joe Eagle Elk, puts it.*

Joe sits in the back of the room, merging into the background. Though a leading figure among the medicine men, he speaks primarily through his actions and ceremonies, not his words, being a quiet, almost gentle man. There are no outward markings of him as other than ordinary—no Lakota jewelry or feathers, no cowboy hat or boots to give him an image that calls for attention. But as I learn more and more over the course of our relationship, he does speak when needed and does not compromise his words, which have force without any loud volume. Joe smiles at times, but most often his look reflects the struggles and difficulties he has faced in growing up and faces in continuing his healing work—sacrifices are many, rest is rare.†

In 1969 I participate in my first sweat lodge; it's in Joe's lodge. He later adopts me into his family; I become his son. And over the years, there are many trips to Rosebud, and many sweats, many pipe ceremonies, and many healing ceremonies, mostly conducted by Joe, some by other medicine men.‡

And it is Joe who, with the help of Stanley Red Bird, puts me on the hill for my first vision quest. During that vision quest one goes into the

---

*Almost the opposite of Joe *on the surface,* Stanley is one sharp-looking guy, publicly displaying his place and pride in being a Lakota through his personage and image. But in essence, he and Joe are together on their spiritual journeys.

†Like so many other Indigenous elders and healers, Joe has had his serious ups and downs. He's a man who struggles honestly with his calling to be a medicine man and courageously tries to face his limitations and failures. And he works hard to keep his balance. In that he is a true Lakota medicine man. Using his struggles as sources of knowledge and reminders of his pursuit of integrity, he remains, for me and many others, a teacher, a guide, an inspiration. See Mohatt and Eagle Elk, 2000, for his searingly honest and powerful life story.

‡In 2015, I attend a sweat lodge at the annual conference of the Society for Indian Psychologists. Dan and Becky Foster from Rosebud (Dan is Lakota and Becky is Blackfoot) conduct the sweat, and it has a deep continuity with the way Joe runs his sweat. More than forty-five years after my first sweat with Joe, more than twenty-five years after his death, I again feel in ceremony with him—I'm still with him.

bush, alone, and often for four days and nights without food or water. Stripped down to basics, it's a difficult journey; one suffers. But now better prepared to face the universe and beseeching with prayer, you seek spiritual guidance for one's life journey; the Lakota call this quest "crying for a vision." Then you share any gifts of teachings with the community that has supported your quest.* It's during one of those healing ceremonies that the spirits speak to me through Joe, the medicine man in charge, as is the way in these ceremonies: "Your voice is a way of healing for you. You use your voice in your teaching. And so your teaching becomes a work of healing." Yes, I can understand that. Yes, that is how I approach my teaching.

Sitting on the South Dakota prairies, Rosebud, and its neighboring, closely related reservation of Pine Ridge, is buffeted by fierce winter winds and swirling snows, by piercing hot summers and the gentle swaying of wild grasses that calm and captivate.† Rosebud offers almost

---

*In his own inimitable way of piercing but honest teasing, Stanley speaks to me as he's helping me prepare for my vision quest—*and* within the earshot of my still impressionable ten-year-old son, Alex, who is with me during these preparations: "Don't know why you're even thinking of going up there on the hill," Stanley starts out slowly, almost reflectively. "Last white guy that tried that never came back," he continues with a crescendo, "yes, never came back . . . died up there!" Of course little Alex is freaking out—and I'm not immune to Stanley's dire warning. But he accomplishes his teaching: Don't take this vision quest lightly; it can test you in ways you've never experienced before. I have to calm down Alex, but first I have to more honestly face my own fears.

†The Lakota people of Rosebud and Pine Ridge bear the burden of being caricatured by the mass media, and especially Hollywood, as "real Indians," generating what seems a never-ending parade of racist-engendered pictures of Indian people in full headdress, speaking in monosyllables and warring viciously or dreaming off into a spiritual never-ending land. But to counterbalance these popular culture examples of stolen identity, there is an especially valuable set of documents by and about healers and elders from Pine Ridge and Rosebud, offering teachings whose influence goes far beyond the boundaries of those two reserves. Most widely read—and too frequently abused or misunderstood—by non-Indigenous people, these writings, many of which are among the first to allow Indigenous healers to tell their own stories, also have influence among Indigenous people (see e.g., *Black Elk Speaks* and *Lame Deer, Seeker of Visions*). Joe's life, caringly and honestly recounted, is one of the more recent of these documents (Mohatt and Eagle Elk 2000). Joe's honesty, humility, and dedication to his spiritual journey speaks volumes in his soft, measured voice.

continual opportunities for sweat lodge ceremonies, as well as healing ceremonies, and during the summer months, vision quests.

As with the Indigenous reserve system in general, Rosebud comes into being as Indigenous Lakota people are forced from their traditional and rich subsistence lands onto designated tracts of land, which are at the time economically marginal,* and then are arbitrarily restricted in movements on and off these reservations and denied opportunities in education and health care. Unemployment is now rampant on the reservation, and poverty dominates, as the forces of colonization continue their oppressive institutional racism. Though there are still some subsistence activities off the land, including trapping and hunting, the demeaning pall of poverty increases the likelihood of abuses and violence.

But as we continually emphasize, that is only one part of the picture, a picture being reshaped by internal forces of resistance and revitalization—still struggling because the overriding poverty and racism retains such strength. For example, the fiercely resistant American Indian Movement (AIM) fights one of its most crucial and tragic battles at Wounded Knee on Pine Ridge. The grassroots movements toward improving education and employment, on a foundation of respect for traditional Indigenous teachings, hold bright promise.

After Verna and I become a couple, we begin to travel down to Rosebud from Saskatchewan to be with Joe and his family, now staying at his house. Verna is now part of his family, his adopted daughter. And

---

*At the time the reservations are established, farming is the economic pathway to sustainability, and reservations are limited to what is deemed poor farming land—keeping the richer land for the incoming settlers. The tragic irony is that this poor farmland often conceals valuable underground resources, such as gas and oil—and in places like Saskatchewan, resources such as uranium and potash. But the oppressive outside control continues, as the government now claims that Indigenous people own or have access only to surface resources on their reservations, and the extraordinary riches of oil and gas go largely to the government despite strong and concerted efforts from the reserve community to demand their fair share of the profits from gas or oil exploration.

then Joe comes up to Saskatoon to perform a traditional Lakota marriage ceremony for us. Each time we visit Joe, he puts on a family sweat at the end of our stay, as a way of our taking leave of each other, so that the spirits can reaffirm our connections and guide us till we meet again. On the day we drive away, we are all tearful, as Joe and his wife, Vicki, stand in their doorway waving, and we wave and wave, until we can no longer see one another.

On our last visit, Joe talks about how his heart is giving him increasing difficulty; we have known for a while now that he has a troubling heart condition. "I could only go for two rounds in the sweat yesterday," he says. He has to leave before the final two rounds. "Let's not have our family sweat before we leave," I suggest. "No, that's how we take our leave," Joe replies. "But . . . but your heart," I almost say in a whisper, "maybe . . . maybe you should rest a bit now." Joe looks at me with kindness and a warm but slight smile. He doesn't interrupt me, but his look makes me pause. "We'll have our sweat," he says, the kindness melting his words but at the same time giving them a finality. And that is what we do. It's a fully hot sweat—and our final sweat together.

Before Joe passes away, I ask him about family and more specifically about home. It's that "where do I belong?" question. He should know about this, I assume, as he and his ancestors have lived on Rosebud for many generations; they have their ancient family ceremonial ground in the hills for their vision quests and fasting, and that's where Joe continues with his ceremonies.*

"I've lived in different places over the years," I begin, "so it's sometimes hard for me to think of what is or could be my home." It's not a perplexing question for Joe, but his answer serves to enlarge my understanding of immersion. "Your home," Joe assures me, "is where your

---

*Earlier, pointing toward that ceremonial ground off in the far distance, Joe tells me, "that's where you'll do your next vision quest." Now that's substance and continuity of place offered into my life. It makes my "where do I belong" question become even starker.

heart is."* I've heard those words before, but they are newly powerful to me because they come from a man who has a strong and enduring *physical location* for family, a location that is a source of spiritual sustenance. Your home is where your heart is: being is more important than locale, and being full of heart needs caring and respectful commitments and engagements. How can I best write this book with and from the heart?

INTO OUR BOOK

There's a growing interest among non-Indigenous people in the traditional teachings and in particular the spiritual knowledge of Indigenous peoples. "We want to learn about your ways," it is said, "especially your spiritual ways, as we in the West have become lost because our spirituality is gone." It seems a legitimate quandary. But is it?

"First you came and took our land. Then you've taken the natural resources from those lands. And now you want to take our souls, our spirits." I often hear this from First Nations peoples in Saskatchewan, and it reverberates throughout Indigenous lands.

And now I'm writing this book, and it draws its strength from Indigenous teachings, which rest on spiritual knowledge. What *am* I doing?

I'm committed to doing the best I can. But I'm also committed to understanding the ways in which this book can inevitably be used as ammunition to bolster the recolonization of Indigenous peoples. Linda Tuhiwai Smith, an Indigenous Maori woman from New Zealand,

---

*On first glance, this seems like a cliché. But what is a cliché? Typically, a truth misapplied or overused or used casually, but it remains a truth when used honestly. Joe's phrase is not a cliché. It's not that land, or his land, is unimportant, but there is not always a land to connect to, and land is animated by the people who live on it, bringing their spirits and histories to the land and its spirit and histories. The heart makes the land a home. Other elders' teachings may seem like clichés, but as expressed through the heart, they remain truths.

writes powerfully and eloquently about "colonizing knowledges," about how knowledge has been historically co-opted as a resource owned and dispersed by the Western colonizers, who insist on the universality and superiority of their particularly Western form of discourse to other forms of knowing, in particular Indigenous forms.* She adds how the written word, almost like a physical weapon of oppression, adds a special leverage to this colonizing among Indigenous peoples whose introduction to reading and writing is more recent. Indigenous oral traditions, she points out, are perfect vehicles for intelligence and wisdom, so that reading and writing itself does not equate with knowledge. By showing the cultural limitation and inherent racism of the universalizing commitment of mainstream Western psychology, I believe this book can be an ameliorating force. But in the end, a degree of recolonization will likely remain one of the costly aspects of this written book.

Respect and exchange are two key elements in my attempts at ameliorating the recolonizing effects. With respect, I try to discuss Indigenous teachings on their own terms as sources of valid knowledge for all. And I focus on principles, not practices; truths, not secrets. Many of these teachings are expressed within and live through sacred ceremonies that are meant only for those in the community, and meant to be learned only through direct contact with elders and their oral teachings. I don't write about any of the sacred elements of ceremonies, now existing within these oral teachings, only the *principles* expressed through these ceremonies, which I've been given permission to share. For example, I'll talk about the teachings of the sweat lodge, such as humility and sacrifice, but not how to construct a sweat lodge.

---

*There are many powerful ideas in Smith's book, *Decolonizing Methodologies: Research and Indigenous Peoples*. Here is one: "The globalization of knowledge and Western culture constantly reaffirms the West's view of itself as the centre of legitimate knowledge, the arbiter of what counts as knowledge and the source of 'civilized' knowledge . . . the story of civilization remains the story of the West" (Smith 1999, 63). Hopefully that quote encourages you to get more deeply into her book.

As a further expression of respect, I don't advocate that a non-Indigenous person take on the ceremonial practices of an Indigenous people, unless he has permission to do so by an Indigenous person who is a legitimate holder of that ceremony. For myself, even though I've been given various healing ceremonies from different Indigenous traditions, I don't practice them, except on occasion in the quiet of a small, immediate family setting, and don't see myself as a holder or practitioner of that ceremony. But I know the sociopolitical context of capitalism will send tentacles throughout the book and its reception, inevitably suggesting, even supporting ways to commodify and commercialize the Indigenous teachings described.

Writing this book has helped me be a better psychologist, a better healing vehicle within the primarily Western context that I live in, where I'm often working with Indigenous peoples. It's my respect for Indigenous knowledge that has kept the focus in this book on enhancing Western psychology, not on providing a definitive account of Indigenous teachings. I'm not teaching Indigenous knowledge; at best, I'm pointing toward that dynamic body of knowledge and its actual teachers, so others can negotiate their own terms of learning.

When I'm leaving Fiji for the first time, after apprenticing as a healer for more than two years with Ratu Civo, I'm somewhat confused about my return to my home in the United States. Ratu Civo has instructed me to continue my practice as a healer based on what he has taught me. "But how can I continue this work," I almost plead, "when the conditions in the U.S. are so different than Fiji?" "I want you to continue with your work as a psychologist," he assures me. "Only now you'll be a better psychologist because you know about Fijian healing." But always searching for more information, I continue on: "But we've talked about Fijian healing herbs. How will I find them when the plants are so different in America?" "No need to worry," he says. "You just go out into the bush and look around, and you will see a plant that speaks to you. Pick it . . . it will be the right one to use. Rely on your inner spirit to guide you." And that both calms me down and gives me a sense of challenge. "You mean I have to do my own inner spiritual work," I think, and then I re-realize that that is the essence of Ratu Civo's teachings, not the particulars of any Fijian ceremonies.*

During my first experience in the Kalahari, =Oma Djo tells me, "Tell our story to your people. We have something of value in our healing work," he adds, "and we want to share it with others." On that first visit I grasp only part of =Oma Djo's meaning. In my first intensive work with an Indigenous community, I naïvely emphasize his wanting to share and don't fully grasp the *process* of exchange that has been initiated. Yes, =Oma Djo *does* want to help my people, but I must assume my responsibility to give back, not as "payment" but as a way of respectful relating.

I have to be realistic about the forces that are working against our ability to hear and apply the Indigenous teachings presented in this book. As long as we are functioning within a capitalistic system, there will be resistance—resistance to fair and honest exchange, resistance to respect, resistance to teachings that speak of psychology and healing not as commodities to be sold but as gifts to be shared. As both an expression of and support for that capitalistic system, the guild aspects of mainstream Western psychology, the structures and motivations that insist that psychology be controlled by certified psychologists, typify these resistances.

Ratu Civo has very sound advice for me. He's given me a tremendous amount of knowledge about Fijian healing. But he and I know that is only a beginning; what matters is what I *actually* learn and what I in fact *do* with that learning. "Say only what you know, no more, no less," he cautions. "Do only what you are honestly capable of doing."

---

*Upon arriving home to Saskatchewan, I find myself having to put Ratu Civo's teachings about "relying on my inner spirit" and "seeing a plant that will speak" into practice. I need to find something for arthritic pain for a family member. I go out into the bush, and yes, a plant does "speak to me." I pick it—and it is later confirmed by Danny as a plant that can work for arthritis. He then instructs me in its proper preparation as a medicine. I realize the important teaching from Ratu Civo will serve me in a wide variety of healing situations, well beyond the use of natural medicines.

The more I can live that advice, the more this book speaks some truths. My knowledge is limited, but if I can share what I do know and have permission to share, I can better serve the elders.

Ratu Civo offers another piece of advice, which though obvious at one level surprises me dramatically at another. When I return to Fiji for a second time, I want to show him a draft of the manuscript I'm writing on Fijian healing and my work with him. We plan the writing of this book early on in our work together; he charges me with that writing responsibility. But I still want to read through the book with him, focusing on certain sections I'm unsure about, and have him tell me where I've gone wrong and where I've gotten it right.

Ratu Civo looks at me a bit quizzically: "You really want me to look at this book?" "Well, yes, I thought you should be sure that what is written is correct." "But Dick . . . writing books is your job. That's your skill," he assures me. "Just carry on with your given talent and your assigned work. I don't need to look at the book. I only have to look at you. I know what you have learned; I've done my job teaching you. Now it is your turn to do your job."

Ratu Civo's words leave me both in awe and a bit afraid; the trust he has in me is overwhelming, and the responsibility he's given me, awesome. And then he adds, "You've spent many hours and days with me learning about and practicing Fijian healing. I trust your knowledge. But if by now you don't get it, then you can write whatever you want, and it won't matter."

The Indigenous elders in this book speak clearly about many things. They are very serious about wanting to share their teachings with others. As these teachings begin to percolate within mainstream psychology, beginning to transform conventional structures and motivations of power and control, all people are better served. These elders say over and over, "We want to help all people." As psychology is being healed and becomes more of a healing psychology, those historically disempowered become more active participants in the processes and structures of psychology, and, thus empowered, are more justly served.

=Oma Djo opens this book talking about "things of power," with the need to understand how they work so they can be healing forces in our lives. Psychology is today one of those "things of power." And there is an appallingly limited understanding of how it works.

This book seeks to better understand mainstream psychology so it becomes a more just and potent healing force in our lives. But our larger aim is not only enhancing mainstream Western psychology but also seeking a multiplicity of healing psychologies, not one universal psychology. There must be openness to the diversity that exists throughout our world in ways of knowing and being. As mainstream Western psychology steps away from its global stranglehold over psychological thinking and services, Indigenous psychologies, too often suppressed and oppressed within the clutches of colonization, have more room to continue growing, to flourish and effectively serve their people as they have for many thousands of years.

Having stepped aside, mainstream Western psychology needs to be a more respectful and responsible partner in the emerging community of psychologies—but only one partner. Becoming less domineering and arrogant, Western psychology can be more open to learning from other psychologies, including its own voices of resistance and exploration. What can emerge is a synergistic community of healing psychologies where the whole is greater than the sum of the parts and where available healing networks, now renewable and expanding, are more accessible to all. Then we can have a collaborative pattern of psycholog*ies* that can be a model of best practices for all. In that way psychology can better honor its commitment to social justice and equity.

In the following chapters, we focus on key topics in mainstream Western psychology and explore how Indigenous perspectives can enhance the way these topics are understood, to provide more revealing and inspiring reflections on human conditions and potentialities. But where to start?

Continually I hear from Indigenous elders about the centrality of spirituality *in everyday life*. They tell me that this spirituality must be experienced in order for there to be a healing of psychology, let alone a healing psychology. But they make just as clear that spirituality is something we live, rather than something that is far beyond or set within an incredibly dramatic occurrence. "Look at it this way," says Ratu Civo, "there's a sacred energy throughout our world . . . and here within us. It makes all things connected. And it's a path toward respect for all things. It's what lets us go beyond our own little needs. Lets us know there is more to us than what we see or hear. And lets us live into places and parts we never knew were possible."

As we move into the next chapter, we can begin to see how this spirituality is both ordinary and pervasive, often subtly life guiding; at times substantially life changing. And most important, spirituality doesn't require or assume religion or special training. For our Indigenous healers, it is simply "the way we are." And just as clearly, spirituality is a dimension missing in mainstream psychology. Can spirituality be a foundation, a perspective that can offer healing to psychology, maybe even help create a healing psychology?

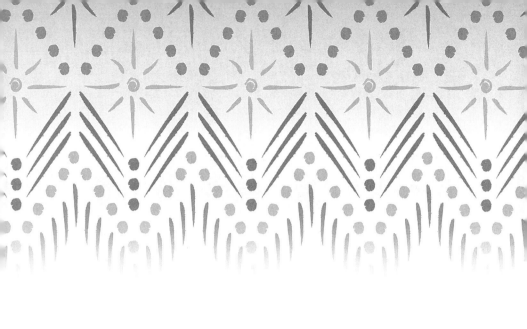

PART TWO

THE WORKINGS
OF
PSYCHOLOGY

CHAPTER THREE

"We Respect What Remains a Mystery in Our Lives"

The Enduring Foundation of Spirituality in Everyday Life

Cree elders Tony and Emma Sand, from Mistawasis First Nation in Saskatchewan, become my first spiritual family upon my arrival in Saskatchewan. Tony adopts me as his younger brother and welcomes me into his sweat lodge. It's really an adoption into their sweat lodge *family,* as the lodge offers a centering point in the everyday lives of their large extended kinship network.

One day Tony and I are driving north toward a ceremonial feast to be held outdoors on his reserve. It's beginning to rain. Then it's raining harder. "Too bad," I reflect, "this rain is going to make that feast difficult." Tony has a different perspective. "You know, Dick," he says without judgment, "I respect the rain. It's the Creator's way of cleansing Earth. The rain has a spirit . . . and the rain is given to us as a blessing."

From Tony's Indigenous perspective, the spiritual dimension pervades and animates everything. The rain and wind, the animals, the trees and rocks, the humans. Everything has a spirit. In my pedestrian concern for getting *wet* from the rain, I overlook being *cleansed.*

But Tony isn't a dreamy-eyed mystic; he's above all a man of common sense and practical focus. When he feels the spiritual dimension throughout nature, he's acknowledging our human ability to go beyond our ordinary perceptions into another dimension that is *extra* ordinary. But it's not a formal or verbalized acknowledgment; it's more simply his felt experience. For Tony the spirit of the rain is part of his daily life— it's not a big deal but a moment of respect shared with but not imposed on me. It's just one path that allows him to move beyond his limited boundaries into a realm of possibilities and potentials. "The rain can remind me to be more than myself, to be more of what I can be. Like being more concerned with others than just my own needs."

I overlook the spiritual dimension ignited by the rain, the opportunity to go beyond my ego needs, because I don't see, or as the Ju/'hoansi say, I don't "see properly." "When I see properly, when I feel the n/om rising inside me," says =Oma Djo, "that's when I can see inside people. I can see what's troubling them; I can see everything clearly."

Experiencing spirituality, =Oma Djo can understand what is typically hidden but is now clearly present. It takes seeing properly, available during our everyday life and not just during special ceremonies, to become open to the spiritual presence in our universe, to experience the cleansing spirit of the rain. "Being open to the spiritual," says Ratu Civo, "brings the spiritual into our everyday lives, simply . . . no fanfare."

Yet in the end, as the energy of the spiritual becomes active in our lives, mystery remains—not all things can be explained, even understood. "We can't really understand all about the spiritual," cautions Ratu Civo. "In the end, we accept it, work with it—and still it remains a mystery. We respect what remains a mystery in our lives."

MAINSTREAM PSYCHOLOGICAL APPROACHES

What is this spiritual dimension we're talking about? We could say the spiritual is a dimension of experience and existence beyond the boundaries of the individual or community; what is beyond yet within daily life; what is ultimate yet intimate. That dimension alludes to both a human experience (spirituality), which is not synonymous with religion or religious practices, and a characteristic of the universe (the spiritual), as in the Indigenous teaching about the sacredness of all things coming from their being infused with a spirit. Experiences of spirituality exist within and connect to the dimension or realm of the spiritual, that which has been variously named God, the Creator, and the Great Mystery. This last term affirms the essential human unknowingness of both the spiritual and spirituality. But from an Indigenous perspective, since the spiritual is so importantly a *concrete yet dynamic experience* any definition becomes a futilely abstract attempt to pin down what remains fluid and beyond words. At best we can use the above definition in the Zen tradition of understanding that describes how when we point our finger at the moon that can direct our attention to the moon, but the finger is in no way equivalent to or even sharing characteristics with the moon.

Whereas Indigenous approaches to psychology go, in the course of daily living, into and within the spiritual nature of the universe, mainstream psychology keeps drawing lines of separation from that journey, insisting on its fallibility, questioning its reality. Historically, to achieve its goal of not only being a separate discipline but a respected one at that, psychology believed it had to remove itself from its roots in religion and philosophy in order to become a "true science," which meant a laboratory-based field of inquiry. Religion and philosophy were devalued as processes of scientific inquiry, their subject matter considered off-limits for proper psychological (scientific) study. The remnants of this historical cleansing persist today and remain a major obstacle to a full and unbiased consideration of the spiritual dimension by mainstream psychology.

Mainstream psychology's primary response to spirituality is to deny or ignore, or at least minimize, the existence of spirituality as an *experiential* phenomenon and, in particular, as emphasized in Indigenous approaches, spirituality as a *personal* experience. John Watson, a founder of behaviorism, an approach that remains a pillar of mainstream psychology, says that consciousness is "neither a definable nor a usable concept, it is merely another word for the 'soul' of more ancient times. . . . No one has ever touched a soul or seen one in a test-tube" (Watson 1928, 3–6). Though today the variable of consciousness and its seminal role in spirituality is being researched within psychology, Watson's dismissive words still echo in current beliefs within mainstream psychology. And when dealing with spiritual experiences in their non-Western contexts, mainstream psychology often degrades those experience into irrelevance or meaninglessness with pejorative labels such as "primitive" or "superstitious."* While the experience of spirituality may be the heart of Indigenous approaches, it's the bane of experimentalists seeking to pin down things into measurable units, with data about groups trumping and thereby erasing data about the significance of any particular individual's experience. But this Indigenous emphasis on a person's experience is not an example of the individualism supported by the mainstream, but an expression of the ultimate valuation of a person's integrity within the context of serving the common good.

When mainstream psychology does deal with spirituality, it uses a number of limiting strategies, each resulting in diminished and therefore more manageable (meaning "more measurable") versions of spirituality. By focusing on *concepts* of spirituality that can be *analyzed,* as well as *conditions* that can stimulate spirituality and *consequences* of spirituality, the mainstream approach makes the "reality" of spirituality increasingly dependent on the degree to which it can be measured.

With its focus on concepts of spirituality, mainstream psychology

---

*I personally feel the force of this reductionism as an unspoken tenet of psychology when I first present my research on spiritual healing among the hunting-gathering Ju/'hoansi to more mainstream, Harvard-type audiences. For example, when I talk about n/om, the Ju/'hoansi spiritual healing energy, to more mainstream audiences, I might hedge my words, saying something like: "It is their *belief* that they work with the healing power of n/om." Very soon, however, I abandon this safe cover of conservative academese and talk directly about the healing energy as an experienced fact of existence—at a cost to my credibility as a "real" academic.

gives primacy to verbal constructions of an essentially non- or preverbal experience.* Data about spirituality or spiritual experiences is gathered from surveys, analyses of diaries, or internal reflections. These data are then analyzed into categories or themes, the sum of which is said to describe spirituality. Among those categories are feelings of awe, a sense of inner calm, and a quality of ineffability. Though the categories are rich in meaning, they remain categories—only abstractions of experiences. Also, the sample of persons providing the data is skewed toward those who are verbally articulate and especially so about that densely nonverbal area of spiritual experience. There is an irony in having ineffability, or an inability to put things into words, as one descriptor—then why even ask the participants to use *words* to describe their spiritual experience?

Mainstream psychology's fascination with what is measurable feeds its focus on religion as an indicator of spirituality rather than, as the Indigenous perspective warns, a mere and often limiting container—if even that. A common research strategy uses attendance at some formal religious service, typically church attendance, as a measure of religiosity, which is then often confounded with spirituality—being able to *count* attendance figures overwhelms reasonable doubts about the accuracy of that attendance even as a measure of religiosity. But flawed as they are as studies of spirituality, this research shows something most interesting: the positive health-supporting effects of attending church are related less to spiritual experiences such as developing a sense of purpose or the strength to cope with deep, existential fears, but more to the opportunities for social networking and support that occur as a result of that attendance.†

The overarching term of choice in mainstream psychology, under which spiritual experiences are typically included, is *altered states of*

---

*In contrast to Zen koans, which use words not for their intrinsic meaning but to evoke a nonverbal experience or understanding, mainstream psychology values its verbal constructions and analyses of spirituality as having intrinsic, even real value.
†See for example, Diener and Seligman (2002) and Salsman et al. (2005).

consciousness. The connotation here is that ordinary normal consciousness is altered, including also being derailed from our accepted ways of being. As a result, spirituality can be unrealistically associated with negative connotations, along with the common assumption that it is separate from, and separated from, the flow of daily life. For example, much of the discussion of altered states of consciousness focuses on negative, drug-induced states, with detailed discussions of the physiology, psychology, and devastating outcomes of being drunk with alcohol or being in a cocaine- or heroin-induced state of consciousness.* Less attention is paid to changes in consciousness during processes such as meditation or healing ceremonies. As a result, the full range of human motivations to change consciousness supported in Indigenous perspectives, which can include the seeking of wisdom, is truncated, reduced to motives such as pleasure seeking, coping with anxiety and depression, or avoiding responsibilities.

This emphasis on drug-induced negative states of consciousness opens the door to a pervasive negative evaluative tone, so that alterations of consciousness are seen not only as bad but abnormal, the latter being used as a substitute for, even an equivalent of, the former. As a result, changes in consciousness are seen as something to be avoided if one is to live a normal—meaning respectable, predictable—life.

Even when considering potential positive effects of spirituality, mainstream psychology tends to be relatively simplistic and superficial, lacking the deep nuances and broad range acceptance of multiple ways toward understanding seen in Indigenous approaches. Although studies emphasize such positive effects as increases in happiness, well-being, positive self-image, or self-esteem, there isn't an equally serious consideration of some so-called negative outcomes, such as confusion or self-doubt, which can be powerful accompaniments of and even preludes to

---

*Rarely does a conventional introductory psychology text mention culturally sensitive and historically effective uses of mind-enhancing substances, such as the use of ayahuasca among Indigenous peoples of the Amazon. And then such examples are layered with connotations of being at best exotic or, more typically, questionable.

the more positive effects. Even more important is a failure to see these outcomes as neither good nor bad, positive nor negative, but more part of an ongoing process in which different experiences exist in dynamic balance. This preoccupation with positive outcomes also tends to be superficial. For example, happiness is conceived of more as being positive or optimistic or feeling satisfied with one's life rather than considering a more existentially nuanced state such as appreciating and accepting the complexity and challenges of life as a foundation for well-being.

Finally, as part of its effort to minimize the importance of spirituality, mainstream psychology marginalizes it, building a rationale for spirituality to be inaccessible and therefore unresearchable *because* it is inaccessible—too out of the ordinary. Even when adopting a more positive perspective, mainstream psychology emphasizes more dramatic and therefore inaccessible forms of spirituality. For example, out-of-body experiences or near-death experiences are described, implying a sharp break with and from ordinary consciousness. Even when using the term *transcendence,* with its primarily positive connotation, the ongoing connections transcendence has with ordinary life situations are minimized. The impermeability of boundaries between states of consciousness is stressed, strengthening perspectives that separate ordinary consciousness from these more dramatic or extraordinary states. Whereas Indigenous approaches see spirituality existing within daily life, it's almost as if mainstream psychology protects itself from a serious, sensitive study of spirituality by configuring it as an unrecognizable, even threatening monster of an experience.

One of mainstream psychology's most promoted accomplishments is to offer a list of the five most important human personality traits—what are ostentatiously called the *big five* in psychology texts. Aside from the cross-cultural flaws that undermine the claim of universality for this list, the list remains instructive about what psychology considers basic to human nature. The five traits are extroversion versus introversion; neuroticism versus emotional stability; agreeableness versus antagonism; conscientio   ess versus impulsiveness; and openness to experience versus resistance to new experience. What is lacking is any mention of the human need or motivation to seek something more or search for meaning beyond the self—let alone spirituality—and to have this as part of our ordinary lives as humans. In Indigenous teachings, this search for meaning is at the heart of human nature.

The trait of openness to experience incorporates motivations of curiosity, imagination, questioning, and creativity. Aren't these particular motivations a source for, and even the beginnings of, seeing beyond the egotistical confines of self, which then can be a springboard into the spiritual? Why is mainstream psychology so conservative and careful? What is there to fear about the almost logical extension of questioning and curiosity into experiences of the extraordinary? That is where Indigenous perspectives take us, without misplaced fear but with respectful deference.

Ratu Civo says, "In our hearts we live in the land of the spirits." If people's spiritual experiences are difficult for mainstream psychology to work with, imagine how hard it must be for this logical, materialistic-oriented mainstream approach to appreciate that the spirits live *throughout the land.* But that is what we see when, as =Oma Djo says, we see properly.

INDIGENOUS APPROACHES

"The spirits are our relatives," Joe Eagle Elk tells me, "and so when they appear to you, like in the sweat lodge, don't be afraid. We welcome them into our lives. They guide us in a good way." Joe also emphasizes that any experience I have in the lodge is a treasure to be nurtured, shared only if I choose, and then for the benefit of all. "Our spiritual experiences are very personal," he insists, "but they all lead to our serving the community."

In performing his sweat lodge ceremony, Joe expresses the importance of the *experience* of spirituality that *can* occur and the directness and simplicity of that experience. He doesn't want people making a "big deal" out of any experienced connection with the spiritual and doesn't encourage an extended analysis of what happens in the sweat. Indeed, when a person does choose to talk about her or his spiritual experience, that doesn't indicate that this person had a more powerful experience; in fact, sometimes talking about the experience can weaken its intensity. "You can remember your experiences in the sweat just by living them," Joe cautions. "Words can be helpful as reminders—but only for some."

Furthermore, Joe emphasizes that spirituality is connected with the depth and intensity of an experience, not the number of ceremonies (or sweats) one attends; counting sweats is not a way to measure spirituality. And most important, the spiritual is not confined to or contained only in specific ceremonies like the sweat lodge: "The spirits are all around. It's sometimes easier to connect with them in the sweat. But we *can* connect—anytime, anywhere."

Rather than requiring a *definition* of spirituality, Indigenous psychological approaches emphasize the *experience* of spirituality and especially its diversity and ordinary life contexts. When the people gather inside his sweat lodge, and the door flap closes—welcoming the darkness that can highlight the still glowing heated stones—elder Tony Sand, my spiritually adopted older brother, starts his ceremony with words of assurance and hope. "What happens inside this lodge is your own business," he begins, "and only you know why you are here . . . and that is between you and the Creator. Your experience in this lodge is yours . . . the story of what happens here is your story . . . yours to tell if and when you wish." By speaking the truth of his sweat lodge ceremony, he is trying to give people confidence to be open to the spirits that would be invited into the sweat, to lay aside fears and experience, directly and simply.

I speak with Danny Musqua about the sparks often seen in the sweat lodge that are said to be manifestations of the spirits. And we talk about how these sparks come about. Out of a sincere desire to know, I slip into my comfortable Western mode and do some analysis. "Are the sparks the actual spirits manifesting?" I ask. "Or can they sometimes be created by the sweat lodge leader, who having become a vehicle for the spirits, rubs objects together, helping to make the invisible visible?"

Danny joins me in this inquiry, knowing that I'm searching for a truth. "I've had similar thoughts and questions. At times I've had my doubts as well," Danny shares, "but to me these questions are splitting hairs. It's a useless exercise because what matters is the honesty of the spiritual search and experience—that's what counts. Not the mechanics of how it all happens. Sometimes we just don't know for sure," he continues. "We can't analyze it into understanding. A mystery remains . . . that's how it is." I smile. "Yeah, that's the way I've been thinking myself . . . but you know," I add, "sometimes that old Western-trained mind just demands a time to come out and do its analysis thing. And it seems one way to calm it down is to let it out." We clasp hands in joyous agreement, having fun watching the analytical mind try to take control.

Joe Eagle Elk makes very sure I understand I'm to withhold judgment about the way in which a particular sweat lodge is conducted. As my spiritual father, Joe feels a responsibility to lead me in a proper way toward the spiritual life of the lodge. "Each of us who does a sweat," he cautions, "does the sweat in the way it was given to him, by his teacher, by the spirits. And each of us, if we do the sweat properly, does it in the way the ceremony was given to us. And so there will be differences in sweat lodges, almost as many differences as sweat lodge holders. Go into a sweat with an open heart," he continues, "and without judgment about whether the sweat is being done the right way, which usually means the way you are accustomed to its being done. Just try as best you can to be in that sweat and, in your own way, to connect with the spiritual." From an Indigenous perspective, the various forms in which spirituality can be experienced and encouraged makes definitions, and especially *a* definition, almost fruitless, without detracting from the reality of the spiritual.

But spirituality is only a small part of the picture—though very important to our aspirations and intentions. There is a spiritual quality or foundation to the universe we live in, expressed in a pervasive way throughout the universe, and spirituality is a way of expressing our connection to that foundation. Danny Musqua speaks eloquently about how the spiritual pervades all life and how all parts of Mother Nature are alive. "Earth is our mother," he says, "and she gives us all life." Danny adds perspective to the Mother Earth teaching: "In terms of a natural order, we are mere humans, we are at the bottom of the chain and therefore need to respect our life sources, the plants and animals, in order to survive . . . Thus in order to understand the Creator and spirituality, we must first understand Mother Earth" (Knight 2001, 37).

As I continue to work with these Indigenous teachings, I'm more able to connect with—to strongly feel—this pervasive spiritual dimension. Danny emphasizes that the plants and animals, the wind and the stars—all of nature—"have spirits with stories to share." Yes, I know this. Sitting in my house, I can see right outside a giant elm tree. It's magnificent in so many ways. Strong, almost unshakable at its base, it grows increasingly subtle and agile as it nears its tips, its tiny branchlets bending to even the slightest shifts in the wind, dancing out invisible forces. The shape of the entire tree is impossibly complex, branching off in never-ending journeys. A strong spirit must live within that tree, especially as I view the several major pruning marks along its trunk, which now seem more like scars than improvements. Scarred yet thriving. And I haven't even considered yet the multitude of services this tree offers to the world, from its warmth-producing firewood to its wind-shielding protection for birds and other creatures to its exchange of carbon dioxide and oxygen.

Yes, this tree—or any tree—could only be so intricately beautiful and useful if it were infused with some kind of spirit, some force that places it squarely in Mother Earth's garden. And it teaches, often unexpectedly if we are not seeing properly, strength and flexibility; being grounded and reaching for the sky; giving in a variety of ways for the benefit of others. I can have these knowings *while still being a psychologist* and, most important, not in contradiction to what psychology can be.

The Kalahari Ju/'hoansi live this pervasive spirituality. At their healing dances, their most important ceremony, the boiling energy of n/om is released throughout the community, all of whom typically are at the dance. =Oma Djo talks about how when n/om is released, it is like the "sparks leaping into the night air from a strongly stirred fire pit of embers." The sparks reach into the night air, touching all as they disappear into the sky. As well, nearly half of the men and one-third of the women become spiritual healers; healing is not a specialized task but a community function, as healers continue with their hunting and gathering survival activities. All at the healing dance are part of the healing network—not just those with more obvious healing functions, such as those dancing or performing laying on of the hands or those women who sing the n/om song. The community goes on a collective spiritual journey: it gives and takes and partakes of the healing now released.

Rather than considering their work an altered state of consciousness, or even an enhanced state of consciousness, the Ju/'hoansi describe their work with the spirits as "something we do." The most common reason for having a healing dance is to give the people a chance to visit, to spend valuable time together sharing the news of daily events to build community, *while* all at the dance receive healing. Healing of sickness occurs, but it is in the context of healing community; as with all communities, there are confusions and conflicts that need concrete, almost daily attention to resolve or at least lessen. The Ju/'hoan acceptance of spirituality as a way of life does not make them into romantic versions of fully realized beings; they are, like we all are, humans preoccupied with human emotions and struggles but now fortified with the healing power of the spiritual.

From an Indigenous perspective spirituality is pervasive and grounded in the daily context of life. Danny Musqua is constantly having to correct Western preoccupations with traditional ceremonies, like the sweat lodge, which are often "exoticized" and seen as being the essence if not the definition of Indigenous spirituality. "The spiritual plane clearly continues to play an important role in Aboriginal life, despite the fact that many traditional ceremonies were banned by law and were deemed heathen practices," he says. "When considering the role of the spiritual plane, we are not dealing with some quaint custom, nor are we dealing with religion as defined in the Western world. To Aboriginal people, the spiritual plane is not simply a belief, which is separate from everyday life; instead, all aspects of life are viewed as having a spiritual dimension" (Knight, 2001, 37). All aspects of life have a spiritual dimension—ceremonies are just another aspect. Spirituality is a way of living.

Because from an Indigenous perspective spiritual journeys are "just something we do," states of consciousness become experiences of reality, with the emphasis on a flowing between states, rather than on whether the state is normal or abnormal. Consciousness is seen more as a neutral energy that takes many forms, and when it is enhanced it can lead to spirituality. Ratu Civo is clear that humans can direct and redirect this spiritual energy toward positive or negative purposes. He explains that some people use their prayers to the spirits to ask for devious or harmful things to happen to others; that can be effected, but always at a cost—the ones seeking harm to others will themselves (or their families) be harmed in the future. "This," he says, "is how what people call witchcraft occurs. There is always an exchange. Nothing is free. Good or bad."

When I speak to Ratu Civo about the book he has asked me to write about Fijian healing and our work together, I still have a deep quandary, though the book is nearly complete. "Will it be a problem that I talk about witchcraft in the book? I know it happened, but will readers, who will mostly be in the West, see this mention of witchcraft as a sign of how 'primitive' these Fijians are?" I ask. "No," he affirms, "you *have* to talk about witchcraft. It's only when we realize the strength of witchcraft that we can then realize the strength of the straight path, our spiritual path that opposes this witchcraft. And our book is about the straight path. There is a continual struggle between these two forces . . . that's our life," he adds, "the spiritual energy is locked in the motion of balance. We need to respect all sides as part of the challenge, the good and bad, the ups and downs, all are part of what it means to be human."

Though the sweat lodge or the Ju/'hoan healing dance can work on people's psychological and physical problems, including anxieties and depressions, its primary purpose is to encourage and support a spiritual journey of discovery. Within the context of that journey, help can emerge for those anxieties and depressions. As a result, what seem like problems can become expressions of existential challenges, the very nature of what it means to be human, the very stuff of life's ups and downs.

A central condition, indeed requirement, for spiritual transformations is that individuals contribute to the well-being of the community. In contrast to a Western indulgence in the depth and drama of an individual's spiritual journey as a sign of that individual's achievement, from an Indigenous perspective, such ego-centered experiences are not supported. For example, the Ju/'hoansi employ a kind of thermostatic principle in dealing with the healing potential of n/om. The aim is to have n/om boil within healers until it is hot enough to release healing but not so hot that it overwhelms the healers, often causing them to fall to the ground, which would short-circuit the potential for n/om to release healing to the community. The Ju/'hoansi can't waste their efforts on training a young healer who can't learn how to modulate his spiritual energy so as to make healing possible. "If those young guys keep falling," says =Oma Djo, "I just can't keep working with them. We need healing, not falling-down guys!"

Though the Lakota vision quest may seem, to Western eyes, like an individual's search for his or her vision or path, that is only a part of the picture. Though an individual returning from a vision quest is encouraged to tell the story of her or his spiritual experience to the community, which has supported the quest, the point of the storytelling is for the individual to learn how his or her path can develop *within* the community to best serve that community. "We want to hear what happens on the hill, what did the spirits tell that person," says Joe," because then we can learn how that person can be of service to us, and that way come to learn who he is." When I come down from my vision quest, Joe talks about some of the teachings of the spirits that visited me up on the hill: "They say your voice is a healing way, that your teaching is a healing work." And that does make sense to me and makes me more sensitive to my community work.

The humor that is ingrained in Indigenous daily interactions doesn't become off-limits during a ceremony. Having fun during certain parts of a ceremony can help ground spiritual experiences that seem ready to leave earth; it makes them more ordinary and thus more readily available to serve the community. At my first Ju/'hoan healing dance, I'm almost embarrassed at the joking and, at times, raucous laughter. What's going on here? I wonder. They don't seem serious. I carelessly judge them, invoking images of the correct religious behavior, based on my Western viewpoint, that one should be deep in thought and contemplation—or at least look that way! Now, many laughs later, I realize by how much I missed the point.

At times when a Ju/'hoan healer is displaying signs of pain and struggle, almost howling his anguish into the night sky, the women, singing healing songs around the dance fire, will shout out jokes, bringing the healer back to earth and helping to ground him into steadiness. "Hey, you," the women will cry out, laughter ringing in their voices, "do you know your business is hanging out there so we all can see?" The dance breaks into joy, as the healer regains some of his contact with the soothing earth of ordinary life and joking.

One day I am at Wanuskewin Heritage Park in Saskatoon, Saskatchewan, with my two-year-old son, who, though still wearing diapers, is now walking with that delightful confidence only those new to walking can display. The park, established on a revered gathering place that had been used by Cree people over many centuries, is now open to the public with exhibits teaching about First Nations culture and spirituality. In the entranceway greeting visitors is a large display of a buffalo and a First Nations man in a position of prayer, symbolizing the sacred connection between the buffalo and First Nations people, the buffalo being a physical and spiritual key to survival. My son walks up to the display and, still standing, looks up at it, a powerful presence to his eyes. He then crouches and—with an intense, almost physical focus, eyes straining as if searching into the beyond—he looks toward the buffalo. A man walks up to me, saying: "It's so good to see the very young ones in prayer. What a beautiful sight." "Well," I agree, "it is so important for the young to know about prayer. But . . . but I have to tell you that right now my son is taking a crap." Nothing like humor to highlight the *ordinary* out of the typical Western emphasis on the *extraordinary* nature of spirituality.

Just as humor can humanize spirituality, while still respecting it, so does the Indigenous approach to the material as a vehicle for and expression of the spiritual. The concepts of material versus spiritual, which suggest separate and even dichotomous realms or phenomenon, a conceptualization typical in mainstream psychology, are essentially non-existent within Indigenous perspectives. The material and spiritual are aspects of the same essential reality, and they infuse each other. During their healing dance, the Ju/'hoansi can pick up the n/om and hold it, drawing on it to bring healing into their laying on of hands at the dance. N/om is a concrete, deeply felt entity or substance. At one level, as they move around their days, they can clearly distinguish between sensed qualities of a log in the bush and n/om at the dance—but the level of that distinction does not have ultimate meaning in their efforts toward healing and well-being.*

Some Ju/'hoan healers leave their bodies to facilitate their healing

---

*The body, for example, is seen as a place for the spirit and vice versa: "Our body is sacred," says Andrew Skin, an Indigenous Inupiaq healer from Kotzebue, Alaska, "and we keep it clean so it can be a home for our spirit." In today's world of devastating temptations, especially to young people, he is pointingly referring to people needing to avoid drug and alcohol abuse.

work. "I slip out of my skin," says =Oma Djo. "This leaving my body is just like breathing, like your breath leaving your mouth." What could be more natural, even ordinary? Breathing. Not some dramatically foreign, even unattainable or exotic experience. Spirituality becomes a thread woven into life.* Indigenous teachings about the sacredness of Mother Earth and her gifts to all species, including humans, tell us that.

COUNTERCURRENTS WITHIN
THE MAINSTREAM

Though the picture we draw of mainstream psychology's tendency toward a reductionistic and devaluing approach to spirituality is accurate, it's not the complete picture. Though some in mainstream psychology say the spiritual is unimportant in the understanding of human behavior, others say it's important but an inappropriate subject of study. But countercurrents within the mainstream are articulating a more complete and nuanced picture of spirituality, stressing its experiential as well as its conceptual qualities, and its everyday relevance in addition to its dramatic extraordinary dimensions. These forces of resistance are thereby making the subject of spirituality a more appropriate area of study for psychology.

Seeds for these contemporary countercurrents appear in William James, one of the founding figures† of contemporary mainstream psychology. For example, William James opens many doors for the acceptable, even inevitable, study of the fluidity of consciousness and its transformations within spiritual realms—a set of doors still not

---

*Melinda García, an Indigenous psychologist and spiritual counselor, uses the image of a necklace to establish this point: "Each ceremony, like the sweat lodge, is a bead in a necklace of other ceremonies—they all are interconnected with each other. And that necklace is worn in daily life."

†I use the phrase *founding figures* to minimize a stark and unfortunate fact; as of now, mainstream psychology texts only identify founding *fathers,* with rarely a mention of the sexist bias that dominated the early history of psychology.

fully explored within the mainstream. In rich and subtle descriptions of different states of consciousness, including ordinary as well as religious and spiritual states, he shows how they are all connected, separated only by the "filmiest of screens," which can be easily crossed, often unexpectedly. Here is James's now famous quote: "Our normal waking consciousness, rational consciousness as we call it, is but one special type of consciousness, whilst all about it, parted from it by the filmiest of screens, there lie potential forms of consciousness entirely different" (James 1985).*

There are also analytically oriented theorists and therapists who resist mainstream psychology's static and dismissive stance toward spirituality.†

With his emphasis on wisdom as the challenging issue in

---

*Though James's insights about the fluidity of consciousness and its potential for spiritual transformations are generally ignored, his quote about the "filmiest of screens" has earned a place in most mainstream texts—it's typically an honorary place, not to be taken too seriously.

James's concept of the filmiest of screens separating transcendent and spiritual experiences from ordinary life is very important. Though his discussions of the more dramatic, extraordinary spiritual states, such as conversion experiences, can shift the focus away from the importance of the *subtle* shifts in everyday consciousness that can move a person beyond her or his usual sense of being self-contained and self-focused, James himself very much appreciates the *ordinary* aspect of the extraordinary.

Placing James sensitively within his particular Western historical and cultural context, the scholarly, groundbreaking studies of Eugene Taylor help illuminate the crucial contributions James makes to the study of spirituality and other enhanced states of consciousness (see e.g., Taylor 2011). Gene, who is a special friend and colleague, also writes extensively on the larger issues of mainstream psychology's problematic relationship with issues of consciousness and spiritual transformation (see e.g., Taylor 1999).

†In his effort to focus on what could be scientifically analyzed and understood, Freud focuses instead on organized religion rather than spirituality. He analyzes religious yearnings and sees them as expressions of an infantile (and unconscious) search for a father or authority figure; organized religions, with their often vaunted leaders, would satisfy this need to be told what to do and how to be.

An active stream of neo-Freudians has expanded upon and enhanced Freud's ideas about religion. For example, the early work of Rizzuto (1981) discusses how representations of God have a variety of sources, not just infantile yearnings for authority, and these representations influence how we see ourselves and relate to our worlds.

consideration of the eighth and final stage of human development, Erikson offers an appreciation for some of the gifts of understanding that come with a sense of spirituality. But it's Carl Jung who walks most boldly and extensively into spiritual realms and mysteries. Though one of Freud's earliest and closest associates, Jung seeks to distinguish himself from what he sees as Freud's limitations. For example, Jung transforms Freud's conception of the unconscious as being largely the place for unfulfilled, typically infantile desires that need to be unraveled in order to achieve well-being into the idea of the unconscious, now also filled with deep archetypal memories, as a springboard into far-reaching searches for meaning and spiritual understanding.

Drawing heavily upon his own spiritual journeys, including intense analyses of his dreams and participation in spiritually induced automatic writing, Jung becomes an explorer, creating a rich tapestry of interwoven spiritual and psychological insights.* He complements and enriches his psychological insights, including his study of personality types, such as introversion and extroversion, with a conception of full, including spiritual, human development (individuation). And Jung's journeys include ventures into arcane and esoteric areas, such as the medieval discipline of alchemy. Jung describes alchemy, presented to the public as a scientific attempt to turn the base metal of lead into the precious metal of gold, as in fact a spiritual search about how to transform ordinary (base) consciousness into spiritual (precious) consciousness.

My encounters with Jung contain a mixture of excitement and wonder. I still remember when his *Seven Sermons to the Dead* makes its appearance as a mimeo document among us Harvard graduate students; it's treated as a piece of contraband by us, since we're eager to learn, and as heresy by our professors. A big part of the attrac-

---

*One good introduction to both Jung's thought and the sources of those thoughts, including his personal journeys, is his autobiographical *Memories, Dreams, Reflections.*

tion of these seven sermons is the fact they result from Jung's unfettered spiritually infused explorations into his unconscious, as he opens the gates to these explorations and lets those journeys speak directly for themselves. Others have called this a form of automatic writing.*

Jung—as we all do—operates within a particular historical context. While his Eurocentric approach yields fascinating insights, it also can impede his full understanding of non-Western approaches. Jung has a strong focus on medieval European spirituality, which is heavily Christian. In fact, in writing about his visit to India and his meetings with local wise men and gurus, he cautions against becoming a student of their spiritual paths. We have our own way, he emphasizes, the spiritual paths in the West, and that's what we should be following. I agree that's an important part of the larger picture, but Jung's position could present an obstacle to fully understanding the wisdom of Indigenous teachings, even though we don't take on specifics of that Indigenous way as our personal practice. As well, Jung focuses on spiritual development more as a journey toward an individual's fulfillment than as a path an individual takes in order to eventually serve his or her community.

Jung makes spiritual inquiry and fulfillment important elements in an effective therapeutic approach, stressing human potential more than obstacles, growth more than pathology. But Jung, and in particular his deeply spiritual side, is still treated with skepticism by much of mainstream psychology. It's said that he's "too spiritual," meaning too speculative or mystical, even mysterious and—in what can be considered even worse from a mainstream perspective— not scientific. Some Jungians prefer to emphasize his psychological

---

*Seven Sermons to the Dead, often seen as a glimpse into his strongly esoteric magnum opus, The Red Book: Liber Novus, is now available in conventional print form as an appendix in the 1989 edition of his Memories, Dreams, Reflections. Quite a difference from our graduate student days of discovering not only a treasure but also, most importantly, a hidden treasure!

concepts as opposed to his spiritual understandings in their desire to have the Jungian approach be seen as more acceptable by the psychology establishment.* Yet Jung's foundational principle, that much of what makes us uniquely human is spiritual understanding, remains.

Another extremely fertile countercurrent, feeding the appreciation and cultivation of the spiritual within mainstream psychology, comes from within the discipline of humanistic psychology and its offshoot, transpersonal psychology.† Building on the groundwork of psychologists like Abe Maslow and Carl Rogers, the contemporary humanistic approach studies variables like a person's motivation for altruism and self-actualization as part of the natural human condition, and seeks to encourage positive and nourishing social environments that support such self-actualization but that are too often compromised by human-made obstacles. It also introduces an emphasis on spirituality as an essential and *inborn* quality of human nature. That emphasis is further cultivated and deepened by transpersonal psychology, a discipline that seeks to go beyond perceived limits in the strictly humanistic perspective. Transpersonal psychology focuses more specifically on the form and nature of spiritual experiences, including specialized practices of meditation, often avoided in mainstream psychology as too mystical, and distance healing and out-of-body spirit travel, phe-

---

*Jungians often emphasize his work on psychological functions (thinking, feeling, sensing and intuiting), as well as his discussion of the attitudes of extroversion and introversion, stressing their more scientific nature, in an effort to bring Jungian ideas more firmly into the mainstream. For example, the Myers-Briggs scale, based on Jung's theory about psychological types, is put forth as an example of a useful and testable assessment instrument.

†Humanistic psychology is now one of the official divisions of the American Psychological Association (APA), and transpersonal psychology is now a regular focus of papers presented at the APA. But I'm still considering the contributions of these two disciplines as examples of resistance within mainstream psychology because generally the mainstream establishment sees them as unscientific or at least soft science—instead of the preferred hard science of the experimental model—and bordering too close to philosophical perspectives on human nature.

nomena dismissively labeled in the mainstream as examples of illusions or even quackery.*

The climate of acceptance is rapidly changing in the area of popular psychology; now it's hard to avoid some mention of spirituality in venues such as the iconic psychology mass media magazine *Psychology Today*.† But these popular conceptions of spirituality tend to be superficial, appealing more to whatever is catchy or in vogue rather than offering a path that demands commitment and struggle—even if it is to learn how not to struggle.

There are, however, some very solid, creative, and promising expressions of this humanistic orientation toward the value of the spiritual. Consider, for example, recent shifts within such fields as the psychology of religion and pastoral counseling, historical staples of mainstream psychology. Where those fields used to focus on variables like church attendance as a way to tabulate spirituality, attendance being easy to measure, or on bringing Christian principles into one's clinical practice, that set of guiding principles being familiar to the vast majority of practicing counselors, research is now emerging that focuses on topics of spiritual transformation. Spiritual transformation goes into uncharted realms of experience, beyond any specific religious framework into a more generic consideration of consciousness, beyond a more static delineation of spiritual states into an exploration of the dynamic and ongoing

---

*There is an outstanding history of scientifically sound and insightful researchers in these transpersonal states, psychologists who generally move from a more specific focus on phenomena such as hypnosis to a more general study of consciousness transformations into spiritual development. There is, for example, the groundbreaking work of Stan Krippner, with his early studies of hypnosis, and Charlie Tart, with his early work in distance healing and out-of-body experiences. Both Stan and Charlie are persons of integrity who bring a creative energy to their ongoing paradigmatic work on spirituality.

†There are, for example, a series of blogs sponsored by *Psychology Today* that include titles like: "Finding Spiritual Treasure in Our Everyday Emotions," "4 Powerful Ways Spirituality Can Ease Anxiety and Depression," and "Are Out-of-Body Experiences Always Spiritual?" Even after reading the material in these blogs, I can't really say what any or all of them mean by spirituality, but I do know their definitions lack the depth found in Indigenous approaches.

effects of spirituality in daily life. The work of Joan Koss-Chioino is central to developing an understanding of this spiritual transformation. She defines spiritual transformation as a "special type of personal transformation in which a deep sense of spirituality is incorporated into an individual's consciousness and cosmic perspective." Seeing this transformation as a change in the "ultimate concerns, values, meaning-making that can reshape life directions,"* Joan explores issues such as spiritual influences on cultural and social transitions and the relationship between spirituality and health.†

Growing out of a humanistic perspective on psychology, and more directly the field of positive psychology, Lisa Miller, a professor of clinical psychology at Columbia University, presents a pervasive and accessible concept of spirituality. "We are born whole, wholly present and holy," she says, ". . . and by being here and now and present, we are present to the universe which is made of love . . . and that is a two-way relationship of love" (Miller 2013). No holding back here!

Lisa directly and unambiguously brings attention to this spiritual dimension, insisting that it is not something "far away" or "beyond" but rather close at hand. By stressing spirituality as an inviting and animating characteristic of our universe, available to all, Miller escapes from the elitist connotations of Maslow's concept of peak experience, an experience of the most intense spirituality that by its very nature is typically separate from ordinary life, and available only to a few.‡ And she remains inclusive and flowing in her descriptions of the spiritual, seeking to be true to the expanding, effusive quality of the experience,

---

*Joan draws upon the research of Paloutzian (e.g., Paloutzian and Park 2005) for these formulations.

†A good introduction to Joan's research can be found in Koss-Chioino and Hefner (2006).

‡Abe wrestles with this elitist connotation, especially as he is firmly committed to concepts of social justice and equity. His concept of the plateau experience, which describes how the dramatic intensity of the peak experience is sustained at a more manageable and enduring level within the ordinary rhythms of daily life, is one effort to open spirituality to a more common existence.

resisting the comfort of words and concepts that are more bounded and verbally manageable—and therefore more acceptable to mainstream psychology.

Miller understands the radical nature of her position, as she asks: "How do we sell this to science, this idea of our inherent spiritual nature, this need for a dialogue with a living, loving universe?" And I might add, "sell" these ideas to a highly respected and fundamentally conservative Ivy League university! Lisa anchors the concept of spirituality into effective clinical practice, stating that spiritual experiences are key to mental health and communal well-being, and into issues of social justice, attempting to infuse her work with at-risk youth with a spiritual perspective.*

There are several long-standing and respected institutions of higher education that focus on spirituality and its contributions to therapy, human development, and social change.† But these institutions are freestanding, and thus their focus on these spiritually infused issues is more easily maintained, even though the economics of their survival remain

---

*Miller is better able to substantiate these practical applications of spirituality through her extensive research program, as well as her institutional positions as director of the clinical psychology program at Columbia University and as head of that university's Spirituality and Mind-Body Institute. She has also cofounded and now coedits a journal called *Spirituality in Clinical Practice;* this is an official journal of the American Psychological Association, the premier professional organization of Western psychologists. Thus the journal carries a mainstream-type stamp of approval. One of its recent issues contains an article entitled "Sacred Moments in Therapy."

†Two such freestanding institutions are Saybrook University and Sofia University (formerly the Institute for Transpersonal Psychology). Stan Krippner at Saybrook and Jim Fadiman and Bob Frager at Sofia are exemplars of how psychologists can create a respectful, committed, and deeply thoughtful approach to the domains of spiritually infused theory and practice.

But these spiritually oriented academic programs, including Sofia and Saybrook, still exhibit a disconnect with the on-the-street problems facing those unjustly marginalized from society's rewards. The programs remain more within the context of privilege than beyond it. But this is also more generically a critique of the mainstream Western culture they exist within and struggle against; both institutions are committed to finding ways to break out of those constraints to work more with the marginalized.

problematic. Yet Miller exists *squarely within* the mainstream, and that context creates an essential component of her significance—and its exciting promise.

In addition to its acceptance of a wider variety of culturally validated spiritual teachings, transpersonal psychology's blossoming can also be attributed to its dedicated series of neuropsychological studies.* These studies, carefully delineating variables for research in controlled settings, describe, explain, and substantiate various states of consciousness, including many with obvious spiritual dimensions. In these neuropsychological studies, it's almost like the best of both worlds—a respectful presentation of spirituality through a (conventionally) respected methodology; namely, the experimental paradigm, which is the gold standard of mainstream psychological research. Now that's a powerful combination, silencing even some of the harshest critics passionate about making psychology into a science—even though the transpersonal researchers don't employ a rigid model of the experimental design, yet they clearly show that very important data about the neurophysiology of spirituality still needs to be collected in more naturalistic settings and with more narrative methods.

The groundbreaking work of Elmer and Alyce Green is an important thread in this ongoing research on neurophysiology and spiritual transformations. Initially focusing on research and clinical applications of biofeedback, leading to the voluntary control of internal physiological processes that are normally involuntary, the Greens open doors to the study of consciousness and spiritual development. For example, they train people—ordinary people—to lower the body temperature in their hands through directing their attention to the hand and thinking about lowering the temperature there. These processes of "thinking about" and "directing attention" are in fact processes of meditation and directing spiritual energy, but the Greens, true to their ordinary specialness,

---

*This work in neuropsychological investigations into spirituality is a small part of the larger explosion of neuropsychological theory and research within mainstream psychology.

don't bring in extra language baggage whenever possible. How did they know body temperature was being lowered? They measured it, with body thermometers. As Alice tells me, "We're just showing the reality of mind over matter." She makes what can be called an extraordinary change into an ordinary, trainable event.*

In 1969, under the auspices of the Menninger Foundation in Topeka, Kansas, the Greens lead a series of wonderfully accepting and invigorating conferences (the Council Grove Conferences) where scholars, researchers, and practitioners exchange ideas and create mutual support networks. Deep in the Kansas prairie, we meet and learn. I feel grateful to be a participant in the opening conferences. We simply spend time together, sharing ideas with informal talks or presentations, reinforcing and enriching each other's understandings. Too bad there aren't more of these types of real exchange.

When Harvard Medical School professor Herb Benson begins to study the effects of meditation† on physiological states in the 1960s, he enlists the help of Joan Borysenko, a highly skilled psychoneuroimmunologist. Benson's research topic is very controversial at the time, especially in such a conservative setting as Harvard Medical School—"what kind of nonsense is that," I hear more than once as a description of the Benson project. Herb is smart enough to hire Joan as an associate, and she provides the theoretical insights and technical experimental research strategies to help give the Benson project a scientific foundation and thus ensure its continued life. The project demonstrates how meditation can have beneficial physiological, neurological, and psychological effects, such as lowering blood pressure and mitigating unhealthy

---

*One of the Greens' earliest reports of their research, *Beyond Biofeedback,* is published in 1977.

†Benson basically studies the effects of Transcendental Meditation, an approach then becoming very popular but criticized by some within other meditation traditions as being too simplistic and superficial. Who knows? Jealousy among meditative traditions does exist and sometimes spills over into such criticisms. Also there is often a gap between the way a tradition is originally taught and the way it is eventually practiced by its followers.

reactions to stress. Most important, it energizes the establishment of the field of mind-body research and practice, while introducing meditation as a therapeutic intervention to a wide audience—though the quality of that meditative practice is questioned by some.*

But Joan expresses her frustration with the limited focus of the Benson project. "How do these effects of meditation shape our lives, deepen our understanding?" she asks one day in her research lab. Joan and I have talked about this kind of question for a while now, so she's not really raising a question as much as setting guideposts toward her new directions. Moving out of Benson's lab, Joan further explores the spiritual contributions of these meditative states, now working in the general area of spiritually based health and well-being, while still respecting her roots in neuropsychological research. Stressing the importance of people developing the energy for their own spiritual journey, she offers guidance in a variety of areas, such as therapeutic meditation, resilience in the face of stress, coping with burnout and fatigue, and the preparation of foods that can promote healing and well-being. Joan is a wellspring of energy, feeding paths of discovery, healing, and spiritual development for many through her books, tapes, and workshops.†

Two other colleagues, Jon Kabat-Zinn and Richie Davidson, are carrying out extensive and innovative research programs on meditation,

---

*Herb's application of meditation to a range of psychological and physiological ailments, introduced in his early book *The Relaxation Response* (Benson 2000), breaks new ground in the field of mind-body medicine, helping establish and give respectability to the field. His approach is especially influential because it attempts to demystify meditation, presenting meditative practice in a simplified, easy-to-apply format, avoiding potentially off-putting technical or esoteric characteristics of the meditative practice in order to make it more attractive to those unfamiliar with meditation. But since he is offering an adaptation of Transcendental Meditation, itself already criticized for being too simplistic, Benson's further simplification is problematic—though it does provide a door for many to enter the world of meditation, and that, in and of itself, can be very important.

†Joan Borysenko's classic, breakthrough book is *Minding the Body, Mending the Mind,* now in a newly revised 2007 edition. She continues producing material in the form of books and tapes and remains active in offering workshops—consult her website for details, www.joanborysenko.com.

consciousness transformations, and well-being. Both focus on what is called insight meditation, often also referred to as mindfulness meditation.* And while both employ impeccable research methodologies—meeting the mainstream standards of being scientific—both are themselves also committed meditation practitioners who work within the general spiritual framework of Buddhist living and practice. They each affirm the rich contribution personal experience can make to a more nuanced and insightful psychological understanding rather than confirming the feared contamination of research data and subsequent compromising of understanding that remains a standard caution in the mainstream.

Kabat-Zinn establishes a program at the University of Massachusetts Medical School using meditative techniques as a key component in the management of pain.† He works with ordinary people who are typically not meditators, nor even necessarily interested in spirituality, but who suffer debilitating pain. Jon goes on to document the life-changing effects of meditative practice, showing how this practice can not only help in pain management but also can enhance positive, affirming attitudes such as compassion and a general sense of well-being. One element of his approach is to teach patients how mindfulness can help them to "uncouple" the way pain actually feels, the sensory dimension

---

*The phenomenon of Buddhist-based meditation covers a wide range of specific theories and practices, and unique characteristics of differing versions are important to acknowledge and respect. But for the purposes of the discussion of Buddhist-based meditation in *Indigenous Healing Psychology*, I'll follow the lead of Jon and Richie and refer to that range of approaches by the common terms of *insight* or *mindfulness meditation*—insisting this is no sign of disrespect for the nuanced and sacred differences the terms are masking. Also, this decision about terminology also overlooks the fact that the term *mindfulness meditation* can sometimes refer to a simpler, even less spiritually infused form of practice that is almost like an enhancing of attention.

†This program, called the MBSR program (Mindfulness-Based Stress Reduction), catalyzes an energetic and energizing series of mind-body and alternative medicine interventions and discoveries that have helped shape and continually expand the fields of mind-body research and alternative medicine practice. Jon's early research, animating that MBSR program, is described in his classic book *Full Catastrophic Living* (Kabat-Zinn 2013).

of pain, from the feeling of alarm and fear about the pain, the emotional and evaluative dimension of pain. Through this uncoupling, the *experience* of suffering can be lessened. Jon's approach is widely accepted and employed in a variety of settings such as schools and health care facilities with encouraging results.

Highlighting the concept of neuroplasticity, or the ability of the brain to change as a result of specific training processes, Richie Davidson researches how experiences with transforming consciousness, such as meditative practices, affect brain structure and chemistry, increasing the potential for positive qualities to emerge in attitudes and life experience (see e.g., Davidson 2004; and Davidson and Begley 2012). He emphasizes the concept of the "plasticity of synaptic connections." Richie's work is especially attractive to psychology, grounded as it is in the hard data of neurological measurements. Richie works with both experienced meditators, including monks from Tibet, and ordinary people, many not especially connected to a spiritual dimension in their lives, measuring brain activity in both. He finds that brain activity during meditation is clearly different between the two groups: the trained meditators show increased activity in those areas of the brain that are associated with happy and calm states. As Richie puts it: "Our brains are adaptable, the 'hard-wiring' is actually not always fixed . . . who we are today is not necessarily who we will be tomorrow . . . as our emotions ebb and flow so does our brain chemistry ebb and flow."* Practices like meditation, he claims, can promote beneficial changes in the brain, changes that help to cultivate changes in our life balance and well-being.†

---

*All quotes are from Davidson (2015).

†Richie Davidson (2015) goes to another dimension in his discussion of potential effects of meditation. Going beyond documenting changes in a person's brain structure as a result of meditation, he focuses on possible changes in the very genetic structure of humans—pointing toward the eventual "regulation of the human genome." This is how he puts it: "There is every reason to believe that contemplative practice will alter epigenetic information and epigenetic regulation and by doing so it will change our gene expression."

But there's still at times an undue stress on the biomedical aspect of this research on neuropsychological aspects of meditation. For example, there is often more of an effort to show that expanded states of consciousness, such as meditation, are "real" by demonstrating their effects in a laboratory setting. Measurements of differences between the brain activity of meditators and nonmeditators becomes the prime data, *supplemented* by interviews about their mental states. A less common research strategy, exemplified by Davidson's work, is to employ careful studies of meditators' personal experiences and the quality of their daily lives—for example, their degree of balance and calm—as primary data in collaboration with the neurophysiological data; what can result then is a *science of* meditation, rather than a *scientific proof* that something called "meditation" exists.

With this rapid increase of psychological work focused on a fuller experience of spirituality, there are inevitable challenges to avoid the dilution of practice and the trivialization of effects.* For example, the field of positive psychology, which now carries forth an active program of clinical work and research within or relevant to the more general framework of humanistic psychology, has been critiqued as being too much an exercise in Pollyanna thinking—always looking on the bright side of things, viewing the world through rose-colored glasses—a criticism very familiar to humanistic psychology in general. If there is an unrealistically positive spin placed on human nature

---

*In what seems an almost inevitable process within Western culture, when an idea or practice is seen as successful, it's easily drawn into a popular cultural vortex. For example, Joan Borysenko, Jon Kabat-Zinn, and Richie Davidson move into a more popular dissemination of their ideas. For example, even a casual exploration of YouTube can provide ample material from these three.

But I know all three pretty well, and they are all actively and honestly facing those challenges of dilution and trivialization, seeking to maintain paths of integrity—in spite of the many commercial lures for their practices. What more can you ask of anyone? Others doing similar work are less dedicated to seeking truths and more willing to turn spiritual understanding into a commodity—an outcome not restricted to Western psychology, as we see with the occasional existence of commercially hungry plastic medicine men within Indigenous traditions.

and functioning, the depths of the human experience, including the struggles and obstacles, the losses and tragedies—which are precious opportunities for learning—are not intrinsically appreciated but seen only as superficial stepping-stones to some desired state like happiness or contentment. "We can't just live for the good times," cautions Ratu Civo, "but we have to live for life."

The popularity of this new focus on meditation and spirituality also brings a dilution of purpose and practice. The explosion of books and workshops on spiritual development—promoting a "proven" technique, promising "real" results—carries with it the inevitable instances of false materials in alluring packages. It will require mature and common-sense judgments and intuitions—and a good bit of realistic research—to separate the charlatans from the real deal.*

Another example where dilution, even trivialization, can occur is in the too superficial, widespread utilization of mindfulness training programs in diverse settings, including schools, businesses, and governmental agencies. These mindfulness programs often offer what is in practice training in *attention,* an increase in the powers and flexibility of ordinary mental processes rather than a release of spiritual insights and functioning. Now attention is not unrelated to classical meditation techniques and can be an effective entrée into meditation, but while remaining on the purely cognitive level, it misses key ingredients of a spiritual and therefore deeply enhancing practice. But for programs in insight meditation to become widely palatable and therefore acceptable, any strong connection made between those meditation techniques and their source in Buddhist spiritual teachings could potentially be perceived as a threat—a religion other than the accepted baseline Christianity being offered to "our innocent school kids." Also, local school boards will actually be interested

---

*Criteria that have aided me in my ongoing challenge of finding authentic or simply honest and knowledgeable elders (see chapter 2) can be helpful in determining what is the "real deal"—or better, what is *attempting to be* the real deal.

in a program that focuses on increasing attention, given the recent epidemic-type increase in attention deficit hyperactivity disorder syndrome (ADHDS) diagnoses. And being more attentive, especially to one's inner states and feelings, can itself be very helpful in cultivating some sense of calm, balance, and sensitivity, all of which can encourage more healthy living.*

Clearly, spirituality is of foundational importance to the Indigenous approaches of our first psychologists. Just as clearly, spirituality's position in Western psychology is unclear. Largely misunderstood, ignored, and dismissed within mainstream approaches, spirituality is gaining a foothold among countercurrents within that mainstream—but even there, confusion and misdirection still prevail.

These countercurrents generally still exist within the context of Western, primarily white privilege so that their spiritually infused processes and projects retain some of the historically common but flawed dynamics of spirituality as a path of self-centered discovery. Seeking understanding and insight through spiritual practice devolves into seeking increased individual understanding and insight for purposes of *personal* and *individual* self-development. I often hear from Western-trained psychologists about the "great journey" they undertake in a spiritual ceremony—or as one colleague puts it, "It was amazing! My eyes were opened to who *I really am* . . . and the many lives I've already lived." But no mention of how that insight into self generated better ways to serve others. Granted, understanding of self

---

*Attempting to deal with this pervasive dilution, even trivialization of the powerful spiritual teachings of mindfulness, Danny Goleman and Richie Davidson (2017), both accomplished psychologists and seasoned practitioners of mindfulness meditation, offer an alternative: a return to and focus on the core of mindfulness, both as it is practiced in its original historical form and as it is further revealed through current systemic neuro-psychological research. They offer ways in which mindfulness can regain its significance as a spiritual path, emphasizing committed practice and substantive results in ways we can live with more compassion and balance. It's like a return to the source to create a more honest and living present.

can serve as the necessary foundation for service to others. Indigenous elders are continually emphasizing the importance of knowing oneself before one can effectively help others. But from an Indigenous perspective, that process of knowing oneself is always undertaken with the aim of serving others. "When these people come to our ceremonies trying to 'find themselves' and focus only on the drama of the spirits that have come to *them,* as if it's a personal accomplishment, I worry," says elder Danny Musqua. "I worry because they seem to be missing the point. We seek spiritual guidance so we can better serve others and our communities."

The sweat lodge of Indigenous elders Walter and Maria Linklater provides a good example of the Indigenous emphasis on spiritual journeying as a path to serving others. Now living in Saskatoon, Walter is an Ojibwe-Anishnabe elder originally from Couchiching First Nation in Ontario, while Maria is a Cree elder originally from Thunderchild First Nation in Saskatchewan. Their connections with their birth communities remain strong and enlivening, but Saskatoon has become their new and most immediately felt community. They are functioning primarily as urban elders, serving the needs of Saskatoon, including offering ceremonies and counseling to city institutions like the Saskatoon Police Service and at Indigenous gatherings in the city at places like the local White Buffalo Lodge. Walter and Maria are dedicated people, serving others with honesty and commitment,* and that's so important given the large number of Indigenous people that have moved from their reserve communities into cities like Saskatoon.

The Linklater Family Community Sweat Lodge is a family-oriented lodge; most frequently, it's attended mostly by extended family and friends. The lodge is filled with young people, including kids, with their bursting and enlivening energy, as well as adults, almost all Indigenous

---

*I tremendously value their commitment to serving others; on several occasions, they are there for me and my family in times of personal suffering and tragedy.

people. They come from all walks of life, including those with ongoing addiction issues or difficulties with the law; for example, local detox institutions regularly support their clients' wishes to attend the sweat. Also, on occasion the Linklater sweat is focused on a particular community group, such as the Saskatoon Police Force, as they seek a better understanding of Indigenous culture, the better to work with Indigenous people.

Following fundamental Indigenous teachings about the sweat lodge, the Linklater sweat is a space of prayer and healing open to all who approach it with respect.* It's a beautiful sweat experience because we're all in the lodge together, trying to support one another's prayers and recovery with our own prayers. "We pray for healing . . . so we can better help others," Walter reminds us. "And we pray for the well-being of others." Everyone matters in the sweat; and that "everyone" means all of our relatives, friends, and communities, including those who are not physically with us in the sweat, as well as those now in the spirit world. Prayers are always offered for those sick in the hospitals or recently departed.

There is no focus on how "spiritual" our experience in the sweat is or what new visions we've had, unless they lead to some way of serving others through our own new understandings, and no talk about an individual level of spirituality attained or comparisons between different individuals' spirituality. All that kind of focus seems the province, and at times the preoccupation, of mainstream approaches, with their individualistic orientation. Instead the emphasis is on experiences in the sweat being for the service to others. The Linklater lodge

---

*Whenever I go to a sweat lodge run by Indigenous elders, I'm reminded of this connection to the whole of life, this openness to all. The sweats are typically very simple, none of the fancy structures that characterize lodges run by some non-Indigenous people who charge a fee. It's not just a class difference, though you do need money to maintain these fancier lodges. It's more importantly a difference of principle; in the Indigenous approach, ceremonies are meant to be simple, and by sitting squarely and simply on the ground, one can be more directly connected to Mother Earth.

is a real family experience because within and outside that sweat all are loved.

But compared to Indigenous approaches to spirituality, when these countercurrents within the mainstream seek to unleash the healing powers of spirituality, the experience of spirituality still remains relatively outside the rhythms of daily life—more add-ons to improve the quality of life rather than becoming facts of life. And so it's appropriate, even compelling, to ask, Where can we go from here? What can be some of the contributions of spirituality to psychology?

FUTURE COLLABORATIONS

One precondition for the application of Indigenous teachings to enhance mainstream psychology is the realization that much of what is already valued in mainstream psychology need not be sacrificed as much as refined and made more sensitive. We're talking about *collaboration* between mainstream and Indigenous approaches to psychology, the dimensions of which we discuss in more detail in the final chapter. All the emphases and themes in Indigenous teachings are not meant for Western psychology; some belong rightfully within their Indigenous context. But now those Indigenous themes can be respected by Western approaches. The Indigenous and mainstream approaches each have things of value to contribute, and through respectful collaboration, and the release of synergy, a whole of psychology that is greater than the sum of the parts can result.

Driven by forces of resistance and promise within, mainstream psychology has already opened doors to spirituality. Though still in a distinct minority, and speaking from positions of marginality, there are voices calling for spirituality to be a proper, even necessary, focus of psychology, to bring spirituality in as a center and centering concern. In this effort, Indigenous approaches can help, suggesting ways to consider the nature and function of spirituality so it can live more effectively within mainstream psychology's domain.

Indigenous psychology's acceptance of spirituality as an accessible enlivening force in everyday life helps bring spirituality more squarely into mainstream psychology's realm. With an emphasis on spirituality as a "going beyond *within* ordinary life situations," it becomes less strange or frightening and more familiar and acceptable. Since we are emphasizing the collaboration between Western and Indigenous approaches, perhaps some of the more intense spirit journeys and intimate connections with spirits throughout the universe, both central to Indigenous approaches, can remain more properly connected to their particular Indigenous paths. In addition, the Indigenous commitment to the experience of spirituality, in its many and varied forms, rather than only analytic categorizations of experience, so prized in mainstream approaches, can be helpful. A more experiential emphasis can bring spirituality closer to home, to something all can connect and work with.

The Indigenous teachings about spirituality can also help move mainstream psychology beyond its individualistic, ego-focused perspectives. For example, the teaching that these spiritual experiences need to be intimately connected to a therapeutic outcome in the community can help move Western psychology away from its focus on spiritual journeys as defining and fulfilling an individual's development. The aim can be to support journeys that seek to bring the individual more clearly to a commitment to serve and help develop the community, wherein individual and communal fulfillment become part of the same process. How can an individual claim individual credit for or ownership of spiritually influenced phenomena if by definition those phenomena pervade our universe?

Spirituality will keep reappearing as central to the Indigenous approach to the various psychological topics discussed in the next chapters in *Indigenous Healing Psychology,* such as research, human development, therapy and healing, and social context. I think legitimate questions might be: Is this book just about spirituality? Does the proposed enhancement of mainstream Western psychology translate into turning it into a spiritual discipline? I know these are legitimate questions for me, and up to the very end of my writing, they remain relevant for me. But *Indigenous Healing Psychology* can't be reduced to a treatise on spirituality. And it's not a question of just looking to the spiritual and thinking that solves everything. Ratu Civo will have none of such wishful, erroneous thinking. "The straight path," he confirms, "is the path of spiritual understanding and growth. But . . . the path doesn't just come to you because you want it. You must find the path—and find it by walking it. And that's hard! There's struggle and disappointment. We have to work to connect with the spiritual—even though it's there all the time."

Indigenous Healing Psychology, as it draws upon Indigenous teachings, offers a series of spiritually infused ways of doing, being, and becoming. With contact based on mutual respect, these ways can help to reshape psychology toward a more healing path. But individual effort and commitment and supportive sociopolitical institutions are necessary mutually enhancing ingredients in this healing process.

As the mainstream and Indigenous approaches each maintain and nurture their specific and at times unique contributions, a greater understanding can occur—in this case the deep openings for the spiritual that exist within us. By becoming more accepting of the spiritual as a realm of study, mainstream psychology can both better appreciate the fullness of human nature and potential and get closer to its own roots as the study of psyche, or soul, within which the spiritual lives.

And whatever the collaborations that emerge, mystery remains a key ingredient in spirituality—a key especially hard for a materialistic, positivistic mainstream approach to accept, if not understand. Can mainstream Western psychology understand that this spiritual core of being, the spiritual dimension throughout the universe, grows from and is entrusted in mystery? Can Western psychology remain open to the Indigenous teaching that this mystery is an expression of what they call the Great Mystery? Open because the Indigenous perspective insists that the Great Mystery, though great or ultimate, is neither forced on nor diminishes anyone; it merely *is.* "We respect each person's journey toward knowing the Creator," Danny Musqua offers, "and each journey is different . . . though we all end up in the same place." Realistically, by collaborating respectfully with Indigenous approaches to psychology, mainstream psychology can acknowledge the reality of the spiritual without taking on the full responsibility for studying it and respect what it considers an unknown without belittling or denying it. Respecting the honored place for mystery, we can respect the ambiguities, complexities, and the unexplained as an integral part of development, a hallmark of being.

I think now is the time to get practical. Here we've been talking quite a bit about spirituality. A mainstream psychologist might ask: "That all sounds good, but how do you *know* these things about spirituality? How do you *really* know these things as *facts?*"

Can I answer such a question—which is really a difficult *challenge?* Because that mainstream psychologist is really asking us a question about the nature of reality and how we know that reality. For mainstream psychology those matters of knowing are the domain of research, and mainstream psychology has a clear concept and structure of research. Research within mainstream psychology can become more concerned with designing a good experiment than with a process of knowing.

But there is more than one way to do science and be scientific. From an Indigenous perspective, there is also a clear concept and structure of research, and it too is scientific. At its core is the valuation of experience, especially personal experience. Indigenous research is careful and systematic, featuring sensitive observations in natural settings. How do we know the spiritual exists? From an Indigenous perspective, we know because we experience it and because those experiences are based on careful observation and reflection, highly valued aspects of knowing.

As we consider research in the next chapter, we can see that research is best understood *as a process of knowing.* How can such Indigenous approaches to research enhance mainstream approaches, deepening their connections to knowledge and understanding?

CHAPTER FOUR

"The Purpose of Life Is to Learn"

Research as a Respectful Way of Experiencing and Knowing

We're talking with Komera about her healing work. She's a middle-aged Fijian woman widely known throughout the urban area of Suva as a powerful practitioner. Much of her power is said to come from her states of possession, where the snake god, one of the most dominant forces in Fijian spiritual life, takes over her person and brings insight and treatments into her healing work. I'm with Ifereimi Naivota, my Fijian friend and research guide, a man well versed in both traditional Fijian healing and Western medicine. Our conversation with Komera is proceeding well, and we're learning a lot about her work.

But now, as we ask about what kinds of illnesses she treats, something unexpected and frightening is happening. Komera's posture slumps, her face becomes contorted, a threatening smile emerges, and her voice slows to a slurred and rasping drawl, words grunting out in between long spaces of silence. The snake god has come into Komera and taken over her end of the conversation.

I turn to Naivota and whisper: "What's going on?" He at first only looks at me, deeply perplexed and clearly nervous. Then he whispers back: "I don't know. Never seen this before." "Well, what should we do?" I almost plead, not covering over my feelings of confusion and fear. "I don't know," he repeats. "It's up to you now." Up to me?! I think. This friend of mine is some friend, I reflect. He's leaving me to figure this thing out on my own.

And that's what I do. Accepting and thus lightening my fear and pushing through my confusion, I decide to be in the moment. I deny the safety my Western mind can provide that says possession states can be mimicked or can be theatrical performances and instead continue the conversation with Komera. But now I realize I could *actually* be talking with the snake god! Knowing that would be such a rare privilege, I feel honored and, without hesitation and out of respect, engage in the moment of that potential exchange.

It's not a conversation that unfolds but a set of teachings, delivered by the snake god in short, sometimes harsh authoritative bursts. And I believe in my heart it *is* the snake god talking—feeling anything less on my part would be dishonoring the possible in a grasp for a familiar reality. The snake god—and I now feel its presence, which I almost settle into—talks about Fijian healing in many ways freshly new to me. For example, I'm told that fear can be a respectful beginning to connecting with the god, as it can lay the groundwork for transformation into a deeply felt respect. No questions from me, not even thinking about what I would like to ask. How do you ask a god something when it's clear the stream of teachings is rushing forward without a break?

The snake god ends the conversation abruptly: "We're done now. You can go." Komera as we knew her before the possession slowly returns—her body unwinds from its twisted state, and her voice regains its human modulations and rhythms. We talk some more, but the appearance of the snake god is not mentioned—Komera considers what was said by the god as being off-limits, and she herself cannot remember anything of what happened during the possession.

We thank Komera for talking with us and take our leave. "Well now, what do you think?" I ask Naivota. "I'm still not sure . . .

never seen that before," he says. "I guess it's up to you to decide."

I remember the words of my teacher Ratu Civo, the respected Fijian healer who has taken me on as his apprentice: "All that I teach you has to be tested by your own experience. If you really want to know something, you have to know it in your everyday life. You have to experience it. You have to understand it from the inside out." Clearly, by being in the moment of Komera's possession, by accepting the reality of that possession, I experience new dimensions of reality and as a result new and important insights about Fijian spirituality and healing.

Yes, I could have analyzed more what was happening, could have stood back—at least in part of my mind—to protect myself from the unknown and from experiencing my vulnerability,* the very vulnerability that Ratu Civo has told me is at the core of remaining alive and thereby open to potentials for understanding and growth. "You stand ready for anything," he advises, "because anything might happen . . . actually *will* happen." What opportunities for learning, for knowing would've been lost if I had closed up against the unfamiliar, resisted being in that snake god reality, even when it's threatening? Embarrassment? Criticism for being naïve, even gullible? A small cost for the potential return of knowledge.

Personal experience, matured through careful and honest self-reflection, nurtured through the fires of vulnerability, is my guide into research; it becomes a vessel for learning and my companion in attempts at understanding. As well, research becomes a journey into and through an ethical, even sacred space and time, characterized by a respectful exchange. Rather than being an exercise in methodological strategies, research becomes a journey into how we figure things out, how we make judgments, how we decide what matters—an expression of our purpose in life, which is to learn. And one ingredient of that journey can, and often does, include mainstream Western research findings.

---

*Another discussion of vulnerability, so crucial to Indigenous teachings about the core and dynamics of psychology, appears in chapter 6, which focuses on issues of therapy and healing.

MAINSTREAM APPROACHES

This Indigenous idea of research as a process of knowing, featuring the ultimate value of personal experience, focuses on *understanding* and the *making of meaning*. It offers a sharp contrast to the prevailing concept of research in mainstream Western psychology, which focuses more on *prediction* and *control* and the development of research *methods* to ensure clear-cut experiments.

The mainstream Western model of research considers the laboratory experiment, with its emphasis on objectivity, control of variables, replication, and causal connections, as its classic, even guiding paradigm. This laboratory experimental approach represents a set of *aspirational principles* rather than a description of *actual practice*. So I offer this description of the laboratory method as a way to characterize a set of ideals, not intending to caricature that mainstream approach. Also, by focusing on this idealized form of mainstream research, a sharper comparison can be made with Indigenous approaches.

Before even beginning to describe this laboratory-inspired model of research, it's important to consider a set of power words this model uses to describe itself and establish its authenticity and authority and in the process dismiss other forms of research as lacking, even useless. The Western approach continually characterizes itself with words like *valid, empirical,* and *objective,* all of which culminate in the self-descriptor of scientific. The Western approach likes to claim sole ownership of these power words as self-descriptors, basically kidnapping authenticity and authority from other ways of doing research. Indigenous approaches then are labeled as invalid or subjective and as a result unscientific.

Knowledge generated within worldviews other than the Western perspective is seen as inferior, not even considered as knowledge. Because mainstream psychology, working out of a colonizing mentality, does not even see Indigenous research approaches as generating knowledge, those power words are used, almost casually, as descriptions of *fact* rather than as opinions emerging from the mainstream's *point of view.*

By contrast, the Indigenous idea of research as a way of knowing broadens the concept of science to include diversity in ways of doing science. When used in this context, these power words become inclusive rather than exclusive, and their meanings richer and more nuanced. For example, if valid means something that is actually what it says it is, then observations and teachings within the Indigenous tradition bear that mark of truth.* And though a personal story is generally considered subjective, if it is honest and truthful, doesn't its truthfulness establish its objectivity, if by objective we mean something that is true or unbiased? Seeing research as describing *differing ways of knowing* can offer *paths* toward validity and the search for truths that can benefit mainstream Western approaches and the enterprise of research in general. To put it another way, there are different ways of doing scientific research.

How might we characterize this Western approach to research? We discuss a classic example of that approach, a research study on cell phone use and driving, much quoted in standard psychology texts and, for our purposes, simplified into its basic components.

As people continue to use their cell phones while driving, and assuming there is suggestive evidence that cell phone use may compromise automotive safety, some Western researchers want to study whether that use does *in fact* affect safety. But first they want to be clear about what they are actually studying. They need a hypothesis, a statement about the possible connections between cell phone use and automobile safety, and then they need to set up an experiment that will control the variables or phenomena under examination so they can gather data just on those variables, in order to prove or disprove that hypothesis.

---

*In its strict, formal sense, as espoused within mainstream psychology, the concepts of valid or validity refer to characteristics of tests and measurements. Validity becomes the ability of a test to measure what it says it is measuring so that, for example, an intelligence test actually is measuring intelligence. This more limited and discipline-based definition of validity—and other power words—is less useful because it keeps the meaning of the word within one discipline, as if it were "owned" by that discipline alone.

To simplify matters, and zero in on what might be some causal relationships between cell phone communication and automobile safety, they decide to study the effects of *actual communications* on the cell phone, excluding cell phone communication behaviors, such as reaching for and holding the cell phone. They seek to isolate that variable of cell phone communication processes, making it the clear focus of the research. The hypothesis becomes that a driver's communicating on a cell phone will lead to a decrease in her or his automobile safety.

Here is the experiment devised to test that hypothesis. There are two groups of subjects: an experimental group and a control group. These two groups are matched; that is, they are similar on as many dimensions as possible, including general characteristics such as sex, age, and socioeconomic status, as well as characteristics specific to the experiments, such as familiarity with a cell phone and driving experience. Each group is then seated in a simulated car interior with a mounted cell phone, allowing for hands-free use, and then takes the same simulated driver's test, which scores their safety record as their car cruises through various traffic situations. The only difference between the two groups is that the cell phone in the experimental group engages the driver in a conversation, while the cell phone in the control group does not, remaining silent. The control group's cell phone then is just like the cell phone that is engaging the experimental group driver in conversation, but without the control group's knowledge, it will not have the active ingredient of an actual conversation. Both groups are told in advance they may receive a call, and if they do, they are to answer it and engage in a conversation.

After the two groups, the experimental group engaging in the cell phone conversation and the control group with no conversation, perform their driving tests, the safety scores for each group are tabulated. The experimental group has a worse safety score. The hypothesis is confirmed: engaging in a cell phone conversation does make driving less safe. Discussion of the results would probably focus on explanations such as the role of focused and divided attention to accidents. Further research would be needed to refine that conclusion, such as varying the content of the communication: Does it make a difference if the cell phone call contains a positive, neutral, or negative message or if members of the experimental group have short or long responses? When there is no cell phone conversation, to what degree do group members pay attention to their driving versus allow their attention to wander? Does it make a difference how long the experiment continues? For example, will a longer time period cause the control group to have more anticipatory responses to the call that never comes, making them more accident prone? These are the kinds of refinements of the basic experimental design that can be a real delight to puzzle out, and they're one of the hallmarks of good, experimentally based research.

Yes, the classical mainstream experiment-based approach to research can provide useful and valuable data or information, especially in pinning down causal links between discrete and concrete variables. The experimental paradigm is especially effective in testing the efficacy of pharmaceutical interventions.* But the very attributes of this mainstream research approach that makes it effective in certain specific areas, such as identifying causality, are also the attributes that severely limit its usefulness in a wide range of important areas, such as quality-of-life issues and questions of human potential.

What are some of the primary characteristics of this mainstream approach? We discuss some of them in chapter 1 when we describe the dominant and dominating form of mainstream Western psychology, including its emphasis on materialism and the flawed pursuit of a limited and limiting concept of science.

The mainstream psychology research paradigm posits *prediction* of behaviors and their subsequent *control* as its guiding principles. If we can

---

*There is accumulating data about how big pharmacy can unfairly influence outcome studies on drugs they are manufacturing. As many studies are still funded by the pharmaceutical companies that seek to prove the efficacy of a drug they are manufacturing, there are multiple pressures on researchers to produce positive results. For example, studies showing negative or no outcomes are not routinely published, and examples of researchers massaging or manipulating the data to show positive outcomes continue—even though that behavior is so clearly dishonest and unethical.

clearly state there is a causal link between cell phone communication while driving and an increase in accidents, then we can predict that drivers who are communication in that manner are at greater risk to have accidents, and as a result, we can propose ways to control that cell phone communication behavior, including making it illegal while driving.

This is a powerful sequence of events emerging from a research study. But to establish this causal relationship certain conditions must be met, most of which compromise the depth and relevance of the research, limiting it to a focus on discrete, concrete, and typically behaviorally oriented variables. The complexity and subtlety of human nature needs to be reduced to simple, at times superficial dimensions, rendering them more capable of being measured, hopefully through some counting procedure. An intelligence quotient (IQ), which is an actual number achieved by an intelligence test, is preferred to a general picture, such as ways in which a person displays everyday intelligence. Many of the issues that plague and fulfill human nature are thereby ruled off-limits.

The mainstream researcher must also be detached from the research enterprise, acting as a neutral, objective observer. Unless the research is conducted in a strictly monitored laboratory setting, this detachment and neutrality is nearly impossible, as researchers, though they claim neutrality, typically have biases that do affect research outcomes. The very concept of *neutral* research or *neutral* science is problematic, more an ideal than a reality. Can there ever be a clear separation between the researcher and what is researched, between the observer and the observed?* My doctoral research is one of the earliest demonstrations of the mechanisms by which this experimenter bias is conveyed, as we showed how a researcher, without conscious intention, uses different body language signals to affect the nature of the data collected, encour-

---

*Assumptions of scientific neutrality often elevate the legitimacy of the observer's perspective. The observer then becomes an expert, the center of discourse, and thus the one who can collect information or data to generate theories, having the power to interpret findings, a power that can turn what might be a range of *plausible* interpretations into *the* interpretation. Those providing the data, now called "subjects," have no voice.

aging the subject to produce responses supporting the experiment's hypothesis (Katz 1965).

Even if neutrality were achievable, the methodology Western psychology uses to attain this elusive quality—the laboratory paradigm for research—sacrifices a realistic connection to ongoing life issues for the presumed clarity of a neutral, controlled setting. There is an attempt to create a sterile environment, isolating what is to be studied from the confusions of its natural context, the better to study only that variable. If well-being is the focus of study, better to administer a questionnaire in the experimenter's laboratory than to enter into the stream of everyday life and observe experiences with and of well-being, including the inevitable unpredictable rhythms of that condition. We all have our bad days just as inevitably as our good days, and the mixture and sequencing are themselves unclear. The mainstream approach's purity of focus only becomes possible in a highly controlled and therefore artificial environment, keeping out "extraneous" variables—which are actually the very substance of daily, complex living. Empirical reductionism is practiced to achieve objectivity, but that objectivity—assuming it's even possible—becomes increasingly focused on smaller and less important issues.

An important ingredient in the classical mainstream research approach is replication: a research finding can be reproduced repeatedly, preferably by researchers other than the original one. Replication is said to cement validity, helping to avoid biases, which can taint the work of any one researcher. But replication, as with neutrality, may be an unattainable ideal.*

---

*Some argue that replication is impossible. How can you exactly duplicate an experiment to see if the same results occur? Simple things like inevitable changes in context—like time of year, personality of researchers, and political-economic conditions—can sufficiently alter the conditions of the original experiment that it in fact becomes, at least somewhat, a *different* experiment. Rather than the rigid requirement of replication, the alternative of *translation* is offered as a measure of the validity or strength of a research finding. For example, does the finding hold up under similar conditions, or even can it be generalized to conditions related to the original ones but now touching on more pressing human dilemmas? This emphasis on translation is part of the countercurrents that are examined in more detail in the countercurrents section of this chapter.

The entire mainstream research enterprise survives, even thrives, on having the researcher maintain power and control—over the topic to be researched, the research procedures, the interpretation of data, and the dissemination of results. The researcher is in charge; the researchee is called a subject—we could say a subject of the researcher, or subjected to the researcher's agenda. Certainly the researchee in being a subject is not fully a person.

This imbalanced power structure maintains mainstream research's power relationship over those being researched. Because the researchers remain in control, they often ignore or minimize their obligation to have research make a positive difference in the lives of those being researched. Indigenous communities are often the sites of research that historically are exploitative, gathering data from the community with minimal commitment to share that data and make a difference in the life of the community. I remember painfully the people in a small village along the Tanana River in Alaska who are still waiting, ten years after a research project is completed in their village about adolescent suicide, not only for the complete results of the study but, more importantly, for changes that can be effected as a result of the research. They get a summary report, but that leaves them only with more questions.

What good does it do to gather data on teenage suicide but not use that data to support appropriate prevention and treatment programs? Mainstream research sees the Indigenous idea of research—a process of exchange characterized by respect and equality among *all* participants in the research process—as a compromise of scientific integrity and impractical as well. Indigenous communities see mainstream research as an intrusion, a rip-off and robbery of precious experience and information. To them, research is a dirty word. "Those researchers just come in and take. It's a rape of ourselves," says an Indigenous student in my psychology class.

This unilateral exercise of power and control is justified by the expertise of the researcher—who better to make decisions about all these research issues and strategies than a person trained to understand them, meaning *professionally* trained in research methodologies, not trained in the dynamics of positive community change, as are many community members. Allowing untrained persons to collect data is common, especially when those collecting data have special connections to the people who are supplying the data, but that hardly breaks the grip of the researcher over the entire research enterprise. Especially in the interpretation and dissemination of data, the researcher remains in charge, as those areas are considered too specialized and too important to entrust to untrained people.

Certainly times have changed: most persons involved in research no longer tolerate a cavalier disregard of their interests, and researchers today are more rarely knowingly insensitive. But power and control still reside primarily in the researcher. Take, for example, the procedure of informed consent, a requirement in mainstream research. Potential participants in a research project are told about possible risks if they become part of the research and are given the opportunity to decide whether or not to participate or to withdraw at any future time after the research has begun. If they agree to participate, they are asked to sign an informed consent document, a formal assent providing the researcher with legal protections against future problems. But how informed are the participants when even the researcher does not know all the consequences that might emerge from their participation? If you are not really informed, how can you really give your consent? The researcher, even without full knowledge of the research process, retains the upper hand, especially when the importance of the project and the value of the participant's contribution are subtly used as incentives. The researcher may typically say: "This work is in the interest of science," or "Your participation will help us solve this important problem."

INDIGENOUS APPROACH
TO RESEARCH

How does this mainstream Western research approach, symbolized by the laboratory experiment, compare with an Indigenous approach? Danny Musqua, the Anishnabe elder who is my spiritual father, tells a story about his Indigenous research effort. As a member of the Bear Clan, Danny is a guardian of traditional Anishnabe ceremonies, caring for the knowledge that underlies the life and nature of the ceremonies, offering support in their actual performance. He's also a traditional storyteller, entrusted with the stories of his people that contain their journeys and spiritual teachings and educated in the ways of remembering these stories and communicating them in the proper manner. Memory and remembering are part of his being, inculcated in him from early childhood. When he was just a toddler, his grandmother would send him outside after he woke up to listen to the birds . . . and the wind . . . and the grass. "These things can talk to you and tell you important things," she instructed him. "Listen . . . listen carefully."

Part of Danny's responsibilities is to learn and know the many songs that activate and accompany the ceremonies. The songs are calls and pleas to the spirits, asking for the blessing and protection of the spirit world. They sing a sacred language. There is a song that Danny realizes he needs to learn in order to more completely fulfill his responsibilities, and he knows the Anishnabe elder who knows that song.

Thus begins his research effort. He approaches the elder with respect because the elder is a man of knowledge. The elder also has sacred responsibilities, one of which is to protect and nurture his songs and offer them to others when appropriate. Danny will be requesting an opportunity to learn a song that the elder is holding dear to his heart.

Danny knows he must approach the elder in a spiritually based ceremonial manner, offering a sacred exchange in order to learn the song. He presents the elder with a tobacco offering, which among First Nations people carries a spiritual message of respect and humility, demonstrating how deeply the offerer values what is being requested. The tobacco offering humbly acknowledges the spiritual nature of what is being requested and invites the presence of the spirits directly into the exchange, giving life to and sanctifying the process. With the tobacco, Danny is honoring the elder's gift of the song.*

The elder is grateful Danny has come because it's the elder's responsibility to pass on his knowledge to deserving others; his knowledge lives only as it is shared with others. The elder sings his song, and Danny listens. He draws upon his lifetime of training, to listen with care, being open to all realms of sound and meaning, so he can hear— and remember. This ability to hear is sharpened as it becomes infused with spiritual energy.

The elder sings the song several times more, and Danny listens and believes he hears. But he has a moment of doubt. He's not totally sure he got it! "Would it be all right if I tape-record this song," he asks, almost immediately embarrassed by his question. The elder looks at Danny with a surprised, quizzical expression. "You say you want to learn this song," he almost repeats Danny's words, "but if you *really* do, you will hear it and learn it. You don't need that tape recorder. If you don't really work to learn the song, it will just go in one of your ears and out the other."

Danny and the elder enjoy a good laugh. "Of course," Danny realizes to himself. Danny now prepares at another level to listen, so he can hear, really hear, and thereby learn. Being more relaxed through the laughter, his ears open to his mind and heart, and listening a few more times, he connects to the spiritual sources of the song. Within a proper ceremonial exchange, the elder has given Danny the song, and

_____

*For a further discussion of the tobacco offering in First Nations cultures, see Michell (1999).

with that Danny now has permission to sing it. The knowledge has been shared.

As Danny embarks on this piece of Indigenous research, he is seeking understanding, not the prediction or control that earmarks the mainstream research approach. He knows that he must approach the goal of learning this new song by engaging his ways of knowing and in the end bringing those ways to a deeper, more spiritually charged level. The entire process of working with the elder is a sacred journey rather than the more technical, even mechanical character of the mainstream laboratory approach.

This Indigenous approach to research is based on principles of respect and exchange; respect for the elder and his knowledge and giving something in exchange to earn the right to learn that knowledge. The research is a process creating and existing within an ethical space, guided by respectful exchanges. Danny and the elder are co-creating the setting in which the learning and spiritual transmission will occur. This is not the unilateral possession of power and control in the hands of the laboratory researcher, but a co-created process of research and learning, which either party can change. The elder is not a subject but a person of respect, and even if Danny wanted to, he cannot become a mainstream researcher because he cannot subject the elder to anything. There are two persons involved, and involved with each other. As the research unfolds, it becomes effective because both become expert in both learning and teaching.

Though Danny now knows the song and has been given traditional permission to sing it during ceremonies, he doesn't own the song—it remains a *gift,* a treasured part of Anishnabe spiritual teachings. He is the caretaker of that song and must nourish it with honest singing and a clean heart, but it is not his property. He can now pass that song on to others, to ones who have earned the right to that song, but obviously he cannot sell it. And pass it on he must, as it is through sharing that knowledge remains alive and enlivening. As Metis elder Rose Fleury puts it, "Our knowledge is useless unless we pass it on." No copyright here; no Western psychology journal statement about ownership of the data reported in a research article.*

The Ju/'hoansi offer us a similar teaching. A Ju/'hoan traditional healer is called a *n/omkxao,* which has been translated, in a misleading manner, as an "owner of n/om." Ju/'hoan healers could never "own" n/om; the very essence of n/om as spiritual energy is that it is beyond the control of anyone. Experienced healers such as =Oma Djo are masters of *knowledge* about n/om and how to activate it for the purposes of healing; in that sense they are knowledge keepers, a role Indigenous elders maintain throughout the world. Yes, some Ju/'hoan healers at various times have attempted to claim they own their n/om, portraying that n/om as a personal possession, as part of an effort to bolster their reputations and thus gain extra rewards from their healing efforts beyond the traditional communal give and take of

---

*The persistent and pernicious influence of colonization impacts this concept of ownership versus stewardship. Though traditionally, as with Danny and his song, Indigenous knowledge has been cared for, shared, and passed on to the next generation, in recent history the commercial-industrial complex of the non-Indigenous world has attempted to exploit (steal) that knowledge and turn it into commodity to sell for a profit. For example, Indigenous herbs, used for traditional remedies, are "discovered" by Western pharmaceutical companies, and their ingredients are analyzed and turned into a marketable pharmaceutical. Typically, the Indigenous source of that plant—including the people, community, and cultures where the plant is grown and whose knowledge guides its therapeutic, sometimes sacred usages—are cut out of the loop and denied any profits.

It's a terrible irony for Indigenous peoples. They know that their traditional knowledge is not a commodity to be bought and sold, and yet they feel betrayed by the unethical exploitation of that knowledge. There is now a movement to obtain copyrights for Indigenous plants, including the knowledge holding its effective employment. It is a last resort, unwelcomed but seemingly necessary—using the Western concept of copyright, which is based on the assumption of private property and ownership, to protect Indigenous knowledge, which is not constrained by any principles of private ownership. They are being forced to use a Western system to legitimize what they know, to prove that their research is truthful and valid; once again, Indigenous knowledge is devalued by being commodified. And yet who can deny that those Indigenous communities deserve—and can clearly use—the money they derive from the sale of their knowledge resources?

the healing dance.* But these efforts at ownership for personal aggrandizement are discouraged. "N/om heals us all," assures =Oma Djo, "and it belongs to us all."

At the heart of Indigenous approaches to research is observation. This may seem odd because observation is also the bedrock of mainstream approaches. But there is observation, and then there is *observation*. Observation in the mainstream approach emphasizes care and accuracy and is primarily a mental and analytical process. Categorizing what is observed into separate, even distinct units is a way to enable more precise measurement. The environment is controlled so that focus can remain on the objects of study; the natural context in which they exist is considered potential sources of distraction.

From an Indigenous perspective, observation must certainly be careful and accurate, but it also must be caring and intuitive, revealing the layers of what is observed and, in particular, what lies beyond, beneath, and within the surface of the obvious. Most important, Indigenous researchers emphasize observing what comes to you with its natural rhythms intact, including its inevitably unexpected turns, and resisting any preconceived notions (as in hypotheses) about how things can unfold. The Indigenous researcher connects with the phenomenon observed and follows its path to learn more about its nature. This careful, connected observation really matters; it is a survival strategy, not a research luxury.†

---

*=Oma Djo has a period in his life where he attempts to turn his access to n/om into a personal possession of that n/om in order to enhance his reputation. As with most elders—and most people—there are periods during their lives where their journeys enter terrains that are far from their ideals. But with elders, those are not detours but the stuff of life and opportunities for learning rather than just mistakes.

†Ju/'hoan hunting-gathering survival depends on observational skills and commitment in order to ensure successful hunting—for example, knowing the migration and feeding patterns of the animals and understanding the coming shifts in the weather so that extremes of cold or heat do the least amount of harm. This survival comes from not only watching the animals and the weather but also feeling the underlying natural and spiritual rhythms that animate those phenomena. As well, living in close interdependent communities, intra- and interpersonal observational acuity and sensitivity is paramount, to ensure that the inevitable challenges to community cohesion and continuity are thoughtfully resolved. Though hunting for survival is less important now, communication for survival is even more important.

Sitting on an upturned log, Danny Musqua is observing the gophers in their colony in the prairie grass outside his house. He is just six, but already he is being taught to observe with care and caring. He sees how the gopher colony is functioning, with certain gophers tasked with the job of protection, popping up out of the burrows, standing on their hind legs, surveying the surrounding land. Is there danger out there? Maybe a hawk circling still high above? Are things OK? Danny notices the ways in which gophers use different holes to arrive at their destination and the special license they take when danger drives them into the nearest available hole. Danny sits there for a long time, maybe an hour, observing. And as he sees the way the gopher colony organizes itself for survival, he observes patterns in their behaviors, connections between the functions.

As Danny, now an elder, is telling me this story, he's animated, excited. "My little boy mind became joined by my heart," he reflects. "Seeing all those interrelations was so wonderful. I didn't have the words when I was little to describe what was happening . . . but I felt it, the awe, the specialness and ordinariness of that gopher community," he continues. "But I know now I was observing the gophers *and* observing the spiritual underpinnings of all life, the intricate web of living." Even as a boy Danny is observing so he can see properly.*

A key aspect of this Indigenous approach to research is the ultimate valuation of personal experience. The Indigenous approach is a journey into our deepest inner spaces and places where we are at one with the animating spiritual forces of our world. Willie Ermine, an emerging Cree elder, beautifully describes the sacred importance of this inner space (Ermine 1995). The personal dimension then becomes not a source of bias but an expression of truth, as

---

*This kind of observation of the gopher reality reminds me of the time I spend in Fiji, where for hours at a time, I sit with the men drinking yaqona, not yet understanding Fijian, but absorbing the atmosphere of the gathering, letting go of expectations so that the feelings of the place touched me. I am learning, not just the beginnings of the Fijian language, but the qualities of Fijian life.

the experience is permeated by a process of honest self-reflection.

When our personal experience evolves from within our sacred inner space, it is a gift; when our stories evolve from our reflections on these experiences, they have ultimate meaning. From an Indigenous perspective, you don't question a person who is telling a story of his or her experience. You respect that story, as it is a creation, in the moment, of a life unfolding. It is pointless, for example, to make specific corrections about life events that you think are being misrepresented or misdated. Our stories are our lives, and we're creating our lives in the moments of those stories.

It's easy to see how uncomfortable mainstream approaches are with this primacy of personal experience; not only is that experience an inner state, without necessary observable or behavioral correlated, but also it's dynamic, sometimes evolving in the very process of its telling. "How do you pin down something existing within an ongoing process of change?" the mainstream researcher might plead. What is a foundation for reality from an Indigenous perspective becomes the very reason it cannot be a foundation for reality from a mainstream perspective.

For the song to live, Danny must sing it, and sing it with respect during ceremonies for the many years to come and in this way bring healing to the people. The Indigenous research model insists on an outcome that will benefit the people. Where the mainstream approach can afford to do "research for its own sake" or "research for pure knowledge," the Indigenous approach always seeks to make a difference in people's lives and hopefully encourage social change and justice.

"The purpose of life is to learn." This is a central point in Danny's teachings. "We're on Earth to learn. . . to experience, to know," he says, "to learn to be good human beings . . . and learn to be of service to others." Learning how to be a good human being is part of the larger process of change and justice. When research becomes a process of respectful experiencing and knowing, we can listen so we can hear and observe so we can see properly. Research is animated by being part of a larger path toward understanding and service; as a result there is less support for the Western fascination with developing increasingly technical methods to control and isolate phenomena in order to better study them. Instead of an emphasis on an accumulation of facts, there is a focus on meanings emerging from facts.

COUNTERCURRENTS WITHIN THE MAINSTREAM

As we have examined the mainstream and Indigenous approaches to research in their relatively classic or pure forms, sharp differences emerge. But that fact is only a beginning. While the mainstream may draw its inspiration from the laboratory experimental model, at least historically, there are long-standing and growing countercurrents *within* psychology. These countercurrents, such as narrative research and community-based participatory research, are typically character- ized as forms of *qualitative* as opposed to *quantitative* research that derives more from that laboratory approach. Too often the discussion about these two methodologies, or general approaches to research, emphasize their differences, even to the extent of seeing them, errone- ously I believe, as dichotomous. But as with most things theoretical, when applied in practice, differences can soften as the actual intersec- tions and overlaps become apparent. I see the qualitative-quantitative distinction as a dimension, displaying differing amounts of each through particular emphases and interconnections.

Qualitative approaches stress the *quality* of phenomena, their more subtle and complex aspects that emerge from within their natural con- texts of flux and interconnections. Quantitative approaches stress the *quantity* of phenomena, the more obvious and simplified aspects of those phenomena that emerge when their contexts are controlled to isolate those phenomena and better allow them to be broken up into discrete units. These discrete units then are more open to quantitate measurements—for example, counting the number of units present. And though practitioners of the quantitate approach often label the qualitative approach as less rigorous, even unscientific, both approaches are appropriate paths toward science, and the emerging vitality of qualitative approaches is impressive.*

These qualitative approaches typically *point in the direction of* Indigenous principles of research, but they are not *synonymous with* the Indigenous approaches. When, for example, qualitative research stresses the importance of personal experiences, it is a less profound and enduring commitment to that experience than appears in the Indigenous approach. Once again, the same words, such as *personal experience,* have different meanings in the two approaches. These qualitative approaches generally lack the *ultimate* valuing of that experience, built on a respect for the meaning generated by the experiencer, which is central to Indigenous approaches.

In addition to the critiques of quantitative methodologies arising from qualitative alternatives, there is also a devastating line of critique emerging from within the quantitative model itself, further encouraging a serious consideration of alternatives. Increasing revelations about researcher-experimenter errors, such as incorrectly entering data and even making up data to support the researcher's hypothesis, undermine the concept that science is a neutral endeavor, a foundational principle of the mainstream quantitative approach (see e.g., Chwe 2014). That neutrality is theorized to be epistemologically impossible if not improbable;† now the less than honest behavior of the researchers themselves makes it practically so!

The qualitative approach espouses a type of research in which power and control are shared between the researcher and researchee. For example, in the qualitative approach of community-based

---

*See Wertz et al. (2011) for an excellent discussion of the theory and practice of qualitative research.

†A major theoretical perspective that undermines this concept of neutrality while offering an active alternative that describes how we deeply influence what we see—how we construct our realities—is social constructionism. Ken Gergen, who is one of my Harvard professors, is a leading contributor to this constructionistic movement (see e.g., Gergen 2015b).

participatory research,* the participants or community that are involved in the research collaborate with the researcher in deciding the topic of research, designing the research instruments, collecting and analyzing data, and disseminating the findings. This sharing of power means that all critical stages in the purpose, intent, and implementation of the research are a collaborative responsibility. No claim of academic expertise can override the consensual decision-making process at each of these stages. Yes, the community can reject the topic of a proposed research because that is not the topic they believe is most important—a possibility that the conventional psychological model of research abhors. The researcher can't blithely override community choices because they "just don't know the research literature that tells us what research is needed." Often, in this case, this researcher has already received funds to perform a particular line of research, which then, in this context, becomes "needed." At the base of this sharing is a respect for the researchee, who is no longer objectified as a subject but becomes a research collaborator.

When power and control are shared, it's most common that the community seeks to do research that matters in the lives of their people. The qualitative approach eschews "research for the sake of research" as a justification, insisting that research at least have an agenda of social change and justice, if not an actual outcome of those changes.

Realizing research as a source of power, Verna St. Denis (St. Denis 1992), a Cree Metis scholar in areas of antiracist education and social justice, is committed to using research as a vehicle for supporting

---

*Community-based participatory research derives from or shares values with a variety of closely related approaches, such as action research (St. Denis 1992). Psychology has this penchant for claiming a contribution is new or innovative when it is often more a relabeling or rebranding of an already existing method or intervention. This is common in the field of therapy, where groundbreaking interventions seem to spring up like the blooms of spring, when they are little more than repackaging, with minor tweaks, of older techniques.

empowerment in Indigenous communities.* But it is not an easy task, given the historical and continuing encapsulation of mainstream research in a racist, colonial mentality, and is especially difficult for an Indigenous researcher who lives the continuing effects of that history. St. Denis frames her deep dilemma with eloquence:

> I'm a Cree/Metis woman who grew up in rural Saskatchewan, Canada. Throughout my "growing up" years, I experienced many of the painful effects of racial and class discrimination, which was fueled, in part, by "knowledge" and policies generated from social science research. This experience is common to most people of colour, women, the underclass and other groups who do not have access to powerful decision-making positions. Therefore, as a First Nations woman who grew up "dirt poor," I have searched for a way to do social science research that would be more responsive to the needs of First Nations communities and disempowered communities in general (St. Denis 1992, 51).

St. Denis sees a community-based approach to research as a way to break somewhat from that colonial mold—and that decision has led to a rich body of sensitive and insightful research, committed to effective social change for Indigenous peoples.† She finds that the

---

*In this section on resistances within the mainstream, there are references to the research projects of a number of Indigenous scholars and activists. I discuss their work in this section, rather than in the section on Indigenous approaches to research, because these Indigenous scholars are trained in mainstream universities and typically identify themselves primarily as scholars—not traditional elders or healers. The same reasoning lies behind the discussion of contributions from Indigenous Western-trained psychologists in later chapters; for example, how these psychologists bring Indigenous teachings stressing the importance of spirituality as a therapeutic foundation in clinical work.

The material by Indigenous scholars discussing Indigenous perspectives on research is exceptionally rich and valuable. In addition to the research of St. Denis, there are, for example, the research efforts of Melinda García, Walter Lightning, Herman Michell, and Tara Turner—all of whose work is discussed in *Indigenous Healing Psychology*.

†See the bibliography for a selection of St. Denis's writings.

community-based participatory approach allows her to work with the community, seeking to support their empowerment. As she does her research, she passes on the skills and strategies that will allow community members to begin doing their own research and thereby better defining for themselves future directions and having the tools and vision for implementation. But the obstacles of the larger capitalistic sociopolitical context remain, and its competitive strategies and disempowering institutions can overwhelm gains made at a local level, making social change less effective and enduring.*

Another aspect of the qualitative approach is an emphasis on naturalistic settings, minimizing the degree to which variables are artificially isolated and environments artificially controlled. Describing the process of research as being like a canoe journey through the lakes and rivers of his northern Saskatchewan home, Herman Michell, a Cree academic and researcher, lovingly and insightfully, offers an Indigenous perspective that illuminates the natural rhythms of research that qualitative approaches could aspire toward.† As it unfolds through its intrinsic dynamics, Michell shows how the research process is filled with the unexpected—demanding resiliency and flexibility, an appreciation of the value of starts and stops, patience and acceptance. It is a process, not a project.

You prepare, Michell says, but only for the unexpected, as the weather determines the speed, even direction of the canoe journey. And you appreciate the need for stopping along the way, avoiding the perils

---

*As we see in chapter 7, community psychology, the countercurrent within mainstream psychology founded just to promote social change and justice, is itself being co-opted into a set of mainstream principles. Encumbered by a need to be "scientific," it is losing its sharp, incisive thrust for social justice. It becomes more the task of critical psychology to carry this mandate for change, indeed a radical restructuring of the status quo sociopolitical institutions.

†Michell (2012, 1) also establishes the spiritual foundation of this dynamic, naturally unfolding model of research by discussing the sacred importance of water for his people: "Water is also sacred to the northern Cree. We all come from water when we come into this world. We require water for our existence. We cleanse ourselves with water."

of bad weather, taking time to reflect on where you have come from and where you will end up. At the end of the trip, you are welcomed home, and the story of your journey is told to the community, as it celebrates the accomplishments and gifts of the journey itself.

The qualitative approach seeks to minimize predetermined foci, encouraging the issues that merit research to emerge from the participants whose lives are being studied. Hypotheses, especially a priori hypotheses, are neither required nor particularly valued, as the direction, even the topic of research, can change, depending on the insights and commitments of the collaborative complex, which now contains both community and researcher.

But the mainstream academy pushes on and exerts a telling influence in settings like thesis committees that often cling to some semblance of expert-driven order and expectation. Imagine a graduate student, committed to doing a piece of community-based participatory research, telling her thesis committee or funder that she can't say exactly what the topic of her research will be until she has a chance to work with the prospective research participants or community. Furthermore, the student cautions her committee that she not only needs the community's input but she also cannot guarantee community members will not change their minds if the research unfolds in a direction they see as less relevant to their needs. Most committees want to know before the research begins what the topic is and hesitate to give the student permission to do the kind of research whose intent is to clarify the purpose of that research. Good luck!

The ethnographic method, one of several research strategies borrowed from anthropology, emphasizes that research should occur within a natural setting minimally disturbed by the research project itself and, as much as possible, attempt to observe the entire context. This, of course, is impossible, as not only do aspects of the context escape the researcher's observational talents, but also the researcher's very presence in a community changes the nature and dynamics of that community.

Participant observation, the central method in ethnography,

then becomes a method that attempts to ease those dilemmas, as the researcher delicately, and often unsuccessfully, balances her or his observations of and participation in the community where the research occurs. My various experiences in participant observation raise impenetrable questions.* Am I participating too much so that I can't observe accurately? But how can I observe what is really happening, unless I participate in it? These are the kinds of questions that keep coming up, though rarely articulated. In the end, I discover there is no clear and clean way of deciding what is the correct balance and, even more difficult, how to obtain that balance. Participation and observation are actually end points in a continuum, never existing in pure form but always in dynamic flux, reciprocally affecting each other. I realize that what is needed is an intuitive leap into the research, with continual reflections on the emerging balance.

At times in my research, I'm reminded that I'm not invisible, that I indeed often stand out—though I strive to be just part of the community. Having lived for nearly two years in a small rural village on

---

*I'll always remember my first experience with participant observation—engaging in that method not so much by choice as by necessity, not so much knowing how to use that method as using it as best I know how. In 1964, I'm hired by the Outward Bound schools, which are one of the original outdoor-experiential education institutions in North America, to describe their educational principles. I'm working at the Colorado Outward Bound School, set within the Rockies and featuring mountain climbing as the activity venue for learning.

In the first few days of the program, I interview some of the boys while we're all staying in the base camp; I'm comfortable with this way of gaining information. Then on the third day, the schedule calls for activities on one of the smaller slopes, working on climbing skills. I'm not into heights, so I'm not excited to go out to those slopes. And also, I kind of like the rhythm of the base camp. I'll just stay in camp and interview those boys when they return from the slope, I muse. And then, looking at myself in disbelief, I further muse, How can I do *that!* I'll miss all the action. I'll get only a recollection of what *actually* happened! So off to the slope I go, and as I participate along with the boys in climbing activities, I'm still somewhat in fear of those climbs. Thus I see and feel some of what they are seeing and feeling. When we do interviews later on back in camp, the exchange is much richer, more insightful. Without preparation or planning, I've completed my first participant-observation project. The full report of that Outward Bound research appears in Katz and Kolb (1972).

a remote Fijian island while doing my research on healing, I'm in the rhythm of village life. My family, with our two kids, are *just* one of the village families—or so I believe. And then two visitors arrive at the village, two white Australians who sail into the harbor. To my surprise, a couple of the villagers bring the Australians to our little hut. What is this about? I wonder to myself. I don't know these people. Why bring them here?

But the villagers have no such doubts or dilemmas. "White people know all other white people," my Fijian friends must think, or at least, "White people always have something to say to each other. And this guy [me!] living with us is the only white guy and family in the entire area of our island and the surrounding islands as well." And then I see myself as if from above, as if from a helicopter. Yes, there is one white family sticking out from all the brown-skinned Fijians in the village. I may be part of village life, but from another perspective, I do stick out. That dose of reality is very helpful in keeping me humble about how much I still don't know about Fijian life.

Within mainstream psychology there is a new appreciation of the value and meaning of personal experience. Joan Koss-Chiono (2010), a distinguished psychological anthropologist with a long history of research in the Puerto Rican spiritual healing tradition of *espiritismo* provides a wonderfully honest, remarkable example of this valuation of experience in the especially challenging—and to mainstream psychology "suspect"—area of spirituality. Though she remains committed to a more conventional research paradigm to generate certain demographic, behavioral, and outcome data about espiritismo, such as the number of *espiritistas* (practitioners of espiritismo) who are also practicing M.D.'s and the efficacy of variants of espiritismo, Joan has become increasingly drawn to research experiences of spirituality and especially spiritual transformations.

Joan has always valued the personal reports of spiritual experiences from the espiritistas she has worked with. But now, after participating in numerous espiritismo ceremonies, she more fully recognizes and accepts the reality of the spirits *for herself*—"appreciat[ing] spirits as part of my world"—though not claiming a precise understanding. As a respected academic, she has the courage to write about this personal knowledge, forgoing positivistic certainties for ambiguous realities, forgoing the conventional, mainstream psychological measures of respectability. "You know, Dick," she tells me, "that isn't easy to do even though I know it's the truth." "Yes," I join her, "I know what you mean!"*

A new research methodology develops to appreciate and understand personal experience and the stories told to express those experiences is narrative inquiry.† Emphasizing the importance of gathering stories from individuals in order to understand their personality and nature, narrative inquiry attempts to bring stories to the fore, unedited as much as possible. The approach also emphasizes the truth value of the story as told rather than resorting to a fact-checking mentality to be sure the facts of the story are true—whether it be the exact sequence of events or the persons in attendance at an activity or whether the feelings displayed then are accurately reported now. Personal experiences take center stage; life stories are the vehicle for understanding these experiences.

As my former student and now close friend and colleague Stephen Murphy-Shigematsu puts it, narrative inquiry "focuses on how human experience is organized, remembered, and transformed through the stories people tell about their lives. . . . Humans give meaning to their lives in narrative terms," he adds, "by seeing themselves as living in the drama of particular stories" (2012, 171–72). Our personal narrative becomes our life story, and there is truth being created in the telling. This is not to deny the realities of facts but to honor a new dimension of reality

---

*Joan Koss-Chioino (2010) describes her journey toward accepting the reality of the spirits with a wonderful story and refreshing honesty. Early in her research with espiritismo, a respected espiritista practitioner tells her: "I don't believe [in spirits] but what exists, exists." I think that's a wonderfully grounded way to understand a phenomenon that is too often abstractly floating in space—usually high above us.

†Some of the particular research approaches within this general framework of narrative inquiry are narrative medicine, autoethnography, and photo-autobiographies.

based on our ongoing constructions of meaning.* How we construct our reality matters more intimately than any consensually formed conceptions of reality; therefore, our personal stories, speaking from the inside out, are to be treasured, nurtured, and reflected on for guidance.

But the *ultimate* valuation of personal experience, and the honoring of one's story truthfully told, is not easily affirmed. From a classical mainstream perspective, how can we trust just one person's views? They could be just opinions, suggests the mainstream perspective, or if they are offered as a true picture of what is happening, how can we rely on only one person? Don't we need to have some corroboration from others to be sure of the real truth? A truth that goes beyond a personal truth?

Even qualitative approaches find it difficult to accept fully the Indigenous valuation of personal experience as an ultimate truth for that person. There is always a bit of holding back in the qualitative approaches, an ongoing temptation for the researcher to add something, some analysis or interpretation, to make sense of these stories of personal experience. Imagine the difficulty of turning in a piece of research, especially a thesis, in which all you present is a verbatim collection of stories. "But where is your contribution to this research?" can be a common comment, assuming that the researcher with her special expertise can add something to the story, at least helping it make more sense or helping to establish its meaning.

Narrative inquiry offers ways in which stories as told can remain as much as possible stories that are gathered as research data. For example, Stacey McHenry, a doctoral candidate in culture and human development, talks about the need to keep a story's "rough edges" in order to honor its telling (2016, 84). She proposes a dynamic, fluid approach to narrative as a way to better represent our stories as we create and tell them, instead of the more conventional linear and sequential approach,

---

*Gergen's social constructionist theory, emphasizing our role in creating the world we experience through our meaning making, gives a firm theoretical foundation for this emphasis on life stories as vehicles for the creation of meanings.

used to control and shape our stories, making them more coherent so that they make more sense—even though a lack of sense, even common sense, is what animates many of those stories. Stacey says that this conventional narrative analysis covers up and blankets the messiness, discontinuity, incoherence, and instability of our lives and the stories that create our lives.

There are important efforts being made to present stories' research data in a form as close as possible to the way they are originally created and told—but there is always lurking the impossibility of ever completely and cleanly accomplishing this aim. The spiritual teachings of elders represent a particular challenge, as the exactness of the words is so often related to the important nuances of meaning. Walter Lightning, a Cree educator, works diligently to present the teachings of Cree elder Louis Sunchild (Lightning 1992). He presents his interview with elder Sunchild as much as possible in verbatim from transcriptions of a tape recording—first in Cree syllabics, then in Cree words, and finally in an English translation, all the while checking out each version for accuracy with the elder. A valiant effort!

Tara Turner, a Metis psychologist, does a beautiful thesis, honoring the realities and meanings of stories and thereby the storytellers (Turner 2011). She comes from a family that is tragically interrupted by an automobile accident; her father is separated from his siblings at an early age. Though the ones that are separated as kids reestablish contact later in life, knowledge of many pieces of their lives is missing—to each other and to themselves.

Tara's thesis is a gathering of family stories that are then shared among the family members. Older sibs help younger ones recover missing chapters in their lives; the older ones remember what happens and can explain that, for example, a sib who seems to just disappear is in fact taken away for adoption in another home. As the stories circulate among family members, there are new views of self, new understandings of meanings through the reflections of others, and a resolution of old hurts through the recovery of memory. Eventually, the stories create a living web of family connections, and the stories keep unfolding. Within this active process, Tara, as the sensitive gatherer of living gems and a reflecting point through which lives pass and reform, realizes one of her aims in the thesis: "I want to find out more about who I am, about who we all are," she says. And as the family story-web grows and lives, all are learning more about themselves as they learn more about each other.

I'm on Tara's thesis committee. I see my job in simple terms: affirm Tara's intuitive genius for the truths and meanings of personal stories. "Don't worry about making your thesis acceptable to conventional psychology," I keep telling her. "Your thesis is unearthing and honoring truths, and that is what psychology should be doing. Your thesis is alive—and continues to grow—re-creating understandings in peoples' lives. What more could we want from a thesis?" I add. "Don't worry whether you are doing enough as a doctoral candidate to show your competence. Just do enough to make the stories speak their truths." Yet I'm clearly aware of the Western academic assumption that unless an expert—in this case, Tara as the academically trained doctoral student—interprets the data collected, then the data has no real or valid meaning. It's almost as if Tara's interpretation of the stories she's collected transforms them into valid data. And then there is the Western academic rule that the writer, or doctoral candidate, must show how *she* has contributed to the writing—to show she can do interpretive work or, to put it more crudely, to show she is qualified to get her doctorate. And so Tara does add theoretical sections to the thesis and does some analysis of the stories—and they *are* helpful, at the very least to create context, but the stories shine out, in their own languages. She writes a beautifully stirring thesis—still, unfortunately, not understood by many in mainstream psychology as research.

An overarching and perhaps most fundamental contribution of the countercurrents within the mainstream suggests that research, at its very core, creates an ethical space, a contribution most powerfully articulated by Indigenous researchers. Research, they insist, is an ethical process and action, connecting people and communities through respectful exchange, creating mutual responsibilities to be of service. Marlene Brant Castellano, a Mohawk psychiatrist, puts it this way:

> In the world of Aboriginal knowledge, a discussion of ethics cannot be limited to devising a set of rules to guide researcher behavior in a defined task. Ethics, the rules to right behavior, are intimately related to who you are, the deep values you subscribe to, and your understanding of your place in the spiritual order of reality. Ethics are integral to the way of life of a people. . . . This is the ground on which Aboriginal Peoples stand as they engage in dialogue about research ethics that will limit the risks and enhance the benefits of research affecting their lives (Castellano 2004, 103).

Cora Weber-Pillwax, an Indigenous Metis scholar and researcher from Alberta, focuses on what is a key element in the teachings about an Indigenous approach to research (Weber-Pillwax 2001). She writes that "I had trouble getting past the idea that I'm an Indigenous person; therefore, what I'm doing is going to be Indigenous research." Then she goes to the core of what she sees as an Indigenous approach: "Any research that I do must not destroy or in any way negatively implicate or compromise my own personal integrity as a person, as a human being" (2001, 168). That makes it all both simple and true; an Indigenous approach must first of all be honest and respectful, whatever the eventual *particulars* of that approach may be.

If, as Danny says, the purpose of life is to learn, then research can be an appropriate space in which that type of deep learning can be valued and can even occur. Research can be a place of living and learning, not merely an arena for the implementation of research methodologies.

FUTURE COLLABORATIONS

At the basis of any collaboration between Indigenous and Western approaches to research, with the hope of enhancing the latter, is a firm recognition that both approaches are legitimate and valuable ways of doing science. My friend Oscar Kawagley describes the elegance and insights of such an Indigenous approach to research in his wonderful book *A Yupiaq Worldview: A Pathway to Ecology and Spirit* (2006). He takes us on a journey of discovery over the land, revealing the deepest nature of things and their intricate interrelationships, through a blending of acute observation and spiritual inspiration. As the mainstream looks toward Indigenous approaches as another legitimate and scientific path on the search for knowledge, it can be receptive—and learn.

A fundamental Indigenous teaching that could enhance mainstream approaches is that research can be a process of knowing and experiencing, connected to the fundamental process of learning to become a good human being. "The purpose of life is to learn," Danny Musqua says. This understanding can help move the mainstream away from an unproductive preoccupation with research as a technical enterprise, cultivating sophisticated methodologies to gather data from subjects. Yes, methods can remain important but not as the sole and most valued focus. Research can be a more humane and human enterprise, dealing with existential life issues, and still be methodologically strong. Research could be motivated more by a sincere desire to know than a need to publish or perish.

Flowing from this more humane focus comes a commitment to see research as occurring within an ethical space, creating a time for reflection and dialogue before activating a research agenda so that, with a respectful exchange between researchers and proposed research participants, inequitable expressions of power and control are avoided.* A key

---

*Ermine, Sinclair, and Jeffery (2004) offer a valuable discussion of how such an ethical space can offer effective opportunities for collaboration between mainstream and Indigenous perspectives approaches as they each contribute, in their own unique ways, to the formulation of a research agenda and the execution of a research project. In practice, the dialogue in this ethical space is presently focused on how mainstream research can be more sensitive to and accepting of the unique contributions of Indigenous approaches. In short, the challenge is how to welcome the teaching of Indigenous research into the formulation of the actual resea   nterprise.

here is the valuing of personal experience, as people can be a special source of information about their own lives. No need to use the labels of *subject* and *experimenter* to do valid and valuable research; those two groups can be more connected within the research process, stressing a collaborative effort.* Participants who offer data can be more than simply objects from which data is *extracted*. And observation, which is central to all forms of research, can be not only careful but also more caring and sensitive—respecting sources of data as intrinsically valuable. Within that ethical space, with its aim of deconstructing the colonial agenda expressed through the domination of the mainstream approach, the need for research to make a difference in people's lives becomes more recognized.

Allowing vulnerability to animate the research process, there is a movement away from the protective mantle of conventions and expectations. As the researcher gives up the conventional role of the expert as being the one in control and nourishes the role of being expert in listening, the better to offer relevant contributions based on his or her specialized knowledge base, other partners in the research process become empowered. As Ratu Civo says, "Share what you know, no more . . . *and* . . . no less." The researcher shares what he or she knows—sharing, not directing.

These Indigenous influences on the nature of research are not meant to be copied by mainstream approaches: such an assimilation would not only be unethical, it would also detract the essential values from those Indigenous approaches. Yes, the mainstream approach can benefit from the *influences* of the Indigenous approach, but it cannot and, we would argue, should not seek to be the same. We need to build structures of

---

*Straits et al. (2012) have written an important document detailing the principles necessary for doing research in Indigenous communities—meant primarily for non-Indigenous researchers who might enter Indigenous communities under the mantle of science without considering the necessary respect for the community. One principle is that of "co-learning and ownership" so that research involves a "reciprocal exchange of knowledge and ideas" between researchers and the community (11).

collaboration between these Indigenous methods and Western methods, each maintaining the uniqueness of its contribution. For example, Indigenous approaches can be supported in their uniquely qualified ability to research the more dynamic, deeply personal and spiritual aspects of human experience, and thus psychological research in general can be more of a fully human enterprise. A richer, more effective and revealing process of research can result from collaborations between mainstream and Indigenous approaches, allowing psychological research to be a more fully human method of seeking knowledge.

This more fluid, respectful approach to research, with its emphasis on one's personal experience and dynamic meaning making, can lay a foundation for psychology to reconsider the wide variety of issues we face in our lives over time and space. Do our lives follow clear, linear, sequential stages of development—as expressed in Indigenous approaches; or is our life journey characterized more by the fluidity of the unexpected and the recurring nature of the fundamental challenges and dilemmas of what it means to be human—as expressed in Indigenous understandings? Indigenous teachings support this lack of predictability in our life's course while still maintaining the importance of natural rhymes and the steadfast nature of guiding moral principles. If this fluidity is to be respected, and hopefully understood, our acceptance of vulnerability can provide a foundation for this challenging life rhythm. Then it's good to know we have the research approach that can allow us to know that fluidity—and learn from it.

CHAPTER FIVE

"All In the Circle of Our Lives Remains Valuable"

Nourishing a Recurring Fullness throughout the Life Cycle

Knowledgeable in both the traditional teachings of his Fijian culture and its contemporary changes, my dear friend and guide Ifereimi Naivota is robust and articulate, a man of large dreams and strong actions. We're now sitting with Ratu Civo, the Fijian healer to whom I'm apprenticed. The conversation turns to our paths in life, our human development.

"I think about Naivota here," Ratu Civo says. "He was born into the responsibility of serving his community. He comes from a line of traditional spokespersons for the chiefs. That's a very important job." With a smile of approval, Ratu Civo adds, "Then he had the good fortune to be accepted into medical school . . . a real honor for us Fijians." Ratu Civo continues: "But it didn't work out . . . he was asked to leave." Naivota nods in agreement. "But that's how it is," Ratu Civo says. "What we *do* in our lives is never in a straight line—we don't expect to just get more and more things. We can't predict what will happen."

"I know what others might say," Ratu Civo reflects, "that Naivota has had *good* times and *bad*. Some might say the honor of medical school is good, the shame of dismissal bad. But for us, all parts of our life are for learning and teaching. There's no good or bad, only different ways to learn."

"Yes, our life *events* don't follow a straight path. All we can do is to try to remain on the straight path, which means trying to remain honest, respectful, and humble—straight in *our attitudes, our being,*" Ratu Civo adds. "And our life's path always seems to circle back on itself . . . and there we are, facing an old, familiar challenge again . . . and maybe in a new way."

"Naivota's continuing his struggle to be straight in his heart. No one told him how to be straight during that medical school journey. He had to find his own path. It's not a *bad* thing leaving that school—it wasn't a *mistake* that he made. It's important only as a *teaching* thing. Naivota is now meeting again the challenges of that school time . . . right now in his life as a spokesperson for the chiefs."

And with a gentle teasing tone, Ratu Civo adds, "Just look at him—doesn't he look a bit wiser now?" Naivota succumbs to an almost instinctive pride and then, with a gentle cough so he can cover his mouth—and his smile—he tries to look modest.

But how do we try to remain on the straight path? Crucial is an understanding that life is in flux, and all parts are valuable for learning. There is no emphasis on what is good or bad as much as what are the different times and ways of learning. It's not so much how we learn from our mistakes but how we learn from life. The challenging fact is that the straight path is in *lived experience;* there is no preconceived plan. As well, the straight path is actually perceived as a circle, as the challenges we face to remain straight keep reappearing, offering the same basic lessons of life in a variety of forms. "All in the circle of our lives remains valuable" is how Ratu Civo puts it.

Does mainstream psychology pick up some of these Indigenous teachings about the dynamically circling nature of human development, which remains committed to an aim beyond individualistic concerns? What does Jean Piaget, an icon of mainstream developmental psychology, have to say about this? Studying children, he comes up with a very linear, sequential, and hierarchical model of development—no circles or circulating rhythms in sight! What is he missing?

MAINSTREAM APPROACHES

I play peek-a-boo with our year-old grandson Jayden as I hide behind the door. It's a captivating, thrilling game for him, joyful and a bit scary, as it feels like I'm gone, but he knows I will return or will be found at any moment, the key being an *unexpected* moment—even though my hiding technique may have some obvious flaws. Jayden screams with delight when he finds me, even more so when I "find" him, as I leap out from behind the door. I scream too—with delight! And though my hiding place has now been discovered, its magic of discovery persists, as we hide and seek behind the door time and time again.

The French psychologist Jean Piaget would say the game of peek-a-boo is successful because my grandson understands the "permanence of objects." When something like an object or person is out of sight, he knows it can still exist, but the actual finding of the object, perhaps because of a suspension of some part of logic, is an act of surprise, if not wonder. The game delights us, as adults, because we get into that wonderful child world of imagination, where what we know becomes less important than the mystery we surround that knowing in. Before Jayden has developed the ability to perceive the permanence of objects, peek-a-boo would not work: if he thinks that when I hide, I'm gone forever, there is no need to look for me and then be in a state of terrified joy because from his point of view, I no longer exist. How can you look for something that is not there?

So Jayden and I both continue with this game of illusion and reality, egging each other on, wrapped up in our elemental joy. But as my grandson moves along in his developmental path—or, as Piaget emphasizes, goes through the cognitive stages that bring him to adulthood—the primal delights of peek-a-boo become rarer and less easily generated, as the tempering and moderating influence of reason grows.

Permanence of objects, as well as other cognitive abilities and perceptual skills such as the conservation of mass,* lie at the core of Jean Piaget's stage theory of cognitive development, a revolutionary model he proposes in the 1960s. Piaget says that we move through relatively discrete stages of cognitive development, passing beyond the concrete to figure out the concrete realities of the previously impenetrable peek-a-boo, moving into more and more abstract cognitive abilities in adulthood, such as being able to figure out a complex math problem or extracting a moral principle from a set of activates and actions. These stages, resulting from the interactions between innate neurophysiological and environmental factors, are keyed to chronological ages.

The stages proceed in a rigid sequence, so we never have to go back to earlier stages to relearn their lessons, but those earlier stages, once learned, serve as the necessary jumping-off point for later stages. Development is linear not circular. The sequence of the stages also forms a hierarchy so that the later the stage, the more cognitively sophisticated we become and thus the more effectively we can adapt to and shape our world. We become better and better at doing what mature, capable adults do; development becomes a successful passage through the challenges and skills that when added up describe what Piaget considers as successful adulthood.†

---

*Before learning about conservation of mass, children think that when the same amount of liquid is poured into two different containers—one tall and thin, the other short and stout—what they think is apparently the larger of the two contains more liquid. When asked why, a child typically says the tall one has more water "because it's bigger." The child cannot yet see that a certain amount of water in a container remains the same even when the shape of the container changes.

†Piaget's conception of the path toward adult cognitive development shares many characteristics with what is often proposed in mainstream introductory psychology texts as the path toward scientific thinking. For example, these texts often talk about the importance of "critical thinking," stressing logical examination of alternatives and

Piaget's original formulation of his stage theory of development is neat and clean, and in the ensuing years there have been many revisions challenging that clarity. For example, the Piagetian model has been modified to make it more sensitive to cultural variations in achieving stages as well as to newly discovered cognitive capacities in infants.* It is more focused on transitions between stages than on stages as discrete entities so that cognitive functions that overlap stages are now considered as important as those that signify a particular stage.

So if Piaget's original groundbreaking theory of human development is now dated, why am I turning to his work as a current example of the mainstream approach? I believe that the essential elements of Piaget's theory constitute a *paradigm* for what mainstream psychology still seeks in its approach to understanding human development. For example, Piaget emphasizes *stages achieved* more than the *processes* of achieving them,† and he sequences those stages in an invariant and therefore predictable order, moving along a hierarchical path as the individual reaches higher (and better) functioning as she or he develops, going beyond attachments to the concrete toward a grasp of and participation in abstract and conceptual thinking—up to the point when declines set in. These emphases represent ideals that still

---

(cont. from page 246) reliance on data before reaching conclusions. This critical thinking is a shorthand way of describing the scientific thinking that lies at the heart of mainstream research. The Piagetian emphasis in adult cognition on logicality and empirically based observation makes me think that he's suggesting that adulthood can be characterized as when we become "good" mainstream scientists. "Unscientific" cognitive processes like intuition are not stressed. The developing child then becomes in large part a little scientist, learning increasingly sophisticated Western scientific processes and methods.

*Baillargeon (2004), for example, demonstrates a form of object permanence in infants as young as two and a half to three and a half months, much younger than the age proposed by Piaget for developing that cognitive capacity.

†Piaget does discuss the critical concepts of *assimilation* (placing new data into old cognitive categories) and *accommodation* (changing cognitive categories to take account of new data), interrelated processes that help explain how we process data and encourage or discourage transitions between stages. But these two interrelated processes are dynamic and fluid, making them less attractive to mainstream developmental research and its preference for static and discrete—and therefore measurable—variables.

motivate researchers in the field of human development. Piaget's theory is even more influential because it proposes a research-based model for unlocking the complex processes of development. He describes a model of cognitive development that can be measured according to mainstream research methods, yielding clear, discrete data, and it can be viewed as generic since Piaget sees cognition as a basic life capacity for everyday functioning, including moral development.

It's important to state here something that's obvious and significant, though that significance is not fully appreciated within mainstream psychology. When the mainstream speaks of human development, the stress is on *human*—as human is the standard of excellence. The development of other species is studied primarily in a specialized area called comparative psychology and then primarily as a way to better understand or illuminate humans and their uniqueness—rather than the animal species studied. For example, research attempts to discover if apes have a language have emphasized the severe limitations to primate communication, reaching the conclusion that apes have no language in the formal sense—thereby bolstering humans' unique linguistic capacity. The Indigenous belief that other species also have a sacredness of life and have their own ways of communicating beyond the specifics of *human* language is ignored. Thus research on development in other species has a severely limited focus.

Western models of human development, focusing on dimensions such as the neurological, cognitive, linguistic, temperamental, personality, and psychosocial, avoid, in general, a consideration of the spiritual dimension.* Instead, there is a special attraction to the biological

---

*One of the examples Piaget offers of how children mature in their cognitive development is when they learn that the moon is not following them as they walk outside on full-moon nights—even though experientially it might seem, and even feel, that way. But I wonder whether a child can come to see that while the moon is not *physically* following her, it is also, and even more closely, *spiritually* following her. From an Indigenous perspective, the moon is a powerful spiritual force, offering knowledge and protection to humans. A child can keep these two dimensions of moon knowledge and be the more whole and developed as a result.

dimensions or underpinnings of development, which would include the neurological and genetic levels. These biological levels, being hard-wired, are more predictably sequential, typically following an invariant, internal logic—all very satisfying to the fundamental commitments of the mainstream approach. Both Piaget and Erikson, for example, stress there is a neurologically based foundation to the sequencing of stages, as innate capacities interact with environmental influences; Erikson calls this foundation the epigenetic principle.

As assuredly as the infant cannot "think" about abstract philosophical dilemma, the adult—if his development is proceeding as scheduled—is not fooled by peek-a-boo. This developmental certitude is comforting to the mainstream approach that emphasizes predictability. It minimizes the ambiguity, complexity, and therefore especially human characteristics that a circulating Indigenous model entails, where tasks of life can occur repeatedly and challenges appear unexpectedly, all within a context of overlapping rather than discrete experiences—life as a moving target resisting efforts to pin down exactly what is happening.

While focusing primarily on adapting successfully, even creatively, to life and its challenges, mainstream approaches generally lack a set of value-rich guiding principles to orient the directions and aims of that development, especially how persons can experience their own ego boundaries. As a result, mainstream approaches emphasize the *adaptive* functions of development rather than the *transformative* potentials that Indigenous approaches see as inherent in development. Adaptation emphasizes constructing healthy and effective relationships within the givens of society and culture, though not necessarily accepting toxic and oppressive conditions. Transformation emphasizes going beyond adaptive responses to the creation of new and transpersonal realms of human experience and relationships with social and cultural contexts. Even discussions of moral development, an area ripe for an examination of spiritual influences, often shy away from a full embrace of the spiritual influences, especially as embedded in our daily lives. For example, as Piaget emphasizes the balancing of the processes of assimilation and accommodation as guiding developmental principles, he speaks about a *neutral* process of emerging strategies for successful adaptation—to whatever the society or culture offers.

The developmental theory of Freud, though it charts the path toward increasing understanding and self-acceptance as an end point, also emphasizes adaptation more than transformation. There is a focus on the person's inevitable struggles to bring elements of the unconscious into consciousness, in order to better understand the crippling effects of the now unconscious experiences of early anxiety and misplaced attachments. The energy of the developmental path can be exhausted by the time these healthy adaptations are achieved, leaving untapped transformational potentials.

Erikson introduces value orientations as guiding principles for development, offering the possibility for transformative changes. For example, in meeting her initial developmental challenge during her first year, the child must face the developmental crisis of trust versus mistrust. "Can I trust the world?" is what the child seeks to learn. "Are those looking after me trustworthy and dependable or undependable, even abusive?" If the former, the child can learn to trust, feeling secure and optimistic; if the latter, the child learns more about mistrust and can become frustrated and suspicious, lacking confidence. Learning trust establishes the basic value of hope in the child's world. The way in which the child meets each developmental crisis determines how effectively he will meet the next sequential crisis; for example, after trust versus mistrust comes the crisis of autonomy versus shame and doubt.

Despite his richly nuanced conception of developmental crises, eight in total, Erikson's early theorizing does not offer the overarching and teleological framework that appears in the Indigenous concept of the spiritual path as a way of life. Though his final stage of ego integrity versus despair promises the value of wisdom with a successful meeting of that final crisis, that wisdom falls short of the wisdom that is central to Indigenous concepts of development. Erikson is speaking about wisdom as more of an expression of knowledge from life experiences, including the preparation for death, rather than an appreciation for the realms beyond individuals and communities, and is more the characteristic of a *particular* stage in life than a *continuing* guiding principle for living, as exists in Indigenous approaches.*

The invariant sequential and especially the hierarchical nature of mainstream models of development give rise almost naturally to a developmental pathway that can be described as following a rising line, reaching a peak, and then declining. Getting better and better—smarter, stronger, more sophistical, more understanding—as one moves to the next and better stage, fulfills the Western fascination with the idea of progress that underlies many of psychology's self-definitions.

Since the linear model does not embrace the notion of infinity, the line does not keep going upward and onward but reaches a peak and then begins to descend, as human functions deteriorate.[†] Just as the higher stages are more positively valued, the stages before and after are less valued. This unequal valuation of stages leads to differing amounts of attention paid and respect given to the various stages. As quick, logical thinking with rapid shifts in focus is often considered a sign of intellectual prowess and therefore a sign of a person's worth, people with more of those intellectual skills, such as young adults, are valued more than older people in their intellectual decline—especially

---

*But as discussed in the Countercurrents section of this chapter, Erikson's model eventually moves toward a spiritual enriching of this final stage, concomitant with his and his wife's own aging process.

†The irony of Maslow's peak experience is that, almost by definition, what comes after and before is not as intense or deep. That's one reason he introduced the concept of the plateau experience, a more sustained state of being, where the values of the peak experience live but not so intensely or purely.

since intellectual prowess can often be used as a measure of a person's worth. As well, transitions into those stages of prowess are more discussed, even celebrated, than transitions into stages of decline—which if discussed are often done in hushed, pitying words or made light of ("look at me; I can't even remember my hat's on my head").

There is also in the mainstream approach a differential valuation of aspects of human functioning. From an Indigenous perspective, four aspects are stressed: the emotional, physical, intellectual, and spiritual. Each is valued for its own qualities, and each is equally valued. But even someone like Maslow, who typically would be a source of countercurrents, demonstrates this Western tendency to differentially value parts of human nature.

When I come back from my first visit to the hunting-gathering Ju/'hoansi of the Kalahari Desert, I go to Abe Maslow's house to show him some slides of the Ju/'hoan healing dance. In that dance, the healers struggle to make available the healing powers of their boiling spiritual energy (n/om); it is an intense spiritual experience, manifested with dramatic physical struggles, including profuse sweating and uncontrollable falling and writhing on the ground. The sweating in fact becomes a fluid of and vehicle for spiritual energy, the loss of physical balance a result of the power of that energy.

Abe is very interested in seeing this Ju/'hoan healing dance but is not able to appreciate its profound spirituality. He wants to learn more about the variety of paths toward intense spiritual experiences; in fact, Stan Grof, whom I first meet when he arrives from his home in Czechoslovakia, is here tonight to talk about his research on psychedelics. But Abe can't quite connect to the Ju/hoan healing dance. "Boy, they really sweat a lot in that dance," he comments, almost as if drawing away from the sweating bodies. "That shows how much their healing activity is still on a physical level," he continues. "They have a way to go before it can reach the higher stages of self-actualization and spirituality." Abe is trapped in his own hierarchy of needs, where physical actions such as those that involve sweating and loss of bodily stability are relegated to the realm of the lower less valued needs.

And in general the stages of development posited by the mainstream perspective still lack depth and richness, offering truncated versions of what is humanly possible. The area of intelligence is one example of these missed opportunities. The mainstream approach emphasizes a concept of intelligence influenced by the convenience of what can easily be *measured;* in fact, it is often said that intelligence is what the intelligence test measures.* And what does that test measure? Memory, spatial understanding, vocabulary, mathematical skills, and verbal language skills. The test gives a score on each of these skills and then an overall score to sum up those skills (an IQ score), and then places that score on a scale that both identifies the intellectual level of the individual (e.g., borderline, average, above normal) and how that individual compares to others (e.g., in the top 10 percent or the lower 25 percent). These rankings allow for any individual to be considered either as a good candidate for potential placements or as someone who should be excluded from those placements; for example, deciding who goes into accelerated learning and who goes into special education—placements that often determine a person's future.†

---

*This function of the IQ test is an example of the mainstream's definition of validity: a test is valid if it measures what it says it will be measuring.

†There is a terrible irony in the history of this IQ test. Originally, it is developed in France by Binet, and is meant to identify children who need more help in achieving normal developmental aims and scholastic requirements. It is meant to *include* more children into the mainstream paths of academic success, not to *exclude* them from such paths. Binet emphasizes that any one child's score is not to be compared to the scores of others, as each child's score is to be used for the benefit of improving that one child's performance and enlarging that one child's possibilities. Finally, he insists the test be delivered on a one-to-one basis so that the tester can better understand how the child is actually responding to the test and better support that child in the task. As the IQ test comes across the Atlantic, the Western influences takes hold, now emphasizing the ability of the test to exclude, the need to compare people to one another rather than looking at individual's own distinctive condition and potential, and the convenience of group testing, introducing testing efficiencies but ignoring characteristically individual attributes.

But the IQ test proposes that a very limited range of skills and aptitudes define a potentially deep and even profound concept of human intelligence that includes emotional, artistic, interpersonal, and intrapersonal aspects. These aspects will become the focus of countercurrents within the mainstream. And where is the dimension of wisdom, introducing spiritual aspects? This dimension will be articulated by Indigenous approaches.

While mainstream psychology is emphasizing the perceptual and physiological development of infants, it is just beginning to study the richness of life infants express as a part of creation, such as their joys of discovery and novelty. Mainstream psychology sees the young adult as someone wrestling with certain moral dilemmas, but it pays little attention to the insoluble dimensions of morality that bring us all to a uniquely human set of dilemmas: for example, how do we realize and even embrace the way the unexpected—an illness, an accident, or a twist of fate—can completely change our worlds? And until recently, mainstream psychology represents old age as primarily a stage of deterioration, along not just physical but also intellectual dimensions.*

INDIGENOUS APPROACHES

Piaget brilliantly describes how children *adapt* to the challenges of the world through their growing intellectual and perceptual capacities, skills, and strategies. But he leaves out so much! So much of what are both the risks and potentials of development go *beyond* the tasks of adaptation; Piaget's model fails to explore the realms of experience beyond the self and community, which reveal themselves through transformational learning. "If we think we know our path," cautions Ratu Civo, as he works to deepen my understanding, "we're not really living our life. We only know our path as we walk it, and it is filled with

---

*Erikson makes a major contribution to work in human development when he extends the range of concern to include the full range of life's stages; in particular, he gives the challenges and potentials of old age a more realistic poignancy and texture.

unexpected turns and disappointments. We have to be alert and ready for anything."

Indigenous perspectives deal more with the dynamic, circulating quality of development rather than its preordered, invariant sequential quality. They stress that development is more about engaging in challenges than figuring them out, more a source of inspiration for creating one's life story than a description of where and how one has traveled through life. If we are to live such dynamic lives, it helps to have guidance—not prescriptions. Development is being and becoming human, which involves all points and phases in life as equally valued challenges, in contrast to the mainstream emphasis on becoming better and better and then drifting into an often-despairing decline.

In discussing particular Indigenous teachings about development, I highlight three paths: the Anishnabe seven fires; the Fijian straight path; and the Cree and Anishnabe approaches to the Medicine Wheel. In each case, I focus on *general principles,* teachings that apply to all of us. Though there are specific developmental tasks and ceremonies for males and females, these different rituals nonetheless encourage particular routes into these general principles.* Therefore, the general developmental path is emphasized, knowing there are always particular variations based not only on gender but also on the fact that each person goes on

---

*With the Ju/'hoansi, the developmental path into becoming healers is different for women and men. For example, women typically become healers only after their childbearing years are over. "When we're already suffering the pain and challenge of giving birth," says the female healer Karu, "we don't need to also get into n/om." Karu also suggests that childbirth is its own enhanced state of consciousness and brings healing to the community; no need for yet another one induced by the boiling n/om. But at the heart of Ju/'hoan healing—turning the boiling n/om into a healing force—men and women face the same developmental challenges, dealing with fears so that acceptance can be nurtured. "N/om is the same for men and women" is a common refrain in the Kalahari.

As another example, there are Anishnabe ceremonies of transition into maturity that differ for boys and girls. For example, for boys there is a transition ceremony that surrounds the first kill in hunting; for girls, it's the start of menstruation. But the general principle of being accepted into adult concerns and responsibilities, celebrated by those particular ceremonies, is the same for each sex.

her or his own specially forged journey. Also, these specific male and female tasks are typically meant more for direct transmission in a face-to-face relationship with a traditional elder; *Indigenous Healing Psychology* only deals with general principles meant for a wider audience.

The Anishnabe developmental model of the seven fires as taught by elder Danny Musqua can be especially challenging from a Western stage theory perspective because it *seems* to have stages, making it tantalizing familiar.* But when Danny talks about the seven fires of life, he is talking about spaces and places along life's journey that are sources of particular energy, allowing the person to be better equipped to meet certain challenges. Though the form of the challenge might differ, its substance keeps repeating. Danny tells me that in Saulteaux the word *fire* is defined as a "woman's heart." How could those seven fires as developmental energy points be contained into discrete stage-like boxes?

The seven fires mark and celebrate seven periods in life, which together describe our learning and growth. They identify chronological times when certain life challenges are more apparent and include conception to birth, birth to walking, walking to seven years, little men and little women, young adults, adult development, and old age and death. The life span is expansive, including times before conception and after physical death: "We don't see life as just starting when we can see it, like a fetus, or a body when the person has died," Danny emphasizes. "We care for the mother-to-be even before conception, being sure she is supported with a positive environment, and there is an important spiritual journey going back to the Creator, after we stop our physical breathing." Whereas mainstream psychology describes some of the physical and physiological aspects of conception, such as the negative effects of ingesting alcohol on the fetus, Indigenous approaches emphasize the importance of a full range of experiences during conception as part of

---

*In presenting Danny's ideas about the seven fires, I'm drawing on his written words as presented in Knight (2001), as well as conversations he and I have over the years. The Knight book, based on tapes of Danny's words, offers an excellent and detailed presentation of those teachings.

development: "As First Nations peoples," Danny Musqua states, "we realize the baby's spiritual journey has already begun with conception—and even before conception." The spiritual atmosphere in the womb lays a foundation for psychological and physiological influences.

The values highlighted during each of the seven fires reflect on each other. "In those first seven years," Danny adds, "we try to nurture our child, to lay a foundation, but we have to show them respect and model what we want them to do by our own behavior . . . otherwise, we can't expect them to be respectful and nurturing."

No developmental fire is more or less important than another; the often reckless curiosity of the child is honored as much as the measured wisdom of the elder. Though each fire is recognized by a celebration of transition, in which its new formulation of recurring challenges is noted, it is the string of celebrations, affecting each other, that constitutes the life journey. "Sometimes it seems we make more of one transition than another," Danny observes, "like when the child first walks, and we have a special ceremony, but whether the transition is dramatic like that or more subtle, like assuming adult responsibilities of caring for others, they are all celebrations—celebrations of life."

One of the ceremonies that help shape transitions is the naming ceremony. Typically, when the child is still young, sometimes early in the first year, the child is given a spiritual name, meant to be a source of spiritual protection and inspiration and a guiding light for the child's life course, emphasizing a particular set of strengths that will help carry him through the inevitable struggles of living.* Through the naming

---

*Though some may yearn for a conventionally powerful spiritual guide, carried with names that include the bear or the eagle or thunder beings, all names given in the ceremony are powerful because they point to parts of creation.

This naming is very different from labeling that can result from the mainstream preoccupation with diagnostic labels, a process exemplified in the *Diagnostic Statistical Manual* (DSM). Whereas the spiritually infused naming ceremony speaks to strengths and potentials, the psychiatrically determined diagnostic labels speak to problem areas needing fixing or therapy. A label of bipolar or schizophrenia establishes limits more than possibilities, a need for help to adapt more than a strength to forge ahead.

ceremony, a spirit is invited into the child's life, not to predetermine our journey but to show the child his path. "Once we have a spirit name, the work really begins," Danny emphasizes, "because we must make the choices and live the struggles that can fulfill the promise of that path." This spiritual guidance doesn't solve an individual's problems for us; it supports her in facing her challenges.

To make the person's travel through the seven fires more harmonious, there is special care taken to recognize and nourish a person's particular strengths and gifts. Danny talks about the role of the oskapayo in Anishnabe ceremonies. The oskapayo assists the elders in their performance of ceremonies, making certain the ceremony proceeds in the right way, being careful to include all the ceremonial elements the elder deems as important. For example, in the pipe ceremony, the oskapayo prepares the pipe for smoking, following the particular ways in which that elder works. The oskapayo responsibility requires attention to detail and respect for consistency.

Danny talks about how the oskapayo role nourishes strengths, including transforming a potential disability into a source of self-esteem. "We look at our young people, and if there is someone who is a bit developmentally slow, who finds comfort in repetition and order and who really thrives when things are predictable, then that person might be encouraged to become an oskapayo. It can be a great fit," he says, "giving that young person a responsibility and a job of great respect. It helps give them dignity. And their careful approach to things is just the kind of help an elder wishes to have when doing ceremonies."

For nearly three years, Ratu Civo guides me in what I label as "my efforts to learn about Fijian healing"; in essence, he guides me along the straight path—a spiritually based set of teachings about how and why we seek to live in respectful and worthy ways.* There is a set of values that exemplify the straight path that can guide one's travels toward

---

*Though Ratu Civo is teaching me about this path as the way healers should live, offering it as the key to my learning about healing, the straight path portrays the way *all* Fijians should live: "This is our way" he says.

fulfilling one's potential as a supportive member of the community. These values, all interconnected, include respect, honesty, humility, single-mindedness, love, and service. Each is to be lived at a depth often missing in Western conceptions of the same value. For example, love (*dauloloma*) means that we feel love for another person in that he is part of the sacred web of the universe; it's an unconditional love that does not demand that we agree with that person's lifestyle or even like that person. It is a love that embodies respect. With such profound meaning to its values, it becomes clear how the straight path is something to be constantly *sought after* rather than *found* or *accomplished*. Ratu Civo's teachings about human development as a journey through and guided by essential values, rather than the particulars of our jobs or achievements, is a common theme in Indigenous teachings, as are the specific values identified.*

There is no book or document describing the straight path; it's a set of teachings that emerge as we develop. We find—and lose—the path as we attempt to walk it. There are traveling companions along the way—not always helpful—but in the end it is our own journey to forge, create, unfold. "I can sometimes help to break your fall," Ratu Civo says, "sometimes give you directions, but I'm not always there. It's your path to find and travel. It's your life to learn. It's like cutting a path through the heavy bush with a machete," Ratu Civo continues. "We would like to go in a straight line, to get to our destination quicker, but the bush is filled with obstacles; big trees stand in the way of that straight line. So we cut a path around those trees. And sometimes we get lost . . . or we're at a dead end. Sometimes we realize, 'oh, we're back where we once were.' We've circled back on ourselves. But we keep going—we work to keep our intentions straight on a path that is never straight."

---

*For example, Saskatchewan Indigenous elders have a tipi brochure describing tipi teachings, where each of the fifteen tipi poles represents a value that is meant to guide our lives (Council of Elders 1988). Values include obedience, respect, humility, happiness, love, faith, kinship, thankfulness, sharing, and hope.

"My life is like that," Ratu Civo asserts. "I have all the support I need to lead a good and respectful life . . . but I keep facing unexpected challenges that divert me, that demand I travel along unexplored routes."

The values guide, but the actual journey comes from each person's life as it unfolds. The straight path has an aim, a value-driven destination, such as being honest and humble, but we learn about the path by walking it, doing it, living it. The straight path is about the process of being straight, meeting continually unfolding challenges, not about reaching a particular stage. If there is undue pride or a sense of accomplishment in reaching what seems like a stage or even a developmental marker, that's often when you're off the path: "That's when you get knocked down" is how Ratu Civo puts it.* He tells me about a Fijian healer who gains the people's respect from years of valuable practice. "People flocked to that healer. They sang his praises . . . and that's the dangerous trap. He began to feel confident, too confident. He lost his humility, and then he became unaware of the constant challenges to remain straight and that the further along you travel on the path the more difficult those challenges become. It was just when he felt securely . . . too securely . . . on the path, that was exactly when he fell off and was no longer worthy of the people's respect." Ratu Civo is teaching me about a moral and spiritual path unfolding.

Straightness is in the dedication to live well and honestly, and this dedication is necessary because life events and experiences do not happen in a predictable, linear way but keep unfolding in unexpected ways. To an outside, naïve observer, a healer's life path might seem linear, even ascending, but everyone's essential path, the inner life's work, presents a continuing series of moral challenges that keep appearing and

---

*Fijian healers encounter particular challenges in their struggles to be straight. Especially as their reputations grow and their pride is fed, the temptations to stray from the path—such as taking money for their work—grow stronger. Charging fees for their services and having inappropriate sexual contact with clients are the two most common temptations for traditional healers in many parts of the world.

reappearing. "You can't be honest or respectful all the time," Ratu Civo says. "All you can do is work toward being that way because what is honesty or respect keeps changing as our life situations change." In practice, those ways of being are more difficult as we work on them; to be honest as an adult involves a more complex and demanding challenge.

The Medicine Wheel offers another Indigenous perspective on development.* Drawing on spiritual principles, the Medicine Wheel is a set of teachings about how to achieve balance, harmony, connectedness, and wholeness within one's life space to benefit the community. It is a set of teachings that become active as one *engages* in them, working them into one's life to better understand them. The Medicine Wheel is typically conceived of as a circle consisting of four *equally valued* sections, each of which expresses many layers of meaning. The sacred number four is expressed in a variety of interconnected, equally important realms and experiences, such as the physical, mental, emotional, and spiritual. The four seasons and four directions also offer guidance about the tasks of living in the four stages of life: infancy, adolescence, adulthood, and old age. The Creator is seen as the center of the Medicine Wheel, animating the entire process.

The developmental challenge of the Medicine Wheel is to establish and continually reestablish balance among its four sectors or elements. For example, if one's emotional life becomes overdeveloped, and even dominates at a certain point, then the other three dimensions must be

---

*My discussion of the Medicine Wheel is based on Anishnabe teachings I hear from a variety of traditional sources, and the teachings of Cree elder Mary Lee. Though I hear Lee speak about the Medicine Wheel a number of times, I quote from her published teachings (Lee 2006a, 2006b). But I want to emphasize that I do not have the Medicine Wheel as a ceremony to practice, nor knowledge of its specific teachings—only knowledge of its general principles that are meant to serve as guiding lights for balanced and right living.

There is some controversy surrounding what seems like a too casual use of the Medicine Wheel symbol; for example, by some non-Indigenous institutions serving Indigenous peoples. A symbolic representation of the Medicine Wheel, stressing its four colors, might decorate an agency wall. But that may not indicate that the actual traditional Medicine Wheel teachings, if they are even used in the agency, are properly and ceremonially given to all those who profess to offer them.

nurtured to establish a balance, which is continually undone because life—and the Medicine Wheel—is dynamic.

The key is how you enter into the Medicine Wheel teachings and, by engaging them, attempt to live them. The wheel is in motion, constantly changing, as is our life. A person enters into the wheel in the place appropriate to his or her present situation and seeks to engage in the tasks of that part of the wheel. For example, as Mary Lee teaches, the West is the time of adulthood, where we become responsible for other people; when we enter the Medicine Wheel as adults, we engage that responsibility intensely as we become parents.

In contrast to the mainstream linear model of development with sequential and hierarchical stages, the Medicine Wheel offers guidance to a circular and circulating path; as one moves around the wheel and its teachings, issues of life keep reappearing in order to be reexamined and re-resolved. For example, you can be dealing with issues of infancy even when chronologically older because you are learning something about trust, typically an early developmental task, at a new level and, therefore, as if for the first time. Mary Lee (2006a) talks about the recurring teaching of our little ones:

> They continue to teach us as they grow . . . they will crawl, stand, fall down and get up again, and learn to walk. My mother used to say: "That child teaches you what life's going to be—you don't just get up once and walk forever—you will fall, and you will have to get up. Maybe you'll need to crawl a little bit, but you will get up and walk again."

My Fijian friend Naivota is living this teaching!

These three Indigenous developmental paths share features and emphases. They do not emphasize discrete stages but *ongoing, dynamic processes* that offer recurring challenges and opportunities and bring the person continually back into and forward onward to her life events and understandings. Instead of stages, there are overlapping and interconnecting *phases* that are initiating points in processes of development, times for celebrating transitions between life responsibilities. All phases are equally appreciated, and the challenges of living, such as committing to a moral path, keep reappearing at different points in life. Meeting any *one* particular challenge is deemphasized because it's just when a person thinks he has achieved something that he is in the most danger of losing it. Rather than becoming better and better, the Indigenous approach can offer opportunities to fill out the aspects of being human. A life lived becomes more important than any stage one is at.

As the lived image of the moving circle dominates Indigenous paths of development, there is an inevitable equality in appreciating all phases of that path: one doesn't get better and better but occupies different positions with differing attributes. It is really impossible to give differential weightings or evaluations to points along a circle; there is, for example, no top or bottom, especially when that circle is circulating and a person can enter at any particular place in that circle to deal with what is appropriate for her at that time. No room for hierarchy here! Each phase has its own ups and downs that are accepted as part of living at that time. And each phase is appreciated for what it is. The aim is for everyone, at whatever stage they're at, to be appreciated for who they are—at that point in time.

A primary characteristic is that Indigenous paths of development apply not just to humans but also to all parts of creation. In fact, humanity's place is at the lowest level of importance and draws sustenance from the struggles of other creatures and natural elements. "We must learn from the animals and other parts of nature," Danny advises. "They carry important spiritual teachings. Take the trees as an example. The trees have a spirit—they teach us about being grounded and being of service to others." Mary (2006a) adds that we "give thanks to Mother Earth for accepting our child to walk upon her."

Identity becomes a central experience in Indigenous approaches to development, an identity emerging from an understanding of who we are and our place in the universe. My friend =Oma Djo tells me about his eagerness to participate in a healing dance, to expand his consciousness so he can travel to the village of the gods to rescue the sick. "I want to dance again soon so I can feel myself," he says with a smile that invites me to join him in that impending journey. This identity, though apparently complex, is at its heart simple. I'm in the coastal Inupiat village of Kotzebue, in northwest Alaska, with local resident and elder Rachel Craig. She is an accomplished woman of the world who is a leader in her community. We're looking at a poster in the local village office that talks about Inupiat people making their way successfully into the modern Western world, which is increasingly diluting and displacing their traditional Inupiat values and world. The poster states, "I walk in two worlds with one spirit"—just what Rachel has done so successfully. "I'm not sure what that means," I say, turning to Rachel. "How does the spirit guide in two worlds?" "Well, you're making it more complicated than it is," she says. "I walk in two worlds, the Inupiat world and the white world. I live and work in both but as one person, a person of one spirit. At my core, in my spirit, I'm Inupiat!"

By stretching the ends of the developmental path beyond where mainstream approaches function and going more deeply into the meanings of developmental attributes, these Indigenous approaches bring more of a fullness or richness to the developmental process. For example, the Indigenous phase of being an elder adds depth to the mainstream Western conception of old age, while the Indigenous description of intelligence as an expression of wisdom gives added meaning to the mainstream conception of intelligence as a primarily logical cognitive function.

With the fully appreciated role of being an Indigenous elder, Indigenous approaches bring a vitality and deepened meaning to end-of-life phases of development. Whereas mainstream approaches are still struggling to document areas of strength in old age and generally do not posit old age as a desirable or desired state, emphasizing the declining of attributes and capacities, the role of Indigenous elder offers purpose, opportunity, and significance to Indigenous people in the final stages of their development, ushering in new forms of engagement and meaning. Indigenous elders are selected *by the community* to honor the wisdom they gain through reflecting on their lifetime of experiences, including their knowledge of sacred and traditional teachings and ceremonies. Being so honored, they have an honored role in the community. And they can feel the joy and meaning that flows from that role: "We elders have a purpose," says Ratu Civo, "and it gives a purpose to my life."

For example, while old age is valued for its potential wisdom, few welcome with enthusiasm the physical infirmities that also accompany that phase. But the infirmities are seen as part of the entire package rather than considered in isolation as purely negative features. The aim is to have the positive and negative balance out to create the phase.

Danny Musqua and I are talking about the inexorable wave of age-related infirmities that are becoming more familiar to each of us. With a mischievous smile, he tells me, "As long as I can still communicate, I'll carry on, even if I have to drag this old body around—or discover some fountain of youth and start acting a bit foolish again! And even though I can't move around very well anymore," he continues, "I can still sit here and look wise." We laugh together, helping each other enjoy the moment, knowing that an odd part of Danny's role as an elder is to *look* wise, as he knows that surface appearance is meaningless and sometimes what others, especially when young yet eagerly searching, expect to see.

There are temptations to place differential valuations to various phases of life rather than valuing differences. For example, there is a common misperception that Indigenous elders occupy a special phase in the journey of human development. People can place elders on a pedestal, approaching them with misplaced awe. But as Ratu Civo insists, "I'm just another person, like others, but my task is to teach, to pass on the knowledge I've been given. That's my task . . . but that's not making me special."

People can often forget Indigenous elders are also old people, not immune to the infirmities of old age. The elder offering his teachings—which can be a wonderful, inspiring time—is the same elder who needs help getting in and out of the car. Likewise, when raising a little one, it can be very demanding of time and patience—so much so that we can forget the gifts of light and energy and innocence they convey. Cree elder Emma Sand, into whose family I've been adopted, is looking at our newly born little one, wrapped snuggly within her blanket. She offers some counsel: "Our children are gifts from the Creator. They are only on loan to us—we don't own them. And as gifts from the Creator we must honor them . . . protect and nourish them . . . because they are sacred. They are treasures." Each phase of the life cycle has its special gifts, but none is more special than any other—only special at its own different time.

The role of Indigenous elder highlights a concept of intelligence that is enriched into an expression of wisdom. Elders offer teachings that combine the heart, mind, emotions, and spirit. Cree elder Louis Sunchild speaks about the "compassionate mind" (Lightning 1992). He explains how feelings like compassion are not separated from intellectual functions but merge with and define those functions. Intelligence is not a strictly cognitive exercise and certainly not a primarily logical one—as is so typical of mainstream conceptions. Rather, thinking is something that helps the development of a good life, intelligence something that matters in the well-being of the community. "I can't say that I'm smart in the school way," Joe Eagle Elk tells me with a satisfied acceptance. "Never did well in school . . . but that's not my way. I just try to have a good heart so my mind can go along and travel together in a good direction." Intelligence becomes wisdom, and that wisdom is expressed in all phases, in different ways—the wisdom of the child is valued, as is the wisdom of the elder, each for its own wisdom ways.

COUNTERCURRENTS WITHIN
THE MAINSTREAM

Having offered the Piagetian model of human development as a starting point, if not paradigm of the mainstream approach, emphasizing the orderliness and predictability of a linear, sequential, and hierarchical stage theory, I think a return to Piagetian models might be a good way to start a consideration of countercurrents to that mainstream. By starting here, I can talk about two of my former colleagues at the Harvard Graduate School of Education—Bob Kegan and Carol Gilligan. Both, being influenced by Piaget's conceptualizations,* seek to relax the rigidities of that model to better reflect the complexities, ambiguities, and potentialities that characterize a fuller understanding of development.

A man with an at times youthful exuberance and intentionally unexpected approach to conventional wisdoms, Bob now proposes a spiral model of development, which though sequential and hierarchical is not rigidly so, as the spiraling processes break out of the more simplistic focus of linearity.† To further emphasize the nonlinearity of his model, Bob talks about the "evolving self," a way of stressing developmental processes that develop more realistically in everyday contexts, displaying stops and starts, unexpected dilemmas, and previously undiscovered strengths rather than a predetermined path.

Intensely curious and dedicated to researching her emerging perspective, as, for example, early on with a group of engaged Harvard graduate students, Carol Gilligan brings a renewed focus on a *more complete range* of fundamental value orientations as guiding principles to development and on ways these values effect social justice and equity.‡ Rejecting the finding in Kohlberg's work that women generally score lower in

---

*Piaget's influence is deeply felt in the Department of Human Development. For example, Lawrence Kohlberg builds his model of moral development on Piagetian principles; he also serves as an early mentor to both Carol and Bob.

†See Kegan (1982) for an early formulation of these ideas.

‡See Gilligan (1982) for an early presentation of her ideas.

tests of moral development than men, she insists that values more often expressed by women, relational values such as caring, need to take their equal place in any assessment of a person's level of moral development, whereas values typically expressed by men, justice values such as what is right or wrong, had previously dominated those assessments—and thereby incorrectly ensured men would be scored as having higher levels of development. Though Carol's work is dramatically embraced by the feminist movement, which she supports, she still wants to talk about relational values as necessary *human* ways of being and especially pathways to social change. Carol and I feed each other's excitement in learning and teaching and grow from that exchange.

Another most impressive example of revisions to the mainstream stage model is provided by the husband-and-wife team of Erik and Joan Erikson. Yes, Erikson's eight-stage model is already discussed as part of the mainstream approach, but it's the work that occurs in the later years before and following Erik's death that introduces important and dynamic changes. There is new realism, appreciating more the significance of the difficulties in each stage, a new openness to the unexpected, and an appreciation for the recurring nature of developmental challenges—all pointing more in the direction of Indigenous emphases.

Much of this new appreciation for deep complexity in human development comes as the Eriksons, and especially Joan, look back over their own lives, now from the perspective of being themselves *old* (see e.g., Erik Erikson 1987 and Joan Erikson 2010, 2012). A ninety-two-year-old Joan says, in speaking about the classic eight-stage model and especially to those who are its adherents, "We owe you an apology. Now that I'm old myself I see things differently. We really didn't know what we were talking about when we wrote about the later years of life when we were ourselves still *young!*" (Erikson 2012).

The original Eriksonian model stresses the ability to revisit earlier stages, to work again on an earlier crisis whose initial resolution was fragile or incomplete or though seemingly firm now reopens in the face of newly overwhelming subsequent life events. For example, the earliest

Eriksonian stage presents the infant with the challenge of establishing trust in her life, establishing a relationship with parental caregivers. But later life events can reopen that challenge of being able to trust one's world, perhaps through the devastating abandonment by a loved one. As a result, earlier successful adaptations can become undone, and new feelings of trust, at new levels of maturity and complexity, become necessary.

With their most recent revisions, the Eriksons propose that this ability to revisit earlier stages where a crisis has been met is more a *need* to revisit and keep revisiting. In fact, they propose a ninth stage, which emphasizes transcendence, during which a person is challenged to revisit all the earlier stages, now from the perspective of a life nearly completed. Reflecting back over his life, a person revalues, reworks, and reestablishes ways in which earlier crises are met and, now with a deeper understanding of those crises and earlier responses, establishes more mature and nuanced forms of adaptation. This reworking of one's life establishes new meanings and a deeper respect for the complexities and enduring challenges of living a full life—a conception of the last stage of life that brings the Eriksonian model closer to the Indigenous conception of the elder as a role someone grows into at the end of her life.

The Eriksons also suggest that each of the eight prior crises be reformulated so that the "negative" end of the continuum be emphasized rather than the "positive" end; the first stage presents the crisis of mistrust versus trust rather than trust versus mistrust. Giving primacy to what they call the distonic form of the developmental challenge rather than the syntonic form allows the Eriksons to welcome into more serious consideration the fact that life is a series of ups and downs, positives and negatives; as both are accepted as part of life, a more realistic form of acceptance can occur.* With this deepened respect for the

---

*Psychology's research on the concept of resiliency demonstrates this renewed interest in both the reality and importance of life's challenges but also the potential for learning within those so-called negative experiences—as more and more evidence accumulates about our ability and motivation to face adversities and, with that, open the door to learning and growth.

challenging parts of life's challenges, including the learning potential inherent in suffering, the Eriksons move toward an Indigenous perspective that there is teaching value in all stages of life and the need to respect the so-called negative parts of the life process, as well as the full form and power of the positive aspects, against which these negative forces are artificially pitted.*

The forces of resistance within mainstream psychology have attempted to enhance its model of human development by adding depth and complexity to the attributes, attitudes, and capacities used to define that development. Revisions to the mainstream concept of intelligence are a prime example. Dissatisfied with the limitations of the mainstream conception, which emphasizes intellectual capacities easily measured by objective tests, psychologists are expanding and deepening what it means to be intelligent—though they still generally fall short of the Indigenous embracing of the merging of the mind, emotions, body, and spiritual and especially how the infusing of the spiritual helps to create the concept of wisdom.

Howard Gardner proposes that there are multiple intelligences.† In addition to the intelligences emphasized by the mainstream and measured by the standard IQ—verbal, mathematical, and spatial intelligences—there are also musical, kinesthetic, interpersonal, and intrapersonal intelligences. A person very skilled in physical movements and agile would be demonstrating kinesthetic intelligence; a person sensitive to the feelings and intentions of others, interpersonal intelligence. When Howard is first developing these seven forms of intelligence, he asks for my comments. "Looks good," I say, "but I think you might have left something out . . . How about spiritual intelligence?" "I know what you mean," he agrees, "but I just don't know how you would measure that spiritual intelligence . . . so for now, I'm not inclined to include it."

---

*Since the epigenetic principle underlying the Erikson model of development is not fundamentally questioned, there remains a sequential order within this newly dynamic Eriksonian conceptualization.

†Gardner 2011 contains the original formulation of these seven intelligences.

I find Howard's work stimulating and, since it is so accepted within psychology and education, worth exploring further about how it relates to Indigenous perspectives on intelligence. For example, when he questions the ability to measure something like spiritual intelligence, Howard means not only the absence, even inability of standard psychological testing instruments to identify and hopefully quantify the actual behavioral, attitudinal, and motivational occurrence of something like spiritual intelligence but also the existence of an area in the brain that can account for its occurrence. I would agree with him: How could we develop standard, mainstream measures to identify, no less capture this constantly shifting, deeply felt experience? Also, it seems to be a misguided effort to locate a brain center or even correlate of that not only shifting but also pervasive and diffuse experience. But with his stance toward the inadequacy of available measurement tools, Howard is expressing the materialistic emphasis of mainstream psychology as opposed to the Indigenous perspective on the merging of realms, including the material and spiritual. Without hesitation, Ju/'hoan healers talk about how they *do* pick up and hold the spiritual energy of n/om.

In his later work, Howard does attempt to explore more actively intelligences that approach more spiritual realms.* For example, he explores the concept of existential intelligence, which speaks to a person's

---

*A form of intelligence that Howard Gardner seeks to add is called naturalistic intelligence and refers to a person's ability to sense patterns in and make correlations to phenomena in nature (Gardner 1999). One example he offers is the intellectual ability of early hunter-gatherers to know which foods are edible and which are not and in what amounts they might become one or the other—a capacity clearly important to survival. But Howard leaves out an important Indigenous teaching about this knowledge of nature; namely, the spiritually infused teachings about life and development demonstrated in the lives of animals, plants, and all of the natural universe around us. As Danny puts it, "It's the animals—really all of nature—that can tell us about how to live in a good way. How to conserve and how to use what we need. And the importance of respect for the animals and plants if we wish to be properly fed by our world. Take the bear as an example: the bear spirit teaches us about healing and the importance of protecting ourselves from threats. Just look at the mother bear with her cubs."

sensitivity to deep questions about human existence, such as the meaning of life and death and the ability to ponder and engage in such questions. But again, because he insists that any form of intelligence needs to be measured—both with psychological testing and brain imaging—he is reluctant to add such an existential intelligence to his original list of seven. Howard also adds that he is not in favor of expanding the concept of intelligence too broadly to include, for example, all the important human values and virtues.* As well, he wants to be sure any form of intelligence he proposes has its own distinct identity, separable from the other forms. This analytical emphasis of Howard's, including the desire to have separate categories defining a phenomenon like intelligence, is again expressive of the Western psychological approach. In contrast, Indigenous perspectives see intelligence not only as a merging of functions, including the mental, physical, emotional, and spiritual, but also including experiences that matter to humans, such as the spiritual. Indigenous elder Louis Sunchild beautifully demonstrates this merging and inclusively in his talk about compassionate mind (Lightning 1992).

Further work on enhancing the mainstream concept of intelligence is done by Robert Sternberg, who, with his triarchic theory, brings in dimensions of street smarts and innovative thinking to make intelligence a more realistic and more valuable factor on a wider range of human activity.† Appreciating the dynamic and creative aspects of intelligence, Sternberg emphasizes that intelligence as an experience develops over a person's lifetime and stresses the critical importance of the creative

---

*With the strong cognitive, even logical emphasis in Western concepts of intelligence, that concept becomes more strictly bounded and limited. It's commonly heard from Western researchers that "you can't put so many things into the concept of intelligence, otherwise you lose the concept itself."

Howard's reluctance to be more inclusive in his discussion of intelligence becomes more fascinating considering the fact that he is positively influenced by Erikson while both are at Harvard. Certainly, Erikson feels no restrictions in his examination of human motivation and development, the concept of wisdom being a prime example of the breadth of his purview.

†An early articulation of his triarchic theory is found in Sternberg 1985.

aspects of intelligence, those aspects that enable us to go beyond the given and create new ways of reconceptualizing old problems (see e.g., Sternberg 2007). Sternberg moves us firmly beyond the static, paper-and-pencil determined concept of IQ, opening up new paths of growth.

And then there is the dynamic line of theorizing offered by Danny Goleman, a longtime colleague. Danny builds on his own deep understanding of what makes us smart, including his long practice of Buddhist meditation, to develop a series of innovative and expansive ways of looking at intelligence, to include emotional, social, and ecological intelligence. Emotional intelligence stresses the ability to accurately assess one's own feelings as well as the intentions of others and regulate emotions so that there is more balance and understanding—abilities cultivated more intensely in Buddhist meditation. Such abilities open a door to the Indigenous consideration of the fullness of intelligence as a wisdom force in life. But though these innovative viewpoints give more life meaning to what intelligence is and what it could become, an obstacle remains. Though strongly articulated on the conceptual level, these viewpoints are held in check by the pervasive mainstream insistence on demonstrating the reality of a phenomenon by being able to measure it quantitatively.

Finally, developmental countercurrents seek to give fuller meanings to basic life values. Positive psychology takes this as one of its tasks, though it often falls short of the depths of Indigenous meanings. One example is the frequent emphasis in positive psychology on the experience of happiness. Positive psychology discussions of happiness, still primarily encased within a Western framework, too often focus on superficial expressions of happiness, such as feeling good,* which ignores the nuances and complexities in life, such as a feeling of happiness that can come with the acceptance of tragedy, a happiness born of equanimity. Also, the proposed centrality of happiness as a determinant of human fulfillment carries too many Western connotations; these

---

*"Feeling good" is typically how this happiness gets constructed in the media.

conceptions of happiness often imply ego or individual satisfaction and are too often fused with feelings of power as opposed to balance—suggesting, for example, that feeling power, rather than balance, makes one feel good or happy (see Datu 2014).

But in the end, the forces of resistance within mainstream psychology generally fall short of the pervasive spiritual dimension in Indigenous perspectives on development, a dimension that underlies development from conception to after death. When mainstream psychology does consider spiritual issues, it typically discusses spirituality as a concern happening in the later or last stages of life, when individuals turn more to questions about the meaning of life. And maybe it's appropriate that pervasive and deep spirituality remains within Indigenous approaches, where it can be properly cultivated and reach its fullest expression. Spirituality can be one of the unique contributions from the Indigenous side to future collaborations.

FUTURE COLLABORATIONS

As with all of our views into future developments, we think more in terms of collaborations between Western and Indigenous approaches to psychology. At the same time, there are ways in which mainstream psychology can be enhanced while still keeping its unique character so that its contributions to future collaborative efforts can be maximized. The Eriksons already demonstrate the gifts of those collaborative dimensions.

There's also so much room within mainstream psychology to broaden and deepen its foci on developmental tasks and issues. How much more understanding can emerge if old age is seen more as an opportunity for becoming like an elder, so that capacities for wisdom and teaching that might typically lie dormant in older people in Western contexts can be explored with more encouragement and sensitivity. This touches on psychologist Ellen Langer's work as she attempts to show the need for a shift from the mindlessness, which prevails in settings like senior care facilities, to a support for mindfulness, which encourages a spiritual dimension to mellow and inform the aging process into more of a wisdom stage. To accompany this, the narrow and narrowing focus on intelligence as a rational, logical adaptation can evolve into a concern for encouraging the emergence of intelligence as a wholistic functioning where wisdom and understanding are cherished.

Certainly, it can be helpful for mainstream psychology to appreciate more fully all aspects of developmental challenges, respecting each for its own tasks, seeing each as an equally valued part of the life journey. A hierarchical approach depreciates while it values, and thereby certain aspects of development are not fully studied or understood. A hierarchical approach, even if it puts a highly valued stage at the top that can represent the highest of aspirations and inspirations, remains hierarchical.

As the focus of mainstream psychology shifts more to this non-hierarchical valuation of developmental tasks and a fuller appreciation of developmental milestones and capacities, the richness—including the unpredictability, ambiguity, and dynamism—of everyday life is better understood. Though a circular model of development may not be realistic and is possibly best left for a more complete expression with Indigenous approaches, a loosening of the sequential rigidity and clearly bounded stages following a linear and upward pathway could open the mainstream approach to a more effective understanding of actual life journeys.

When the spiritual dimension of development is recognized and respected, there can be a fuller acceptance of these complexities, ambiguities, and challenges in life and the responsibility of each person to work toward dealing with them. As my adopted father and Lakota medicine man Joe Eagle Elk always demonstrates, we're not in control of our life's course, and our spiritual strength can sustain us within the unexpected. "I didn't choose to be a medicine man," he tells me. "That path was chosen for me. It's become my spiritual journey. Even though it's real hard. And there are times I wish I didn't have to do all those ceremonies.

But it isn't up to me to decide . . . And now I have to live that life with my own efforts—to make it work." As his life unfolds with many unexpected, often daunting challenges and losses, Joe's spiritual journey holds things together and gives him the strength to endure.

As the spiritual dimension supports the equal valuation of all phases and tasks in life's journey, giving each its own respect, it can also add substance and meaning to those phases and tasks. Child-rearing has the potential, even the imperative, of being work in the name of the Creator. But even without such an explicitly spiritual connection, the process of child-rearing, so crucial in developmental histories, can be enlarged and enriched with a perspective beyond human concerns and understandings, can be enlarged by going beyond a strictly mainstream psychological perspective.

An explicitly and extensively spiritual dimension in development may best be cultivated with Indigenous approaches. At the same time, spiritually inspired influences, such as recognizing the deeper meanings and responsibilities of child-rearing or the equal valuation of developmental tasks, can help mainstream approaches more generously see potential. Yet there remains an important caution—the need for balance. The Indigenous teaching is not to "be spiritual"; the teaching is having balance, where spirituality works in harmony with the physical, emotional, and mental dimensions of human nature. "Balance is what we seek. Balance is what allows us to be fully human," Danny Musqua cautions. "Yes, spirituality is key, perhaps the key, but without feeding our physical, emotional, and mental lives as well, we're out of balance. We're not healthy. We're not preparing for our return to the Creator."

Balance and its necessary correlate of imbalance are together intrinsic to and defining of the circular and circulating Indigenous model of development. In that model, each developmental task or opportunity or phase of life is valued equally since no points in a circle can stand apart or above, especially as that circle is in motion; each task or phase, as equal partners in life's journey, contributes to the value of the other tasks and phases, as it balances out and with them.

This dynamic of *balance* and *imbalance*—so crucial to fully human development—along with principles of respectful *exchange* are keys, as we'll see in the next chapter, to Indigenous approaches to health and well-being. These Indigenous approaches stress *healing* rather than *curing*. Yet mainstream psychology remains preoccupied with the more limited aim of curing, emphasizing the removal of symptoms rather than the more expansive aim of healing and a transformation of consciousness. For the mainstream to accept balance, along with exchange, as keys to its efforts in the area of health and well-being, is a mighty challenge—and opportunity.*

Joe Eagle Elk lives this connection between processes of human development and healing. His life is not smooth and predictable—he has times within the grasp of alcohol or the confines of jail, as well as times, much more intensely and extended, of dedicated and deeply honest service to the people. But it's a balance he's always sought, and that balance—built on his respectful exchange with the spirits that guide his work and the people he serves with his healing and his inner dedication to honesty—nurtures his healing energies. Despite all his deeply admired work, despite the essential role he occupies in his culture, I always feel in Joe a simple, almost unshakable humility, a key value in Indigenous understandings of full human development. He makes clear he is a *messenger* of the spirits, which provide the healing lessons, and thus only a *vehicle* for healing, so that, in the end, as he puts it, he's "just an ordinary guy."

---

*Our son Adam, a social work student at First Nations University, is taking a class from Danny. Danny is feeling his age these days, and Adam, choosing to sit beside him, leans over, inconspicuously whispering, "Let me know if there's any way I can help you out." And each time the class meets Adam takes his seat beside Danny, and each time asks him—once again—the same question. Danny loves how Adam, his adopted grandson, humbly enters into the respectful exchanges between and of life stages—and Adam loves being there in those exchanges. They both feel good and in balance.

CHAPTER SIX

"Health Is More Than Not Being Sick"

Balance and Exchange as Foundations of Well-Being

"Visiting . . . that's what we do. Just visiting." Mary Lee, a Cree elder originally from Pelican Lake First Nations in Saskatchewan, is describing how she does traditional Indigenous counseling. I've invited her to come to the culture and healing seminar I teach to clinical psychology doctoral students at the University of Saskatchewan.

In addition to her counseling, especially of Indigenous youth who are struggling with identity confusion, depression, and loss of hope, exacerbated by substance abuse, which sometimes develops into suicidal tendencies, Mary is also a respected source of traditional Cree teachings, especially in areas of female development and responsibilities.* One ceremony of living and healing in which Mary remains active and from which she draws many teachings is tipi making (see Lee 2006a).† Always expressing the spiritual meanings of that ceremony, she supervises the

---

*Mary Lee currently works as an elder at Oskayak High School in Saskatoon. Oskayak is a learning space available to Indigenous students who can thrive in an alternative school setting devoted to infusing the standard curriculum with a strong First Nations' cultural dimension, including opportunities to participate in pipe ceremonies and sweat lodges.
†A brief graphic presentation of tipi teachings can be found in Council of Elders 1988.

harvesting of strong, straight trees, which serve as the tipi poles, guiding those taking the trees to ask permission to use what the forest provides and ceremonially offer sacred tobacco,* and then continues her guidance in the erecting of the tipi, ensuring the poles are raised in a sacred manner and order. The care and respect she teaches as essential to tipi making also exists at the core of effective traditional counseling . "That's the way I was taught," Mary explains. "We worked in the bush to gather what we needed to survive—but always taking what we needed in a respectful manner."

Looking at Mary, you may wonder how she still does that kind of forest work since she's slight of build. But her appearance is deceptive: her strong will and moral commitment, poised beneath her soft voice and gently moving presence, give her physical strength as well. Mary is especially firm in ethical and spiritual areas, and when she finds something questionable, I've heard the solid note within her soft voice that is like saying, "I can't agree with what you've just said or done," or the resolute silence that speaks the same message. "I just follow what I was taught," Mary says. "I'm not adding things or leaving out things."

The clinical psychology doctoral students are a bright, engaged, and committed group. None of them are Indigenous, neither have they had much contact with Indigenous approaches to health and healing. For them, traditional Indigenous counseling is simply a different method from what they are being trained to practice—rather than a specific set of principles and techniques. But the students are open to learning, realizing that Indigenous counseling is not only a therapeutic approach but also an expression of Indigenous culture. This learning is more imperative since, unfortunately, most of their clients will be Indigenous people. As one consequence of racism and continuing colonization, Indigenous people in Canada are tragically overrepresented in the settings where these students will practice, such as jails and mental hospitals, as well as

---

*See Michell (1999) for a discussion about the meanings and ceremonial significance of tobacco offerings in Indigenous communities, with a focus on Northern Saskatchewan.

in doing testing for psychological referrals from the courts and schools. Connecting these students to Indigenous and especially Canadian First Nations approaches to healing is the primary purpose of the seminar, and I'm eager to have the dialogue begin.

But Mary's expression "just visiting" alerts the students to something unexpected. The phrase confuses them, as they silently wonder how this "visiting" can be considered counseling or even therapeutic. Mary's use of the word *just* is not intended to minimize the process of visiting but to emphasize it, placing visiting at the core of healing—visiting allows listening and hearing to occur.

The clinical doctoral students are trained in mainstream psychological therapies, such as cognitive behavioral approaches, which emphasize the *technical* aspects of therapy more than the *processes* and *values* of therapeutic relationships, such as empathy, stressing that experts, especially Ph.D.-trained clinicians, are needed to master those techniques. And even though they don't always fullheartedly accept these assumptions of their training, the students remain uncertain about what they're about to learn. But Mary's calm and knowledgeable presence brings them into unknown territories. Mary and the students are working within different therapeutic worlds, and their meeting in class becomes eventful and dynamic.

As Mary describes in more detail how she does this traditional counseling, the clinical psychology students begin connecting more to her work. They realize her counseling work is not *reduced* to visiting but *enhanced* by that process. "Sometimes young people can be overwhelmed by their lives. They find it hard to cope," Mary cautions. "And they want to talk with someone. They need to be heard. They come to my office, and I sit with them . . . and listen. I listen so they know they are *heard*. I don't see them as my patients or clients," she adds, "and I don't tell them what to do. They come to get some guidance in their lives . . . and then *they* decide what to do with that advice."

Yes, the students realize, listening is crucial to what they are already being taught, but it takes on a deeper meaning with Mary—listening because you respect the person who comes to you to be heard and listening without judgment. This respectful exchange cultivates the *listening* into *hearing* which can become *healing*.

Mary also talks about how she's come to do traditional counseling. "This listening, this visiting is what we do as elders," she continues. "We try to bring some of our own understanding of life's crises to the person seeking help. It's like sharing what we've learned, what our mistakes have taught us, the strengths our cultural teachings can offer." The students already know, from our previous class meetings, that being an elder requires lots of experience; it's a position that evolves from self-reflection on a long life lived. So they know Mary, as a traditional counselor, is highly trained—hers is a rigorous life training in contrast to their academically oriented guild-certified training. And because she is an elder, her counseling derives from her spiritual understanding and its healing nature.

"When these young people come to see me, they are out of balance," says Mary. "Balance is what's needed for health. Each part of the person—the physical, emotional, mental, and spiritual—needs to be expressed and to be in balance with all other parts. I can't solve people's problems," she continues. "I only do the best I can to care for others. Healing is a gift to be freely given," Mary emphasizes. "It isn't my power that heals but something beyond me, something spiritual that works through me."

The clinical students realize their commitment to diagnosis, so central to their training and eventual practice, can become prey to the medicalization of life's challenges. Clinical diagnosis is a powerful form of judgment, especially since it carries so much stigmatizing in addition to its prescription toward treatments. But Mary's concepts of being "out of balance" and "overwhelmed"? How can such concepts provide "proper" diagnoses? I remind them that while Mary's concepts stressing the importance of balance are not professional psychology diagnostic talk, they do convey how many people actually describe their problems—as difficulties or challenges to be worked on, not as diagnoses to be burdened with.

After Mary leaves, one of the students asks me: "But what about serious mental illnesses? Don't we need *more than* listening? What about psychopharmacology? What about those people who need to be committed to a mental hospital? What about schizophrenics?" "We always have to consider serious mental illnesses, and the real suffering they entail, and what might be appropriate treatments," I respond, "but the respectful listening that becomes hearing is not only therapeutic in itself but also remains a foundation for further clinical interventions, including, when appropriate, those mainstream ones you mention." And Mary Lee is not imperialistic in her approach: she respects and works with other therapists who use very different interventions.

Later that day I get an e-mail from another student; she asks: "Isn't this listening that Mary talks about what we are supposed to do as good clinicians? Isn't this what Carl Rogers emphasized?" "Yes . . . and no," I reply. "There's listening . . . and then there's *listening so one can hear.* Rogers talks about listening as an essential ingredient *in* good counseling; Mary talks about listening *as* good counseling."

Despite their questioning of Mary's approach, her humility and commitment to service strikes a poignant chord in the students: it's what they aspire to be in spite of the way their training pushes competence and expertise to the point of overconfidence. "Why do we always have to show how competent we are?" laments one of the students. "I don't always feel that way . . . at times I'm not sure what or why I'm doing something in my therapy sessions. I'm overtrained in competence." I suggest that Mary's talk actually shows how understanding and then accepting those confusions can help him be a good therapist.

At the end of our class, I seek both closure and inspiration: "We can work . . . and work hard toward better collaboration between traditional counselors and ourselves. As future clinical psychologists you'll have power in the mental health system. And you can make a difference when you see this traditional counseling as a model of best practices and a way to welcome Indigenous people into services they deserve and are still denied. And that would bring psychology into its important task of offering healing as social justice."

Mary Lee's work as a traditional counselor exemplifies how *healing,* as opposed to *curing,* is more characteristic of Indigenous approaches to therapy. While curing focuses more on fixing what is wrong with people (e.g., some diagnosed illness), typically through the removal of identifiable symptoms, healing is a broader, more dynamic, more open-ended, and respectful process. Healing can be seen as a movement toward meaning, balance, connectedness, and wholeness. Symptoms may not be removed— though few would oppose their removal—but healing can still occur. Meaning, for example, can be created in a life still carrying the symptoms of an illness. Rather than fixing someone, healing seeks to support and enhance ongoing life adaptations and transformation. Though healing and curing are not mutually exclusive and can influence each other in practice, curing is more frequently a focus in mainstream approaches.

Most important, Mary's acknowledgment that the source for healing is "beyond herself" opens the door for healing to become a renewable, expanding, and widely accessible resource—the kind of resource that encourages synergy, a cornerstone for a healing community. She still insists on the necessity for her own skill and understanding and her dedication to doing her part in the healing process. By being a caring listener and respecting her clients—challenging and demanding work— Mary becomes a clearer vehicle for the entrance of healing.

MAINSTREAM APPROACHES

In the wide variety of therapeutic approaches* in mainstream psychology, cognitive behavioral therapy (CBT) stands out. CBT emerges

---

*I will be using the terms *therapy* and *therapeutic* as general and inclusive terms to refer to processes, approaches, and techniques, primarily practiced within Western settings, intended to bring about healthier conditions in people, who are seen as clients. Other terms will be used for more specific purposes, such as *counseling* instead of therapy and *patients* instead of clients.

dramatically toward the end of the twentieth century as an alternative to the prevailing psychodynamic therapies.* Offering a short-term approach that seems immediately comprehensible with its logical and rational principles of functioning, CBT is seen as a more welcoming, user-friendly, and cheaper alternative to the psychodynamic approaches, which, with their emphasis on the long and difficult work of uncovering the unconscious causes of mental illness, can seem too demanding and inaccessible. Featuring an oft-documented—though at times limited—effectiveness,† coupled with an ease of application, CBT has flourished. It is undeniably helpful to utilize a therapeutic intervention like CBT, which can end symptoms that can be painful and debilitating and even life-threatening—such as phobias of being outside or destructive behaviors such as adolescent cutting—regardless of whether we understand underlying causes. CBT does not exclude therapeutic work on those underlying causes, appropriately dealt with from within

---

*Though emerging originally from a strict behavioral approach, as exemplified by Skinner's focus on observable behaviors, CBT blossomed into its more contemporary form with the inclusion of thoughts and emotions as proper foci, considering them also as behaviors that could be worked with therapeutically. Albert Ellis, with his rational emotive behavior therapy (see e.g., Ellis 1993a), and Aaron Beck, with his behavioral therapy (e.g., Beck 2005), are two of the leaders in this broadening influence.

†Often in research comparing various Western therapies, CBT is demonstrated to be more effective. But that comparative effectiveness of CBT can be a bit misleading. First of all, that effectiveness is typically limited to removing symptoms and curing specific and more limited mental problems, such as phobias and specific anxieties, rather than more generalized and serious conditions, such as schizophrenia. Yet there is also research showing the effectiveness of CBT in treating more serious conditions like depression (see e.g., Beck 2005). Second, there is more research done on CBT because it is more amenable to being researched—especially within a mainstream outcome paradigm. For example, CBT inputs and outcomes are typically cast in terms of concrete, measurable steps or variables, such as the presence or absence of a particular symptom or the lessening severity of that symptom (e.g., the increasing ability for a person suffering from agoraphobia—a fear of being outside in crowds—to enter increasingly crowded situations). And third, there are still too few solidly substantiated comparisons among different forms of therapy. For example, outcome or "success" in most studies remains poorly defined—except in the limited terms of symptom removal and then not often in a long-term study.

an analytic or humanistic-existential framework, which can be pursued more fully once destructive symptoms are dealt with. In my own therapeutic work, I use CBT techniques in just that way, to remove debilitating and threatening symptoms so there is space and motivation to deal with other more internal psychic issues. Today, as a stand-alone treatment or as part of a larger therapeutic package, CBT is indisputably the most common therapeutic approach in mainstream psychology. For this reason, I'll be highlighting CBT as a dominant paradigm of the mainstream approach.

What is this CBT? I pick a purposely simple, well-defined, and clearly bounded example, treating a phobia of flying, rather than one of the various more complex CBT interventions; and then I highlight critical aspects of that phobia treatment rather than giving a more nuanced, detailed description. Hopefully, this provides an accurate and *accessible* understanding of the therapeutic principles involved in CBT—accessibility is in fact one of those key principles.

Henry, a forty-year-old middle-class male, with a wife and two children and a job in sales, comes to see a CBT therapist to deal with his debilitating anxiety about flying in an airplane.* Henry is so afraid of flying that he can't use airplane travel and has to drive long and exhausting distances for his job, as well as driving days to visit his close relatives. He decides that he wants to change. "I need to get over this anxiety," he says, "because I feel my life is crippled now." He's heard that CBT is an effective way to deal with his airplane anxiety, which he has learned is called a phobia, and that the treatment is relatively quick. He makes an appointment with Dr. Salmon, a clinical psychologist who is a certified, trained CBT therapist with a reputation for successful work with phobias, including flying phobias.

As he enters Dr. Salmon's office, Henry is impressed with her professional appearance, as she sits comfortably behind an attractive

---

*This case of using CBT to treat a phobia of flying is constructed from clinical materials, but pseudonyms are used throughout.

wooden desk, surrounded by a number of diplomas on the office walls, attesting to her advanced training and degrees. In a straightforward but caring voice, she gathers background data from Henry about his phobia, such as when it first appeared, what sets it off, and how it impacts his life. "I can help you," she says with assurance, and Henry feels reassured.

"We'll use what we call systematic desensitization," Dr. Salmon says. "It's good at treating the kind of phobia you have. I'll guide you through some exercises and give you some work to practice at home, some 'homework' we call it, and probably within a month or two we should see some good results."

Henry is ready, even eager to hear more about how the therapy will work. He appreciates that Dr. Salmon gives him a clear description, including the formal terminology for the different interventions. Her confident demeanor immediately calms Henry, and he feels optimistic.

"This treatment goes in stages," Dr. Salmon explains, "and I'll bring you into increasing contact with elements of the flying experience, pulling back if you feel too anxious and moving to the next stage when you feel ready. Our goal is get you into a plane, flying without debilitating anxiety, even comfortable enough so you don't feel you have a problem."

"Now we'll start with your thoughts," Dr. Salmon continues, emphasizing a simplicity of analysis. "When you think about flying, those thoughts can create anxious feelings, and then you are so totally anxious, you can't even consider flying."

Henry likes the way Dr. Salmon lays out the treatment plan— ordered, sequential, result oriented. He's always prided himself on being an "organized type of guy."

Over the next two months, Dr. Salmon brings Henry step-by-step into contact with experiences relating to flying. With each experience, she gauges Henry's anxiety and attempts to keep it under control by backing off the experience if Henry is still too anxious and then, when he's ready (not too anxious), going on to the next experience, which is closer to flying.

She starts just by having Henry think about flying, which he confesses is already making him sweat. "Now look at those thoughts," she counsels, "and see them as only thoughts. You're not in the plane, not even close." After some working with these airplane-flying thoughts within the calming context of Dr. Salmon's office, his thoughts become less terrifying, less overwhelming.

Another step in the CBT treatment is having Henry sit in an airplane seat, which sits in another room in Dr. Salmon's office. Henry quickly shares ways in which sitting there makes him anxious. "I think right away of the plane this seat could be in . . . and that terrifies me," he says. Dr. Salmon works with Henry on these thoughts, trying to have him become more rational. "It's only a seat," she assures him. "It's not going anywhere." As Henry works through this anxiety so he feels under control, Dr. Salmon introduces him to the next in a series of steps bringing him closer to the actual experience of flying: sitting in the airplane seat with the seat belt on, and then with the sounds of an airplane taking off and flying, and finally having the seat shake as if it were in a plane taking off.*

At each step, she helps Henry deal with the irrationality of his thoughts, such as "I'm falling out of the air" or "I don't have enough air to breathe." Since steps to calm his anxiety usually need practice to become functional, Henry also does some CBT exercises at home (homework); Dr. Salmon tries to regulate the intensity of these home exercises so they give Henry practice without releasing anxieties that could overwhelm him and possibly set him back in his treatment progress.

Treatment is concluded when Henry is able to fly in a plane, a short distance at first, and then on a longer flight. And he leaves with a series of mental and body exercises he can employ if he feels his anxiety rising again. "I feel like I've now got a toolbox of techniques to bring to my work of flying," he says with some bit of pride.

---

*As a CBT therapist with a specialty in phobias like flying, Dr. Salmon has access to physical settings, like airplane seats and airplane sounds, which help her create experiences close to actual flying.

This work between Dr. Salmon and Henry would be an example of a successful CBT intervention. The door is always open if Henry subsequently needs some additional CBT sessions if his fear of flying begins to return—perhaps a rough flight due to weather will bring back his anxieties. These booster or refueling sessions are not considered a sign of failure but as necessary corrections to or restrengthenings of the initial therapeutic input.

The primary mainstream therapy alternatives to CBT, and their many and varying offshoots, are the analytic approaches, such as the Freudian- or Jungian-influenced therapies, and humanistic-existential approaches, such as Rogerian or person centered. Since we consider the humanistic-existential approaches more as examples of countercurrents within the mainstream, we save a more detailed discussion of them for later.

The analytic approaches are more concerned with healing than CBT; they take into consideration the *significance* and *meaning* of anxieties and crises and how they can affect the quality of a lived life. These analytic therapies focus not on a client's externals—unlike CBT's focus on a client's behaviors, including treating the client's thoughts and feelings *as behaviors*—but instead on the client's internal processes, especially early childhood anxieties and repressed feelings that are now held captive in the unconscious. CBT would consider the unconscious irrelevant since it would not be seen as a determinant, or even explanatory mechanism, of behaviors.

During the relatively long process of analytic therapy, the client is encouraged to explore early childhood traumas and confusions, expressing the accompanying anxieties, sometimes initially symbolically, in the now safe therapeutic environment. For example, Henry's airplane phobia might be interpreted as an early childhood fear of abandonment by or independence from his parents, now repressed because that deep fear makes him feel too anxious. He has transferred his fear to flying, which has come to symbolically represent independence (in this case, literally breaking free of earth) or taking an uncharted path.

As the suppressed and repressed unconscious material now becomes conscious, a catharsis of expression results, releasing the maladaptive and previously unrecognized hold of the unconscious material over the patient's everyday life. A highly trained and legitimized professional, the therapist or analyst is as much artist as scientist, relying on intuition as well as training. She guides the client toward these forays into the unconscious, helping the client uncover the unconscious and bring it into consciousness, thereby making its contents more amenable to the client's control.

While the CBT therapist is more of a practitioner applying a prescribed set of techniques, the analytical therapist takes a transformational journey along with her patient. My wonderful friend Niti Seth, an analytically oriented psychotherapist, has helped me understand about this collaborative journey. "Analytical therapy," she says, "is a search, an exploration into the heart of those who feel dominated." Niti describes the psychological transformation she has experienced in the process of becoming a healer. "Something is occurring during my therapy work," she adds. "I become an instrument . . . there is a joining of souls, a receptivity by therapist and client as we both are transformed so that it's no longer me and you." Niti is perhaps more existentially oriented than many analytic therapists, and her work might be more rightfully considered as an example of analytically oriented countercurrents within the mainstream, but she does highlight the potential for transformation within the analytical model.

From an analytical point of view, CBT would be deemed superficial and reductionistic because it ignores the root cause of mental disturbance—namely repressed and illness-provoking unconscious anxieties. The CBT focus on behaviors and relative lack of emphasis on early childhood traumas is seen as "missing the point." Analytic therapy views symptom removal as merely a cosmetic change, while the deep root of the problem remains unresolved—and as a consequence the unresolved underlying problem is likely to be re-expressed in another symptom.

Fully committed to the primary importance of healing, rather than curing, the humanistic-existential therapies focus on potentials to be fulfilled rather than deficits to be fixed. The humanistic perspective would also see CBT as superficial, reductionistic, and even dehumanizing because it does not consider issues like the meaning of life and denies the power of free will in the evolving landscape of human development, thereby ignoring the fullness of human potential, including our spiritual challenges and journeys. Humanistic-existential therapies view analytic approaches as overly focused on pathology and too deterministic, especially in the powerful influence they assign to the earliest years of development. In the humanistic approach, the therapist is more of a partner in the therapeutic process, supporting and joining with the client as he confronts issues that define the very structure and texture of living—such as vulnerability, loss, and failure—and seeking to transform these natural life crises into life challenges and opportunities for growth.

Though substantial differences exist between CBT and analytical approaches, there are some commonalities between these two methods that can help us better understand the mainstream approach.* At the base of these two mainstream approaches is the therapists' conviction that they are the primary source of therapeutic change, if not in their personal skills and understandings, then in the therapeutic techniques they have mastered and now administer.† This assumption makes healing a limited resource bound by the conviction that a therapist is needed to fix clients who are broken. Implicit in both CBT and analytical approaches is a deficit model of human functioning. There are

---

*For now, we focus on CBT and analytic approaches in their classic forms in order to sharpen the eventual comparisons that are made between mainstream and Indigenous approaches and thus highlight dimensions that can be the basis for fruitful collaborations.
†The more classically trained analytically oriented therapists are committed to a "didactic analysis," wherein they undergo therapy themselves to better understand their own issues and the dynamics of the therapy process, and thus are better able to understand the issues of their patients. As therapists they then have the expertise to be a sensitive listener. CBT therapists have access to a variety of technical and unambiguous therapeutic techniques, often contained within manuals that make explicit the forms and stages of their interventions. The detail of these manuals, providing an ease of execution, can even make the personal expertise of the CBT therapist herself less important.

things wrong or broken with the person that need to be fixed; these deficiencies, expressed in diagnostic categories, define that person as a patient. The focus is on a *problem* to be solved to bring about adaptation more than *potential* to be realized to bring about transformation.*

Still, these mainstream therapies recognize the importance of the therapeutic alliance as a critical ingredient in therapeutic effectiveness. For example, Dr. Salmon attempts to bring a calm professional atmosphere into the therapy as one way to weaken Henry's anxiety, and she employs her highly directive approach in a sensitive manner. In analytic therapies, unless there is a sensitive connection between therapist and patient, the process of transference, which occurs during therapy, cannot feed into an effective outcome. Transference is the process by which a client "transfers onto" his therapist thoughts and feelings associated with the client's problem, such as feelings of anxiety about his father or mother. With a therapeutic alliance in existence, the therapist's offer of a neutral, nonjudgmental, and accepting environment can allow the client to now project those feelings, initially instigated by a childhood figure of importance, onto the therapist. But now the therapist is providing a safe or holding environment for the client to work on those problems, which heretofore remained either inaccessible or unmanageable. The client can then safely bring these repressed problem thoughts and feelings into consciousness and work toward accepting and dealing with them.

In the end, however, therapeutic techniques retain their unique importance.† The CBT therapist remains "in charge." She is the expert,

---

*The mainstream therapeutic intake process—which typically asks the prospective client questions like, "What brings you here?" or "What are your problems?"—supports the client in taking on and strengthening this deficit model thinking.

†This is an unfortunate emphasis because the research on all types of therapeutic interventions, including CBT, shows the nature of the therapeutic relationship between therapist and client (e.g., the degree of empathy) is more important for outcome effectiveness than the therapist's use of a particular technique. But this emphasis on technique can give the therapist a sense of control over his work and a sense of "knowing what he's doing"—even though moments of not knowing can be a critical part of an effective therapy process.

leading the client through a preconceived treatment program containing clear, concrete tasks the client is asked to perform. The analyst alone possesses certain skills, based on her extensive professional training, which are essential to successful therapy. For example, as dreams are critical in analytic therapy, being seen by Freud as the "royal road to the unconscious," the ability to interpret dreams becomes essential. Dream interpretation is a complex skill, which, though allowing for intuitive thrusts, relies heavily on a set of translations of the unconscious meanings. Dream interpretation is the province of the therapist—and carefully guarded as one of her more advanced interventions.

Training for therapists in both CBT and analytic approaches emphasizes *competence* over *vulnerability*. The therapist is meant to be in control of the therapeutic process, minimizing doubts or confusions she might have in the interest of being, or at least appearing to be, professional and consequently not fully honoring exchanges with the client that could seriously change the trajectory of the therapy process. As the Indigenous approaches demonstrate, closing off the almost inevitable feelings of vulnerability that occur in the healing exchange removes opportunities for deep learning and unexpected potentials for growth.

In contrast with Indigenous approaches, where the counselor and client establish a kinship relationship, the mainstream therapist *as therapist* is relatively isolated from segments of her community. She is taught to maintain a "professional distance." And while that concept's intention—to avoid moral and ethical transgressions, especially possible with therapists being in positions of power and control—is critical, it also shuts off important avenues of human contact that can cultivate a more natural human relationship. If, for example, a mainstream therapist and her client run into each other at the supermarket, the protocol is to avoid each other, even with eye contact. "It's freaky if I see my therapist," confides a person in analytic therapy; "they know so much about me. I feel naked." Therapists voice similar reservations: "It's a bit awkward if I see one of my clients. Best just to pretend we didn't see each other." What is there to hide? Does a commitment to ethical behavior within the therapy relationship rule out ordinary and ethical human connections?

With this emphasis on the therapist as expert, and her expertise as shaping the course of the therapy process, certain Indigenous emphases are absent. For example, therapists are under no obligation to be humble about the source of their ability to heal or to emphasize the service aspect of their therapeutic work. Instead, a fee-for-service mentality prevails, supported and even initiated by the capitalistic structure of mainstream human service work; and therapists can enhance their fees by promoting a personal ownership of their expertise to help sell their product. Generally absent is any acknowledgment, so central to Indigenous approaches, that some power and understanding beyond and not owned by the self is the source of healing.

Pervading the mainstream approach, so much so that it has become a foundational principle, is the importance of diagnosis and the need to apply an "approved" diagnostic category to the client. A diagnostic imperative is fostered and a diagnostic empire created with the *Diagnostic Statistical Manual* (DSM) as its centerpiece. Referred to as the "clinician's bible," this thick word-laden manual sits, ready for use, on the desks of mainstream clinicians across techniques and settings, offering them a multitude of diagnostic choices. An insurance-reimbursable diagnosis is typically required in order for any treatment to begin, leading to instances where a formal diagnosis may be made just to establish a need for treatment—the human expression of anguish may not be sufficient.

Beneath this commitment to diagnosis lies the increasingly long shadow of the health insurance industry, which requires a diagnosis for reimbursements, and the often hidden reach of the corporate pharmaceutical world, which has been accused of encouraging the maintenance, even creation, of certain diagnostic categories for which they have patented drug therapies. The DSM is heralded by its proponents as a scientific set of categories for diagnosing mental illness and dysfunction while critiqued by its opponents as an unscientific set of procedures for controlling the mental health industry through often arbitrary and stigmatizing labeling.

Mainstream therapy approaches are also increasingly influenced by the increasingly popular, yet still controversial, psychopharmaceutical interventions or drug therapies. As CBT is coming to dominate treatments offered by psychologists, drug therapies now occupy a similar role with psychiatrists. Though only a medical doctor or psychiatrist can prescribe these medications, psychologists have many interfaces with this biomedical treatment, often referring their clients to psychiatrists for drug therapies.

The plethora of drugs on the market makes a pharmaceutical treatment available for a wide variety of ailments and complaints. It's hard to escape being confronted with advertisements for quick and easy drug solutions for whatever ails you, ranging from serious conditions like clinical depression to what seem like serious but inevitable life conditions like worry about financial pressures. The problem is not the pharmaceutical intervention itself—as there are enough instances of effective drug therapies to continue the research for even more—but the emphasis on these drug therapies as quick and easy "fixes" for "whatever ails you," to fix what is broken. Also, the effectiveness of drug interventions depends on their being appropriately prescribed and carefully monitored, with dosages regulated depending on the specific conditions and changes experienced by a particular client. And the side effects of these drug therapies must always be respected—even though they are deemphasized or even hidden as much as possible in the advertising.

This process of medicalization, the turning of inevitable existential life problems, such as worry over our futures, into diseases that must be professionally treated, such as anxiety disorder, helps to support the overuse of pharmaceutical interventions. This is not to deny that some conditions deserve appropriate professional interventions, such as people who feel overwhelmed, even doomed, by essential human concerns, those who suffer from debilitating and enduring anxieties, or those whose depressive mood could turn into more serious clinical depression, including suicidal thinking. But *careful* considerations are always important, with an emphasis on the *caring*, including the full exploration of nondrug alternatives before or during ongoing drug interventions. A common wisdom is that one helpful use of drug therapy is to bring enough calm into a person's life and emotions so that some form of talk therapy becomes more possible.

"Quick and easy" can be an attractive label for those seeking health and well-being. What are the alternatives? Slow and hard? Would it were that simple! No, when we consider Indigenous alternatives, they remain complex, defying such clear labels—but in the end it seems Indigenous approaches are more connected with the shifting realities of our lives, and especially their furthest-reaching potentials.

INDIGENOUS APPROACHES

The light of near dawn warmly illuminates the Ju/'hoan healing dance at /Kae/kae. The dance is winding down, as people slowly stretch, soon to enter the rest of sleep. It's been hard work, hard but joyful. Lots of powerful healing, lots of good visiting, lots of unbridled laughter. And =Oma Djo, now sitting next to me, has not held back the last few hours, dancing gently, and then fiercely, healing all, his sweat reflecting the glowing fire in the middle. "Healing makes our hearts happy," he tells me.*

=Oma Djo is filled with joy; he is more than happy—his heart is happy. And this means he's glad he's able to serve the people, to help bring healing to those at the dance. It means he feels connected to, at one with his community, as during that healing, with its intimate laying on of hands, there is a deep and respectful exchange of healing between him and others. Since the source of healing comes from beyond him,

---

*Translation is a delicate, crucial act. If the translation of =Oma Djo's words is literal, it would be "healing makes me happy." If the translation is accurate, taking into account subtleties of cultural context, it becomes "healing makes my heart happy." For the Ju/'hoansi, a "happy heart" exists in a deeper, more community and spiritually influenced place than merely being happy.

from beyond the community, it's inexhaustible. =Oma Djo releases that healing energy, leaving aside ego concerns that could bottle it up. He knows that as he heals one, he makes it more likely someone else will heal another, as the boiling n/om moves from person to person through exchanges and connections. As =Oma Djo brings healing to others, others support and feed the intensity of that healing energy, that boiling n/om. The differing rhythms and intensities of the women's singing has helped him balance the heat of the boiling n/om with the task of healing, so he could heal rather than being overwhelmed by the searing pain of the boiling energy within.

Inevitably, the healing established at the dance is challenged and diminished by the obstacles and textures of daily life. Healing is not a once and done phenomenon—nor easily marked by the removal of symptoms—but a continual negotiation, a back and forth between the balance established by healing and the existential imbalance that is part of the flow of daily life. Long-standing conflicts reemerge: perhaps a person who so intimately helped =Oma Djo during the dance now complains about =Oma Djo's perceived failure to share the meat that came to his house. And new ones can develop. Eventually, the community feels a need for healing as imbalance weighs more and more heavily over balance. Healing communities are constantly re-created and re-creating communities.

How could mainstream psychology possibly measure, even understand, what =Oma Djo has just experienced and affirmed? Healing as balance is so dynamic, constantly being worked and reworked; healing as exchange is so filled with interconnections, continually reciprocating its effects; and healing as a renewable and expanding phenomenon is so expressive of a source beyond the restrictions of ego-bounded concerns like taking personal credit for outcomes. For the Ju/'hoansi, the source of healing is the gods and the boiling n/om, but there are many names for the beyond—which is why Indigenous approaches to health and healing are so richly promising, pointing toward potential rather than just removing obstacles.

"Health is more than not being sick," Ratu Civo tells me. "Health is something active. Healing brings health. And this healing places the good next to the bad, the joy next to the sadness. It balances them out. But that balance doesn't last. That's not life. Just because I don't feel sick, that's not enough. If I want to feel well, something must be created. I need an active exchange of energy."

When I'm living in Naqara, a rural village in Fiji, there are strongly suspected cases of *vakatevoro* (witchcraft). On hearing about that situation, Ratu Civo is forcefully clear. "We don't attack the person we think is doing that vakatevoro. Respect is important . . . even to such a person. You know, we don't know why he's doing those bad things. Our only job is to get protection from the vakatevoro. We go to our healers to help build a protective fence around ourselves so the evil forces can't hurt us. We try to cancel things out, strength against strength." Balance is the path of health as well as healing.

There is always imbalance. If this imbalance is on the path toward attaining balance, that is the nature of development. But if that imbalance persists, "if the person is stuck," says Danny Musqua, then some counseling is needed. From an Indigenous perspective, that counseling is not to cure or to deal with a "sick" person but to heal, to offer guidance to a person in the place where he is, which may be, as Mary Lee puts it, "feeling overwhelmed by life."

With the terrible toll of racism and colonization in the Indigenous community today, experiences of being overwhelmed are more frequent, especially among young people, adding now to the destructive legacies carried by residential school survivors. It's a life hemmed in by racism that can become overwhelming. Feeling overwhelmed by life is enough to begin a healing connection; a psychiatric diagnosis is not necessarily needed. "I don't believe in diagnosis," says Mary. "I only believe in helping people find their true path." But as a traditional counselor who really does guide, Mary will refer people to other resources, including psychologists and psychiatrists, when she encounters something that is more troubling and severe.

From an Indigenous perspective, healing is the way to restore and support balance. Healing is seen as a movement toward *and* away from meaning, connectedness, balance, and wholism. I've never heard an Indigenous teaching saying it's better to have the symptom than not—who needs symptoms! But their existence or removal, though connected to healing, does not define it. There are many Indigenous ceremonies focusing on this healing, and though they appear to have a separate and separated identity, they are in fact integrated within their surrounding community and culture;* they express as well as shape that context. These ceremonies are not important in and of themselves; they represent the community attempt to provide people with guidance for living a balanced life.

I often hear the expression among Indigenous elders in Saskatchewan that "culture heals"; it's often misunderstood by those outside the Indigenous community to mean that ceremonies heal. For example, take a person suffering from an addiction to a sweat lodge, and he can be healed. In fact, the phrase *culture heals* means that bringing a person with addictions into the entire web of traditional cultural values and actions, including participating in ceremonies, can heal. Being in the sweat can open a heart, be a spark for change, but that spark must be nourished through continuity of support. The web of relational and community supports builds the fire of recovery.

The traditional Fijian healing ceremony is an example of a ceremony representing, in fact being, the way the community seeks to live. Fijian culture emphasizes the sacred importance of exchange. For example, when one wishes to enter another village, you perform a sevusevu ceremony, presenting a sacred plant (yaqona) to the villagers and formally requesting permission to enter. Though performed by people, the ceremony is actually a sacred exchange, as your guardian spirit is communicating with the guardian spirit of the village, seeking permis-

---

*There are instances where the ceremony seems at odds with the general culture, but there is always an immediate supportive cultural-community context.

sion to enter in return for your honoring all those within the village.

Another example is the ceremonial exchanges of material goods to mark and energize special occasions such as a marriage or the visit of an important chief.* In a marriage ceremony, the family of the bride and that of the groom take turns presenting gifts to each other, with a period of time passing between each gift exchange. The gifts are intentionally similar, as the exchanges are meant to maintain balance. That balance is critical because the material exchange is an expression of a spiritual contract and connection between the two family groups. Some Western psychologists have said to me: "Why bother with all that ceremony stuff? Each group ends up getting pretty much what they gave." They fail to see that the exchange process itself is the point of the ceremony.

I realize that this intimacy of the spirits in daily life is crucial, woven deeply into the landscape of Fijian life. "Our vu [the gods] are our relatives," Ratu Civo tells me." They are our ancestors. We know where we've come from with our spiritual roots. Though we deeply respect the gods—we revere them and can be in awe of them—they are our relatives and will look after us. That's why they are welcomed into our lives."

The classic Fijian healing ceremony is at its core a spiritual/sacred exchange. The person seeking help presents a yaqona to the healer or dauvaqunu. As the yaqona is presented, the guardian spirit of the one seeking help is requesting healing from the healer's guardian spirit. In

---

*In these major Fijian ceremonies materials are exchanged that are needed for basic survival or are household furnishings, such as woven mats, bottles of coconut oil, reams of cloth, and barrels of gasoline and kerosene, or certain sacred or ceremonial items. From an Indigenous perspective, the exchange emphasizes the heart—intention and commitment—of those who give and receive rather than the size or value of the materials exchanged, though lively discussions about relative size and value still occur, representing the human side of ceremony. Ratu Civo, talking about bringing yaqona to a healing ceremony, offers a crystal clear example of this emphasis on the heart: "If you can't afford to bring a full yaqona root to the healer, you can offer even a yaqona twig . . . or a glass of water."

the very act of the healer accepting the yaqona, a commitment is made between the respective guardian spirits to do the healing work. It is in that exchange that the healing is activated.*

As mentioned in chapter 2, the healer typically prepares a beverage from the yaqona, and the healer and client, and others who may be present at the healing, drink the beverage. The healer may also do some massage, give some herbal remedies, or prescribe some changes in the client's daily life rhythms or activities. But these subsequent activities are merely carrying out the substance of the initial sacred exchange, an exchange built on spirituality and nurtured by respect and balance, and cognizant of the need for a continuingly recalibrated exchange.

In my time in Fiji, I visit other traditional healers, and some of them seem not as familiar with the spirits as is Ratu Civo. "One of the healers I went to seemed afraid of the spirits and then tried to control their impact on the healing," I mention one night to Ratu Civo. "I really felt uncomfortable in that healing session . . . as if strong powers were being released but without a moral direction. I feared for my life's balance." "Yes, that can happen," he replies. "If a healer is not trying to follow the straight path, to be honest and truthful, and does a ceremony to call upon the spirits, the spirits can become wild . . . they can be unpredictable because they're being called upon by a person who can't be trusted. Those are the healers you stay away from. It's not healing they are doing but playing with fire." Joe Eagle Elk put it so clearly: "Nowadays there are medicine people who are trying to do too much. They believe they have more power than they actually have. They're doing ceremonies they shouldn't perform. They are without the vision. There is no 'instant coffee' in this business" (Mohatt and Eagle Elk

---

*Often in Indigenous approaches, out of respect for the power that fuels the healing work—the power that exists beyond the self and the community—healers and the activity of healing are not directly and explicitly labeled or even identified. For example, in Fiji, healing is called *na cakacaka,* meaning "the work," or *na veiqaravi,* which means "the service (to others)."

2000, 42). As Ratu Civo reminds me, "Tell only what you know . . . no more . . . and no less."

As the Indigenous approaches exemplify a sacred exchange, spiritual challenges, including these spiritual journeys, meet *both* the healer and the ones coming for healing. Welcoming the spiritual can make it more familiar: "We invite the spirits into our sweat lodge," says Danny. "They bring the healing energy into our midst."

This is not to say that every journey in consciousness is spiritual; such journeys can descend into an unforgiving and unrelenting losing of the way, at times expressing severe psychological confusions and loss of balance, even being invaded by psychotic elements. But Indigenous approaches are more accepting of journeys beyond the ordinary, resisting a quick DSM-type label of psychosis to more patiently explore whether positive and productive outcomes can emerge after passing through the terrors and unknowns of lost consciousness.

In Indigenous communities throughout the world, the answer to the question, "What is it that heals?" is simple and direct. Whether it's called mana in Fiji, n/om among the Kalahari Ju/'hoansi, or *wakan* by the Lakota people, the source for these various concepts of spiritual power is the same: "There's only one Creator," says Joe Eagle Elk. "We may call that force different names and approach that power different ways, but there's still only one Creator, and that's the source of my healing."

Indigenous healing approaches stress that healing occurs through this power beyond the self, this spiritual power, with the healer being only a vehicle—but the healer must be a "clear and clean" vehicle, says Andrew Skin, an Inupiat elder who is a tribal doctor in Kotzebue Alaska.* A wiry, somewhat reticent man, still active in his hunting and

---

*The tribal doctor program has been established in the NANA Regional Native Corporation to support Inupiat healers to carry on the traditional Inupiat healing work, emphasizing the laying on of hands and deep massage. Collaborating with Rachel Craig, a fluent bilingual Inupiat elder from the coastal village of Kotzebue, we do research on the nature and functioning of these tribal doctors. All our interviews are conducted in Inupiat, and under Rachel's guidance, there are numerous visits to engage with tribal doctors during their work, or what they call their "doctoring."

fishing survival activities, Andrew is open about his work, wishing to share even details because he wants to "show others how serious our work is . . . that we really are doctors."

Acknowledging this spiritual source does not mean a compromising of technical skills and knowledge. Andrew emphasizes the critical importance of his knowledge of how to use his hands—the essential instrument in his healing approach—in his search for the nature of the illness a patient brings and the necessary and proper treatment.* These tribal doctors probe the body for causes of problems, using deep massage to bring relief, rearranging internal organs that might be sticking improperly along their surfaces.† They draw upon their lineage with ancient shamans and engage in careful and intensive study in mastering their massage technique; they prepare themselves technically before turning to the healing power that comes from beyond their lives.‡ "Before I work on any patient, I pray to the One Above that my hands will heal, and not harm," Andrew says. "I have to be clean in heart and spirit or else the healing won't work." The training period for Indigenous healers is long and arduous, including not just the acquisition of technical skills and even more importantly the development and deepening of character. I'm grateful for this combination of spirit and skill because when Andrew gives me a massage, going so deep into my

---

*Healing hands remain the basic medium and vehicle for healing in Indigenous approaches throughout the world. But mainstream therapists have largely lost that healing resource because it has been abused by some, including inappropriate touching and sexual contacts with clients. Physical contact is now limited, and strictly at that, to the so-called body or somatic workers, and they struggle to be accepted by the mainstream.

†Andrew states his frustration in not being allowed to witness autopsies at the Western hospital so he can better understand the human anatomy beneath the skin: "Those Western doctors keep saying we're not *real* doctors." Presently, he gains his knowledge in the traditional manner by studying the internal anatomy of the seals that he still hunts for food.

‡In my research with traditional doctors in the Kotzebue area, I find that these Indigenous healers are reluctant to publicly acknowledge, sometimes even talk about, the healers among their ancestors, whom they acknowledge as their lineage and source of family training and call shamans. The judgments of the earlier Christian missionaries in Alaska, who labeled shamans as "workers of the devil," still cast a powerful shadow.

stomach that he "touches" my spine, I could easily develop a "protective shell"—even though whenever I work with Indigenous healers I will inevitably participate in their healing ceremonies. I trust Andrew as his hands go into my insides, and that helps me relax enough so he can work effectively.

Acknowledging, really honoring, this spiritual foundation of healing prevents Indigenous healers from taking credit for their work; humility is the aim. The commonly heard term *gifted healer* therefore means being a good *vehicle,* not, as when used to describe healers who are seeking recognition and clients, to mean a gifted person or someone who *personally* owns the ability to heal. Indigenous healers typically do not seek healing work; it seeks or finds them—and often they try to avoid the responsibility of becoming a healer but can't. They know there will be increasing and continuing challenges and sacrifices in their work, without the massaging of their ego.

Healing then becomes what Ratu Civo calls "silent work."* Though deserving of respect and recognition because he is an important hereditary chief and effective healer, Ratu Civo never advertises his healing work. He's hard to locate and never talks about his healing in any public context, or even among people that he interacts with in his regular

---

*Indigenous education teaches the healer to be content with the silent recognition that comes of good work; rather than being rewarded with public degrees or certificates, Indigenous healers know inside, silently, when their work is on the straight path.

But there is a desire among certain Indigenous healers for some kind of official accreditation, perhaps something like a diploma attesting to their authenticity and professional skills. It's an understandable desire as it can help combat the widespread skepticism and discrediting that occurs typically from the mainstream institutions, such as hospitals, that deal with health issues. The irony is that often those in official positions of power within the culture are in fact clients of those Indigenous healers, their visits kept as well-guarded secrets.

But any kind of accreditation runs the risk of undermining the traditional values and ethics of Indigenous healing, which can't be captured by these more mainstream legitimizing procedures. The important variable of expectation, such as the client's believing she is going to see a "powerful healer," can't be ignored, but that expectation can be encouraged by community reputation and word of mouth as effectively as the stamp of approval from a formal certification.

employment. He's simply known by those who need to know—those who need help.*

A pediatric psychiatrist working in a mainstream mental health center asks me for advice. "I can see what's troubling my little patients even before they come into my office," she says, obviously concerned, "and I don't know what to do with this precognition." "I wouldn't do anything," I suggest. "Continue to use these special ways of seeing into a patient's problems and work with that special seeing. Work more and more to see effective treatments. But," I caution, "don't mention this special seeing to others because it will just confuse things. Colleagues who won't understand may begin to undercut your work. And if the wrong persons hear of your work, they could easily make your healing into a spectacle . . . and there goes the healing. Just continue healing, and continue silently. It's your patients' health that really matters."

Though now widely recognized and respected as a medicine man among his Lakota community and others around the world who are visitors to his ceremonies, Joe Eagle Elk's path to that healing place has been long, difficult, and filled with frustrations and disappointments— which continue in spite of his respected recognition. Despite the fact that the gift of medicine is in his family—his grandfather was a highly respected healer—Joe resists taking up healing work, even though the spirits, in visions, are calling him to the work, and keep calling in spite of his resistances. Even when it seems inevitable he has to follow the medicine calling, he continues to resist. He knows the life of a medicine man is filled with challenges and sacrifices, such as sicknesses that cannot be treated, serving the community at all hours, questions about his efficacy, and long periods of time away from his family. When Joe finally yields to the call to become a medicine man, he does so with

---

*Historically, Indigenous healers are known because they work in small village settings, where everyone knows everyone else, or they have people who speak on their behalf, letting others know of their healing talents when necessary. Now, especially in transitioning and transitional urban settings, where a healer may not be as well known or when there is no one to fulfill that traditional role of speaking on behalf of the healer, Indigenous healers may be more engaged i   ›moting themselves.

some regret and resignation, but yields he does so he can serve the community, not so he garners attention and rewards. In fact, in the end he has no choice—either follow the call of the spirits or suffer sickness and harm to himself and his family.*

When Joe finally begins to practice, he already has substantial and invaluable training. Tested as he is in the many years leading up to that decision to practice, his character deepens in its honesty and humility. Reflecting on the inevitability of that eventual decision, his understanding of the necessary protocols and techniques in the Lakota approach is sharpened and expanded. And he keeps reflecting on his healing work, always questioning his resolve and his truthfulness, always needing to know he is still following the "red road"—the good and ethical life.

Serving the people brings Joe into the healing work, and that commitment to service stays with him to the end. Through the years of performing his ceremonies, including many exhausting trips to Denver to see people he has treated who need surgery or other Western interventions, and often being called for ceremonies when he seems most to need time for rest and restoration, he develops a series of ailments, including a heart condition to which he eventually succumbs.†

To truly serve others, humility about one's own prowess becomes a key. Being a sacred exchange, healing becomes a gift—something earned but not possessed by the healer, something given to the healer to serve but not to hoard or boast about. Healing being a gift, the Indigenous teaching is that one therefore can't charge for a healing ceremony. But that's not always the case. "This mana [sacred power] is given to use to help," Ratu Civo insists, "though I know some people are trying to use that mana to their own advantage, things like charging money in order to get rich. We're not perfect," he insists, "none of us. We *all* struggle, *all* the time."

---

*In the Lakota way, denying this call of the spirits to the healing work has those negative life consequences—that call takes precedence over human choice.
†The importance of self-care for Western therapists to maintain their effectiveness remains true, but Joe's work represents a path where the needs of those who seek his help can overwhelm, their struggles so devastating and their resources so scarce, that his caring for himself gets neglected.

Since healing is a gift, gratitude is a natural response—from both the healer and the recipient of the healing, as both are connected by the healing energy. But today, especially in urban settings, complications can arise. For example, Indigenous healers are often given money sometimes—called honorariums—for performing their ceremonies for urban institutions, such as hospitals or schools. But honoraria can become expected compensation, and then the gift dimension is weakened.* Danny Musqua states fundamental principles: "Traditionally, our healers would be given gifts to help them survive, like blankets, or food, or on special occasions a gun, or even a horse . . . that's how we lived. Nowadays," he continues, "we give money, which is what is needed to survive in today's world. You buy your food, your survival, with that money." Danny pauses. "I know money can get sticky; it can lead us astray. But if we give the money as a gift, that's just what it is . . . a gift. We honor the healer with that money."

I learn about that teaching a number of years earlier. I'm in Rosebud Reservation, preparing to go to a healing ceremony I've requested from Joe Eagle Elk. Before the ceremony, I approach my friend Jerry Mohatt, who lives on Rosebud, is fluent in the Lakota language, and works closely with the medicine men there. "How much should I give Joe?" I ask, a little bit embarrassed by my question. Jerry just nods and says, "Whatever you want to." "But just give me an idea," I respond. "Really, it's up to you." "But what do others usually give?" I continue in my usual persistent manner. Jerry has to relent. "Oh, $50 or $100 or whatever." That helps, and I decide on the amount I give.

A year later Joe performs another healing ceremony for me. At the end of the ceremony, I reach into my pocket and take out all the money

---

*There is typically an expected amount of honorarium for the various ceremonies or talks elders give. It becomes complicated when, for example, an elder is given a certain amount of money to perform a sweat lodge in the penitentiary. This goes against traditional practice, but given the artificial and at times inhumane constraints in the penitentiaries, having a sweat available to inmates, even though perhaps somewhat compromised by the fee structure, is still ultimately of value. Some kind of sweat, especially assuming the honesty of the sweat holder who does the best he can under very restrictive conditions, is preferable to no sweat at all.

I have and give it to Joe—now more realistically expressing my appreciation, honoring the ceremony. To this day I have no idea how much I gave him, but I know my pocket was full, better to honor the fullness of that healing ceremony. Though a year earlier I thought I was giving Joe money as a gift of appreciation, it became less than that, layered as it was in my calculations about "what *should* I give."

Indigenous approaches to healing stress the deep and enduring connections among healing practice, healers, those coming for help, and the community that surrounds. The Ju/'hoan healing dance exemplifies this pervasive interconnectedness, as everyone at the dance, or even within hearing distance, receives healing—whether or not they receive the healers' specific healing act of laying on of hands. The dance creates an atmosphere in which the healing energy circulates among the people; there is no scarcity of healing, no need to compete for access. This interconnectedness energizes the exchange that lies at the core of the healing. "We're all in this together," says =Oma Djo.

"Whenever I do counseling," Danny tells me, "I first put the person seeking guidance into a kinship relationship with me. I'll say something like, 'I'm glad you've come, my daughter or granddaughter . . . my son or grandson.'" When Danny adopts the person seeking help, he's establishing an ongoing relationship of exchange and mutual responsibility, one that endures beyond the specific setting of the counseling. "You don't stop being someone's grandfather," Danny cautions. If he sees the person he's counseling in the course of his day, they greet each other; rather than avoiding contact as in the mainstream model, they're happy to see each other because they are related—and the contact reaffirms the counseling exchange. "But you know," I add, "psychologists would say you are in danger of violating a central principle, what they call professional distance. You're not supposed to have an ongoing relationship with clients or else you risk the chance something inappropriate or unethical could occur." Danny knows I'm not judging him, only putting the mainstream reality out there for us to examine. "Yes, that's how they do it," he responds, "and they miss so much. If we're good counselors, we honor our position . . . we don't abuse it."

Indigenous healers are not typically isolated from the ongoing fabric of their community's life. The Ju/'hoansi who've become healers continue to hunt and gather, to participate in community functions and responsibilities. They are *Ju/'hoansi* who heal, not *Ju/'hoan healers*. The entire Ju/'hoan community is involved in sustaining the healing tradition, and the cultural stress on egalitarianism counteracts healers being seen as special, a position more commonly pursued in the mainstream approach. As healing becomes a respectful exchange among members of the community, balancing needs and responsibilities, struggles and aspirations, a healing community can be formed. *Community as healer* becomes an important overarching principle of Indigenous approaches.

Though the connection between Indigenous healers and their clients is an intense exchange, it's appropriately guided by structures like the adoption process Danny talks about, as well as the spiritually infused compassion that exists within that connection. For example, the Fijian concept of dauloloma (love for all), essential to the straight path, is feeling a love for another because that person, like oneself, is a part of creation. As dauloloma infuses the healing exchange, a compassion emerges that creates and honors respectful boundaries far beyond what can sometimes be a formulaic interpretation of professional distance.*

One way Indigenous communities help direct themselves toward being healing rather than toxic is through the way healers are educated or trained—and by extension, since healers are in and of the community, how

---

*There is a beautiful, touching story told by Saulteaux/Ojibway elder Alex Wolfe (1988) that I keep close to my heart, creating the experience of compassion. In that ancient teaching story, called "The Orphan Children," two young Indigenous children are lost and hungry; found by the buffalo people, they are immediately adopted and brought fully into the life of the buffalo community. Adopted without question—because of compassion. After being raised by the buffalo people, the two children, now grown into adulthood, are encouraged to return to their original people. But now the two are filled with the wisdom teachings given to them by the buffalo people so they can be of service to their own people. Adopted, loved, and then given up—so they might serve others.

the community is educated. "Our healers have to be role models,"* Ratu Civo stresses. "We have to work hard . . . so hard to follow the straight path. And the further along we travel on the straight path, the more difficult it becomes to keep on that path. As people see us as being more and more powerful, we can begin to believe them . . . just when we're sure we're on the straight path, well, that's *just* when we lose our way."

At the heart of the educational process for Indigenous healers is a transformational experience moving them into a spiritual realm beyond themselves, allowing healers to feel compassion with others and to serve them. "We're all part of creation, part of the Creator's work," Danny stresses, "and that connects us all with compassion." Joe Eagle Elk's experiences with the spirits calling him to the healing work would be an example of a more dramatic transformational experience, but that transformation can also involve a subtle shift in a consciousness to the beyond, which also becomes deep within.

From an Indigenous perspective, technical knowledge about healing is crucial and is passed on with care and respect, but that knowledge must be applied within an ethical context; ethical character—striving for honesty, humility, generosity, and compassion—guides practice, in contrast to the mainstream focus on specific techniques. Indigenous approaches emphasize the gifts of *vulnerability* rather than *competence,* which is the primary aim of training mainstream therapists.

By vulnerability I mean a radical questioning of one's worldview, such that one no longer holds onto what is assumed, often implicitly, to be valid, obvious, and common practice.† This experience of vulnerability entails giving up the often comfortable and comforting protection of questioning and can be a source of fear, even at times terror.

---

*The term *role model* is very commonly used—sometimes overused. As Lenard Monkman (2015), a young Indigenous activist, says, "What we need is *real* models not 'role models.'" With her intense dedication and hard work to become a surgeon, our daughter Hannah is seeking this path of being a real model.

†See Katz and Murphy-Shigematsu (2012b) for a more extended discussion of vulnerability.

But accepting one's vulnerability—rather than denying it or becoming paralyzed by it—can open the door to special knowledge about the limits of the self and one's control over the world, as well as potentials inherent in the larger whole.

It's a vulnerability in *both* the healer and client that makes Indigenous approaches so committed to unpredictability and its potential insights—the openings to growth that cannot be planned. Even experienced Ju/'hoan healers can find themselves unexpectedly overwhelmed by the intensity of their boiling n/om; they may have to allow that n/om to become less painfully hot so that it can be directed toward healing. The straight path is more about vulnerability than assuredness, about being prepared for the unexpected. There is no formula for being *and* staying on the straight path.

I describe the way Indigenous healers are trained as a process of "education as transformation."[*] Education as transformation can inspire education of therapists within the mainstream. But wherever it is utilized, a dialectic with *institutional* education and more pointedly *institutional* change must be addressed. The process of transformation needs to occur on multiple levels, whether sequentially or simultaneously, whichever part of the dialectic functions as an initiating force.[†]

COUNTERCURRENTS WITHIN THE MAINSTREAM

Within mainstream psychology there are countercurrents pointing toward directions identified in Indigenous approaches as essential to health and communal well-being. Often they touch on particular therapeutic aspects, such as the need for compassion and vulnerability; in some cases, they offer entire therapeutic approaches, such as existential-humanistic therapy

When I look at the aims and functions of existential-humanistic

---

[*]See Katz (2012b) for a fuller discussion of this process of education.
[†]This dialectic is further considered in the next two chapters.

therapy, there is a relevance to Indigenous approaches.* As Louise Sundararajan, a former president of the humanistic psychology division of the American Psychological Association, puts it: "[Existential-humanistic therapy] asks about the meaning of life." She quickly adds that therapy doesn't promise to answer that question but can help *both* clients and therapists frame their questions around the larger, deeper issues at work behind identified mental problems such as depression, as well as a more general disconnection and dissatisfaction with life. Louise goes on to say that existential-humanistic therapy offers a more wholistic approach, beyond just addressing symptoms. As existential-humanistic therapy stresses the importance of human choice and feelings of awe toward life, she describes it as an approach that seeks to increase understanding of what it means to be a human being.

Kirk Schneider, an existential-humanistic practitioner, says the concept of presence is essential to that approach. He describes presence as a process in which both clients and therapists enter into a heightened awareness of self, opening up to learning that truly matters, and experiencing in the here and now both barriers and opportunities for change. "Presence helps us to understand and attune to the fuller range of a person's experience . . . You learn to co-exist with your anxieties" (Schneider, 2011).

Yes, existential-humanistic therapy does go in the *direction* of Indigenous approaches, moving away from a deficit model entailing a fix-it mentality and toward a fuller appreciation of health—and life—as expressing a reciprocating relationship between imbalance and balance.†

---

*See Price (2011) for a concise overview discussion of the existential-humanistic approach. Points made by existential-humanistic proponents Sundararajan and Schneider are also discussed in the Price article.

†It's important to note that the existential-humanistic approach is also influencing other Western therapy approaches, including CBT, especially in the area of therapeutic values. As Schneider says, "[W]ith the advent of existential-integrative therapy, increasing numbers of practitioners are feeling welcomed into the existential-humanistic tent. Increasing numbers of practitioners . . . are appreciating that while most recognized therapies 'work,' their effectiveness is multiplied by embracing a wide-ranging philosophy of what it means to live, to struggle for something profound, and to feel a part of a vast and unfathomable journey. This is the existential-humanistic journey" (Schneider 2011).

And yet there are still critical pieces missing. As mentioned before, the word *respect* typically has different meanings when used in Western and Indigenous contexts. For example, the respect that characterizes the existential-humanistic approach lacks the deep spiritual connection that is at the core of Indigenous respect. As Danny Musqua puts it, "Respect goes beyond, way beyond, respecting each other. Respect means protecting the environment and all its creatures . . . and realizing we must fit into that natural order." Also, the existential-humanistic approach does not emphasize as much the crucial importance of service nor the ongoing connection and exchange between counselor and client that comes from their being related through an enduring kinship process.

Representing another path toward Indigenous approaches to health and healing, there are a number of treatment programs, specifically designed for Indigenous peoples with addiction problems, that are based on Indigenous teachings and ceremonies while also offering psychological interventions. One of these is the Pisimweyapiy Counseling Centre (PCC) in northern Manitoba, Canada.*

Drawing heavily from Cree traditional teachings, ceremonies, and counseling, as well as employing Western-based individual interventions, PCC is a community-based treatment program seeking to "normalize, universalize, and depathologize . . . participants' negative life experiences symptomatic of the residential school syndrome . . . [such as] unresolved and often untreated grief characteristic of posttraumatic stress disorder."[†] Participants have long histories of "relational turbulence" and "personal distress," intensified by issues of substance abuse (Gone 2009, 151). Those words *normalize* and *depathologize* speak powerfully to the Indigenous emphasis on moving from labeling (diagnosing) to living.

The PCC speaks of being a "resourceful community healing place that maintains our Cree language, culture and spirituality." Strongly

---

*My description of the PCC is based on an in-depth evaluation done by Joe Gone, a citizen of the Gros Ventre Nation and a highly trained clinical-community psychologist now teaching at the University of Michigan (Gone 2009).
†PCC mission statement (Gone 2009, 133).

tied to Indigenous identity, the program seeks a "reclamation" of the "Indigenously unique" "symbolism of our people," so as to "reconstitute a robust cultural identity" that in turn would lead to "healthier lifestyle decisions" (Gone 2008, 155).

Proposing an integrated and holistic therapeutic approach utilizing Western and Indigenous practices, the PCC offers fundamental Indigenous practices, all guided by Medicine Wheel teachings, such as smudging, talking circles, pipe ceremonies, sweat lodges, and fasting camps; but the Western contributions are anything but mainstream and include the Alcoholics Anonymous twelve-step program, inner child explorations, meditation and visualization work, reiki, neurolinguistic programming, and acupuncture.* A number of Western-oriented terms are used to describe both the espoused of the PCC, including "client self-expression," "healing discourse," "cathartic disclosure," and a "process of positive existential transformation."

The PCC has lofty aims and brings in a wide variety of resources. In fact, it can serve as an example for the synergistic collaboration between Indigenous and Western therapies that are dealt with more fully in chapter 8. But the PCC program also illustrates some of the obstacles and dilemmas almost inherent in that collaboration. For example, there is a subtle devaluation of the Western interventions among the mostly Indigenous staff so that one of the main principles of synergy, a mutual respect for all parties to the collaboration, is not fully realized—which is not an indictment of the PCC program but a recognition of how difficult it is to generate and maintain this mutuality of respect. As well, it's a strange mix of interventions that are considered Western, including some offerings with a decidedly new age coating—perhaps this led to some of the staff's misgivings. There's also hesitation among some of the more traditionally oriented staff about the use of Indigenous teachings. As one program administrator put it:

---

*Techniques such as reiki and acupuncture, though derived from Eastern healing traditions, are grouped under the Western rubric, suggesting more perhaps that they are non-Indigenous.

"We see ourselves as paving the Red Road [the Native American path of spiritually guided good life] to wellness . . . [that] might be regarded by many people as heresy. 'You're messing with age-old customs' . . . but paving the Red Road speaks of an attempt to demystify Indigenous processes and make it a lot easier to grapple with this monster called identity" (Gone 2009, 134).

Finally, the PCC sharpens one dilemma of collaboration between Indigenous and Western approaches. If you want to do mainstream outcome research on such an Indigenously and spiritually infused program, be prepared for frustration if not failure. I know the evaluator Joe Gone: in addition to being a careful researcher, he is familiar with Indigenous teachings about health and healing and participates in healing ceremonies such as the sweat lodge. When he says it's hard to evaluate PCC, especially in terms of client outcomes, he's pointing to intrinsic characteristics of the Indigenous approach that can't be adequately described by mainstream research. How do you "measure" whether Cree spirituality is maintained or whether there is a "reclamation" of the *unique symbolism of our people*"? I say you don't measure those things; at most you *describe* them. And even though sobriety can serve as an important outcome variable, as an outcome is possible, that tells only part of the picture, as new issues of health and healing emerge with sobriety.

And what about CBT, the dominant mainstream therapeutic intervention? It, too, is being enhanced by countercurrents. Elements such as mindfulness training are being brought into CBT programs; as well, CBT elements, such as systematic desensitization, are being included within more humanistic therapy approaches. But these changes generally leave intact the prevailing system. For example, when mindfulness is used as part of a CBT program, the underlying therapeutic structure of a clearly sequenced step-by-step procedure, aiming toward prediction of outcomes with clearly demarcated goals, including the removal of unhealthy behaviors (symptoms), persists—the mindfulness becomes an extra tool toward those objectives. When a CBT technique enters an existential-humanistic approach, it's subsumed within a process guided by existential-humanistic values such as a search for meaning—the CBT technique becomes one more tool to facilitate that search.

At the same time, there is an increasing emphasis on a more structured programmed approach to CBT, wherein the therapist follows a protocol for the stages of therapeutic work, including a sequence of suggested probes for eliciting required information and responses from clients. I know this enables some kind of quality assurance, even though the therapist may not be that experienced, but it also seems to make the CBT therapist even more a technician than a healer.

Is the Indigenous approach to training healers—education as transformation—reflected in countercurrents within mainstream psychology? For example, is there an emphasis on a transformation experience that encourages therapists to go beyond their boundaries of self, into a transpersonal connection with and commitment to serve their clients and community? One area in which countercurrents are active is in emphasizing empathy, extending into compassion, as a core element in the healing process. As empathy is felt, therapists go beyond their own ego constraints, connecting intimately with the life experience of the other.

Carl Rogers, working out of his humanistic framework, helps to lay the groundwork for this role of empathy. He presents a powerful example of the fear he sees in certain clinicians he supervises when they have clients who have done terrible things, such as pedophilia; Rogers says these clinicians-in-training are afraid that if they are empathic in those situations, they may be caught, even trapped, in the dangerous currents of their client's perverted world (Rogers 1982). "Is this something too awful to empathize with?" But Rogers emphasizes that it's just in those situations that empathy is most needed; rather than risk losing themselves, therapists can affirm to the client that despite feeling he has done something beyond the pale of human behavior, he is in fact still human. By journeying with the client into his dangerous places, the therapist affirms to the client that he "can be human and still have those [terrible and terrifying] feelings." This is therapy on the edge.

But Rogers's work has a fundamental limitation. After the counseling session ends and the client walks out the office door, the empathy ends. When Rogers's famous client Gloria questions whether Rogers is pretending to feel, as he says, "close" to her, he responds: "All I know is what I am feeling, and that is I feel close to you in this moment" (Raskin et al. 2010). Yes, the feeling is true "in this moment," but that, by definition, is not a feeling that can endure, as the two are not connected in a long-term relationship.* Likewise, the presence that is essential to the existential-humanistic approach is bounded by the actual therapist-client contact and context. There are no kinship connections to extend those feelings of empathy and presence. Even though Rogers's primary work occurred many years ago, I offer his example because it still guides some of the most important countercurrents of today.

Joan Koss-Chioino (2006) extends the concept of empathy into a deeply spiritual dimension. Studying the central role of spiritual transformation in Puerto Rican healers (espiritistas), she finds that their capacity for relation, empathy, and altruism emerge from that transformation. Many experience what she calls "radical empathy," in which individual differences between healer and sufferer are melded into one field of feeling and experience. This produces a type of altruism in which spirit healers feel compelled to be altruistic in responding to suffering whenever they encounter it. I immediately think of the Fijian concept of dauloloma, which has the same almost instinctive bonding experience. Clearly, these healers are moved strongly and immediately, without question, beyond their ego boundaries and concerns.

This radical empathy is very different from another controversial but exciting countercurrent; namely, the discovery of mirror neurons. It is suggested that humans, and other primates, are hardwired to respond to the feelings and situations of others. For example, if we see someone in pain, we feel their pain; if we see someone laughing, we have a smile

---

*This lack of a long-term relationship is a general critique for Western therapies, including Rogerian and other humanistic approaches; somewhat unusually, Rogers and Gloria do keep in contact after the counseling ends.

come across our face—without even trying. Some suggest that mirror neurons provide us with the neurological basis of empathy—again, there is excitement because, still influenced by mainstream principles, this neurological evidence is so-called hard science.

But there are certain limitations to these mirror neurons; for example, you need to like the person before you feel what she feels, and you must understand the intention of the other's behavior—that a smile means joy rather than being a mask for fear. Most important, if these mirror neurons initiate instinctive behaviors, can they really be seen as the foundation for empathy? Doesn't empathy require some degree of choice? We choose, for example, to ignore all those many other motivations and even instincts, such as for self-survival. With the mirror neuron explanation, we, apparently, have *no* choice but to be empathic.

More generally, does empathy cover the deeply felt and intimately connected nature of compassion? The Indigenous experience of compassion seems more emotionally and spiritually touching—both being touched by that compassion and touching others with that compassion.

Vulnerability is another element of the Indigenous approach.* There is an increasing stress in the mainstream on the importance of vulnerability in the education of health professionals, especially in contrast to the prevailing emphasis on trainees' competence. Sheila Harding, the associate dean at the University of Saskatchewan School of Medicine, delivers a lecture entitled "The Hidden Curriculum in Medical Education" (2010). It's important for medical students to know how to fail, she says, so they can then handle the inevitable experiences of failing in their professional work and, as a result, admit and accept their mistakes so they can learn from them and correct them. Through encouraging the self-reflection that can uncover vulnerability, health care professionals can better appreciate their own limitations and thus be prepared to be more empathic—with their clients *and* with themselves.

---

*See Katz and Murphy-Shigematsu (2012b) for a more extended discussion of these concepts of vulnerability and cultural humility.

Cultural competence training is also being transformed into cultural humility training. Both seek to sensitize providers to the growing diversity of their clients, but whereas the former can instill a false sense of competence that mistakenly treats culture as a predictable explanatory variable, the latter is a process of continual self-reflection that requires providers to be humble as lifelong learners, always seeking a fuller understanding of their clients' worldviews while simultaneously examining the cultural assumptions they too bring into the treatment encounter.

Health providers are now encouraged to be more open to their clients' stories about what brings them to seek help and to treat these as stories of their life condition—rather than immediately retreating into the security of making a diagnosis of the client's illness. The field of narrative medicine has fostered such an openness. Vulnerability allows providers to loosen their grip on the therapist-client process, giving room for the client's story to be heard—and valued. As a practitioner of narrative medicine, Stephen Murphy-Shigematsu describes the therapeutic power of these stories (2012). "My intention in using narratives of self and other," he says, ". . . is to humanize the patient and reduce what the practitioner sees as alien or exotic to the ordinary and understandable" (2012, 172). Steve stresses the importance of hearing patients' stories— about their illness, about their families, about their fears and wishes— as a critical ingredient in effective treatment and caregiving. He goes on to state that "[h]umans give meaning to their lives in narrative terms by seeing themselves as living in the drama of particular stories" (2012, 171–72). Clients' life stories contextualize their particular complaints or symptoms and open the door to future evolving stories.

There are clearly limitations to this organic and evolving client-patient context. Rarely is time available for the stories and exchanges to fully evolve. As well, vulnerability is not easily nor comfortably accepted. And there is always the complaint from the providers' training facilities that an emphasis on vulnerability will take away from "valuable" time needed to teach the "essentials," meaning the basic sciences or the details of therapeutic techniques. Yes, time is typically in short supply in mainstream health care institutions, but there can be some flexibility introduced; also, psychological and existential supports can be offered to allow people to take the risks to become vulnerable. And finally, there is evidence that introducing concepts like vulnerability into a health provider curriculum not only does not take away from basic science learning but also can enhance that learning, as the student can better deal with the anxieties and confusions that are a natural, almost intrinsic part of what is a very demanding learning environment.

A final countercurrent critiques the mainstream emphasis on clinical labeling, including the power to define a person and her potential through a mental illness diagnosis—there's a lack of mainstream attention to mental health or *strength* diagnoses. Featuring the increasingly influential DSM, the mainstream labeling process is in sharp contrast to the Indigenous approach of accepting a person for who she or he is at that time. The Indigenous approach is more concerned with understanding a person's particularities and turning those particularities into sources of strength, such as giving someone specific tasks that depend on those particularities. The inherent paradoxes in life are explored rather than wrapped up with an illness label.

The existence of the DSM raises a series of complex problems. There are now increasingly vocal and articulate critiques of the DSM, both from within psychiatry, the historical seat of the DSM, and allied health professions, especially psychology.* These critiques seek to make the

---

*Many of the professional health-provider associations, including divisions of the American Psychological Association, write their own critiques of the new DSM-5. These individual critiques share much in common, and Brent Robbins (2011), in the form of a petition to those in charge of the DSM-5, offers one example of an excellent summary of both concerns about the present DSM-5 and suggestions for its revision and improvement. I quote large sections from that Robbins-authored petition, because, though it contains technical specifics necessary to making the petition effective, it remains an eloquent and persuasive statement.

The petition offers a general critique of the questionable scientific basis of many of the DSM's diagnostic categories and their cultural and socioeconomic biases, which unfairly target those outside mainstream Western perspectives as well as those whose marginality,

DSM more broadly responsive to issues and struggles we face by being *human* rather than narrowly focused on how those issues and struggles need to be classified as mental problems or diseases. The first edition of the DSM, published in 1952, is only 86 pages long and contains about

---

(cont. from page 319) including poverty, contributes to their being more likely to be diagnosed with a mental illness.

As well, the petition points out the failings in specific DSM diagnostic categories. For example, it states that attenuated psychosis syndrome "describes experiences common in the general population, and . . . was developed from a 'risk' concept with strikingly low predictive validity for conversion to full psychosis." In regard to major depressive disorder, the petition criticizes the proposed removal of the current bereavement exclusion, which has prevented "the pathologization of grief, a normal life process." As to the diagnostic category of attention deficit disorder, the petition says that the proposed reduction in the number of criteria needed to make that diagnosis contributes to what is already an overdiagnosis or "epidemiological inflation" of that category. The same kind of epidemiological inflation is foreseen for the DSM-5's reduction in the symptomatic duration and number of criteria necessary for making a diagnosis of generalized anxiety disorder.

The petition also deals with how vulnerable populations, such as children and the elderly, are made increasingly easy prey for inappropriate and therefore damaging diagnostic illness labeling:

> For example, [the diagnostic category of] Mild Neurocognitive Disorder might be [improperly] diagnosed in elderly with expected cognitive decline, especially in memory functions. Additionally, children and adolescents will be particularly susceptible to receiving a diagnosis of Disruptive Mood Dysregulation Disorder or Attenuated Psychosis Syndrome. Neither of these newly proposed disorders have a solid basis in the clinical research literature, and both may result in treatment with neuroleptics, which, as growing evidence suggests, have particularly dangerous side-effects—as well as a history of inappropriate prescriptions to vulnerable populations, such as children and the elderly.

The Hobson-authored petition sounds a clear call for sensitivity and responsibility not only to those suffering and in need of professional therapies but also to those suffering and in need of ongoing familial and community support and exchange:

> Though we also have faith in the perspicacity of clinicians, we believe that *expertise in clinical decision-making is not ubiquitous amongst practitioners* and, more importantly, cannot *prevent epidemiological trends that arise from societal and institutional processes.* We believe that *the protection of society, including the prevention of false epidemics, should be prioritized above nomenclatural exploration.*

(Note: I have inserted italics in the above quote for emphasis. Also, supporting references within the material as quoted have been removed but can be consulted in the full original petition.)

one hundred diagnoses; the most recent edition, DSM-5, published in 2014, is 947 pages and contains nearly four hundred diagnoses. In addition to the more long-standing and core diagnoses such as schizophrenia, depression, and anxiety disorders, there are new additions, such as attention deficit/hyperactivity disorder (ADHD), referring to people who are impulsive, restless, and easily frustrated and have trouble concentrating. The ADHD diagnosis has become the fastest growing disorder in North America, with over 80 percent of the ADHD cases being boys. Are boys "sicker" than girls? Is ADHD a "boys' illness"?

What's happening? Yes, it's complex. It could be that our world is getting more and more stressful, resulting in more and more mental illnesses, and the range of reported illnesses has also increased, requiring more diagnostic categories to understand them. But do those stresses specifically cause, for example, ADHD? It could be that providers, especially those committed to psychiatric diagnostic work, are getting better at identifying mental illnesses, not only through the use of new categories but also in their ability to skillfully identify incipient or hidden disease categories. It could also be that the process of medicalization, expressed in an imperialistic thrust of the DSM, has invaded the professional responsibility to work with people therapeutically and sensitively; especially considering the pressures of the pharmaceutical industry and their constant discovery of drug treatment for newly discovered diagnoses—heavily fueled by their profit motive. The pharmaceutical industry's business model thrives on maintaining lifelong customers, people who must keep taking a drug to keep their illnesses in check by controlling or removing symptoms but never removing the causes.

With the easy access of so many diagnostic categories, are providers overdiagnosing? When seeing a person who is dealing with life challenges in a less than smooth fashion, punctuated by periods of stress, confusion, and even despair, does the provider too quickly see a mental illness problem, especially if he can prescribe a medication that is thought to be relevant? But I want to emphasize that this medicalization critique does not deny the anguish people can feel with mental imbalance nor oppose the appropriate and effective use of treatments, including medications. Overlabeling and overprescribing are the target. Are we becoming sicker, or simply increasingly *labeled* as sick? The DSM demonstrates the power and prison of the labeling process.

One response to the intrusions of medicalization is to engage in a process of "delabeling." There are, for example, attempts to see hallucinations, conventionally considered symptoms of schizophrenia, as experiences with potential for increased understanding and even growth. This reconceptualizing of hallucinations as a form of consciousness has been discussed thoroughly—and championed vigorously—by a grassroots movement called the Hearing Voices Movement, powered by persons diagnosed with schizophrenia who tell their stories. As an outgrowth of movement, an international network called Hearing Voices Network was established.*

One powerful and revealing "hearing voices" story comes out of the life of Eleanor Longden, a young woman in the UK (Longden 2013). At first, she hears one relatively benign disembodied voice commenting on her actions in the third person and manages to hide her deep anxiety. But she eventually spirals out of control into a "prolonged and toxic sense of hopelessness and despair" and is diagnosed as schizophrenic and hospitalized. It seems that the diagnosis and hospitalization contribute to the worsening of her condition. The voices, labeled as symptoms of her schizophrenia, now multiply and become more aggressive and terrifying—to the point where she attempts to drill a hole in her head to get rid of the voices. "I was labeled, medicated . . . and left," she states in bare language.

But with the help of others, Eleanor finds her way back; she realizes her "shattered self could become healed and whole" and pursues a successful career path working "on the other side the desk" as a psychologist. Central to her healing path is a new understanding of her voices—

---

*"Hearing voices" is one of the more popular search phrases on YouTube, yielding a wide variety of stories, whose quality and content vary widely. As a grassroots movement, the Hearing Voices Network provides a forum for these stories.

which still exist. "I began to see my voices as meaningful responses to painful early life events," she says, "not my enemies. They were a source of insight into soluble emotional problems." Now, as Eleanor listens to her voices, she's learned to "live with them in peace and with respect—and in turn, I've developed a growing sense of compassion and respect toward myself."

Eleanor offers a final teaching about her voices: "I see them as a creative and ingenious survival strategy . . . a sane reaction to insane circumstances. Not as an abstract symptom of illness to be endured but a significant meaningful experience to be explored." Eleanor expands her sense of self to include those voices; they become part of who she is, and she commits herself to making them a potential source of knowledge.

The Hearing Voices Movement doesn't suggest that the voices people hear are not harmful or that they are not part of a painful condition that has been labeled as schizophrenia. Speaking about one's voices, even accepting them as a workable part of oneself, is not a cure-all approach, nor does it exclude the use of other therapeutic interventions, including drug therapies. And Eleanor's specific path is not a prescription for others; one size doesn't fit all. But the Hearing Voices Movement can open doors to new ways of perceiving, making transformations of consciousness the focus, trying to make sense of experiences that are beyond sense, rather than boxing them off prematurely.

FUTURE COLLABORATIONS

Indigenous teachings about health and healing offer points for guidance, even inspiration, in enhancing mainstream approaches. Mainstream approaches can more fully embrace the idea that health is more than not being sick and that health and sickness aren't "on-off" conditions; both are experiences of *continuously* being in and out of balance. By relaxing the need to have certainty in a basically uncertain world and trying to meet that need through excessive diagnostic labeling, and a focus on removing symptoms just because they can be easily understood, mainstream approaches can more fully appreciate potential rather than deficits and healing rather than fixing or curing. And the ethos of visiting, as described by elder Mary Lee, could further enhance the mainstream by deepening a respect for the client's life situations and the stories that convey them.

Education as transformation can impact the mainstream training of health professionals, opening doors to learning a more effective practice. Basic to this transformation is cultivating humility in the practitioners, the realization that they are not the sole or even primary source of the healing outcomes. Positive outcomes will not be reduced if the provider takes a less self-centered, self-promoting role. A full embrace of Indigenous teachings about the spiritual source of healing isn't necessary; such an embrace becomes more appropriate when nurtured within something like an Indigenous context. But some acknowledgment of the limits of personal power and skill in outcomes is needed. As the mainstream practitioner more clearly sees these limits, she can more clearly see connections to others, which can lay the foundation for a stronger commitment to serving others. A key to the education-as-transformation model is the ability to accept and experience one's own vulnerability, and cultivate one's humility; neither are easily experienced or encouraged within the mainstream, but both are definitely possible.

Many years ago, while teaching at Harvard, I'm invited by a student (who's enrolled in the Harvard-MIT program that's granting a combined M.D. and Ph.D. degree) to talk with some of his colleagues about Indigenous, spiritually based healing. A most prestigious program! And my topic is a most marginal one for that pinnacle of the mainstream. But the student is open to ideas about healing, and so—naïvely, but hoping to share what I feel would be important ideas for medical students, especially those high-powered ones—I accept.

Then I find out the talk will be held at the Harvard Faculty Club; an ominous sign, but I had already accepted. As I walk into the faculty club, dressed in my typical informal style, I realized I'm walking into the lion's den: the room is filled not just with students but also with their faculty who, to the man (no women then), are wearing formal professional attire of tie and suit. Yes, I feel vulnerable, and literally plan how I can run away. And then I breathe deeply, feel the anxiety, and ready myself to become the sacrificial lamb—talking about Indigenous material, and spiritual material at that, to a strictly white Western group with a firmly materialistic perspective—ready because looking at the students, I still believe I might have something of value to say.

The talk proceeds, with the professors being unexpectedly polite but clearly not interested, while the students are open and wondering. Then, drawing from Indigenous ways of educating healers, I begin speaking about the importance of vulnerability as opposed to competence in medical training. The mood in the room changed—mostly for the students. Sitting on the edges of their seats, they listen closely. After the talk, a student tells me: "It's such a relief to hear someone talk publicly about vulnerability. We feel that all the time but can't talk about it. It's competence, competence, competence. They keep telling us we're at the top of the heap, and we must show we know . . . and know *all the time . . . even* when we don't. We're being shut down to our human feelings!"

If even those high-powered, high-performance Harvard-MIT students are seeking the opportunity to be vulnerable—to *just be themselves*—and learn specially from that experience, why not others?*

Indigenous approaches to health and healing emphasize balance and exchange, the connectedness of all people and all parts of the living universe. These teachings prepare the ground for the focus of the next chapter where reciprocities among individuals, communities, and the environmental surround are examined, establishing the need for a reciprocal interchange between psychological *and* social-structural change in order to encourage for actual and enduring well-being and social justice.

---

*This story comes from the 1980s before the more recent emphasis on vulnerability in the training of health providers and the more frequent acceptance of that often terrifying experience.

Indigenous approaches also emphasize the emergence of healing as a renewable, expanding resource, as balance keeps the process of healing a continual work in progress and exchange initiates a process where reciprocity encourages new forms. A particularly ironic but worthy challenge for the mainstream is the concept of healing as a movement toward and away from meaning, connection, and wholeness—healing encompassed within both directions, all of which is synergy in action. In the next chapter, we will see that when such intrinsically renewable resources, like healing, are supported within a sociocultural structure committed to equity, a healing or synergistic community can result.

CHAPTER SEVEN

"All My Relations"

Honoring the Interconnections That Define Us

Now, toward the end of our journey, we come again to the Kalahari Ju/'hoansi and their hunting-gathering way of life. I keep returning to their teachings because of the unique privilege I have in 1968 of being with them when they are still relying primarily on that way of successfully meeting the challenges and opportunities of their environment. Now, with gratitude, I can again honor the knowledge given to me from living among a people who offer this special view into the *evolutionary foundations* of our contemporary lives.

Much has happened since 1968, and I see for myself the forces of colonization introduce more intense structures of the dominating Western urbanized, capitalistic world into the Ju/'hoan life space. As they develop new patterns of resistance, adaptation, and empowerment, the Ju/'hoansi can again teach us. But I can confirm what I've been taught—their teachings must in the first instance be directed toward their own survival, and because of *their* commitment to sharing knowledge, and then given for the benefit of all.

In 1968, the Ju/'hoansi in /Kae/kae are still living a primarily hunter-gatherer existence, characterized by extensive sharing, including instances where needs are met both within and among communities through reciprocal support. Located in a desert environment, with the often just-adequate and shifting availability of resources, the Ju/'hoansi fashion a series of structures that allow for the sharing of those resources. Though each group has a well-defined territory (called a *n!ore*), there is reciprocal accessing of one another's territories when resources become scarce in one group's own area while being more available for another group: for example, when migrating game leaves your own territory and enters another group's territory; or when, because the rain may be spotty, berries located in a neighboring territory ripen sooner; or if, while out on a hunting expedition, the closest available water source is in another's home area. "This is the way we help each other," says =Omar Djo. "We let each other take from the riches of our land." Though boundaries to territories are not rigid, they are respected, and permission is needed to access resources in another group's territory—a permission that's routinely granted, knowing and trusting that it will be reciprocated when scarcity comes to one's own area.

This sharing of available resources also occurs within any one group; for example, food brought into camp is distributed throughout the group so no one goes hungry. This within-camp sharing is supported, even demanded, by the Kalahari environment. Without refrigeration, meat will soon spoil in the desert heat—drying meat into strips only delays this spoiling process somewhat. Thus to share meat brought into camp becomes a community given.

One day a young hunter comes into camp with—for a Ju/'hoan— uncharacteristic pride. A dead baby gemsbok, a prized local antelope, is draped over his shoulders. He's saying, without words, "Look at me and see what a thing I've brought here to feed you all!" Immediately, two older women greet him, derisively and decisively putting him in his place: "What's the big deal here? You think that scrawny thing you're going to give us is *real* meat? You might as well take it back into the bush. It's of no use to us!" Then pausing a bit, as they see the young man feeling the sting of their comments and physically deflating into a wish to just give them the gemsbok, the women conclude: "Just leave that animal here. We'll see if we can even *use* it. And you go on your way." The young hunter leaves, learning anew the importance of community and how individual achievements are nothing compared to community survival—which is the key to his own survival. The women, with inner glee, their faces barely showing any pleasure, begin to butcher the gemsbok—they know it will feed people in a good way, "in the Ju/'hoan way."

A key Ju/'hoan concept is that of *kxaosi,* meaning "stewards" or "owners." Ownership is a form of responsible stewardship. An owner is also a master in the sense of knowing fully. This concept of ownership as stewardship extends to many resources of value in Ju/'hoan life; there are, for example, *g!ukxaosi* (owners of water), informed persons who care for water resources so they can be shared rather than exclusive holders of rights to that water, and there are the *n/omkxaosi* (owners of n/om) or healers, who have that same role of stewardship and sharing in regard to n/om. As all are fed as well as possible, rather than a few well fed at the cost of others going hungry, so are all offered healing rather than a few receiving special and exclusive healing attention.

Since an extended Ju/'hoan family group will move several times a year to follow the path of migrating game and ripening root crops, there is a premium on keeping possessions to a minimum—the less to carry. Most of the essentials for survival, including one's home and hunting-gathering tools, can be made from the environment the group moves to, so there is little need to accumulate possessions beyond essential heavier items. This devaluation of accumulation is initiated by and supports the Ju/'hoansi ethic of egalitarianism and the dynamic of sharing.

The melon toss,* a game played mostly by Ju/'hoan girls and young women, exemplifies this practice of sharing and reciprocity. Its aim, structured by elegant and energetic dance movements and joyful songs,

---

*See John Marshall's 1970 film, *N!owa T'ama: The Melon Tossing Game,* for a graphic presentation of this dance/game.

is to achieve harmony among and within individuals and the communities they inhabit. A group of girls may gather to play the game, tossing the melon from one to another, with as much playful grace, at times even acrobatic, as possible, at the same time trying to ensure that any beauty in their toss doesn't undermine the more important aim: to be sure the melon, once tossed, can be caught by another member of the group, hopefully with grace, and then tossed again to another so as to be catchable. As the game proceeds, and the melon is caught more and more times, the participants' mood becomes increasingly joyful. The melon toss is great fun because of each person's successful, even acrobatic catching and tossing—a success that is ensured as much as possible by the skill of the girl tossing. When the melon is dropped—as it always will be—that particular iteration of the game is over. But no one is blamed, and the game can—and eventually will be—carried on. There are no individual winners or losers; the group plays the game and creates a web of reciprocating moves. What one enjoys, all enjoy; when all enjoy, each individual enjoys even more.

Beautiful and respectful exchanges are the valued renewable resources in this game, and the more they are created, the more exquisitely the web of reciprocal interconnections is woven. Individual and social tensions, swept up into that joyful exchange, can be mollified, even resolved, though they are not typically the reason for beginning the game—which is simply to reaffirm, in an exciting and fun way, the connections that make up community.

But this description of Ju/'hoan life is not meant to present an idyllic picture of pervading generosity. Is there anything in human society that is so perfect? The more we extol a culture or community as "pure" this or that, the more we essentialize that culture and in that process demean it by ignoring its realities, which are the complex aspects of being alive. As Indigenous teachings keep reminding us, balance—and its consequent well-being—*intrinsically* contains imbalance. Yes, the sharing ethic that pervades interpersonal relationships nurtures the reciprocity and collaboration that emerges among individuals and their community. When individuals work together to keep each other well and as well fed as possible, that harmonizing moves to the level of individuals and their community.

But scarcity of valuable resources is a part of Ju/'hoan life; for example, periodic droughts diminish the supply of food and water. These external scarcities put a severe strain on the feasibility of this sharing ethic and challenge the durability of the harmonizing relationships among individuals and their community. Within the community itself, there is a continual level of complaint or dissatisfaction with the "generosity" or "social responsibility" of others, most often expressed in complaints, sometimes bitter, about not sharing in the Ju/'hoan way, especially in regard to food. Sometimes it can seem like few people ever get enough, and someone else is always being stingy. "How could he have given me such a tiny piece of meat? Doesn't he know what I deserve?" is an almost common refrain, at times publicly and dramatically aired. The drama, often containing a mock-exaggerated hurt, can help reduce tensions through its very outrageousness. The disappointment or criticism can disappear the next day once there's a proper sharing of food.

But these almost routine complaints can also move into irritating disagreements or more severe arguments and even long-term antagonisms, conflicts, and on occasion, though rarely, violence.* Typically, before they become open conflicts, disagreements are subsumed within the general framework of sharing and reciprocity that governs Ju/'hoan life. The point is that this sharing is earned, not assumed; it's often the result of dealing with conflict, not just doing what comes naturally. Whatever harmony is achieved between individual and community takes effort to cultivate and is continually open to being dismantled.

Certainly, generosity is at play, but it's practiced within, even enmeshed within, a socioeconomic structure that typically demands sharing. So generosity then becomes something more complex than an

---

*See Lee (2012) for a discussion of conflict and its resolutions, and how conflict, and especially aggressive and violent behaviors, increases with the increasing sedentism of the Ju/'hoansi, exacerbated by their increased consumption of alcohol.

individual's personal motive to share—more complex but no less valid. Whatever harmony is experienced between and within the individual and her or his community exists within these *structural imperatives* that generate, even demand this generosity. Thus the generosity that is a reality of community survival is in part necessity driven, not totally freely chosen.

The Ju/'hoan healing dance, with its renewable, expanding, and accessible n/om, is a paradigm both for Ju/'hoan healing and more generally for a healing community. That healing ceremony is within and part of daily life, a point of intensity in the ongoing fabrics of living. The healing ceremony is created by the reciprocating balance among individuals at the dance, thereby creating a collaborative relationship among individuals and community, where what is good for one is good for all and the whole is greater than the sum of the parts—the key elements in a *synergistic community,* the paradigmatic healing community. As the community, fueled by the harmony among its parts, creates and supports the dance, the dance then structures the n/om, the renewable, expanding valuable resource, so that it is equitably distributed to all—the further defining characteristics of *synergy.* Of course, the collaboration and harmony is not permanent and needs continual reenergizing.

MAINSTREAM APPROACHES

This experience in the Kalahari opens my eyes and heart to an ancient and enduring truth—the dynamics and possible functioning of a healing community. Where the Ju/'hoansi teach us about synergy, as healing transformations of consciousness are released within a socioeconomic structure committed to sharing and social justice, supporting reciprocating pathways among individuals and communities, mainstream approaches stress the opposite: the separations and eventual conflicts among individuals and their communities. The mainstream operates more within a *scarcity paradigm* than the synergy paradigm and therefore stresses that valuable resources are experienced as scarce, with limited access, necessitating a competition for access, with the advantage given to those with power or prestige, which is a recipe for social injustice. Yes, we need to understand competition and conflict—and there seems to be too much of it these days, especially with increasing urbanization—and the separations, stresses, and fractures that underlie it. But unless we also delve deeply into experiences of sharing, and the dynamics of collaboration, as expressed within the experience of synergy, a large part of our human nature, especially in regard to its potential, is ignored.

Here is one example of this mainstream focus. A person is lying on a busy urban street, clearly in distress. People pass by, a number close by. Who—if anyone—will notice the distressed person? Who—if anyone—will offer help? This situation is now one feature of urban life. People endure accidents and suffer from destructive influences of life in the public sphere. Our motivation to assist or help is challenged.

Mainstream psychology has taken this real-life tragedy and the social-moral dilemma it provokes and made it into an experiment to find out how and why help is or is not offered. Researchers pay actors to lie in the street and act like they are in distress, moaning for help. It's totally realistic. The passersby are unaware of the deception. By staging this reality situation, it becomes a classic mainstream experiment—controlled and focused, with an emphasis on behaviors and outcomes.* Using videotaped footage taken by concealed cameras, researchers can focus on the behaviors of passersby, uncontaminated by other issues, and study who stops or fails to help, how quickly, and why.

Some of the results are disheartening. One experiment takes place on a crowded nonresidential urban street, near a subway station. In one instance, the actor, a young male, is wearing casual clothes. Despite his very realistic moaning, it takes nearly twenty minutes for

---

*There are many instances researching this concept of bystander apathy, employing various contexts. The results I'm presenting here come from a study described in Cool Psychologist (2009).

someone to stop and offer help; meanwhile, thirty-four people pass by without helping. When the actor is a young woman clearly show-ing signs of distress but also casually dressed, help is offered in four minutes. When the actor, the same young male, acting similarly dis-tressed, is now wearing business clothes (tie and jacket), help is offered in just a bit over *four seconds!* Sexual bias and social class prejudice are at work. The passerby who so quickly bends down to help the well-dressed actor is also, not surprisingly, wearing a business suit. When asked why he stopped to help, he said: "I'd hate to be in his position of feeling ill and nobody stops to help him." He's very comfortable helping one of his own.

Passersby use many devices to avoid helping, including even refusing to look at the actor even though they are close enough to touch him. Their explanations for not stopping to help are sometimes banal ("I didn't have the time") and sometimes fear based ("It's dangerous to get involved with strangers")—though such a response is getting increas-ingly understandable with the increase in random acts of violence. There's also a counterintuitive explanation. It turns out that it's more likely a person will be helped if there is no one or only one other person in the vicinity rather than many. In this case, the rationale offered for failing to help, if there are other people around, is, "I figured someone else was going to help." This is called *diffusion of responsibility,* and it thrives in a social environment that lacks intimate and meaningful con-nections among people.

This mainstream line of research provides valuable information about helping strangers in public, urban environments. Except perhaps for the tightly knit neighborhood and cultural niches within the city, the urban environment typically represents a temporary, makeshift, fluctuating, distant, and anonymous community, one in which path-ways toward harmony would be very difficult to forge. Because the research focuses on the separations and conflicts among individuals and the reasons they don't help, rather than meaningful connections and their reasons for helping, it's examining more of what is, the status quo, rather than what can become—such as potential for reciprocity. Yes, this mainstream research is valuable, but it remains biased. In fact the research topic is more accurately described by its more widely used label of bystander *apathy,* rather than by its more formal and professional but misleadingly neutral label—the bystander *effect.*

This tendency for mainstream psychology to focus more on conflicts between individuals and their communities is supported by a series of assumptions. For example, mainstream psychology assumes there is a separation, even separateness between individuals and their communities, and that separation is caused by and feeds conflict, or at least functions as an obstacle to reciprocity. But in real-life situations, the boundaries between individuals and their communities are typically more fluid than static, more flexible than rigid, and, most important, more permeable than protected. As a result, there are frequent and ordinary interactions between individuals and their communities—the two are more points along a shifting continuum than isolated, clearly defined entities.

I often tell my community psychology students, "I've never seen a community," emphasizing the typical absence of sharp boundaries to communities that are essentially experiences more than organizations. For example, we often can't pinpoint when we enter or exit from a community, as we've typically already thought about the community before we physically enter its domain—we're already having an *experience* of that community.

Beneath the lure, even attractiveness, of this mainstream assumption of separateness lies a pervasive fear of loss of self in the experience of the group or the collective—the threat, made realistic in history, of the authoritarian group mind or the mindless collective. The classic Asch experiment, in offering striking evidence for conformity within a group, provides data supporting this fear.* The typical design of that

---

*The Asch experiment is one of those staples of introductory psychology texts, usually appearing with the discussion of social and cultural contexts. It's been repeated many times over different decades, with very similar outcomes. See Asch (1965) for an early presentation of the experimental paradigm.

experiment has eight people sitting in a circle. They are first shown a drawing of a line, let's say 10 inches long, and then another drawing of three lines—one 7 inches long, another 10 inches long, and a third 13 inches long. One participant is asked to say which of the three lines in this second drawing is closest in length to the first line he was shown. The correct answer is obvious; only one of the three lines is clearly a good match. But unbeknownst to this participant, the other seven members of the group are research accomplices. They are all asked the question before the participant, and all intentionally pick one particular wrong answer (for example, that the 7-inch-line is the most similar)—because that is the way the research is rigged. As these purposefully incorrect answers unfold before the only naïve participant, he may at first disbelieve the incorrect answers being given. But as more people in the group give the same incorrect answer, the participant begins to doubt his own vision and judgment. By the time the question is posed to him, he may be thinking to himself: "I'm not sure what's going on, but I might as well go along with what the others are doing." And so he, too, against the evidence of his own eyes, gives the very same wrong answer as the previous seven accomplices did.* The term "conformity" is personified and solidified.

The political message of this Asch-type research can realistically be that we must be on guard against the tyranny of the masses or avoid "brainwashing," especially when it's a covert cover for real political traps and cages. The responding emphasis on rugged individualism or the courageous whistle-blower point to legitimate responses to group tyranny. But again, though realistic, this message is one-sided; in focusing the analysis on conflict and denial of individual integrity, it can overlook many of the opportunities to explore ways reciprocity can emerge from this denial.

---

*The typical breakdown in the Asch experiment is that only 20 percent of the naïve persons tested remained independent of the group's pressure to answer incorrectly; 33 percent conformed to the group's incorrect choice more than half the time they were tested; and the rest conformed at least some of the time.

I want to stop here to deal with an important point that still calls for my attention. The dangers of groupthink are frightening enough to always take seriously. But the concept of reciprocity, so essential to the Indigenous perspective, actively works against a groupthink mentality or the formation of an authoritarian community. In the Ju/'hoan healing community, individuals are active contributors to the formation of community, and the dynamics of that community are structured to equitably and openly serve its members. There are constant checks and balances to keep reciprocity alive. The challenge is to establish such active and activating reciprocity in larger, more urban settings. But as we'll discuss later in this chapter, it's possible, especially if we start small, moving one careful step at a time.

Another mainstream assumption is that because the world beyond the individual is unpredictable, we employ various cognitive and attitudinal strategies to bring a sense of predictability to our larger socioeconomic environment. By bringing order, even logic, to this condition of unpredictability, we gain a sense of control over our external world, thereby diminishing our fear of the unknown and gaining confidence in our actions. Mainstream psychology has developed concepts of attitudinal attributions or strategies that people use to introduce this sense of predictability into their world. For example, the "just-world hypothesis" describes how many people need to believe the world is fair and just, where bad people are punished and good people rewarded. Unfortunately, this describes a need for predictability rather than a fact of existence.

With these attitudinal strategies, we're supported in our belief that our social environment is now understandable; we can control, even manipulate it, and thereby set the rules for interactions with that world. These attitudinal strategies for bringing order and control into our world mirror the basic tenets of mainstream psychological research and its laboratory-influenced model of data collection. The implied aim is adaptation rather than transformation, carrying out the mainstream tenets of development and therapy. To accept and appreciate the unpredictability inherent in these relationships, as proposed in Indigenous approaches, can open the door to the creation of a balanced reciprocity so that neither the individual nor the community controls the other.

Central to mainstream psychology's emphasis on the separations and conflicts between the individual and her community is its concept of self. Though any consideration of relationships between individual and community must understand both sides, mainstream psychology, especially with its emphasis on theories of the self, focuses more attention on the experience and practices of self than those of community. Whereas there are abundant and well-developed terms relating to the self, such as "self-knowledge" or "self-awareness," terms relating to community are sparse and typically underdeveloped and often carry a negative connotation. The term "community *norms,*" which connotes pressures on the individual to adhere to or conform to society's roles and rules, is commonly used, as opposed to "community *empowerment,*" connoting the liberating force of community for its members.

With these more ill-defined—even shadowy or adversarial—concepts of community, it is easier for mainstream psychology to pin its hopes for health and well-being more on the individual and in particular a concept of self that is firmly set within a Western individualistic framework. The self as the initiator and repository of a person's experiences, motivations, and expectations is typically seen as a bounded concept, emphasizing a degree of separateness that can help the individual stay isolated from external forces. The emphasis is on the development of self within the individual rather than the interchanges with community that define community in the Indigenous world. Self-fulfillment, for example, is vulnerable to being reduced to a description of how personal desires can win out over communal pressures to conform, leaving aside things like the meaning making that comes from collaborative efforts. The ability to stand up and do it on your own is extolled over the ability to work with and within one's group. It then becomes ironic to criticize someone for being too self-centered when that person has been encouraged to look out for "number one" or ask, "What's in it for me?"—constant messages amplified in the media, especially compelling because they are so often stated implicitly, but also accepted in many real-life situations, despite calls for generosity and social justice. This emphasis on the individualistic self, working more against others than with them, prepares a person for battle in the scarcity world accepted—at times promoted—by mainstream psychology. In that world, where valuable resources are kept scarce, access to these resources is determined by competition—authentic collaboration becomes irrelevant.*

Mainstream psychology's discussion of the individualistic-collectivistic dimension has reinforced the value and validity of individuals as compared to—at times over and against—communities. This dimension was originally introduced as a way to recognize the importance of community in a field thus far fascinated with individuals and their growth. But soon the dimension came to be more of a dichotomy, setting the stage for theories of conflict between opposites. Again, mainstream psychology sees the individualistic end of the continuum as more clearly and subtly articulated and implicitly valued than the collectivist end, which the mainstream at times seems to perceive as a vague arena in which one can lose one's self, meaning lose one's ultimately valued individuality.

Reciprocating collaboration between individuals and their communities requires a full and accepting condition from both ends of a

---

*Mainstream psychology's fascination with achievement motivation offers an instructive case study. The person who scores high on achievement motivation has nurtured and even glorified characteristics residing within the self, such as being a self-starter or goal-directed person. Achievement motivation deals with individuals making their mark on the world, in large part by implanting their personalities and personal desires on that world. The world as community becomes more an arena for self-achievement rather than as a partner in the creating of harmonious relationships between the individual and the community. Even when being an effective coworker or team player is extolled as part of achievement motivation, these attributes are still subsumed within the larger goal of self-enhancement.

continuum. For example, if the concept of self is based on openness and acceptance of difference and unpredictability, seeing the connections with others as a reality beyond any boundaries of self, then it can open the door to participation in and with one's community—and vice versa. For example, if a concept of self allowed for the nurturing of generosity, compassion, or altruism, there would be a way out of self-centeredness and into interconnectedness. Such deep connections with others would create the community that would by its very nature exist in harmony with its participants.

But thus far, mainstream psychology has not committed itself to a full-scale study of such motivations, and the research that is available is focused on reductionistic, limited versions of those motivations. In one series of experiments, little kids are shown picking up dropped clothespins that the experimenter, who is hanging clothes, pretends to "accidentally" drop and then struggle to bend down and recover. The child can easily pick up the clothespin, and when she does and hands it back to the experimenter, it is seen as a sign of empathy, if not altruism. Really? What about the desire to please an adult?

Mainstream psychology is fundamentally ahistorical and apolitical; it spends most of its energy describing the status quo—which is important especially in pointing out problems—but has little energy left for working on ways to change it. Not fully committed to exploring community and especially its healing potentials, mainstream psychology has limited its strong commitment to understanding the individual ways people can avoid the unreasonable pressures of the group rather than grow from within their communities. Though the newly formed discipline of critical psychology has attempted to reverse this pattern by considering the social justice potential of communities, the effects of that subdiscipline are not widespread throughout psychology.

As a result, mainstream psychology remains trapped within its colonizing history, failing to work actively toward social change through its underappreciation for the dynamics of change, especially the need for change on the institutional or community level. Viewing challenges from a more individualistic perspective, with its emphasis on the separated and bounded self, mainstream psychology tends to see problems as individual issues rather than considering the institutional aspect. This can be a devastating approach. Though clearly the individual's effort and commitment are critical, they are not automatically explanatory. For example, it does little good to say to a group of Indigenous people, existing within a racist environment and suffering from unemployment and poor health care, that they should just get it together and make more of an effort. Blaming those individuals is a further expression of that racism, since despite their efforts toward constructing a better life, racism continues on the institutional level, exerting a force that overpowers those individual efforts. Substance abuse is affected by individual choice and responsibility, but they both exist within a larger and more problematic social, economic, and political environment, where systemic racism is overpowering. Indigenous approaches, in stressing a healing balance between individual and community, create opportunities for more harmonious relationships between the two—a harmony gained from recognizing that the individual and the community are two levels or parts of a single biome. With that recognition individuals are inspired to make a commitment to social change.

INDIGENOUS APPROACHES

In the bay that our Fijian village of Naqara faces, I'm perched on the barrier reef that sits about one-quarter mile from our village beach. Though punctuated by openings to the rough open ocean waters beyond, the encircling reef creates a natural, accessible water space for the village, its much calmer waters allowing for communal fishing efforts. My family and I have been living and working in Naqara for the past two years, so it's totally natural that I've joined about twenty-five other villagers—male and female, with ages ranging from older to teenage. We're hovering above, sometimes standing on the reef, losing and regaining our balance as the open ocean waves break over the reef, sending their forceful spray onto us. We're all part of a traditional Fijian fish drive.

Standing on the reef we form a large semicircle, joined together as we each hold a section of a large fishing net in our hands. As we move off the reef and toward the beach, keeping our spacing, our net moves toward a more fully formed circle, trapping more and more fish into a tighter and tighter space. If someone slips, another close by picks up the net so it doesn't go below the surface, allowing fish to escape. Aided by mostly the younger participants, who are very animated in beating the surface of the water with sticks to drive the fish toward the encircling net, we're closing in on a really big catch. Only the reef, with its razor-sharp edges, dangerous if stepped on the wrong way, seems to be an obstacle. I can only be grateful to avoid cuts from the reef, knowing I don't have the skill others have from their years of fishing along the reef.

"Hey, don't let the net go down there! Keep it high!" someone shouts. Instructions of where and when to move, how to move together, punctuate the air, voiced with authority by the more experienced participants. The net becomes organic, like we're all breathing together with and through it, and it naturally grows smaller to be more effective. Each of us has a role; each part counts. Screams of joy in the fishing, the fishing together, and the fishing with success bring us all closely together. "We know what we're doing today," one woman affirms, and others slap hands in support. That communal joy spreads across me, as Sevuloni flashes a broad smile of connection my way.

Finally, the net, now forming a large teardrop, closed and bulging with fish, is brought over to the waiting boat, anchored close to shore. And then the net, with the fish inside, is dumped into the boat, producing a chaotic pile. The smiles of excitement speak of the energy we just expended and expended as a community.

The fish drive, though successful, is not over. As the net, heavy with fish of all kinds, is brought onto the grass of the village and the fish are dumped out into a large, sprawling pile, the distribution begins. Two older women are in charge. They direct the young men to throw fish into a number of piles, each one representing one household in the village. The women seek to have piles fairly represent the needs of each household, larger piles for larger households, smaller ones for smaller households. The piles are created independent of how many people from each household were actually on the fish drive—or even if no member was on the drive. There is one older couple in the village, and neither was fit enough to participate—they have their pile. At the end of the distribution, the two women look over the piles and make some final adjustments—adding a bit to one pile, taking away from another. "It's done," one of the woman states, and then each household carries away its allotted pile—and each household knows exactly which is its pile. It's all out in the open—no secret deals for specific community members.

More fish have come in today than typically come in from the regular fishing techniques, where a few people going out in their individual boats, or the women go out as a group into shallow water with their two-women nets. But there are no heroes in this fish drive. No one is boasting about how well he did his part of the drive, nor even talking about his specific job, except maybe to joke with or tease another: "If you hadn't been sleeping out there on the reef, I could have caught even more fish," one of the adolescents says with mock seriousness to another. It's clear that the village succeeded in getting food, and the village shares in that success; it's equally clear that the village succeeded because its members worked together. Villagers and village are one unit, reciprocally supporting each other. And nobody makes a big deal out of it. "This fish drive is how we live together . . . helping each other," Sevuloni tells me. I feel a quiet joy to be part of "how we live together."

As each person in the village is fed through the pervading and prevailing ethic of sharing, competition among individuals for access to this valuable resource is reduced: "Now we all can be well fed," says Komera, one of the senior village women. Interpersonal sharing nurtures and is part of the harmonizing interconnections among individuals and their community and culture. As ends of a continuum, with multiple interconnections and permeable boundaries, individual and community now become one in experience. Synergistic community exists as the whole is greater than the sum of the parts, and what is good for one is good for all. The community is energized by the valuable resource of collaboration; as one, they work the *social* net, which is renewable and expanding. Ironically, as the group works collaboratively to catch the fish, the actual fishing net shrinks to more effectively trap them. At the end, the fish caught from that collaboration are distributed equitably.

Vanua is one of the most important words in the Fijian language, describing the heart of Fijian culture. Vanua is an experience; it means the "land" but more concretely "the land and the people who live on it" or "our place, our culture and its traditions." "Vanua gives us a place in our world," says Ratu Civo. "Where you are living now, in Naqara, that's your vanua," he continues, "and when you return home, I hope you will be in your vanua." Self and community, in tandem and working together, are needed to make the land a people and a culture, a vanua, which then refeeds the people and the community, in continuously reciprocating cycles.

When I first meet Tony Sand, he's interested to know where I come from, who is my community. "In our traditional Cree way," he says, "when we meet someone for the first time, we shake hands and tell each other not just our names but, more importantly, who we're related to and where we come from. That way we know who we really are."* Acknowledging kinships, hopefully going back at least to great-grandparents, and traditional home community, which today is typically a reserve, demonstrates the links and unity among the individuals and their communities. Drawing on history and culture creates identity, while respecting community enhances a person,

---

*In special situations, especially sacred ceremonies, one may also share one's traditional First Nation's spirit name.

enlarging his or her fields of meaning and purpose. Also, Tony says, "Shaking hands is a way of showing respect to the other person . . . because you just don't know if this might be the last time you see them."

Tony affirms this pervasive connectedness in regard to the sweat lodge. When he begins his sweat ceremony, he says: "Let's try to be of one mind in this lodge. If we all focus on why we we've come to the lodge, what we're seeking, we can be of one mind. That makes the sweat more powerful. We all come for different reasons, but we make a whole when we're of one mind." This is not mindless groupthink but the opening of each person to the worlds of others to make a rich community of worlds, nourishing paths, all beyond individual boundaries, toward spiritual understanding.

In Indigenous cultures, the circle, as a dynamic and vital centering point, helps initiate this respectful reciprocity among individuals and their communities; it serves as an enlivening symbol of that reciprocity, a symbol that is an actual experience. "The drum is the heartbeat of our people," says elder Tony Sand. "The drum and the drumbeat is our life. When we hear the drum we come alive." Yes, that's for sure! My little grandson, Jayden, not yet two, moves like an inspired veteran when he hears the drum beating in the Cree powwow or round-dance music. He's inside that drumbeat, as together they move so rhythmically.

The drum Tony is referring to is a sacred drum, used in ceremonies, to call on the spirits for help. The drum is also the encircling nature of the Cree community, where all around and within the circle are equally valued. "There are many sacred circles for us," Danny says. "There's Mother Moon and Father Sun, and our tipis and sweat lodges are constructed to be circles." Ceremonies such as talking circles and healing circles bring people together, connecting them as one.

These circles often have a fire as a centering point, as in the sweat lodge and the Ju/'hoan healing dance. The fire is more than a literal one; it is an *experience* of warmth, light, and life. The fire breathes life into the community, touching all. As the Ju/'hoansi say, "The boiling n/om touches all at the dance . . . it leaps out to everybody like sparks that fly into the night from our fires." Though none would deny the life-giving and, at times, lifesaving properties of that actual fire, with its ability to cook and keep one warm, it's the experience of connectedness that is also treasured.

Another element in this Indigenous reciprocating network is the activation of service toward others; as one sees the reality of the other within that connective web, there's an appreciation for reaching out, and especially in the context of a history that is kept active, forming a backbone as well as context for contemporary living—in contrast to mainstream psychology's ahistorical approach.

In Canada, the era of residential schools exemplifies the dehumanizing and destructive effects of institutional racism on Indigenous people. From an Indigenous perspective, history helps determine identity, and that identity contains political and cultural dimensions. Indigenous survivors of the colonializing residential school system are increasingly telling their stories, stories of abuse suffered at the schools, stories of struggle with addictions that are fed by that abuse, and stories of survival and growth and renewal that demonstrate the strengths of hard-earned well-being and empowerment.* Their lives are a living reminder of the lessons of history, the need for social justice to fight the racism that continues today as a legacy of abuse surfaces. Social justice becomes an everyday necessity and something history will keep boiling to the surface.

I'm constantly reminded how community can respect the individual, especially by encouraging each person to find her or his place of service in the larger whole. As he puts me up on the hill to do a hanbleciya (vision quest), Joe Eagle Elk brings this Indigenous teaching to me concretely, the better to learn. He speaks to me carefully but firmly: "You go up there to find out things and maybe learn from the spirits . . . and when you come back down, you'll tell us what you learned."

---

*There is a powerful and expanding source of materials presenting these stories, as well as analyses, of the devastations caused by colonization and descriptions of paths toward renewal. One of the earliest sources is the Assembly of First Nation's *Breaking the Silence* (1994).

When Joe comes up the hill to bring me home at the end of the vision quest, he takes me to the ceremonial setting in which are gathered those who have personally helped and supported me, including singers who in ceremony are part of the spiritual guidance for my trip to the hill, many of whom I don't know. Joe turns to me and asks me to tell the people gathered about what I learned in those days of "being alone with the Creator"—his phrasing humbles me. "If you can . . . and if you wish, tell us what you saw and heard so we can all learn. Your time up there can help you . . . it can also help us.

As instructed by Stanley Red Bird, Joe's helper, I have also purchased a number of gifts to give away at this ceremony of return that is bringing me back into the community, gifts to express my gratitude for the support and prayers of others. I buy special gifts to give to Joe and Stanley—to me they stand out in the depth and meaning of their support.

As we sit in the circle, and the ceremony celebrating my return is nearing its end, the time has come for me to give my gifts. I lean over to Joe and whisper: "How do I distribute the gifts I've brought? And I'd like to give something special to you and Stanley." "Well, we're in a circle now, this is the way we take you back into the community," Joe says. "So just put all your gifts in a pile, and we'll just pass the pile around the circle . . . then each person who is here can get something." Definitely surprised, with my intention of showing Joe and Stanley how much I appreciate their help apparently thwarted, I do just what Joe suggests. The pile of gifts goes around the circle, as always clockwise. The "special" gifts I have brought are taken by the second and fourth persons in the circle; Joe and Stanley, who sit at the end of the circle, take what from what is left. In this way, they live their humility and respect for community.

"This is how we do this gift stuff. Everyone who is here at the ceremony, even ones you don't know, is part of the ceremony community. They're here to support you, to pray for you when you're up on the hill, to welcome you back when you come down from the hill. They're your community," he ends simply. Yes, this is my community; their prayers and support nourish me on the hill, and they are all equally members of that ceremonial community, all equally valued by my gift-giving process.

Joe establishes the underlying community context for individuals' spiritual journeys. I go on the hill and, as the Lakota say, "cry for a vision"; the difficulty, the suffering in that journey is mine to accept, but I feel the support of others. The vision I have, the teachings given me, are to help me lead a good life—a life committed to service—not for self-enhancement and gaining spiritual development creds. Still a hard teaching for me to practice! In fact it is through that service to others, whether it be healing or teaching or teaching as healing, that spiritual understanding becomes concrete for it's a higher power that fuels that healing.

Mitakuye oyas'in means "all of my relatives" in Lakota. It's not something Joe teaches me explicitly; it's something I learn by observing and doing. After every prayer or prayerful action, Joe says, "Mitakuye oyas'in." It's the Lakota way of acknowledging the web of connections between and among all parts of the universe, all animated by spiritual energy; with those words, one acknowledges one's place in that web and one's humility and respect for the honor of being so connected. "It's placing ourselves in the proper place—as just one part, one little part of the spiritual world we live in," says Joe. As we humans are connected to the universe spiritually, so we are to all parts of that universe, the elements, the plants, the animals, and other humans.

Joe lives the teachings of "all my relations" teachings; and through the proper ceremonial process, he has invited me to join him on the path of how these teachings can exist in and inform my life. In the first instance, I do as he does; then the doing becomes a committed practice. Since those first days in 1969, I work toward incorporating "all my relations" into my life, not just in ceremonies like the sweat lodge but also within the texture and rhythms of my days and nights. If I hadn't been given those teachings, or attempted to make them real, I wouldn't use the actual phrase *all my relations* in this book.

When I first experience these reciprocating and harmonizing relationships among individuals and their communities *as an ongoing part of daily life* while living with the Ju/'hoansi, I struggle to put that experience into words—it seems both so ephemeral *and* practical, so richly complex *and* utterly to the point. I'm committed to writing about such "beyond words" experiences to help carry out the task I'm given by the elders to bring their teachings to others who may need inspiration and practical words to change. The concept of synergy seemed appropriate to at least suggest or point to features in those harmonizing relationships.

Synergy occurs when apparently conflicting elements come together, in unexpected patterns, to form a harmonious whole.* From a mainstream perspective, individuals and communities are just such *apparently* conflicting elements. When synergy is released, a synergistic community is created. In a synergistic community, what is good for one is good for all; in the Fijian fish drive, each community member's collaborative participation not only feeds himself but also feeds every other member. Also the whole is greater than the sum of the parts in a synergistic community; as a result of the entire village's participation, a fish drive can exist, an event whose effectiveness goes beyond a mere adding up of the efforts of each member on the drive—the encircling net that catches the fish, held at different points by individuals, symbolizes this greater whole.

The engine that powers synergy is the existence of a valued resource that is renewable, expanding, and accessible, equitably to all. In the Fijian fish drive, this resource could be village collaborations; in the Ju/'hoan healing dance, n/om becomes that renewable resource. Being renewable, those resources can continue to provide benefits to the community— the more they are made available, the more they are available. The more

---

*For a fuller discussion of synergy and the synergistic community it can create, see Katz and Murphy-Shigematsu (2012a) and especially chapters 1 and 2. The idea of synergy, for example, has a distinguished conceptual history, including discussions by Buckminster Fuller, an original theorist (see e.g., Fuller 1963), as well as Ruth Benedict (see e.g., Maslow and Honigmann 1970) and Abe Maslow (see e.g., Maslow 1971).

the valuable resource of n/om is activated and applied, the more there is available to be activated and applied. Because the release of synergy creates an experience beyond the concept of a limited and limiting zero-sum game, competition for valuable resources can be transcended so that what is good for one becomes good for all.

"Our voices can reach the gods," says /Wa, as she describes how the singers can be energized to sing stronger with the rising strength of the n/om activated at the dance. And she knows that strong singing is part of the reciprocating connected environment that makes the n/om strong in the first place. "We can get those dancers going," she proudly states. The n/om leaps out like sparks from the fire, touching all as they vanish into the dance's atmosphere—and thus the whole of the Ju/'hoan healing community becomes larger than the sum of its individual parts.

Synergy, and the synergistic community it encourages, can be hard to grasp, until it is experienced—and then it seems rewardingly obvious. From a Western perspective, it can seem almost magical, conjuring up ideas about perpetual motion, or the illogic of the phrase "the more you use something the more you have." But that's just one of the main points. Synergy can move the Western worldview toward and beyond its conceptual boundaries, releasing—often exponentially—healing potentials. As a catalyst, synergy cannot only make things happen but also make them happen in an expanding manner. An ideal can become real.

Valuable resources created by or released through human activity and intentions are more suited to the synergy model. For example, healing or knowledge or community collaborations are resources that are intrinsically amenable to becoming renewable. Other valuable resources, such as land, function less easily within the synergy paradigm, though changes in socioeconomic structures can also make this happen. For example, with their reciprocal and reciprocating access to land, the Ju/'hoan create patterns of sharing set within harmonizing relationships. In *Indigenous Healing Psychology,* we're focusing on those valuable resources created by or released through human activity in order to better understand the synergy paradigm and therefore how it might generalize more appropriately to other resources such as land.

Though we are stressing resources created or released by human activity as the most likely sites of synergy, there are strong indications that synergy is inherent in and intrinsic to the nature of the universe (see e.g., Fuller 1963). If synergy already exists, then it is more a question of how we release it into the human community.

But how does this synergistic community actually happen? Realistically, there is no simple or even clear-cut answer. There seems to be no *particular* beginning point or originating cause that *predictably* brings about this community. Personal and interpersonal factors such as feelings of generosity or motivations to share, or institutional and structural variables, such as policies against racism or laws distributing resources equitably, can both serve as starting points. Nor does there seem to be a linear, sequential model of how this change to synergy occurs, nor a clear indication of causal factors.

The personal, interpersonal, community, and cultural factors that encourage the emergence of a synergistic community are continually interacting, making it unlikely one could identify a consistent set of factors that are either necessary or sufficient. For example, if socioeconomic structures dictate the survival necessity for a sharing ethos, when sharing does occur it can't simply be because of *personal* generosity, especially a generosity founded only in choice. The Ju/'hoansi teach us that. This is not to diminish or discredit their pervasive sharing but to seek to understand it more fully. If there is a strong set of personal motivations for sharing, they can begin to reshape institutions, especially at the ground level. The Ju/'hoansi feel concretely—and fundamentally at a deep level—their bonds with each other and the comfort, even joy, in supporting one another; the healing dance is certainly maintained by that sharing ethic and likely emerges in part from that ethic. When =Oma Djo says his "heart is happy" after participating in a healing dance, he acknowledges this personal generosity, a generosity nurtured in service. Both the personal-interpersonal and community-cultural-institutional ends of the continuum must be engaged if enduring change is to result.

Indigenous perspectives cultivate both ends of the continuum between individual and community, enriching each end so that it has more depth and power and strengthening each end so that it can be less defensive toward interactions with the other. For example, there is an emphasis on the deep and loving bonds possible among people, which helps move one beyond the experience of a delimited and separate self, seeking self-justification or self-aggrandizement. Compassion is highly valued, an unquestioned compassion whose depth goes beyond empathic feelings into nurturing altruistic actions.

In Fiji, dauloloma is central to being on the straight path. But knowing how easy it is to love a person I like or admire, and how difficult it is to have similar feelings for someone I don't like or even find reprehensible, I need to understand the full meanings of dauloloma. "Suppose someone comes to you for help," I ask Ratu Civo, "and you know this is not a good person; this is a person who maybe has abused children. How can you still practice dauloloma?" "No one ever said dauloloma is easy," he cautions, "but when we know that everyone is a part of the sacred, everyone comes from our spiritual ancestors . . . then . . . well then, what seems so difficult becomes possible. We have to respect the spirits of our land." "But do you work differently with a person like that, someone who has done something so bad?" I ask. "Not really," he says with a sigh, "we just work as we work . . . I might feel like not being with him, like pulling away, but then I remember his spirit . . . and then I do the best I can to support such a person in finding the straight path." Yes, I think to myself, that's how compassion connects and heals.*

---

*The Dalai Lama discusses the phenomenon of compassion, so central to Buddhist practice. He says there are different forms and levels of compassion; for example, compassion toward one's enemies needs training and dedication to cultivate, whereas compassion toward loved ones or family is more of a naturally occurring phenomenon. The Dalai Lama's writings on compassion are extensive; one example is Dalai Lama (2011); see also Goleman (2015) for a discussion of some implications of the Dalai Lama's approach to compassion.

Though there are times when a particular event or confluence of factors seems to spark or even initiate this synergistic community, those apparently discrete starting points or tipping points or points of a critical mass, while they may accelerate, even jump-start ongoing processes of change, are themselves embedded in those processes. It seems we're left with a realistic picture of change in a world filled with unpredictability—with the Indigenous perspective of knowing that not everything can be analyzed down to understanding, that mystery remains to have its place. Instead of focusing too much on pinpointing what or who superficially causes this synergistic community of psychology, we can work on understanding practical principles about how that community evolves or emerges and endures.

COUNTERCURRENTS WITHIN THE MAINSTREAM

The benefits accruing to the release of synergy and the creation of a synergistic community are many and impressive, especially when we consider the alternative, which could be called the scarcity paradigm or situations where synergy is (relatively) absent. When scarcity prevails, valuable resources are *perceived as if* and then function as if they are scarce. In fact, their value often depends on this scarcity. Competition among individuals and individuals and their communities is encouraged, because there is a limited amount of the desired resource. Access to the resource is typically determined by power and prestige, so that those in power and with privilege get there first and continue getting there until the resource is used up. Clearly, what is good for one then conflicts with and takes away from the good for all.

The mainstream Western health system exhibits many of the structures and principles of this scarcity paradigm. Professionally trained health providers are generally in limited supply; the very demanding requirements of their training places a limit on numbers available, and their reputation is fed by this very nature of access: "That therapist is really good . . . you should see how hard it is to get an appointment with her!" Yet access to professional providers is improved if the one seeking access has power or prestige—or money! Waiting lists function most rigidly for the poor or marginalized; those lists seem to "magically" disappear when someone has connections—usually flowing from already being in a position of power. These inequities in health care access result in poor care for the marginalized, affecting other areas of life (longevity, ability to work) and reinforcing other existing inequities.

This scarcity paradigm, which largely determines the nature of the mainstream approach, is a logical, almost necessary expression of twenty-first-century Western capitalism, which extolls commercialization of all resources, even unlikely ones such as healing, so that they become commodities and therefore more easily bought and sold. This form of capitalism is a system built on assumptions of scarcity feeding value and the need to compete for valuable scarce resources. It is built on the foundational pillars of power and control, possessed and tightly guarded by those already in power and control—the springboards from which those in power seek to exclude those who are presently without or close to attaining power. Existing with a zero-sum game model, the scarcity paradigm encourages competition because the more one person or group uses a valuable resource, the less of that resource is available to others.

Culture and psychology reciprocate their influences, reflecting each other's values and aspirations. Changing psychology more toward synergy is also a question of broad changes within the culture—no easy task. As contemporary capitalism continues to nourish colonizing forces, whereby the colonizers—now in the form of many multinational corporations extracting resources without a fair exchange, especially within Indigenous worlds—the challenge for change becomes exceedingly challenging.

As capitalism is supported by a consumer-commodity-oriented approach to all resources, even those resources most amenable to becoming renewable, such as healing, are cast as being scarce and thus necessitating competition. Making healing a commodity to be pur-chased prevents that healing from being appreciated as a renewable, expanding resource—the heart of the synergy model and the nemesis of the commodification-for-profit model. Though some Ju/'hoan heal-ers have tried to capture n/om as a personal possession, thus making it more available to be "bought," n/om as an inherently renewable and expanding substance escapes those commercializing limitations—or else it turns into something that is far from the renewable resource released in the traditional Ju/'hoan healing dance. Likewise, if a self-help group were to charge admission—selling the group as a commodity—it would violate the fundamental definition of such groups; namely, free access to its healing experience.

The difficulty of this capitalistic trap can't be underestimated, but the challenge is very much worth mounting. The emergence of com-munity healing networks and, in particular, self-help groups that can function as synergistic communities offer one pathway out of that trap.

Before we talk in detail about self-help groups, it's useful to consider two other countercurrents that can help set the stage for that discussion: social construction theory and its concept of relational self, and the disci-pline of critical psychology and its commitment to social justice. Though the individual and the community are realistically inseparable and inter-acting points in a continuum, we can see social constructionism as focus-ing on the individual and his or her experience of self as a starting point, while critical psychology focuses more on community and institutional structures as starting points. Both countercurrents nourish psychology's appreciation for interpersonal reciprocity and institutional equity as nec-essary to promote service within a social justice framework.

Essential to establishing the reciprocating connections between indi-viduals and their communities, a commitment at the core of Indigenous approaches is the need to move beyond the mainstream concept of self as a clearly bounded egocentric and individualistically centered experience, primed for the competitive pursuit of what are managed as scarce resources. The social constructionist approach to self provides a promising alternative, stressing the permeability of self-boundaries, and the fluidity in self-experiences; a connection to others becomes a given and a motivation for reciprocal understanding.

Ken Gergen is at the creative forefront of the social constructionist position, and I'm especially excited to present a view of his work, since he is one of my favorite professors during graduate school. A prolific writer and theorist, Gergen is deeply concerned with praxis, the connections between theory and practice.* Through the Taos Institute, which he helped found, he is an energizing part of a network of scholars, policy analysts, and practitioners exploring ways of applying social constructionist insights into applications, especially as directed toward reconciliation, respectful connections, conflict resolution, and community renewal and global peace.†

As a foundation of his approach, Gergen develops the concept of "relational being" that locates the source of meaning, value, and action in the relational connection among people;‡ he sharply contrasts it with the mainstream approach to self, which is created from an individualistic experience guided by rational thought and functions as a

---

*Of Ken Gergen's many books, I will just refer to a few: Gergen 2009 and 2015a; there's also a very interesting recent article (Gergen 2015b). A special journal has also been dedicated to his work (Misra and Prakash 2012).

†The website for the Taos Institute is www.taosinstitute.net. The institute is not primarily a place tied to a physical location but a space living through a networking web of collaborations. The Taos Institute is guided by an enthusiastic commitment to social change based on understanding collaborations among individuals and their communities.

The openness to relationship and respect for collaboration that the Taos Institute espouses is clearly manifested in the way the institute functions. It has a sincerely inviting character, encouraging participation in its wide variety of events and activities, and there is a noticeable absence of a hard sell or even the more widely used and gently misleading disguises meant to mask a fee-for-services structure—individuals can participate for a very reasonable fee or even for free. For example, I've found their newsletter on positive aging very informative, and there is no charge for reading its regular postings.

‡Gergen also offers the related concept of *multibeing,* which points to the importance of the intersection of multiple relationships rather than the individual person.

relatively autonomous center of activity. Indeed, the relational process is seen to exist prior to the concept of the individual.*

This idea of the relational being lies at the heart of the social constructionist approach. The Taos Institute's website expresses this connection with its characteristic commitment to collaborative social action:

> Constructionist theory and practice locates the source of meaning, value and action in the relational connection among people. It is through relational processes that we create the world in which we most want to live and work. . . . as people create meaning together, so do they sow the seeds of action. Meaning and action are entwined. As we generate meaning together we create the future.

The concept and experience of meaning take on a special significance. As Gergen says, "We live in worlds of meaning," and these are intimately connected to action and constructed within relationships.[†] He goes on to lay the theoretical groundwork for involvement in social change. "To sustain what is valuable, or to create new futures," he says, "requires participation in relationships," and "creative care for relationships" can help reduce or transform the "destructive potentials of conflict."[‡]

Social construction theory, as it nurtures its connection to action, offers mainstream psychology a way to recognize the inevitable interconnections among people and, from a respectful appreciation of those

---

*Hazel Markus, a professor of psychology at Stanford University, who writes about the Eurocentric limitations of mainstream psychology concepts, claims that some of the most effective work critiquing those limitations is in the reformulation of Western concepts of self to better appreciate cultural variations that stress, for example, more permeable as opposed to more rigid self boundaries. Gergen's work exemplifies that reformulation.
†See more at www.taosinstitute.net/theoretical-background#sthash.T1BJCRlc.dpuf.
‡A brief overview of some of the Taos Institute activities demonstrates the variety and breadth of this commitment to social change, such as in the reduction of social conflict. The institute focuses on themes such as relational learning in education, the demedicalization of psychotherapy, a multivoiced world, and appreciative inquiry as a way to introduce social change within organizations.

interconnections, offers a path of reciprocal and collaboration actions toward social change and justice. If relationships are where meanings are created, and therefore where realities are defined or constructed, then these co-created realities imply and entail a concern for others that can eventuate in a striving for peace.

Yes, that's quite a bit to promise. But how practical is it? And to what degree is this practice directed toward those marginalized and imprisoned in poverty, a situation too often experienced by persons of color and Indigenous peoples? But at least the commitment to move beyond intention into action is there.

I remember my excitement with the creating of community psychology as a discipline: here is a forum for a direct and committed connection with social change. But I remember even more my disappointment as community psychology soon devolves into a dimension of mainstream psychology. The growth and evolution of community psychology is a classic example of an innovative approach first becoming recognized, and then approved, and finally accredited by the mainstream. Now that community psychology is recognized as a formal division within the American Psychological Association, much of the vitality of the field has collapsed, its social change commitment weakened. Its own professional journal favors research that conforms more to conventional models such as quantitative-based outcome studies, rather than to researcher-community interactive action research models.

My early work on the front lines of a community-based addiction prevention—we run a "drug prevention" program—would now be considered by the community psychology establishment as being too practice oriented, especially in our commitment to social change, and lacking in "accepted" measures of success. Whereas the mainstream now insists that intervention programs keep reams of quantitative data, especially outcome measures, to determine "success rates," and thus provide justification for a program to continue, the very nature of our community outreach program, which features gatherings of youth in an open and welcoming center, calls out for the use of qualitative data so as not to "scare off" youth, who might resist being heavily monitored. The point of the program is to be accepting of the kids as they are. We do gather lots of qualitative data—stories, evaluations, commitments—so we know "what's going on" in the program; and that data gathering is part of encouraging youth in their journey to change rather than having them "stand still" while data is collected.

As community psychology abandons its original focused, even radical commitment for social change, critical psychology has taken on that challenge.* Fox and Prilleltensky, two of the founders of that movement, state their aim succinctly and without adornment: they are criticizing mainstream psychology for supporting social institutions that "perpetuate injustice and promote selfishness" (Fox and Prilleltensky 2009, xiii). Formed as an identifiable movement in the early 1990s, critical psychology emphasizes social justice and human welfare, stating that mainstream psychology such commitments, especially in regard to oppressed groups who suffer more from those inequities. Proclaiming its own inherently value-laden status and open promotion of social justice, critical psychology dismisses the mainstream claim of being neutral or scientifically neutral and seeks to expose the mainstream approach as itself value laden, with an aim—usually covertly—to support the status quo and, by doing so, reinforce unjust conditions. Psychologists are encouraged not to become detached from their specific sociopolitical contexts because they have an obligation to face the moral, social, and political implications of the situations they live in.[†]

Critical psychology seeks to bring to the fore issues typically ignored in the mainstream yet essential to any efforts toward community health and social justice; namely, issues of race, class, gender, disability, colonization and globalization, social justice in postconflict settings,

---

*See Fox, Prilleltensky, and Austin (2009) and Austin and Prilleltensky (2011) for more detailed descriptions of critical psychology.

†One article dealing with the need for psychology to acknowledge itself as a political discipline, with sociopolitical responsibilities, has a telling title: "Repoliticizing the History of Psychology" (Harris 1997).

and oppression and empowerment in mental health systems. Finally, we hear voices within psychology trying to face realities of colonization and oppression; such realities are central to any fair hearing of Indigenous teachings as they often construct the context of those teachings.

I find the aims of critical psychology very congenial. For me, psychology and life in general have always been inseparable; both present us with challenges to encourage social justice instead of masking inequities by espousing the "way things are" or, even more discouraging, "the way things are *supposed to be*. The real challenge for critical psychology is to make social justice an actuality, especially for those most marginalized.*

All phases of mainstream psychology are considered within the critical psychology critique, such as developmental, clinical, and social psychology, as well as research methods. As well, emphases such as feminist and gay and lesbian psychology are supported. Of particular interest is the critical psychology critique of community psychology.† While admitting that community psychology has shifted the emphasis from seeing social and mental health problems as person centered, and thus calling for individual-based responses, to a more proper emphasis on institutions and systems, such as schools and organizations, thus calling for structural interventions, critical psychology still sees a problem: community psychology seeks to change systemic sources of suffering in an *ameliorative* rather than a *transformative* way. Reforming structures to ameliorate suffering without challenging the status quo's underlying legitimacy is in the end ineffective. Critical psychology insists that oppression can only be eliminated if oppressive institutions are transformed and the basic premises of unjust systems changed.

As one expression of this necessary movement from amelioration

---

*As those who identify with critical psychology are typically professionally trained psychologists who are experts in their particular fields, there is a tendency for their writings to be theoretical and academic and to lack a connection with or data from the actualities of living among marginalized and oppressed groups. This shortcoming applies, however, to Western psychology in general.

†This discussion of the critical psychology critique of community psychology draws upon Prilleltensky and Nelson (2009).

to transformation, there's a need for what are the historical values of community psychology, such as caring and compassion, and more recent values, such as self-determination and diversity, to face a new and more radical challenge, symbolized by the value of social justice. Social justice goes directly to the core of economic and political inequity, demanding a fair allocation of power and resources to all people. This is a very welcome development, as it's those who are presently marginalized who are consistently denied access to resources that can help establish that equity. As the Ju/'hoansi so clearly tell us, it takes more than generosity to create a sharing, reciprocating community; sociopolitical structures must also be transformed. I know that it's easy as a psychologist to rely on personal values and motivations—such as generosity—to power and guide change, but unless those personal motivations entail institutional and structural changes as well, enduring change seems remote. When I hear about the importance of compassion from Joe Eagle Elk, I hear about the importance of compassion throughout the culture, how personal compassion grows out of and feeds compassionate institutions. "We know how to be there for each other . . . because we know how it is to be helped," he reflects.

This emphasis on sociopolitical and economic equity could move psychology as a discipline toward a liberatory and empowering force *for all*. By activating the Indigenous teaching of "all my relations" within the discipline, the healing resources of psychology are brought to all. Again, this is an enormous task because it's not just theory but also concrete— the fair distribution of economic and political resources, including money and property. An ideal, but an ideal worth the struggle of working toward—a psychology that values life as it creates opportunity.

This ideal is even more attractive because even within Western capitalistic cultures, there are concrete signs of hope. The self-help movement, which is a vital grassroots countercurrent within the mainstream, offers an example of what can happen when people are open to their ongoing interlinkings: reciprocating and respectful exchanges can then occur among people, and the energy of synergy is released. Within these self-help groups, participants' stories of struggle and change, the essential core of healing within the group and beyond, are a valuable resource that is renewable, expanding, and accessible to all. Self-help groups can function as synergistic communities, so that what is good for one is good for all, and the whole is greater than the sum of the parts. These are wonderful processes to initiate, but substantial obstacles within the mainstream continually undercut that synergistic vision, including restricting self-help groups to niches in society.

I'm one of many professionally trained health providers, but even that "many" is not enough. The critical shortage of such providers is devastating, especially for those already marginalized from access to such health care. Operating within the mainstream scarcity model where valuable resources like healing are in short and limited supply, those already marginalized become more deeply marginalized.

Clearly, something else is needed. There is no shortage of human suffering and the search for meaning; professionally trained providers will always be needed to help meet those existential needs. The challenge remains to create a respectful collaboration between grassroots self-help movements and professionally led services.*

I want to focus on self-help groups that do not have professionals serving in formal leadership or expert roles within the group. Instead, these groups employ a peer-participatory model.† Professionals do not

---

*I know my case is a bit unusual, since I've never charged for any of the services I've offered, so I'm not financially motivated to maintain or expand my clinical practice, but the point about there being more than enough health care work to go around remains true.
†The generic term for these kind of groups that emphasize the contributions of its non-professional members is *support groups*. I'm using the term *self-help group* to emphasize the type of support group that functions without professional input, groups that emphasize the importance of participation among equal peers within the group. Some support groups have professionals serve as leaders or regular sources of supplementary input, and they, too, provide valuable services.

A fuller discussion of self-help groups and their functioning as synergistic communities can be found in Katz and Murphy-Shigematsu (2012c), chapter 13, "Will There Always Be Enough? Self-Help Groups as a Renewable Healing Resource." The present discussion draws upon material in that chapter.

attend meetings of these peer-participatory groups unless they share the group problem and attend *as members* or unless they are, on rare occasions, invited as speakers. This model of self-help offers a most radical challenge to conventional Western health services, yet is a most promising approach, allowing for collaboration between two distinctly different forms of health care.

Most important, the research supports the effectiveness of these self-help groups. A wide variety of such groups is shown to encourage important aspects of well-being, including self-acceptance, self-esteem, and empowerment; as well, these self-help groups achieve comparable or better outcome success rates than most widely available conventional interventions for conditions, such as addictions.* In addition to functioning as alternatives to these conventional interventions, these groups can also serve as complements or supplements—whether as preparations for or parallel treatments with or follow-ups to those interventions.† These complementary roles are most appropriate for groups such as cancer patients, where curing cancer is not the focus but learning to live as well as possible *with* cancer, however it evolves, is. I'm offering this example of self-help groups not as a cure-all or as a substitute for every conventional approach. The value of these groups is based on a realistic assessment of and a respect for the variety of already existing groups, which can help foster effective approaches within a Western perspective.

---

*The healing effectiveness of self-help groups for a range and variety of settings and conditions is well documented (see e.g., Moos and Timko 2008; and Kyrous and Humphreys 2002). Yet measuring outcomes for these self-groups remains a challenging task. The criteria for effectiveness remain fluid and hard to define, as those criteria are often merged with *implicit* and *generalized* life-changing experiences; in addition, the informal nature of the groups can even at times prevent the collection of outcome data.

†It's very important not to assume that words like *complementary* or *supplementary* imply that these groups are not as effective as the real, main, or standard treatment, thus diminishing the complementary approach. A complementary intervention is best judged on its own merits, including its own professed aims.

In these self-help groups, specific modes of social support emerge. Members share a common problem, often a disease, addiction, life crisis, or loss. Their mutual goal is helping each other to deal with and, if possible, to heal or recover from this problem. Through self-disclosure, members share their stories, including talking about stresses, feelings, issues, and recoveries. They learn that they are not alone; they are not the only ones facing the problem. This lessens the isolation that many people experience and can encourage motivations and actions toward empowerment, the seeds of which might be sown within their initial decision to come to the group.

Designated leaders are merely facilitators for a particular meeting—and the role of facilitator rotates throughout the more experienced members. Experiential knowledge becomes more important than objective, specialized knowledge.* Services are free and reciprocal rather than commodities. Equality among peers, rather than provider and recipient roles, is practiced. Information and knowledge are open and shared rather than protected and controlled.

---

*This emphasis on experiences and their accompanying feeling states can provide a sharp contrast to the many conventional medical settings, where now, in the interest of transparency or the desire to share knowledge with the patient, doctors overload their patients with technical information about their conditions. As a result, patients are often left more bewildered than informed; when the technical knowledge comes in such large doses, it can be too technical to comprehend, no less integrate. Patients may be left yearning for some human connection that meets their needs for care and comfort.

My dear younger sister Alice Goldstein captures this dilemma and its possible resolution as she begins her treatment journey for her cancer with visits to her prospective medical team. "I'm so grateful my internal medicine doctor will be part of my treatment team," Alice says. "She talks to me in a good way, caring about what I'm feeling, calling me back even after hours . . . and she does know her stuff." Then Alice adds, "And the doc in charge of my cancer treatment, he's also special. He's patient and takes time to talk with me so I feel he *is* talking with me . . . and he too knows his stuff. They both take the time to talk to me," Alice reemphasizes, "and most important, they *listen* to me. And they bring humor into things when it seems so appropriate. Yet I'm not missing out on any technical information I need . . . I wouldn't want to compromise that side of things. But along with that necessary information, I still feel cared for. And that *really* matters."

Peers can model healing for each other. The group member who has already been there can help the newer member, offering guidance without unnecessarily explicit instructions. As the newer member learns that the problem can be dealt with and how, the older member who helps also benefits.

One possible effect of this peer-participatory model is empowerment (see e.g., Rappaport and Seidman 2000). Self-help group members are connected to and reliant on themselves, each other, the group, and typically a "power beyond themselves" or a spiritual power. Together they can learn to control the problem in their lives. Those who share a common shame and stigma can come together, without judging, to offer a sense of identity and community. They can give emotional, social, and practical support to each other. Exploring and learning to understand and to combat the shame and stigma together, there are varied opportunities for enhancing self-esteem and self-efficacy. Through participation, members can also enhance their social skills, promoting their social rehabilitation. Through this empowerment of members and the self-help groups as a whole, a potent force for social change is created, featuring the unique strengths and prospects of grassroots change and liberation. Scarcity models beware!

Self-help groups are continually emerging as new dilemmas and issues challenge people's well-being. The very nature of these groups encourages such a dynamic organization. Alcoholics Anonymous (AA) with its classic twelve-step model to recovery offers a paradigm for processes and structures that forge the nature of self-help groups.* As well, this AA model has been the

---

*Because AA and its twelve-step program has been such an important influence on and inspiration for the self-help movement, I'll quote the AA material on those steps, as presented in Anonymous (1952):

1. We admitted we were powerless over alcohol—that our lives had become unmanageable.
2. Came to believe that a Power greater than ourselves could restore us to sanity.

most common inspiration for the self-help movement in general.*

Some might feel uneasy about the "religious stuff" that seems to permeate the twelve-steps literature, and might even, knowing

---

(cont. from page 365)

3. Made a decision to turn our will and our lives over to the care of God as we understood Him.

4. Made a searching and fearless moral inventory of ourselves.

5. Admitted to God, to ourselves, and to another human being the exact nature of our wrongs.

6. Were entirely ready to have God remove all these defects of character.

7. Humbly asked Him to remove our shortcomings.

8. Made a list of all persons we had harmed and became willing to make amends to them all.

9. Made direct amends to such people wherever possible, except when to do so would injure them.

10. Continued to take personal inventory and when we were wrong promptly admitted it.

11. Sought through prayer and meditation to improve our conscious contact with God as we understood Him, praying only for knowledge of His will for us and power to carry that out.

12. Having had a spiritual awakening as the result of these steps, we tried to carry this message to alcoholics and to practice these principles in all our affairs.

*Besides Al-Anon, there are numerous twelve-step groups modeled after AA, such as Adult Children of Alcoholics, Cocaine Anonymous, and Gamblers Anonymous. These anonymous groups help their members to recover from their various addictive behaviors while maintaining member confidentiality. This confidentiality extends to not recognizing members as members when they encounter each other outside meetings. Most groups are self-supporting, do not have dues, and decline all outside support to maintain their independence; they do not engage in any controversy, and they neither endorse nor oppose any cause.

Increasingly, there are groups that work toward recovery from addictions but reject certain tenets of twelve-step programs. For example, the Secular Organization for Sobriety rejects AA's emphasis on spirituality. Parents Anonymous (PA), for family members to combat child abuse and neglect, is not a twelve-step group, and there is no religious commitment.

Another type of self-help group focuses on medical diseases or problems. Examples of such groups that help families include: AFTER AIDS (for people who have lost a loved one to AIDS), Candlelighters (for parents of young children with cancer), and National Society for Children and Adults with Autism (for children with autism and their families).

There are other types of self-help groups that sit within organizational structures that

the origin story of AA, just assume that AA is in part a cover for a Christian approach to spirituality.* In practice, different AA groups may have different emphases in regard to these concepts of religion and spirituality. With AA's official commitment to religious tolerance,† a particular group, depending on its regular participants, may have people expressing their stories through the framework of a particular religion, and within a Western context, that can often be a Christian framework. Indigenous elders and addictions counselors point out that there is a need for AA groups that avoid such a Christian perspective for those Indigenous peoples who are committed to strengthening their own Indigenous cultural identities as their path toward sobriety and wellness. But this tendency for some AA groups to have a Christian connotation has not led those Indigenous elders to dismiss the generic value of the AA process for Indigenous peoples. I hear many stories of Indigenous elders who have turned to AA, especially in the earliest phases of their path toward recovery, to be supplemented by and sometimes even eventually replaced by Indigenous traditional healing resources. Another obstacle for many Indigenous people to their participation in typical AA groups is socioeconomic, as well as cultural. The AA model originated with people of relative

---

(cont. from page 366) provide other forms of help and assistance. Organizations that, in addition to supporting family-oriented self-help groups, also provide services, such as information and referral, advocacy and lobbying, grant funding, research support, and practical assistance (e.g., providing hospital beds for home care), include The Compassionate Friends (for bereaved parents) and Tough Love (providing support and mutual problem solving for parents troubled by teenage behavior).

We're only intending to suggest some types of self-help groups and some particular examples of these types. It's in the very dynamic nature of self-help groups that any typology is only a temporary and approximate one. As these self-help groups are dynamic in nature, the future existence of any specific group can't be predicted. Future lists are guaranteed to be different, and we think likely expanded.

*According to the history of the founding of AA, two Christian men, struggling with their alcoholism, sought help, recognizing they had to submit to a higher power if recovery was to happen (Anonymous 1939).

†The AA website claims that "AA is not allied with any sect, denomination, politics, organization, or institution."

socioeconomic privilege trying to piece back together lives shattered by their alcoholism; that particular context and path toward recovery still is common. But for many Indigenous clients, that background and present context of privilege is absent; their paths toward recovery can thus miss some key elements of group support.

There are many paths toward spirituality, and AA groups demand no particular membership in any one path or, really, in any path. AA's core belief in a "power greater than ourselves," as well as its emphasis on the need for a "spiritual awakening," is an affirmation of the centrality—and common-sense meaning—of spirituality in our daily lives. When they are true to their operating principles, these self-help groups function as synergistic communities. In these groups, people come together to provide mutual support for each other. Telling one's story candidly—honest self-disclosure—is the valued resource in the group; expertise in the group is generated through that honest sharing. Therefore, all members are potentially experts and have access to that valued resource, which, functioning within that structure, can become renewable. An egalitarian system of generating and distributing the valued resource prevails, enhanced by the anonymous nature of the group. It is believed that through honest sharing, a member can help himself or herself, and only through self-help can a member then be able to help others. The personal experiences members bring to the group, transmitted through their stories—whether they are expressing their overall healing journey or reporting on events and feelings of that day—become a shared resource, stimulating other group members to connect with one another to better understand their own experiences. The stories, and the personal experiences they convey, are an expanding and renewable healing resource, now accessible to all in the group.

Within a mainstream Western health care system mired in the scarcity paradigm, these self-help groups can exemplify the existence of niches or islands of synergy, with healing and empowering effects radiating out from those isl s. Synergy *can* occur inside self-help groups because of several interacting and mutually reinforcing group characteristics that encourage the release of renewable and accessible resources of value.

These self-help groups function within and upon a basic spiritual premise: a belief in a power greater than oneself, whether within or beyond the self. This belief is a source of both understanding and healing. A transpersonal healing resource is created, which is endlessly available and can help members attain new perspectives on their own issues, as well as an appreciation for the issues of others.

Each member of the self-help group is her or his own expert, the member's area of expertise being his or her own issues and healing journey. Without relying on a formal leader, who is considered the expert, groups can place ultimate value on the contributions of each member and, in particular, each member's healing story. All that is needed to join a group is the desire and willingness to participate: all are welcome. Therefore, the valuable resource of group members is renewable.

The ultimately valued resource of members' personal experiences can also renewable. Experience is something everyone has. As each day unfolds, it is inevitably composed and colored by one's experiences, so there is an inexhaustible supply of them. By choosing to come to a self-help group and share, participants have experiences relevant to the task or focus of that group, which is to share one's story. You can talk about what you've been doing that day or how you're feeling, as well as more specifically about aspects of your healing journey. All stories count and are accepted; it is their honesty that gives them value.

Telling your story encourages others to do the same, increasing and expanding that resource of experience. The nature of the group's storytelling is such that each listener is encouraged to take from the story being told what is meaningful *for himself,* letting that story encourage the emergence and hopefully the increased honesty of the listener's story. The group principle that there is no critiquing of another's story helps foster the ultimate and unique value of each story and increases its potential as an encouragement for others to share. The stories heal by letting people connect with their own stories, which can bring understanding. Thomas King (2003), a highly respected Aboriginal storyteller, says: "Stories are the medicine that fills in the gaps of the self." As the stories affect others' storytelling and by extension their lived experiences, influence of the stories expands, and they are a renewable valued resource.

Within these self-help groups a synergistic community can emerge and exist, however briefly. In the healing environment of the group, what is good for one is good for all. By focusing on one's own healing, one can potentially help others. Members are cautioned that they can't control what others do, so they should not focus on trying to help (i.e., control) others. Helping oneself, they are reminded, is the best way, in the end, to help others. As one's stories are shared with others, one's stories heal by touching others' stories and understanding. One person's story feeds not only her or his own healing efforts, but also the healing journeys of others. One rarely hears anyone say, "The meeting didn't work tonight because there were no good stories"; all stories are good as long as they are honest and real. This mandated sharing of resources is usually buttressed by the egalitarian social structure of the groups.

Self-help *groups* themselves are a renewable healing resource. If a group focusing on a particular issue becomes too large to accommodate all its members, a new group, in amoeba-like fashion, can easily form, splitting off from the original group, with the skills to run and maintain this new group already in place. In sharing their stories, members learn not only about their problems but also how to take responsibility in guiding future groups. If a new issue emerges around which people wish to share their healing stories, the initiation of such a group is relatively easy—including finding a new meeting space.*

---

*The new group sometimes needs to overcome attempts of others to discredit it, setting aside comments that the new group is not dealing with a real problem.

FUTURE COLLABORATIONS

The release of synergy, and its functioning to create and maintain a synergistic community, expresses the Indigenous perspective of respectful and reciprocal collaborations between individuals and their communities—truly an aim worth pursuing in the West, especially given its domination by scarcity paradigm principles. As mainstream psychology focuses more on separations and conflicts between individuals and their communities, creating situations where valuable psychological resources are scarce and competition for them is weighted in favor of those with power and privilege, the possibilities for such collaborations become especially necessary. Yes, on occasion, there are synergistic communities formed within this dominant Western scarcity paradigm, but they are typically short-lived and too often are in response to a community tragedy or natural disaster.* Yet the experience of synergy within these brief occasions can be a seed for future and more sustained collaborative experiences—nothing like a powerful taste of that experience to initiate a new synergistic way of being in the world.

Self-help groups as a countercurrent within mainstream psychology offer great promise: through releasing synergy in the creation and distribution of healing resources, they can energize forces toward social justice. In establishing the collaborations that can support synergy, it's helpful to recognize contributions from one group that are uniquely suited to collaboration with another. Are there, for example, contributions that seem to arise most specifically and effectively from Indigenous approaches? Spiritually infused connections among and within people and most fundamentally among and within people and all elements of the universe seem to be one contribution that is especially nurtured within an Indigenous perspective. Recognizing and honoring a life of

---

*During tragedies such as hurricanes or floods and instances of collective human suffering, as well as less devastating situations such as snowstorms in urban areas, people can gather strength through mutual exchanges, offering concrete help to their neighbors and sacrificing personal needs for the common good. Spaces of synergy are cultivated.

spirit throughout the universe thrives within the general Indigenous approach to life and living and to the psychological expressions that can animate that way of living.

It can be hard to comprehend from a Western mind-set how both total and ordinary this spiritual dimension is. Each part of the day is filled with its influence, without interrupting the flow of the day. "My elder told me that when we first wake up, before our feet hit the ground, we pray . . . we thank the Creator for the day," says my friend, elder Walter Linklater. "And before we go to sleep, we thank the Creator for the day we have just had," he continues. Danny Musqua talks about how the elders offer spiritual thanksgivings throughout the day, whether it be offering tobacco when picking medicinal herbs, or blessing the food they are about to eat, or thanking the wind they feel on their cheeks, knowing it helps to carry away their scent as they hunt for their winter food supplies.

While spirituality in this *deeply pervasive* form may best be expressed within an Indigenous perspective and be at the heart of an Indigenous contribution to a healing psychology, spirituality in a form more amenable to a Western perspective can still be encouraged. It's reasonable to see that a mainstream approach increasingly emphasizing issues, motivations, and experiences that exist beyond the individualistic self now dominates the mainstream landscape. For some living within a mainstream Western worldview, the word *spiritual* may have off-putting connotations, such as being too mystical or new agey or even cultish. But staying simply with the experience of going beyond the self can release a truly and honestly spiritual experience and perspective, bringing caring substance to psychology and making it a more healing enterprise. For example, from an Indigenous perspective, the circle represents the heart of the people and the fire within the circle a spiritual center. Working more with circles within the mainstream, whether in clinical interventions or educational structures, without strong and explicit connections to the spiritual, can still introduce an element of equity and relatedness that is a common accompaniment of spirituality.

But in order to encourage collaboration and synergy, we need a keener awareness of the obstacles to those possibilities—and they are formidable! The primary obstacle is the socioeconomic context, which both feeds and feeds off that mainstream approach; namely, the contemporary form of capitalism that features the commercialization and commodification of all resources of value. There are also various more specific obstacles to synergy, all of which emerge from this more general capitalistic context.

Looking at self-help groups as one example of a potential synergistic community, we can identify some of these more specific obstacles, obstacles that have *general* relevance to creating synergy. One group of obstacles involves issues of medicalization. Clearly, self-help groups cannot provide certain essential health services, such as surgical and drug interventions. Also, they are not equipped to offer certain kinds of psychological treatments that presuppose extended professional training, such as cognitive behavioral or psychodynamically oriented therapies. But the evidence is equally clear that the health and healing provided in self-help groups, in addition to their own intrinsic value, typically facilitate the healing effects of these other interventions, representing an excellent supplementary or complementary approach. But the danger of medicalization remains, as there is pressure from professionally trained health disciplines to label life issues focused on by self-help groups as problems and then label these problems as illnesses, which need professional interventions. Persons who attend a self-help group can be victimized by this labeling, becoming just what they may seek to avoid; namely, a patient needing to be helped by a professional.

Self-help groups must continue to insist on the validity of what they do offer, no more and no less, seeking to avoid either a too virulent attitude of antiprofessionalism or the ever-present desire of the medical establishment to co-opt them. Attempts to assimilate self-help groups into a professional caregiving system can be very invasive because they seem so attractive, even innocent—strategies of co-optation are often masked in apparently well-intentioned phrases, such as, "If you come into our institution you can have more power to make changes," or "We want to help you do a better job." There is so much suffering and pain in the world that health care professionals really need not worry they can lose their clientele, especially when they realize that self-help groups offer not only a different way of looking at and dealing with pain and suffering but also a complementary way. Within the synergy model, the self-help group and the professional health provider can collaborate, providing consumers with enhanced health options.

A second group of obstacles deals with potential for the professionalization of personal experience. Certainly I *can* succumb to the assumption that, as a trained psychologist, I have something special, even authoritative, to add to the group, in addition to my own story. "After all, I've heard these kinds of group comments and stories in my therapeutic work," I *can* muse to myself, "and I can even put a clinical label on some elements of the stories." If I want to bring my own prejudgments into the meeting—which I almost inevitably do in the beginning—that's my loss. I sharply remember I'm here in the group for help with a painful need, not to pass judgment on the dynamics of the group. Regardless of its various side benefits of comfort and prestige, being a professional is not my path; seeking help, by helping myself, is. My aim is *being* in the group *as just another member.*

Though self-help groups by definition do not have professionally trained leaders and, in fact, eschew any formal leadership roles, there is a tendency in these groups for informal or de facto leaders to emerge. The "old-timers" can ease, sometimes intentionally, into leadership roles that can become formalized or at least routinized. Newcomers can unwittingly provide validation for this process, as they naturally turn to people who seem to know, such as those with "lots of experience." A professionalization of experience can emerge, creating and then validating positions of leadership. This process is rarely intended to undermine the self-help aspect of the group; often these old-timers or specially qualified members are just trying to be helpful—though undoubtedly many also enjoy the recognition and rewards of being a leader or being in charge. While leadership cannot be based on a professionalization of experience, members of a group can still benefit from the special understandings that come from other more experienced members. Also persons can assume the necessary administrative and logistical tasks in the group without implying more substantive or formal aspects of leadership.

To avoid this obstacle of the professionalization of experience, self-help groups must ferociously guard the value, even the sanctity, of each person's personal experience and the stories each one tells about these experiences. The valuing of personal experience makes the profession-alization of experience impossible, as there are by definition no experts except the expert of and on oneself. Here a teaching of First Nations elders becomes relevant: there is intrinsic and ultimate value in each person's own experience, and that experience cannot be undermined by another. Elder Danny Musqua offers some thoughtful guidance: "There's no greater truth for each of us than what each of us knows from our own experience. We must respect that in each other and not criticize what another experiences. We listen and learn. And we don't just blindly follow what an elder says but first make sure what he says is something that has made sense for you."

In the mid-1960s, I have an opportunity to work with a group of women diagnosed with lupus erythematosus who are seeking to form a self-help group at a time when that diagnosis is just emerging into public consciousness. As they are stabilizing their self-help group, they also wish to expand into educational programs for professional medical practitio-ners about sensitive care for lupus patients. This educational direction is fraught with danger because those medical professionals, sometimes with the best of intentions in offering their expertise, or at worst not believ-ing in the women's own strengths, can be inclined to take over roles and responsibilities that are now provided in the self-help group. The women come to me, a mental health professional with a Ph.D. in clinical psy-chology, and seek my advice. Through my knowledge of the health sys-tem and my commitment to the value of self-help groups, I am able to offer effective consultation, suggesting ways for the group to maintain its integrity and unique healing resources. Sometimes it takes a professional to step in for a moment to help self-help groups guard the ultimate value of their own experiences when interfacing, as they inevitably must, with the professional health establishment.

A third set of obstacles self-help groups face, which can limit their ability to release synergy within a Western context, is the trivialization of experiences and the stories conveying those experiences. In a self-help group I attend there is one member, an old-timer, whose stories are what I judge as routinized and formulaic—and therefore of little or no value. Each week he starts and ends his story the same way, using nearly the exact same language each time, while the middle of the story, which remains very short, might vary only slightly from week to week. Even though I *know* each person's story is to be valued as a unique offering, I can't avoid listening less than fully to that old-timer and at times turning off my attending. I'm just being the human part of me! Instead of listening, I look for other stories from other members, even waiting for a fireworks story, where there was some dramatic revelation, or a story from a newcomer to the group. But by turning off my attention, really my caring, I am deadening that old-timer's story for myself and thereby diluting the healing potential of the group.

After several meetings, I'm able to catch myself not fully listening. I recommit myself to being there for each member's story, to avoid judging a story as "interesting" or "boring," and to simply listen and learn whatever I can. In this recommitment I'm helped by a teaching from elder Danny Musqua. "Our stories," he says, "take on meaning as listeners take what means something for them and try to apply it in their daily lives." Stories gain their meaning and are enlivened by the listening process.*

---

*Thomas King, an Aboriginal writer, says, "Once a story is told, it cannot be called back. Once told, it is loose in the world" (King 2003, 10). As novelist Michael Ondaatje writes: "We live permanently in the recurrence of our own stories, whatever story we tell" (Ondaatje 2008, 136).

By refusing to give in to the ease of ignoring what seems to be the same old story and instead listen with as fresh an attitude as possible, one can avoid the trivializing of stories and keep learning alive. Indigenous elders often repeat the stories they tell, and it might seem repetitive. But they offer this caution: "No matter how many times you may hear a story," says elder Danny Musqua, "there is always the opportunity to learn from that story because each time you hear the story you are in a different place and state. The story can then offer a new meaning to you."

Aware of all of these potential obstacles, self-help groups can move beyond them, though they require constant vigilance to protect their unique contributions. Offering special opportunities for synergy, self-help groups fill a huge role in providing invaluable health and healing assistance to many people in the world. Generating expanding, renewable, and accessible health resources, these groups can function, at least on the microlevel or within societal niches, as one paradigm for a synergistic community. And as a grassroots path toward individual empowerment and community health and development, they can be positively contagious, offering great potential for introducing synergy into the larger society.

These potentials for synergy can also be expressed within the field of psychology, offering a vision of a synergistic community of psycholog*ies* that, respecting the distinctive contributions of approaches such as the Western mainstream and the Indigenous, can create a range of psychological options and opportunities that are larger than the sum of its parts—not a newly created universal psychology but a true diversity of psychological pathways. This can be one way of returning to =Oma Djo's call for sensitive knowledge about and use of things of power. This can be a foundation for healing psychology.

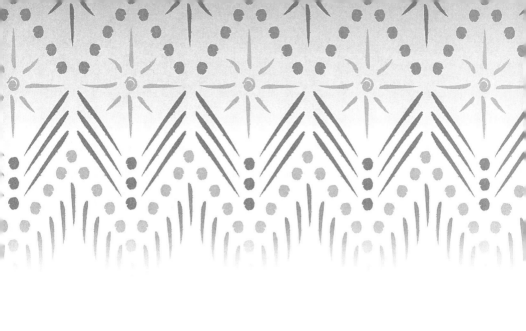

PART THREE

A FUTURE
OF
PSYCHOLOGIES

CHAPTER EIGHT

"There Is No One Way, Only Right Ways"

The Renewing Synergy of Multiple Psychologies

=Oma Djo, my friend and teacher in the ways of Ju/'hoansi healing and community well-being, ignites the spark that has evolved into this book. "Whenever we're given a thing of power by our ancestors," he cautions me, "we're always told how it works and how to use it." From his hunting-gathering world, he speaks special words of wisdom, words that can guide us with fundamental evolutionary perspectives into effectively, even creatively, meeting our contemporary challenges. But as a "thing of power" in the lives of many people, mainstream Western psychology is often misunderstood and therefore misused. Its powerful strategies and structures for defining human nature often ignore a commitment to explore a fullness of human potential and to practice social justice so that all can benefit equitably.

I hope that *Indigenous Healing Psychology* can be one vehicle for activating =Oma Djo's perspective on things of power. Seeking to honor Indigenous teachings, such as those offered by =Oma Djo and other first psychologists—a presently underappreciated source of wisdom—this book suggests ways mainstream psychology can better meet these commitments to potential and equity and thus become a source of power whose use is more respectfully and fully understood. Such commitments can bring psychology closer to its roots as a careful and caring study of all within and touched by the human psyche—the rich variety of everyday motivations, functions, and aspirations that guide our lives, including our spiritual experiences.

Indigenous Healing Psychology aims not only for this enhancement of mainstream psychology but also for the creation of a synergistic community of psycholog*ies* rather than a more inclusive "universal" psychology. Within that synergistic model, different psychologies that seem *apparently* in conflict—including even a now-enhanced mainstream and Indigenous approaches*—flourish *in their own uniqueness* while collaborating respectfully with each other. This productive connecting of apparently conflicting elements is a hallmark of synergy in action. A whole of psychology, greater than the sum of its parts because it respects the integrity of those parts, can then emerge—to benefit all, especially those historically denied valuable psychological resources and services.

The Indigenous Psychology Special Interest Group, recently organized within the American Psychology Association, provides an important example of attempts being made to move mainstream psychology away from its Eurocentric colonizing biases. The group functioning primarily through a list-serve forum for discussion and debate, offers a concept of Indigenous psychology that "supports the need for non-Western cultures to develop psychological constructs and practices that address local problems and generate theories that promote global discourse." Under the inspired and insightful leadership of psychologist Louise Sundararajan, the interest group offers philosophical analyses, clinical discussions, and calls for sociopolitical action.

---

*This synergistic community of psychologies is certainly not limited to these two approaches emphasized in *Indigenous Healing Psychology*. This book can encourage the articulation and respectful acceptance of other approaches to psychology, further enriching the emerging collaborative network of psychologies.

Some in the interest group consider whether a new universal psychology should be developed, now more attuned to and accepting of cultural diversity and Indigenous perspectives. The evidence in *Indigenous Healing Psychology* cautions against this call for a new universal psychology. The lure of a universal psychology that encompasses all different approaches is strong, but the dangers of premature assumptions of unity are great. Too often the true distinctiveness of non-Western worldviews and the psychologies they express can be underestimated, as the Western approach, being unaware or even hiding its connections to sociopolitical power and control, erases what makes these less politically powerful alternatives so distinctively valuable in the first place. How can a Western approach to self as a bounded experience of the individual fully comprehend an Indigenous approach that sees the individual as a reciprocating existence within community without a lessening of respect for any one person?*

This collaboration of psychologies is practical, though many

---

*The interest group also debates the meaning of the concept *Indigenous*. Some claim that the concept should be reserved for describing the first people who inhabit a territory or place; while others claim that it should be used to refer to *local context*, so that discourse and action that arises from psychologists working within their own local culture and environment, whether or not they are historically the first people from that land, would be considered Indigenous. While respecting the importance of local context, especially as it counterbalances the colonizing weight of the Western perspective, *Indigenous Healing Psychology* seeks to focus on Indigenous as meaning the first people of different lands, wanting to highlight their still ignored but valuable contributions, especially with their evolutionary insights.

As well, the interest group focuses on the tensions between theory and practice. There is a strong philosophical and analytical emphasis in the group, supporting the idea that we have to be clear about concepts, like "self" and "diversity," before we can state positions about the cultural meaning underlying psychology. There is also a small but increasingly influential voice within the group, energized by Indigenous people who have become professional psychologists, calling for concrete programs of social justice for Indigenous peoples to rectify inequities and strengthen movements of empowerment from within. *Indigenous Healing Psychology* supports this call for social action, and seeks praxis, insisting that theory and analysis be performed in the service of actually ensuring health and well-being, especially to those historically disenfranchised from psychology's powerful resources.

obstacles must be faced.* It's not easy to support substantially different psychological worldviews within a respectful and reciprocating relationship, treating their uniqueness as a source of strength rather than a characteristic to be erased in a more superficial path toward unity. A deep need to defend one's turf, especially among psychological providers whose core identities derive so much from their specific professional competencies, is a common response—though it can be masked in arguments about maintaining quality of care. It's hard to experience the vulnerability that supports accepting the validity of differing points of view—even points of fact. Power and control can be jealously guarded weapons, especially in the hands of those who already have that power and control—most typically the service providers and academic researchers, not those needing support and encouragement.

When a discipline like psychology unduly focuses on individual motivations and functions, including blaming individuals for failures that are institutionally influenced, the view becomes limited. Expanding that focus to include institutional changes, to both initiate and support changes in the personal realm, is not always perceived as an option: "Isn't that focus on social structural issues the task for sociology?" I've heard some psychologists say. But personal motivations to change *in concert with* institutional structures of change is the pathway of realism—and it is psychology that needs to change to be more realistic.

PATHWAYS TOWARD COLLABORATION

Danny Musqua helps me activate an experience within this collaboration of psychologies. We're both teaching in the Master of Indigenous Social Work (MISW) program at the First Nations University of Canada

---

*A more detailed presentation of these obstacles appears in chapter 7; see, for example, the discussion about the difficulties of creating and maintaining self-help groups, which illustrates one particular form of this respectful collaboration process.

(FNUC).* Created in response to the failures of mainstream therapists to deal with issues in the Indigenous community,† the program seeks to prepare Indigenous students to work effectively with Indigenous clients and communities, utilizing both Western and Indigenous approaches to counseling.

We follow the oft-heard advice of Indigenous elders given to their young people on entering the non-Indigenous world: "Take the best of both worlds . . . but always remember who you are." This is not a path for the dilettante, picking and choosing nuggets of practice, working superficially in various perspectives, but a path for the dedicated searcher. Nourishing their fundamental Indigenous identity, they can more sensitively explore counseling options to better serve the people. Though our students are not traditional Indigenous healers—a role earned with special training and spiritual gifts—they can bring Indigenous influences into their Western-influenced approaches. As liaisons between the two worlds, they can bring a richer, more effective offering of therapeutic environments to their Indigenous clients and in the process develop an approach that offers a model of best practices.

As one way to encourage this "taking of the best from both worlds," Danny and I teach two sister courses together within the MISW program: "Traditional Indigenous Counseling" and "Western Approaches to Counseling." Expressing our differing experience and qualifications, Danny takes the lead in the former, structuring the

---

*See Katz, Musqua, and Lafontaine (2012) for a more complete description of the MISW program, which was first known as the Masters of Aboriginal Social Work program when it was created within the Saskatchewan Indian Federated College, the original name of FNUC.

†Danny Musqua put the need for the MISW program simply and sharply: "There's too much pain and suffering in our reserves. Too many of us are hurting. We need a special therapy program, one that would train our students to work effectively within the two systems, our traditional Indigenous way and the Western way. We've had therapists in our communities before, Western-trained therapists. But they didn't work out. They didn't understand our way of life, our history. The results were *so* disappointing, sometimes disastrous. Our people didn't receive the help they needed!" Along with Sid Fiddler, then dean at SIFC, Danny and I launch the MISW program in 2001.

course in a traditional manner, such as starting with a smudging ceremony; I take the lead in the latter, employing a more Western classroom protocol, transformed by dialogue, which I encourage as our mode of learning. We each support the other with reflections, questions, and comments, when and where appropriate; we collaborate rather than attempt to integrate our work, respecting the distinctiveness of our perspectives: Danny is not a Western psychologist (though he is clearly one of our first psychologists), and I'm clearly not an Indigenous healer (however much I may be open to Indigenous knowledge). Danny and I participate actively in each other's classes, which may pose some difficulties logistically and in terms of time commitment in the typical university setting. But even without that mutual physical presence, there still can be mutual respect, especially for the distinctiveness of each approach, which nourishes the teaching and learning environment.

Today we're teaching "Western Approaches to Counseling," and the focus is on Freud. "I'm not a Freudian," I say, "but I studied Freud in graduate school and respect and utilize some of his concepts—such as the unconscious." We talk a bit about the deep knowledge and healing potential residing in that area of human experience that Freud labeled the unconscious.

"Danny," I turn to my colleague in learning, "was this unconscious thing part of the old peoples' way?" I already intuit the answer because the "old people" (or Danny's elders) were people of knowledge whose understandings remain valuable today. "Yes, we knew and know the unconscious," he affirms. "And it's in part like you say Freud described it, a place where the junk of our everyday lives can build up and without our knowing it hold us down . . . *in part,*" he pauses, "and yet there is also another part, another dimension to that unconscious . . . a deeper, more spiritual part. Yes, we know the unconscious stores old memories and hidden meanings . . . and they need our attention . . . we can't just ignore that stuff," Danny continues, "but the unconscious is *also* the pathway through which the spirits and spiritual understandings can sometimes enter into our human world."

But Danny also insists on realistic caution. "The unconscious is not *always* a pathway for the spirits," he adds. "Sometimes we're so troubled we can't feel that spiritual presence—sometimes our unconscious spills into our lives with these bad memories and anxieties. It's a little like our dreams," he reminds us. "Yes, dreams *can* be places for the spirits. Sometimes our dreams give us messages from the spirit world. Sometimes our dreams can help us see into the future. And sometimes our dreams are *just* dreams—they can be just filled with the ordinary stuff of our troubled days."

Danny emphasizes that the Indigenous perspective is not *the* key to understanding, though it may sometimes be wishfully cast in those terms. "Our way is just *one* way to understanding" is how he puts it. He is showing how the Anishnabe understanding of the unconscious does not negate the Freudian view but enhances it.

I'm reminded of a story Danny tells me about his great-grandfather, a traditional elder and holder of the sweat lodge ceremony; it's a story of acceptance and respect for differing worldviews, an acknowledgment that there are many paths toward the truth. One of the Catholic priests that serves his great-grandfather's Anishnabe First Nations reserve approaches his great-grandfather one day, asking about the sweat lodge. At that time the church portrays all traditional Anishnabe spiritual ceremonies as sites of the devil, as things to be stamped out and certainly avoided. So that priest is unusual and is taking a risk when he says to Danny's great-grandfather: "I'm interested in that sweat lodge—yes, interested—but kind of afraid to get too close . . . I've been told it will try to defeat my priestly mission." Danny's great-grandfather smiles with both pleasure and kindness. "Come to the sweat," he says. "Come . . . you're invited." They look at each other, the priest now relaxed and yielding. "You'll come into the sweat as a Catholic priest," Danny's great-grandfather continues, "and you will leave the sweat a Catholic priest. You don't have to give up your way to be in the sweat, but I believe . . . I really believe you'll leave the sweat as a better priest."

Now I know why it's so exciting to work with Danny, and I can see our students bubble with discovery because so far they have only heard the Freudian side of the unconscious. Now we're all richer in our understanding about ourselves, about how to work more fully with clients.

This knowledge about the unconscious emerges because Danny and I are collaborating on our learning-teaching journey. We respect the distinctiveness of each other's knowledge base and history of learning—whether it be traditional elders' teachings or university and clinical training—and though we have each participated in the other's way of knowing, we try to avoid connections that prematurely or superficially erase the distinctive elements of our knowledge histories; instead, we aim to enrich the distinctiveness of each other's way of knowing through respectful exchange—all the while appreciating resonances of commonality.

On the surface, Freud's and Danny's ideas about the unconscious are different: for Freud, the unconscious is a hidden storehouse of unresolved issues that, through therapeutic work to bring them into consciousness, can encourage psychological health, while for Danny, the unconscious is a way in which we can be open to and influenced by the spiritual dimension. If we take into consideration that Freud does not validate the spiritual, let alone espouse its therapeutic potential, the two views *do* seem in conflict. But by connecting the two viewpoints through a collaboration that respects the simultaneous existence of both perspectives and their distinctive contributions, emphasizing ways to build on rather than contradict each other, we're offered a view of our nature that is expansive and comprehensive. Danny's additive approach, enlarging the terrain and meaning of the unconscious, is one possible path toward creating a whole of understanding that is larger than the sum of its partial views. With this mutual respect, understanding each perspective can open the possibility for understanding the other, so that what is good for one becomes good for all.

While the reciprocating exchange of apparently differing worldviews creates the *structural* integrity of a synergistic community within the MISW, further Indigenous teachings about knowledge and healing as renewable and expanding valuable resources infuse the program with the *energy* of synergy. Within the MISW program, knowledge is treated in the manner of the elders, as a valuable resource whose value *depends* on its being shared. Knowledge is not owned by any individual; at best, we are guardians of that resource, seeking ways to give it to others.

As it is shared, knowledge becomes contagious rather than hoarded; an expression of communal knowing rather than a measure of individual prowess; a renewable resource for all within a synergy paradigm rather than a resource fiercely guarded against the competition within a scarcity paradigm. For example, joint student projects are encouraged within the MISW, without obsessing over what each individual actually contributes to the final project. We don't emphasize the conventional university objective of assigning credit to each individual for his or her individual knowledge base, as if knowledge were an individual's personal resource to possess, always available to display or confirm her or his level of intelligence, worth, or status.

Healing as a renewable resource becomes another cornerstone of the MISW program. Following the guidance of the elders, the program emphasizes the primary importance of self-knowledge as a basis for knowing and being on a healing journey as critical for developing accurate and fundamental self-knowledge. "How can we understand others," Danny says, "if we can't understand ourselves? To be helpful to others we have to know how to be helpful to ourselves." In addition, as the MISW program is created to deal with the many troubling issues stemming from the colonization of Indigenous peoples, including our students, healing journeys as educational catalysts receive further necessary and heartful support. There is no barrier for students to bring their healing journey work into the classroom, only encouragement to have that contribution bring life and meaning to the learning aims of the institution, including its academic curriculum. But in the end, though healing is a cornerstone of the MISW, it is most often silent work, and work that has no end. Mary Lee, one of the MISW elders, always reminds us: "I'm still working on my healing journey—and that work will never end."

The renewable resources of healing and learning reciprocate and feed each other's increasing availability. Reflected personal experience becomes a paradigmatic knowledge resource, lending an examining eye toward other more conventional university knowledge sources, such as books. "No one can critique my personal experience," says Tania Lafontaine, a graduate of the MISW program. "It's from my heart and it feeds my academic work." The students' healing journeys are honored as a central dimension of their university learning experience, and when one student shares that journey with others, the telling inspires others to not only share their stories but also strengthen their commitment to change. Synergy prevails.

The MISW program expresses a model of collaboration, wherein multiple worldviews, including ways of learning and healing, coexist in a reciprocating and respectful relationship while nourishing their distinctive contributions. Patterns of collaboration, supporting the emergence of synergy, are particularly supported at the microlevel, specifically within the MISW niche that sits within the larger integration-emphasized university and even more dramatically within and between the two Indigenous counseling and Western counseling courses that Danny and I teach; these courses epitomize a flourishing of collaboration within a niche even more focused on collaboration. These niches of collaboration, more common spaces for synergy to emerge, can then be seeds of change at larger levels.

The collaborative MISW model is immediately challenged by the model of integration that expresses the primary aim and intention of the University of Regina, the larger and more powerful conventional Western university setting within which the MISW operates.*

---

*Though functioning locally within FNUC, an Indigenous postsecondary institution guided by the instructional processes of Indigenous elders, the MISW program is formally set within and accountable to the conventional Western structure of the University of Regina. The University of Regina tries, often subtly, to integrate the MISW into its mainstream academic routines, causing a number of obstacles and restraints.

That model of integration seeks to bring a unity of purpose and function, at the cost of diversity, asserting the dominance of the world-view held by those in power and control, forcing the assimilation of differing views into the mainstream that is typically labeled as the right or valid way. For example, the commitment of the MISW to elders' teachings and elders as teachers is resisted since they are not "real" professors, which ignores their long years of training in Indigenous knowledge. In our program we emphasize the validity and value of elders' teachings by encouraging students to cite them in their papers: oral knowledge becomes honored as real knowledge, assuming its proper place beside that recent invention of the written word and its progeny of articles and books. As well, the MISW emphasis on knowledge as a shared resource is seen to undercut the university's conception of knowledge as a product of individual effort, with the prize being some claim to individual ownership: the Western-trained scholar is rewarded when she is recognized for having created a particular theory, especially when her name is associated with that theory. Finally, the MISW commitment to the healing journey as central to education is dismissed in the Western university setting, which considers healing as secondary or even unrelated to the core of learning, which is seen as an intellectual accomplishment. Furthermore, healing is considered an essentially useless marker or goal because it is impossible to measure its effects or outcomes.*

Though the MISW program is committed to excellence in education in its most fundamental sense, the larger Western-oriented

---

*One of the key elements in supporting students in their healing journeys, while still heeding the Western university demand that students be graded in order to be sure they pass a course, is to focus on the issue of character. In the MISW program, this is especially important, as we believe developing an honest and honorable character is essential to becoming an effective therapist.

Elders offer a way of judging this elusive phenomenon of character. They insist that character be understood in the particular context of the individual being considered, since an admirable character can be expressed in a variety of ways. Also, the elders say that you judge a person in terms of where they started (e.g., at the beginning of a course) and where they end up (e.g., at the end of a course); in that way, character becomes

University of Regina, under the banner of intellectual excellence, seeks to erase the distinctiveness of the MISW program, seeing its unique contributions as primarily obstacles to its concept of intellectual excellence rather than opportunities to expand and enhance that very concept of excellence. With its mainstream institutional power and control, the university seeks to dominate rather than accept, pursuing a false sense of unity at the cost of a richness of diversity. Models of collaboration will allow for a synergy of psychologies, honoring the richness of diversity in psychological approaches, whereas models of integration will discourage that synergy, pursuing a uniformity based on a false assumption of universality.

Danny's own educational history brings a poignancy and clarity to the way the dominant and dominating system works to extinguish differing views and pathways, pursuing integration—in this case crushing Danny's aspirations to know because, as an Indigenous seeker of knowledge, he is not an accepted part of the dominant educational establishment and culture. Through his own suffering and persistence, he shows not only how hard it is to create this collaboration and synergy but also how, against many, too many, odds, it is also possible to create.

Danny has had to fight through the vicious colonization of his culture, including his individual journey toward knowledge. Pummeled with racist labels that hurt as much as the physical beatings he received at residential school for merely trying to be himself—speaking his Anishnabe language or questioning the school nuns—Danny hears

---

(cont. from page 390) even more a phenomenon of individual challenge and growth. Finally, these elders speak of their confidence in making such a judgment of change or growth in character, emphasizing efforts one makes to change as well as change itself.

Though issues of character and its assessment are part of what elders can and do deal with, that fact does not really ease the concerns of the Western-oriented, intellectually focused university. Though the MISW program doesn't formally employ elders' judgments about character into the calculation of grades, we're continually emphasizing the validity and insight of that elder contribution to the general understanding of our students' progress and readiness, always in opposition to the Western university's ethos and administration.

the constant refrain about the Christian, Western educational system being superior or simply and more dangerously "the way *we as educated people* think." Continually humiliated and dismissed as an adult, his intelligence degraded and his curiosity and quest to know ignored, Danny is submerged in the "white is right" ideology—where predictably he is never white enough. Yet he knows what he has been taught by his grandparents, he knows his culture, he knows he is Anishnabe, and he remains justifiably proud of that inner core; and so he persists, he endures, and he struggles to fulfill his innate capacities to learn.

Forging his own path toward knowing, he's constantly and passionately reading, thinking, and analyzing with unending curiosity, respecting what Western scientists and philosophers have considered while nourishing his Anishnabe teachings through his own practice. He is living within an expanding universe of knowing, building on it with this collaboration of ways of knowing, and he experiences connections with Western knowledge that are quite remarkable, such as his conversations during a conference we attend with the renowned theoretical physicist David Bohm, a close collaborator with Einstein.*

Danny is very excited to meet and talk with David. "What a special gift," he says, "to have a chance to be with someone . . . someone who worked with Einstein!" The feeling is mutual: "Now I can learn more about a way of knowing which is still unfamiliar to me," David says, "a way of knowing that I have such deep respect for . . . especially for the

---

*These meetings take place during a conference organized at the Fetzer Institute in Kalamazoo, Michigan. The conference theme is the relationships between Indigenous and Western science, which at its core is about relationships between Indigenous and Western ways of knowing and being—with the important understanding that Indigenous spirituality is a form of science, meaning an honored and careful way of knowledge. Guided by the physicist David Bohm's principles and structures of dialogue (see Bohm 1996), participants with serious training and respected knowledge in either one or the other aspect of the conference theme sit around a large oak table, exchanging ideas, seeking to learn about new ways of knowledge. The foundation of the gathering is the respect each has for his or her own way and the others' ways of thinking and being.

way it's tied into spirituality, which I know is a critical part of our universe. A way of knowing tied into spirituality," he muses.

At one point Danny lets his enthusiasm carry him into a bit of overdrive, as mutual respect peaks into excited admiration. Going up to David, he expresses his joy in their meeting by enthusing: "It's just great to be with you . . . and to be so near to you." David is a bit on the shy side and though typically uncomfortable with such an open show of intimacy, he now responds with his own enthusiastic and intimate appreciation for Danny and his way of being. "And me too, being able to talk with you," David gladly offers. Quickly, however, David's wife, Sara, brings their connection back to Earth, where they both actually feel more comfortable. "Oh, I don't know," she declares, pointing to her husband. "He's just an ordinary guy, you know." Yes, the necessary reminder that we *are all just human*. And we all have a good laugh at our excesses—again, just being human.

Danny knows what he's doing, but as someone growing up on the reserve, isolated from the Western worlds of knowledge, who first hears about Einstein only as a very distant, even formidable symbol of a great genius—supported by the iconic photo of Einstein with his wild hair going out in all directions—he's excited none the less. Danny and I continue to have fun about this close encounter with greatness. "Maybe if you got too close, he would evaporate," I tease. "Maybe . . . maybe, but it was just close enough," he says, smiling. "I didn't want to scare him away because then can you imagine *what* would people say!" But we both know that this "touch of greatness" means more than touching; it represents the expansion of worlds that becomes possible when barriers are lifted and contact made. "I'll tell my grandchildren about this meeting with a man who worked with Einstein," he adds. "They already know about our traditional ways and deep knowledge. That's their foundation. Now this will just make them even stronger in that foundation."

David Bohm walks away from the conference in equal awe. He has met authentic carriers of an ancient and honorable path, a path he has only read about and could therefore only imagine its depth and clarity. David, too, is unbelievably enriched. "This is one of my lifetime experiences," he tells us.

Not that it corrects the injustices Danny has known nor eases the pain of the humiliations and beatings, but there is a balancing of sorts when Danny is awarded an honorary doctor of laws degree from the University of Saskatchewan in 1995. The university is acknowledging Danny's contributions to Indigenous education and culture, but in the spirit of the *communal* origins and guardianship of that Indigenous knowledge, the text announcing the honorary degree speaks also about the contributions of Danny's wife, Thelma, portraying their partnership in learning and sharing. "That's the degree I wanted to *earn*," Danny says, "but I'm still honored . . . even with the honorary part." He would have written one amazing thesis!

While living within the midst of the long-term oppressions of the dominant Western system, Danny retains his Indigenous values of acceptance and inclusion. He doesn't dismiss alternative viewpoints, either through outright rejection or a subtle critique that seeks to erase the alternative's meaning or even right to exist. "There is no *one* way," he believes, "only *right* ways."* *Indigenous Healing Psychology* seeks to activate that teaching.

"Not one way, only right ways." Yes, this teaching lays the groundwork for a synergy of multiple psychologies. But what about the mainstream approach to psychology as described in this book? Would

---

*This idea of "no one way, only right ways" applies not only to the acceptance of Western as well as Indigenous approaches but also to the acceptance of the variety of valid and truthful ways in which Indigenous teachings and ceremonies can occur. Danny is clear he can't support any notion of a culture police, wherein people, including Indigenous people, judge the acceptability, even authenticity, of ceremonial approaches other than their own according to whether or not they adhere to their own ways of doing things. He sees authenticity differently.

For example, Danny and I are at a conference that includes both Indigenous and non-Indigenous people, most of whom we don't know. Before the conference begins, I ask Danny if we should do a pipe ceremony to prepare for our participation. "Now that's

such an approach be a valuable partner in this collaborative network? *Indigenous Healing Psychology* certainly points out many of the short-comings of that mainstream approach. Partly that is to sharpen the difference between the mainstream and Indigenous approaches, better to appreciate their differences. Also, the described countercurrents within the mainstream approach, demonstrating its potential for enhancements reflecting Indigenous values, can encourage that mainstream toward a more careful and caring paradigm. So the synergy model assumes collaboration between approaches, which are both, in their own distinctive ways, trying best to serve all people.

Putting that collaboration into practice can be an exciting endeavor. When I'm teaching introductory psychology at the University of Saskatchewan to a special cohort of Indigenous students, the opportunity is there, and the challenge is worth the effort. That introductory course demonstrates the importance of niches where collaboration can be nourished so that synergy can be released. Within the larger context of the university, which is committed to integrating that course into its mainstream educational principles, the course ignites sparks of synergy—and who knows how many fires of creative learning can be fed. Using a standard Western textbook, the course also offers a parallel and interacting track that considers Indigenous approaches to psychology. As topics in mainstream psychology are discussed, there is a related discussion of Indigenous perspectives on that very topic. The Indigenous perspective critiques the mainstream approach, highlighting

---

(cont. from page 394) a good idea," he enthuses. And he takes off to a small bluff of trees, generally out of sight from the rest of the conference participants, and there we do our pipe ceremony. It's like no other pipe ceremony I've seen with Danny: it's short, very short. "That's quite a ceremony," I both comment and wonder. "Yes," he offers, "it's what is needed here . . . I don't want to be too public in this place or call attention to ourselves." All the key elements of the pipe ceremony are performed but tightened into a briefer, yet fully spiritual structure. It's a ceremony meant for that particular context. It's a right way of doing the pipe ceremony; the ceremony though brief is intact spiritually, and in addition, because it's brief it respects others at the conference who might find a pipe ceremony difficult to understand.

both its contributions and its limitations, while offering an expanded version of the topic.*

This interaction is symbolized by the lecture given, at the beginning of the course, by two Indigenous elders, Walter and Maria Linklater. Building upon their life stories that continually weave in and through their talks, Walter and Maria speak about culture and well-being, spiritual understandings and identity. They talk about their development, marked by the terrible abuses suffered during their stay in the residential schools and their later growth into years of empowerment and balance; about their culture and its sources of strength; about spiritual understandings and identity.

As an introduction Walter offers the ways in which spirituality is the foundation of an Indigenous worldview and way of living. "Our spiritual identity is our inherent right," Walter emphasizes. "It's what feeds us and gives us strength." But Walter is not just offering a philosophy; he is speaking about a practical way of being and a way he learned only through struggle and suffering. Without seeking any kind of praise, he details his journey to sobriety from a long period of alcoholism and its attendant destructive influence on his family responsibilities. "I was lost to the bottle," he states, "and didn't begin to know myself, and what I could really become, until I began knowing my traditional Ojibway teachings. Now, I've been sober for thirty-eight years, and my spirituality keeps me strong," he affirms.

Maria follows up Walter's talk with her own remarks about the importance of fighting to put those spiritual teachings into practice today in order to serve the most vulnerable, especially kids. She shows the class her fighting spirit. "I really gave it to those nuns," says Maria, as she details some of the ways she resisted the pervasive abuse of the nuns in charge while she was a student in the church-run residential school. "They couldn't keep me down. I just had to fight back because of what

---

*Teaching this special introductory psychology course is one setting where *Indigenous Healing Psychology*, in an early form, serves as a guide. While I am teaching that course over a now ten-year period, the book continually develops.

they were doing to me and the others," she adds, "and even though I was still just a little kid, they came to know they couldn't just mess with me." A clear picture emerges and inspires the class, especially the Indigenous women students, who, typically, are in the majority. Here is a woman who stands up for her rights and the rights of Indigenous people, and she continues using that fighting spirit to animate her ongoing work to seek justice from government institutions, to make them more respectful of the needs and aspirations of Indigenous kids and youth. "If someone in social services is just trying to lie, to cover up their mistakes or racism, I can see it right away! I've got a nose for smelling out that stuff," she adds.

Obviously, the elders don't come to the class as conventionally certified psychologists, nor do they even talk about Indigenous approaches to psychology. That's the beauty of their visit: they talk about their life *as lived,* their teachings *as activated* in that life, and that is what psychology should be more about. Through that process they offer a very different perspective on issues covered in the mainstream textbook used in our course.

I introduce the elders to the class as our first psychologists and later emphasize that their talk deals with topics and perspectives that are the proper foci for psychology, providing foundational insights; they are offering an Indigenous perspective on psychology that is essential to our search for understanding. I stress, for example, that the dimension of culture, so often an add-on consideration in the text, can be the heartbeat of existence. The contrast between these elders and the text is pretty dramatic, and that's the point. We only need to compare these elders with the standard founding psychologists portrayed in the textbook—primarily European males who are clearly not Indigenous! I emphasize that these elders' teachings have the same status as information provided in the text and other readings: their teachings can be discussed and cited in course papers. Simultaneously, I emphasize their special time-honored and experience-honed and spiritually infused significance.

When we consider the topic of identity in the course, students can see a wider and more nuanced picture of identity; without subtracting anything, we just add new insights and perspectives. In addition to discussing mainstream points about the variety of factors contributing to identity formation—including the psychophysiological impacts on temperament, the cognitive effects of mental schema, and the social constructions of gender typing—we now see the largely unrecognized but vital contributions of cultural values and history, including the pernicious effects of colonization, as well as spiritual teachings and practices, contributions characterizing the development of identity in most of the non-Western world. The whole of understanding is now much richer. The more essential aim of teaching an introductory psychology course, namely, engaging and exciting students about the importance and creative potentials of psychology, is encouraged rather than the more limited and discipline-based aim of covering all the basic introductory concepts, themes, and research findings—knowing that what is considered basic evolves over time.*

A note of realism can be helpful at this time. It may be that collaboration and synergy within the mainstream will come only with small steps, which could stimulate larger ones. Perhaps, for now, we should look to examples of collaboration wherever they exist, including what is a common example; namely, patterns of collaboration existing in niches

---

*A number of conferences and gatherings comparing Indigenous and Western ways of knowing and education, health, and healing are occurring; these gatherings nourish this collaboration within niches that have potential for yielding a wider influence. The gatherings feature traditional Indigenous elders and healers as core participants, with an emphasis on their teachings as guiding principles, in dialogue with Western-trained psychologists and educators. My longtime friend Jerry Mohatt, a Lacanian-oriented therapist living on the Rosebud Reservation, organizes such gatherings for many years, inviting his medicine man colleagues from Rosebud Reservation. There is also the Fetzer Institute Conference that brings together Indigenous elders and Western trained physicists. And recently I attend a conference organized by Joe Gone, a Gros Ventre psychologist at the University of Michigan. I feel honored to be part of the respectful exchanges at these gatherings, and *Indigenous Healing Psychology* seeks to follow the intentions and commitments of those gatherings.

within larger structures where integration persists.* These microlevel collaborations, infused by the energy of synergy, could initiate reverberations in the larger systems in which they exist—the promise of self-help groups carries such a message.

But the respectful collaboration of psychologies, though challenging, is also necessary. Though some influence of the integration model likely exists, collaboration can still help release synergy, especially within a focused niche environment. With this collaboration, psychology becomes more of its intended practice; namely, an approach to *a way of living,* and in particular a way of honest, equitable, and caring living for all. The lure of a universal psychology that encompasses all different approaches is strong, but the dangers of premature assumptions of unity are great. Too often the true distinctiveness of non-Western worldviews and the psychologies they express can be underestimated, as the Western approach, being unaware or even hiding its connections to sociopolitical power and control, erases what makes these less politically powerful alternatives so distinctively valuable in the first place.† How can a Western approach to self as a bounded experience of the individual fully comprehend an Indigenous approach that sees the individual as functioning within community without a lessening of respect for any one person?‡ The synergy

---

*None of the Indigenous elders who teach in this book are totally unfamiliar with or immune to Western influences.

†There are many thoughtful attempts to create a unified or universal psychology. For example, systems theory, drawing heavily on the early work of von Bertalanffy (1968), attempts to place the various aspects of psychology within one coherent theoretical structure; Gestalt therapy is one expression of that systems approach. More recently, there are theoretical frameworks offered to create a universal psychology, now less beholden to the assumed correctness and dominance of mainstream Western psychology and more attuned to the existence of various alternative views, including non-Western and Indigenous perspectives.

‡The profound differences between the Western and Indigenous concepts of the self are made dramatically clear at the Fetzer conference on Western and Indigenous approaches to science. Indigenous elders and Western scientists go to the heart of questions about reality, exchanging their distinctive conceptions of space, time, and matter, including how we know about those subjects. In their metaphysical explorations, both express foundational differences for distinctive, at times finely nuanced, considerations of self.

of psychologies emphasizes not the loss of contributions but the addition and consequent enrichment of contributions. For example, the present mainstream approach, which views psychology as a specialized and increasingly technical professionally defined discipline, can contribute to this collaboration, especially as it directs more of its energies into creating these caring and equitable ways of living. Future applications of this synergy model might provide paradigms for how various synergistic communities of psychologies might function, including brief experiences of that synergy, as well as more extended synergistic structures. That can be an exciting path of exploration and commitment, and hopefully *Indigenous Healing Psychology* can offer some suggestions and motivation.

INTERRUPTED IDENTITIES AND THE PROMISE OF COLLABORATIVE HEALING

Though slight of build and in his midsixties, Howard Luke, an Athabascan elder living on the outskirts of Fairbanks, Alaska, remains fiercely strong.* Refreshingly independent and deeply knowledgeable about traditional forms of subsistence and ceremony, he lives mostly in his fish camp, which sits on the banks of the swift Tanana River, surrounded by heavy brush and forest. Growing up, he was trained to be a runner, the one who runs from village to village to deliver important messages—no Internet then, not even telephones! With that traditional training, he was not allowed to compete in the frequent races that would be held in his village for the kids—his spiritually based talent makes him ineligible. Later, though, as a young adult, he is an active participant in dogsled racing. Even now, Howard remains youthfully vigorous; chopping wood and hauling in fish are just part of his day, and he doesn't wait for others to join him, as they often lag behind his swift actions.

---

*Howard tells his life story, detailing his development within a traditional Athabascan lifestyle, as well as his contemporary efforts at cultural empowerment (Luke 1998).

At his fish camp, Howard still functions within a traditional subsistence lifestyle.* He tries to show me elements of that subsistence approach, including running down moose, carrying in the beaver from traps, and hauling salmon from the river—I'm an eager student, but far from accomplished. From 1986 to 1989, I learn from and with Howard. Elders are typically older people, and they need help with ordinary life tasks; for Howard that meant things like helping to get groceries or advice in filling out government forms. Some people would call that being a gofer, but being an elder's gofer is actually essential.

Howard, though generally muted and often quietly within himself, appreciates humor, which is so critical to Indigenous ways of connecting and healing. But as he reminds me, humor is funny only when its context is sensitively understood. One day Howard is making the most delicious salmon I've ever tasted, cooking his fresh catch over the woodstove on a tray steeped with honey and other goodies. I'm joking with him—can't remember now about what. He turns to me and with a stern, uncompromising look says: "Never joke about that again!" I feel cut to my bone—and learn my lesson. There is joking that is joyful and life affirming and joking that is not funny at all.

Howard demonstrates the way of elders' teaching: you earn the right to be taught. We spend lots of time together, doing chores such as collecting firewood at his fish camp, riding around the city on errands, and just being together. We don't jump into any teachings. The teachings come when he feels it's appropriate and when I'm ready—and they often come unexpectedly, not always in some sit-down sessions. Howard exemplifies the elders' commitment to the principle that we learn through doing. Through engaging with him in his subsistence activities, I'm walking and working with him in a world infused with the spirits. "These salmon are our food," he says, "and we respect them. We pull them from the river and clean them in a good way, not wasting anything . . . just grateful for their feeding

---

*Fish camps in Alaska are typically more active during the summers, especially with the rich salmon runs that occur then.

us." As with the other elders I've worked with, living on and with the land is the primary spiritual practice and source of knowledge, no explicitly labeled or specifically demarcated healing ceremony with Howard this time around.

Collaborating our differing worldviews, including approaches to health and healing, Howard and I become engaged in therapeutic work with a group of six young Native males diagnosed by the local hospital as schizophrenic. It's an appropriate Western diagnosis, as all of them have delusions, disorganized thinking, and fluid, tenuous connections with requirements for normal everyday tasks; word salad or severely idiosyncratic speech intrudes into their daily conversations, and they have suicidal tendencies, including attempts. Addictions, mostly to alcohol, regularly dominate and destroy any semblance of balance they can create.

Most sadly, even cruelly, they are also labeled as chronically mentally ill. "These guys* are only in their early twenties, two still in their late teens," I reflect. "How could they already be chronic?" But since all were at present homeless—coming into the hospital on an outpatient basis, primarily to receive daily medications—and had few if any options for recovery, maybe that chronic label was more to signify the depth of their despair rather than the duration. All having grown up in rural Indigenous villages, they are immersed in their cultural values and traditions but are now cut off from their cultural roots; they're wanderers in an urban environment, only vaguely speaking of those values and dominated by a racist environment that labels them as just another example of "those dirty Native guys on the street." Their inborn identities no longer offer strength of character nor the will to live well.

The staff at the hospital is trying to help these young men—but with little success. In addition to the medications, there are occasional

---

*I'm using the term "guys" since that's how these young men always referred to themselves and each other; it is no way meant as a sign of disrespect but to honor the intimacy of our connections.

life skills workshops focusing on making their everyday behaviors, now alienating and even frightening to others, more adaptive and sensitive to normal interpersonal interactions. The hospital is providing what is seen as an example of best practices, but they know something is missing. The staff turns to me for assistance, knowing my long years of experience in working clinically with Indigenous people. "Would you want to run a group for these guys?" they ask. "Maybe bringing in more cultural material?" I know what they are searching for and accept the challenge. "Even if I can do a little bit more with their cultural teachings," I assume, "it can be better than nothing . . . which is what's happening now."

And so we begin our work together, those six young men and I, and our group forms quickly but not smoothly. The second meeting they decide as a group to get rid of me. Murmurs and confidential asides speak of "sending him up there" and "we can launch him now." As a group, they subtly begin moving their chairs around as if to encircle me, eventually jerking them toward me. I realize they're building a rocket in order to send me out into space. "This way will do it," Jimmy,* the oldest guy, says, "and at least he's out of here." Immediately I decide I'm going to stick it out with these guys and go with the flow of the group energy, facing a developing alternative without fear, realizing the worst that could happen is some manhandling. I respond calmly and respectfully to the spaceship atmosphere and intentions—which then deescalate and disappear. "I guess you're now one of us," says one guy. "I guess so," I respond.

We're now a group, and Justin, the youngest guy, formalizes that condition by assigning us all a place in a traditional kinship structure: I become the father, the others being sons. "This is how it's meant to be," Justin says. "It's good having older brothers here in the group." We're living out a relationship familiar to them from village life, which brings a certain stability to the group, though I remain sensitive to times those

---

*Pseudonyms are used to identify those in the group to protect their privacy.

kinship connections can impede our therapeutic work.* The diagnosis of schizophrenia becomes a background variable, respected but not emphasized and certainly not reified. The focus is on who these young men are now, including their growing-up years in the village and their current struggles on the urban sidewalks. But something important is still missing—a more direct connection with traditional cultural values and guides. And this is where I turn to Howard.

Inviting him to attend a group meeting, I trust he will be himself. Not only is he stubbornly true to his values, but also as a caring elder, he knows those who inhabit the Fairbanks Native street scene. I emphasize, "The group is yours . . . talk about whatever you want to." Howard understands: he knows he is coming *as an elder* to a group I'm working with *as a psychologist*. But we both know we're closely connected and respectful of each other's ways—highlighted by my active learning on his traditional land. I trust he will bring an elder's perspective to the group, offering an essential cultural grounding, and I'm right.

As we all sit down in the group room, Howard goes around the circle, greeting each young man in a traditionally appropriate manner. With each he has a connection, a deep connection based on kinship. "Oh, yes, I know your dad," he says to one. "We're related, you know," he says to another. "Your grandma and my mom were cousins. How is your mom?" he asks a third. "Is she still living by the river out there?" With each greeting and connection, a foundation is established, a warmth is created. The eyes of the guys are excited, they attentively lean into the group, and they relax into themselves, feeling and looking whole. It's quite remarkable, yet so simple to comprehend.

A deep and spontaneously satisfying connection emerges between Howard and each of the six men. Their home culture—the continuing subtext of their existence—is affirmed and nourished. Their identities as Indigenous men—still very important to them but unacknowledged in

---

*One important meaning level associated with my becoming the father in the group is that none of the guys have a positive relationship with their biological fathers and none are now in contact with them. Issues of transference become more salient.

the hospital—are confirmed and affirmed, well beyond the partial and mostly debilitating identities of patient or street person. Even though our group is still meeting inside the larger context of the hospital—which continues to offer its therapeutic services—collaboration grows as Howard is able to introduce an Indigenous environment within the group setting. An Indigenous identity that nurtured them as children is reconfirmed, sparking a childhood innocence and strength into their newly damaged adult frames. That spark of knowing who they are—transforming now into knowing who they *still* are—will keep appearing in the group, often initiated by Howard's presence.

Later on, I take the six guys out to Howard's fish camp, where he practices his traditional lifestyle. It is there that collaboration blossoms. Howard is on his ancestral land; it is his home living space, and the subsistence requirements of the place determine what we'll be doing. I can only assume at some point he'll talk with the boys—but where, how, and when, I have no idea. The day unfolds with the rhythms of the land, no clock-scheduled markers. The guys help Howard in a variety of tasks that they are already skilled at from their early years of living in their villages, whether it be setting fish nets, preparing fish for the smokehouse, or chopping wood for the stove—and I join in as best I can. The guys engage in these tasks not at Howard's behest but because they have been taught how to be helpful, and in particular how to help an elder. I marvel at how easily, one could say naturally, these men are being helped by being helpful. Their ways as Indigenous men, still with them, are being respected.

At one point, Howard goes to sit by the river to talk a bit about traditional teachings and the challenges of living in Fairbanks. I worry about whether his words are being wasted because all the guys are still busy doing different things out of earshot, including one who is fishing with a homemade rig (a stick and a hook) and is getting the hook caught in his hair as he throws out his line—though wonderful things are happening at Howard's camp, it's not all smooth sailing. But Howard is not *just* talking to the river—facing the river as he talks is part of his teaching. One by one, without being called over, the guys come and gather around Howard, listening intently. These are the same guys who, when in group, are often distracted and unfocused.

That time at Howard's fish camp epitomizes the gifts of collaboration. With the six young men at home in their familiar and encouraging world, positive aspects of themselves emerge. For example, Randy, who during our group meetings at the hospital continually and seemingly inappropriately bursts into group discussions with remarks about the weather, makes similar weather remarks at Howard's camp, but *now* they are totally appropriate and well timed—they are accurately related to the immediate river environment.

As collaborations with Howard continue, the group meetings at the hospital become energized, with the men being more engaged; they participate more in other hospital services, such as field trips. Stimulated by Howard's presence, I suggest more activities to reinforce that positive side of identity he nourishes. We go ice fishing as a group. My ignorance of ice conditions, including whether to drive our truck onto the ice and where the best spots to dig our fishing holes are, is nicely matched by the guys' expert knowledge of the ice—they are just doing what they have always done as kids. Competence breeds confidence; confidence nourishes self-esteem. As we walk on the ice and it begins to bend, I have a clear moment of doubt: "Is this OK?" I ask too tentatively. "No worry, we know this ice," more than one guy responds. And what do I know? I don't doubt them; they are ice fishermen now, not schizophrenics.

Later we start a firewood business, cutting mostly fallen trees into logs and loading them on a truck to deliver them to always eager customers—many homes in the area rely on woodstoves for their heat and cooking. As we're heading out one day—six guys, myself, and our three chain saws—a hospital staff member whispers in my ear: "You're going out with six schizophrenics . . . with chain saws?!" I can forgive that crippling stereotype as it comes from a staff member who, though uninformed, truly cares about the guys.

Yes, with the guys and chain saws because, again, cutting firewood is their normal, even natural activity. That's what they did growing up in the village, and especially when they provided firewood for elders and others unable to get their own, they are expressing their cultural values of sharing and service. Driving the truck because only I have a license, I'm still more a member of the team than a top-down leader. "It's good to be out here," says Jimmy, who as the oldest guy often verbalizes a group feeling. "I'm feeling strong again . . . and this is a way we can help out others." Responsibility nourishes mature feelings; being of service encourages self-esteem.

The psychologically infused group work I introduce continues, intersecting with, reinforcing, and reinforced by these cultural experiences. We seek to identify feelings, especially sadness, anger, and hopelessness, reflecting on them within their life spaces, seeking transformations into feelings of calm, hope, and acceptance. We also recognize and nourish the community that is emerging, and I stress it can be a community of helping and healing, supporting one another in positive ways rather than inviting one another into abusive and addictive pathways.

We also talk about the voices they hear: Who are those voices? What are they asking for or demanding? Our aim is to make those voices more familiar, more a part of who they are and therefore more amenable to being changed if not shaped. A central concern is how to tell the voices you don't want to do something if it will be destructive or hurtful. In this effort to understand the voices, I take guidance from Rachel Craig, my close friend and Inupiat elder. "If these young men had been in the village when they began hearing voices," she relates, "we would've known how to help them. We would've guided them, helped them to see those voices are not to be feared. I want to be clear," Rachel continues. "It's not that those young guys would have necessarily become healers—using those voices to guide healing work. That only happens once in a while and with special voices that can guide. But at least those guys could have lived their lives knowing that our ancestors do speak with us . . . that voices *can* become an important part of who we are."

I offer my work with this Alaska group as an example of some of the dynamics of collaboration. At first, though my work with the group emphasizes Indigenous principles of respect and sensitivity to cultural issues, we're still working within the larger hospital setting and its conventional Western-oriented therapeutic services model—a form of forced integration on its way toward a fuller process of collaboration exists. Then, with the introduction of Howard to the life of the group, collaboration blossoms, especially as the unique healing rhythms of Howard's fish camp are treasured. As the group continues, less and less tied into the hospital ethos, more and more merging with meanings in their Indigenous life spaces, we break increasingly out of the bindings of the integration model, becoming less and less a recognizable hospital program.

I'm not describing this group of Alaska guys as a success story but as a story of promise and potential. When I go back to Fairbanks four years later, three of the men have improved their adaptations to urban life, one holding a steady job; two were still mired in the street life, and one had taken his life. But positive change has happened; it is possible. And maybe our little family group played some small role in that possibility, maybe generating a spark of feeling once again of the sense of wholeness the guys knew in their early village years.

This collaborative healing effort, involving all of us, not just Howard and me, highlights certain working principles that can encourage or discourage synergy. While living in the rural island village of Naqara in Fiji, I experience these principles, as I'm part of a collaboration between healers and helpers of differing orientations that creates a healing network larger than the sum of its individual parts—to the benefit of all who seek help.

In Naqara, the two main sources of healing are Sevuloni, the traditional Fijian spiritual healer who uses the yaqona healing ceremony, and Sereana, commonly called *nasi* (nurse), a Fijian woman trained in

Western approaches to medicine to become a nurse who now runs the local nursing station, which has a very strong presence in the village.*

But now I've become a somewhat reluctant part of this healing network, originally not wanting to impose my ways of help and healing on the local village environment. Sevuloni, my closest friend, whom I also work with in his healing ceremonies, as we both have Ratu Civo as our teacher, asks for my help: "My close relative Asenati† is suffering from a bad disease . . . it's vakatevoro [caused by bad spirits], so I'm doing my healing work with her. But she's still afraid of people—afraid to even leave her bed . . . been there for days now. Nasi has been sending over some medicines, but she's still afraid to move. Can you help her? Can you see what your *veiqaravi*† will do?"

Sevuloni knows I'm a doctor—being a Ph.D. came as part of my introduction to the village—but for him being a doctor means being a physician, an M.D. "What can I offer?" I wonder. "My knowledge of the Fijian language is just beginning . . . and how helpful can I be within this context of Fijian culture?" But I remember what Ratu Civo tells me: "Do whatever you can honestly do—no more but also no less." It's the "no less" that convinces me to try. "Yes, I'll do the best I can," I respond with conviction. At the same time I make it clear to Sevuloni that my intervention would work primarily with Asenati's mind—the best way I could describe psychological interventions—and that I would be alongside him as I continued to respect the important traditional Fijian spiritual healing work he's doing with Asenati, as well as the medicines Nasi is giving her from the nursing station.

I visit Asenati in her home. She's lying on her bed in a fetal position, mostly covered with a blanket, too frightened to move. In my halting

---

*Two other sources of healing in Naqara are Nanise, an older woman who dispenses herbal remedies, and Mere, a female healer who works with massage, both of whom draw their knowledge from spiritual sources.

†Again, I'm using a pseudonym here to protect the person's anonymity.

‡Sevuloni uses the word *veiqaravi*, which means "service" or "help," to describe both his healing work and what he hopes I can offer.

Fijian, carried more strongly by my nonverbal connecting, we work together. We connect as Asenati peeks out from her covers. As we talk a bit more, brief but real connections emerge. She agrees to try some things. Using guided imagery and the cognitive behavior technique of desensitization, I seek to encourage Asenati to move, and then to move toward the end of her bed, and then to place her feet on the ground—finally to walk, still tentatively, on the floor. These movements, very tentative at first, occur over two sessions, better described as visits. By the third visit, Asenati is now outside, though still withdrawn, reaching out quietly. Eventually, she returns to much of her routine activities, though she remains reticent, sometimes withdrawing into herself.

All during my work with Asenati, I remain clear to myself that my intervention was functioning within a primarily Western psychological paradigm. At the same time, I recognize the strong spiritual dimension that had always been part of my usual therapeutic work, a dimension that is now being further fed during my ongoing healing connections with Sevuloni. I have respect for and experience in the traditional Fijian spiritual healing system as practiced by Sevuloni, as do Asenati and Nasi; and Sevuloni, Nasi, and Asenati have respect for the therapeutic intervention I am making. We're parties to a collaboration that preserves the unique contributions of each of the three healing systems offered. Asenati is the one to benefit, now having access to a richer, more extensive array of healing resources, creating a whole healing network that was greater than the sum of its individual parts.

Now from the inside of that healing network, I can see some of the principles that seem to make it function to serve the entire village. First, none of the healers see themselves as able to deal with all problems; no one is imperialistic in the way they conceptualize their work: "I do the work I've been trained for—that's what I can do," says Nasi. "I know what my medicines can—so much, but not everything—and Sevuloni works on things I can't do . . . and that's good. And you, Dick, you do your thing . . . and that can be very helpful." Second, there is mutual respect among the different healers for both the distinctive aspect of one another's work and its particular effectiveness—being good for particular ailments. Sevuloni refers to his and my work with the same words: veiqaravi (service or help), na cakacaka (the work). It's his way of showing respect for different paths toward healing. Third, each member of the healing network knows the proper protocol for referring clients to the other healers when appropriate: this ease of referral emerges naturally from their lack of imperialism about healing and their mutual respect for one another's ways. When Nasi goes to Sevuloni for help, she presents him with a yaqona, acknowledging the traditional way spirit healers like Sevuloni are approached. "I have no problem with that," she says with ease. "That is our Fijian way—and my nursing station lives comfortably by his side."

The foundation for Howard and me collaborating is based on these three principles—though I never think about it in such a logical way when we're actually working together. For example, when I ask Howard for his help, I do so in the traditional Athabascan way of requesting his guidance and support. And he knows enough about my work as a psychologist to understand what I might be able to offer. Neither of us believes we alone can do it all, as we each respect what the other can uniquely offer. Moreover, we never even consider inviting Howard into the hospital in a formal, more bureaucratically centered manner. He does not have an office in the hospital and is not expected to submit some account of the work he does and with whom—ways in which someone like Howard can compromise the work he does as an elder on the land and that eventually can undermine the synergistic relationships we seek to nourish. Howard's fish camp and the hospital group meeting room are intentionally kept as two separate worlds of healing—separate but reciprocally supportive. The powerful beauty of the synergy model is just this collaboration between *apparently* conflicting worlds and their worldviews.

The collaboration among all in our Alaska group, not just between Howard and myself, also highlights some of the challenges it evokes. There are many such challenges, ranging from personal motivational issues such as defending professional turf to institutional issues such as systemic racism. It would be comforting to know how best to overcome these obstacles so collaboration could prevail and a synergistic community of psychologies could emerge. The contemporary power structure within psychology dictates some of the options. Do we focus on nourishing the expression of the inherent strengths in Indigenous approaches that are now being denigrated and disregarded? Do we focus on owning the imperialistic aspects of mainstream psychology that foreclose possible appreciations of those Indigenous approaches, thereby creating space for their contributions to count? It seems we need to focus on both, as they are constantly interweaving and supporting—or detracting—from each other. How best to initiate the process of change toward synergy? Perhaps all we can say for now is that the process is rarely linear and typically unpredictable. Whichever focus is most productive as a point of departure *at the time,* considering context and history and other variables of the moment, *if* such judgments can actually be made, would be the focus to emphasize. And whichever is the point of initiation, the other focus will inevitably become a necessary space and place of action as well.

But it may be helpful to consider one of the more subtle and therefore elusive obstacles to collaboration, just to demonstrate the enormity of the task of challenging these obstacles. This obstacle can be described, in its most well-intentioned vein, as the desire to *incorporate* what are viewed as positive elements from one, typically less dominant, system into another, typically more dominant, system. From a more critical and even realistic perspective this obstacle can be described as a need to *assimilate* or *appropriate* elements from the less powerful system into the more powerful one, masking the effort to erase the less powerful system by extolling the virtues of bringing that less powerful system into the mainstream—as if that were the dream of all the underserved!

At times an open-mindedness to aspects of practices from another culture can, though well intentioned, be naïve and actually activate an appropriation. A common acquisitive example is when Western therapists begin practicing elements from Indigenous approaches. I often hear statements like, "I'm just trying to learn more about healing," or "I just want to show respect for my Indigenous clients by bringing part of their ceremonies into my practice" as explanations or justifications for this use of Indigenous therapeutic elements. But the failure of the Western therapist to understand the depth of Indigenous cultural *assumptions* that underlie a particular healing practice turns the use of that Indigenous practice into a superficial performance.

A common instance of this appropriation is the use of an Indigenous talking circle or healing circle by Western therapists. They justify doing this by remarking that these circles seem so straightforward or simple to perform. But I've been told these Indigenous circles are sacred ceremonies; they must be properly given, steadfastly earned. "We have a proper protocol for those healing circles," says Danny. "They are ceremonies, not just gathering people in a circle to talk." Unless a ceremony holder gives the Western therapist one of these Indigenous ceremonies in the proper manner, the Western therapist's performing one of the above circles would be a case of appropriation—a degradation of the ceremony. Which is not to say that gathering people in a circle to talk openly about their feelings cannot to be practiced without having the actual healing circle ceremony; the circle, in a quite ordinary sense, opens doors to strong and honest sharing and is a wonderful therapeutic practice for all.

At other times there can be a more blatant acquisitive motive, perhaps masked by a façade of good intentions, such as "being respectful to their culture." But in fact, the process is taking something from the other approach, without respect, merely to add value—often monetary value—to one's own practice. As we have seen, such appropriations seem to be alive but not so well in a variety of situations, involving all types of people, both within and outside a particular cultural tradition.

Joe Eagle Elk tells me this story of a well-intended appropriation in regard to his healing work. Some of the people who come to Joe for a healing ceremony at Rosebud have a condition that requires Western surgery. Joe always supports such surgeries when they are necessary, adding that a Lakota healing ceremony before the surgery can help clear the spiritual way and thus support the success of the surgery. Joe also goes at times to the hospital to follow up with a client after surgery and then performs another healing ceremony in the hospital. Though he can't do the full ceremony in the hospital, he does what he can, and the hospital makes certain accommodations for Joe to perform his ceremony. Within certain institutional constraints, it becomes a supportive environment.

Joe gets to know several of the doctors from his visits to one hospital, and they express an interest in learning more about his healing ceremonies. When they ask him questions, Joe remains evasive, saying things like, "It's just something I do," or "It's my way," always avoiding giving these doctors any details about the ceremony since they haven't *earned*—through the struggles of dedicated participation in the ceremony or a full apprenticeship—the right to hear those details and certainly not permission to practice elements of the ceremony.

After Joe has completed one healing ceremony in the hospital, a doctor who was friendly with Joe asks him: "I noticed you use a liquid in a glass during your healing ceremony. I wonder what's in that glass? I'm real interested in learning about healing substances. Joe responds, 'Oh, it's just some stuff.'"

The doctor continues: "Well, I hope you don't mind, but after you finished your healing ceremony and left the hospital, I took a little of that liquid you left in the glass and analyzed it. But maybe I made a mistake because the liquid turned out to be just plain water."

Joe looks kindly but knowingly at the doctor. "Yes," he said, "I knew you would try to find out what kind of liquid I was using in my healing ceremony. So I decided this time to use just plain water. And you know, that too can help to heal! Look, I think you're doing a good job with your surgery and stuff. Keep doing it your way. That's what you do. And I'll keep doing my work, my ceremonies. That's what I do. Don't be so curious to find out what I do—just let me do my work. I let you do your work . . . without interfering."

But often patterns of integration dominate, providing the general context within which collaboration emerges, because that is the only way the alternative, collaborative approach can be made available to prospective clients. A typical example is when Indigenous healers and elders work within a Western hospital or penal institution to offer counseling and healing ceremonies to Indigenous patients or inmates. There are numerous instances in the Canadian penal system, a Western institution that incarcerates a disproportionate number of Indigenous inmates, where sweat lodges, an essential Indigenous healing ceremony, are conducted by Indigenous sweat lodge leaders and offered to inmates.*

The prison maintains control over all services offered inmates, including the sweat lodge and what is commonly seen as the standard prison therapeutic intervention, some form of cognitive behavior therapy (CBT). Sweats become a prison program to help inmates, like the CBT workshops in topics such as anger management and social skill training, diluting its significance as an Indigenous spiritual healing ceremony. When sweat lodges are offered, they are typically labeled by prison officials as a secondary treatment, less valued than the CBT, which is itself not that highly valued. In describing the sweat lodge, one prison guard said, "It's just something the Indigenous clients seem to like. I'm not sure what good it does. It's a hassle for us to supervise." Working under the supervision of prison staff, who are typically non-Indigenous, Indigenous sweat lodge leaders must make many compromises in how they perform their ceremony. For example, they must agree to have records of attendance at the sweat kept and even in some cases are asked to report on what generally happened in the

---

*Randy Mason (2000) wrote an excellent thesis on the use of sweat lodges and cognitive behavioral therapy at the Regional Psychiatric Centre in Saskatoon, Saskatchewan, and I'm drawing on that research in my discussion. I serve as Randy's thesis adviser and learn a great deal, especially as he struggles against a less than accepting graduate school environment and I struggle to offer whatever support I can—we've avoided the common academic process where the student's thesis carries out too literally a part of the larger research program of the supervisor.

sweat ceremony itself. Outside the prison, attendance is never taken at a traditional sweat nor is there any discussion about what occurred during the sweat, unless a participant chooses to share his story. As Tony Sands, an Indigenous sweat lodge leader would say to those who entered his lodge: "It's nobody's business that you're here but your own. Only you know why you're here in the sweat. And that's between you and the Creator."

But Indigenous sweat lodge holders do work inside the prison walls, making compromises, just so they can access a very needy and vulnerable population. An Indigenous man who runs lodges inside the prisons put it this way: "It's not the best of worlds when we do a sweat inside the prison. But those sweats can be so important to the Indigenous inmates. Sometimes it's all they have. And sometimes it can help them to turn their lives around."

There are countless examples of patterns of integration, more so than patterns of collaboration. Patterns of integration seem easier to establish because those in control, typically using the Western approach, have very little to give up, as they remain in control after the integration. Also, the compromises the Indigenous approach must make to integrate are considered unessential by the dominant institution because the Indigenous practitioners come to the integration with less power and remain in that relatively powerless position during the integration. Unfortunately, and inequitably, the distress of the less powerful counts for less than any discomfort felt by the more powerful, at least in terms of those defining the dynamics of the relationship; namely, the more powerful.

Integration can be a step in the right direction; it can help to loosen the grip of psychology's stranglehold. But it can also represent a slippery slope of misdirection, where integration can succumb to assimilation. Then the potential for synergy becomes severely limited. In collaboration, there is a relationship of mutual trust created between two apparently conflicting therapeutic services; a whole is created that is greater than the sum of its parts. Clients, especially Indigenous clients, have a greater array of healing options to access, and as these options support each other, they are enhanced. But we should not underestimate the importance of instances of integration that provide the only way Indigenous healing approaches can be made available to Indigenous clients, whether it be because those clients are too sick to leave a Western hospital setting or are incarcerated in a prison. These instances of what might be called no-choice integration must be respected.*

The existence of the sweat lodge within the Canadian prison system is a good example of a form of integration with definite value—even though it may be seen from one perspective as only a first step toward full participation of Indigenous inmates in that prayer and healing ceremony. Within the restrictive context of the prison, causing adaptations to their sweat lodge that impacts its functioning as a resource, Indigenous elders are still reaching out with their sweat lodge to meet the deeply felt aspirations of the inmates—and healing occurs (see e.g., Mason 2000). When Danny and I teach our respective courses in traditional Indigenous and Western counseling, clearly collaboration is occurring, and just because it occurs within a larger environment that seeks to integrate our teaching efforts more firmly within a Western model of education doesn't thereby negate its potential contributions.

There is one more example of ways in which collaboration and integration can at times blend, and this is a most important and provocative example. At the initiation of the Society of Indian Psychologists (SIP),† and under the creative and committed editorial leadership of Melinda García, a document has been prepared that examines the core of mainstream psychology from an Indigenous perspective and finds that core not only severely limited but also a vehicle for colonizing Indigenous

---

*There are attempts to deconstruct this pattern of integration by having mainstream psychology own and disown its colonial relationship toward Indigenous people, thereby seeking to open a door for the honoring and emergence of Indigenous perspectives within that mainstream (see e.g. Australian Psychological Society 2016).

†The term *Indian* in this context refers to Indigenous people in North, Central, and South America, though SIP membership is primarily from the United States.

people. A Meso-American Indigenous woman, Melinda is a dear friend and colleague in arms; she lives an integrated life as a sacred ceremonial leader, clinical and community psychologist, and social justice activist. Entitled "Society of Indian Psychologists Commentary on the American Psychological Association's Ethical Principles of Psychologists and Code of Contact" (García and Tehee 2014), the document focuses on the ethical principles and standards of practice that mainstream psychology—as represented by the APA, its official professional organization—presents as the defining characteristics for the field. Systematically following the articulation of those principles and practices, the document, point by point, devastates the lack of cultural sensitivity promoted by mainstream psychology.*

The document is a true tour de force, and its blistering yet measured criticism exposes the deep arrogance of the mainstream approach, preventing psychology from being a resource for all the people, not just those in control of psychological institutions and functions. To support its critique, the document relies heavily on stories of mostly Indigenous psychologists who recount their personal experiences with stereotypes and racism in the mainstream. Personal experience is honored as not only valid but also essential data: "We had to embrace who we are and communicate in the language of stories. Stories bring the abstract to life. Stories bring out struggles to life. Stories communicate across cultures" (García and Tehee 2014, 8).

Here are two of the many stories:

I had a clinical supervisor at an IHS [Indian Health Service] rotation site who said, I "need to moderate my Indianness." As a Native student I was devastated and angry. How could I moderate my "Indianness" when I am who I am? The disrespect of that psychologist, a seasoned IHS employee, was truly incompetent. I always won-

*A further discussion of the intent and implications of this document can be found in García 2014, 2015a, and 2015b. The document is available from SIP.

der how many Native American students have experienced what I went through.

> As an intern, I saw a Native woman who was struggling with a bad medicine dream. Afterward, I went to talk with my supervisor because the session was disturbing. First, she asked when the client was coming back. When I told her the appointment time, the supervisor said she just wanted to be prepared if the pictures on the shared wall between our offices began spinning around at that time. Her response was one of dismissal of the spiritual and cultural aspects of the subject for the client and for me as the intern. She then proceeded to tell me I had a problem with spirituality. I didn't feel safe to bring up cultural or spiritual issues for clients in supervision after that for fear of being ridiculed. (García and Tehee 2014, 68–69)

There is a beautiful and powerful connection in the document between the sacred and spiritual and the practical—in this case the practice of psychology. Among the essential concepts proposed as a foundation to the document are spiritual concepts (García and Tehee 2014, 14–15): "all things are sacred," "everything is connected," and "mystery, awe, wonder, intuition, and miracles occur naturally in everyday life." Other essential concepts stress social action and justice (García and Tehee 2014, 15): "sustainability is essential for all of us to survive and thrive," and "it is important to consider how to act deliberately and thoughtfully." This is truly deep praxis, as the spiritual is seen as an empowering part of daily life—a belief far from the mainstream. The call for APA to include two principles presently lacking—cultural relevance and humility—speaks volumes about the ironic insularity and isolation of the mainstream as it is shown to be an *outlier* in terms of health, healing, and social justice.

The SIP document offers a groundbreaking example of collaboration and integration. While offering valuable ways psychology can become more truly a resource for all people, it adheres to the structure, the outline of the way mainstream psychology presently defines itself.

Melinda tells me this shadowing of the APA ethics code is to make the SIP critique more accessible to those within mainstream psychology that can make changes; namely, the psychology licensing boards and accreditation agencies. "We need to speak their language by using the structure of their code of ethics," she says, "if we want to maximize the chances they will even read our document, no less act upon it, it has to have a familiar feel to it. Then," she says, "in the future, we'll do our own stand-alone document. A fully and truly indigenous document." I'm so impressed with this SIP effort! Not sure where it fits on the collaboration-integration continuum, but I know it is a document that really matters and promises to not only enhance mainstream psychology but also richly feed the articulation of an Indigenous approach to psychology.

Now that the characteristics of collaborative and integrative patterns of relationship are hopefully clearer, it's a good time to bring up a most important point. As Danny often observes, "Just look around today. There are so many different respectful and honest efforts at learning and growth. So many . . . you look at these different efforts without prejudging them, and then I think that all ways *can* be good." All respectful and honest efforts having the potential to do good. And that includes attempts that could be characterized as being more toward the integration end of the integration-collaboration dimension. Depending on the specific context in which different ways of doing psychology occur, on the particular resources available to those seeking to create some relationship between these different ways, and on the actual aspirations of the clients or communities being served, the pattern of relationship can be more or less collaborative, more or less an example of integration—and if respectful and honest, all ways can be good.

Yes, collaborative patterns of relationship among approaches to psychology are more likely to encourage the emergence of synergy, a uniquely powerful healing vehicle and experience. But healing, as a movement toward meaning, balance, connection, and wholism, can occur in a variety of ways and at varying levels of intensity. Patterns of integration can and do encourage their own forms of healing, including serving as a precursor, even trailblazer, toward synergy, as they challenge stifling structures of power and control.

BEGINNINGS, ENDINGS, BEGINNINGS

At Joe Eagle Elk's funeral, he teaches once again. He knows his time is limited, and he plans his funeral to show his respect for all ways toward the Creator and to honor his relatives and community. He requests that a sweat lodge be held behind his house, honoring his and his family's path; a peyote ceremony be conducted in the basement, honoring his wife's involvement in the peyote road or way of the Native American Indian Church; and a Mass be held in the living room, honoring the Catholic Church that means so much to so many on the reserve, though it doesn't have a strong connection to his family.

These three vehicles for prayer and healing are not offered at the same time—anyone can attend any one or more they wish to—and all are offered in the context of being worthwhile and valued. This becomes important given that, especially historically but continuing on today, each of these three ways is in conflict with one another, sometimes painfully so, in destructive and unyielding ways. But Joe wants to show his respect for all ways of reaching out to and toward the Creator. "The Creator comes to us through many ways," he once says, "and who are we to judge that another's path to the Creator is any worse or better than our own. When you're honest and really trying, your path becomes good."

"All ways are good," he often says, and now, in a final action, he shows how that can be a reality.

Tony and Emma Sand, Cree elders who have adopted my family and me into their family, are strong in their acceptance of me and my psychology training. Tony acknowledges my efforts to connect with the Indigenous community in a respectful way: "We like you," he says to me as we leave after completing his sweat lodge. "In that sweat you're just like us." And Emma adds, not correcting but offering a neutral, encompassing perspective: "But we like you because of who you are . . . as a person." To be more honestly connected to my highest potential— that's what I strive for. To be more honestly connected to its highest potential—that's what psychology can strive for. In being itself, honoring its roots and potentials, psychology can become a source of strength and healing for all, a way of life connecting the everyday and the spirit as one. This can be a healing psychology.

I remember a sweat lodge ceremony Joe Eagle Elk runs at his home on the Rosebud Reservation. As is the custom, each person in the lodge offers a prayer in one of the rounds. One of the participants is Gerhart, a man from Germany. As he prepares to enter the sweat lodge, Gerhart apologizes to Joe. "I'm not sure I can do the whole ceremony," he says humbly. "I can't offer my prayers in either Lakota or English . . . only in German. So my prayers won't be understood by others in the sweat. Maybe I shouldn't offer my prayers when we all pray." Joe shares none of Gerhart's confusion and doubt. "You don't have to worry," Joe assures him. "The Creator knows all languages."

Bibliography

Note that many of the references listed for theories from major figures in psychology, such as Carl Rogers, or data presentations on major concepts, such as those on conformity, are early works. I feel that in those cases the early work represents not only a historically important event, but also, in many cases, the clearest and most fundamental presentation of the theory or data.

Aleccia, JoNel. 2010. "Surgery Error Leads Doc to Public Mea Culpa." NBCNews.com, November 10. www.nbcnews.com/id/40096673/ns/health-health_care/t/surgery-error-leads-doc-public-mea-culpa/#.WSX4WhRrbpg.

Anderson, Kim, and Bonita Lawrence, eds. 2003. *Strong Women Stories: Native Vision and Community Survival.* Toronto: Sumach Press.

Anonymous. (1939) 2001. *Alcoholics Anonymous: The Story of How Many Thousands of Men and Women Have Recovered from Alcoholism.* 4th ed. New York: AA World Services.

———. (1952) 2012. *Twelve Steps and Twelve Traditions.* 77th printing. New York: AA World Services.

———. 1981. *This Is Al-Anon: Al-Anon Family Groups.* New York: Al-Anon Family Group Headquarters.

Asch, Solomon. 1965. "Effects of Group Pressure upon the Modification and Distortion of Judgments." In *Basic Studies in Social Psychology,* edited by Harold Proshansky and Bernard Seidenberg. Canada: Holt, Reinhart, Winston.

Assembly of First Nations. 1994. *Breaking the Silence: An Interpretive Study of Residential School Impact and Healing as Illustrated by the Stories of First Nations Individuals.* Ottawa: Assembly of First Nations.

Austin, Stephanie, and Isaac Prilleltensky. 2001. "Diverse Origins, Common Aims: The Challenge of Critical Psychology." *Radical Psychology* 2 (2).

———. 2011. "Contemporary Debates in Critical Psychology: Dialectics and Syntheses." *Australian Psychologist* 36 (1): 75–80. doi: 10.1080 /00050060108259634.

Australian Psychological Society. 2016. "Australian Psychological Society Apologizes to Aboriginal and Torres Islander People." Media Statement September 15, 2016. www.psychology.org.au/news/media_releases/15September2016

Baillargeon, Renée. 2004. "Infant's Physical World." *Current Directions in Psychological Science* 13: 89–94.

Balter, Marie, and Richard Katz. 1991. *Nobody's Child*. Cambridge, Mass.: DaCapo Press.

Battiste Marie, and Jean Barman, eds. *First Nations Education in Canada: The Circle Unfolds*. Vancouver: University of British Columbia Press.

Beck, Aaron. 2005. "The Current State of Cognitive Therapy: A 40-Year Retrospective." *Archives of General Psychiatry* 62: 953–59.

Benson, Herbert. 2000. *The Relaxation Response*. With M. Kipper. Revised ed. New York: Harper Torch.

Bertalanffy, Ludwig von. 1968. *General Systems Theory: Foundations, Development, Applications*. New York: George Braziller.

Bhatt, Ela. 2006. *We Are Poor but So Many: The Story of Self-Employed Women in India*. Oxford: Oxford University Press.

Biesele, Megan. 1993. *Women Like Meat: Folklore and Foraging Ideology of the Kalahari Ju/'hoansi*. Bloomington and Indianapolis: Indiana University Press.

Biesele, Megan, and Robert Hitchcock. 2011. *The Ju/'hoan San of Nyae Nyae and Namibian Independence: Development, Democracy, and Indigenous Voices in Southern Africa*. New York: Berghahn Books.

Bohm, David. 1980. *Wholeness and the Implicate Order*. London: Routledge.

———. 1996. *On Dialogue*. London: Routledge.

Bohm, David, and F. David Peat. 1987. *Science, Order and Creativity*. London: Routledge.

Borysenko, Joan. 2007. *Minding the Body, Mending the Mind*. Revised ed. Cambridge, Mass.: Da Capo.

Brown, Sidney Ann Stone. 2014. *Transformation beyond Greed: Native Self-Actualization*. Self-published; contact drstonebrown@gmail.com.

Bruner, Jerome. 1990. *Acts of Meaning*. Cambridge, Mass.: Harvard University Press.

Cajete, Gregory. 2008. "Sites of Strength in Indigenous Research." In *Indigenous Knowledge and Education: Sites of Struggle, Strength and Survivance*, edited by M. Villegas, S. B. Neugebauer, and K. Venegas, Cambridge, Mass.: Harvard Educational Press.

Caplan, Paula. 1995. *They Say You're Crazy: How the World's Most Powerful Psychiatrists Decide Who's Normal.* Reading, Mass.: Addison-Wesley.

Castellano, Marlene Brant. 2004. "Ethics of Aboriginal Research." *Journal of Aboriginal Health,* 1 (1): 98–114. www.naho.ca/journal/2004/01/08/ethics -of-aboriginal-research.

Chansonneuve, Deborah. 2005. *Reclaiming Connections: Understanding Residential School Trauma among Aboriginal People.* Ottawa: Aboriginal Healing Foundation.

Charon, Rita. 2006. *Narrative Medicine: Honoring the Stories of Illness.* New York: Oxford University Press.

Cheever, Olivia. 1995. *Education as Transformation in American Psychiatry: From Voices of Control to Voices of Connection.* Doctoral dissertation, Harvard University, Cambridge, Mass.

Chodorow, Nancy. 1978. *The Reproduction of Mothering: Psychoanalysis and the Sociology of Gender.* Berkeley: University of California Press.

Chwe, Michael Suk-Young. 2014. "Scientific Pride and Prejudice." Opinion piece, *Sunday Review, New York Times,* January 31. Retrieved from www .quantumactivist.com/scientific-pride-and-prejudice/.

Colt, Henri, Silvia Quadrelli, and Lester Friedman, eds. 2011. *The Picture of Health: Medical Ethics and the Movies.* New York: Oxford University Press.

Complete Dictionary of Scientific Biology. 2008. Encyclopedia.com. www .encyclopedia.com/topic/Henry_Alexander_Murray.aspx.

Cool Psychologist. 2009. *The Bystander Effect.* Video file. Recorded June 4. www.youtube.com/watch?v=OSsPfbup0ac.

Corsini, Raymond, and Danny Wedding, eds. 2010. *Current Psychotherapies.* 9th ed. Belmont, Calif.: Brooks-Cole.

Council of Elders. 1988. "The Tipi." Brochure. Saskatchewan Indian Cultural Centre, Saskatoon.

Cox, Harvey. 1965. *The Secular City: Secularization and Urbanization in Theological Perspective.* New York: Collier.

Dalai Lama. 2011. *The Dalai Lama's Little Book of Compassion.* Newburyport, Mass.: Hampton Roads Publisher.

Dalai Lama, and Paul Ekman. 2008. *Emotional Awareness: Overcoming the Obstacles to Psychological Balance and Compassion.* New York: Henry Holt.

DasGupta, Sayantani, and Rita Charon, R. 2004. "Personal Illness Narratives:

Using Reflective Writing to Teach Empathy." *Academic Medicine* 79: 351–56.

Datu, Jesus Alfonso D. 2014. "Why Power Does Not Guarantee Happiness across Cultures." *Online Readings in Psychology and Culture* 5 (3). //dx.doi .org/10.9707/2307-0919.1131.

Davidson, Richard. 2004. "Well-Being and Affective Style: Neural Substrates and Biobehavioural Correlates." *Philosophical Transactions of the Royal Society (London)* 359: 1395–1411. https://centerhealthyminds.org/assets /files-publications/DavidsonWell-beingTheRoyalSociety.pdf. doi:10.1098 /rstb.2004.1510 .

———. 2015. *Richie Davidson on Mindfulness, Neuroscience and Epigenetics.* Video file. Recorded April 28. www.youtube.com/watch?v=2qaJnBp4ZFg.

Davidson, Richard J., and Sharon Begley. 2012. *The Emotional Life of Your Brain: How Its Unique Patterns Affect the Way You Think, Feel, and Live— and How You Can Change Them.* London: Penguin Books.

Davidson, Richard J., and Anne Harrington, eds. 2001. *Visions of Compassion: Western Scientists and Tibetan Buddhists Examine Human Nature.* New York: Oxford University Press.

Davidson, Richard J., and Antoine Lutz. 2008. "Buddha's Brain: Neuroplasticity and Meditation." *IEEE Signal Processing Magazine* 25 (1): 176–74.

Diamond, Jared. 2012. *The World until Yesterday: What We Can Learn from Traditional Societies.* New York: Viking.

Diener, E., and Martin E. Seligman. 2002. "Very Happy People." *Psychological Science* 13 (1): 81–84.

Duran, Eduardo, and Bonnie Duran. 1995. *Native American Postcolonial Psychology.* Albany: State University of New York (SUNY) Press.

Ehrenreich, Barbara, and Deirdre English. 1978. *For Her Own Good: 150 Years of the Experts' Advice to Women.* Garden City, N.Y.: Anchor Press.

Ellis, Albert. 1993a. "Changing Rational-Emotive Therapy (RET) to Rational Emotive Behavior Therapy (REBT)." *Behavior Therapist* 16: 257–58.

———. 1993b. "Fundamentals of Rational-emotive Therapy for the 1990s." In *Innovations in Rational-Emotive Therapy,* edited by W. Dryden & L. K. Hill, 1–32. Thousand Oaks, Calif.: Sage.

Erikson, Erik. 1950. *Childhood and Society.* New York: W. W. Norton.

———. 1969. *Gandhi's Truth: On the Origins of Militant Nonviolence.* New York: W. W. Norton.

———. 1987. *Childhood and Society.* Extended version with new chapters on the ninth stage of development by Joan Erikson. New York: W. W. Norton.

Erikson, Joan. 2010. *On Old Age I: A Conversation with Joan Erikson at 90.* Video file. Recorded July 13. www.youtube.com/watch?v=00DUXNQLAjQ.

———. 2012. *On Old Age II: A Conversation with Joan Erikson at 92.* Video file. Recorded July 19. www.youtube.com/watch?v=158CneVeJkk.

Ermine, Willie. 1995. "Aboriginal Epistemology." In *First Nations Education in Canada: The Circle Unfolds,* edited by M. Battiste and J. Barman, 101–12. Vancouver: University of British Columbia Press.

Ermine, Willie, Raven Sinclair, and Bonnie Jeffery. 2004. *The Ethics of Research Involving Indigenous Peoples.* Report of the Indigenous Peoples' Health Research Centre to the Intergency Advisory Panel on Research Ethics. http://iphrc.ca/pub/documents/ethics_review_iphrc.pdf.

Estrada, Alvaro. 1981. *Maria Sabina: Her Life and Chants.* Santa Barbara, Calif.: Ross-Erikson.

Evans-Wentz, W. Y., trans. 1927. *The Tibetan Book of the Dead.* London: Oxford Press.

Fanon, Frantz. 1965. *The Wretched of the Earth.* New York: Grove Press.

First Nations University of Canada. "Who We Are: Vision and Mission." https://fnuniv.ca/overview.

Fox, Dennis, Isaac Prilleltensky, and Stephanie Austin, eds. 2009. *Critical Psychology: An Introduction.* 2nd ed. Thousand Oaks, Calif.: Sage.

Freedman, Estelle. 2002. *No Turning Back: The History of Feminism and the Future of Women.* New York: Ballantine Books.

Freire, Paulo. 1968. *Pedagogy of the Oppressed.* New York: Seabury Press.

———. 1970. *Cultural Action for Freedom.* Harvard Educational Review. Monograph Series. Cambridge, Mass.: Harvard Graduate School of Education.

Freud, Sigmund. (1900) 1955. *The Interpretation of Dreams.* Translated by James Strachey. New York: Basic Books.

———. (1905) 2000. *Three Essays on the Theory of Sexuality.* Translated by James Strachey. New York: Basic Books.

———. (1923) 2010. *The Ego and the Id.* Seattle, Wash.: Pacific Publishing Studio.

Fuller, Buckminster. 1963. *Ideas and Integrities.* New York: Macmillan.

Gabriel Dumont Institute. 2010. Biographical portrait of Rose Fleury, Order of Gabriel Dumont Silver Awards Ceremony, Saskatoon, SK, November 19, 2010.

Galanter, Marc, and Herbert O. Kleber, eds. 2008. *Textbook of Substance Abuse Treatment.* 4th ed. Washington, DC: American Psychiatric Press.

García, Melinda A. 2014. "Implications of the Society of Indian Psychologists' (SIP) Commentary on the APA Code of Ethics Are Many, Broad and

Deep." Part 1 of 3. *Communiqué News Journal*. APA Office of Ethnic Minority Affairs. www.apa.org/pi/oema/resources/communique/2014/12/indian-psychologists-ethics.aspx.

———. 2015a. "Cultural Humility: Process and Content of the SIP Commentary on the APA Code of Ethics." Part 2 of 3. *Communiqué News Journal*. APA Office of Ethnic Minority Affairs.

———. 2015b. "Who Would Have Thought? Similarities in the Findings of the SIP Commentary and the Hoffman Report." Part 3 of 3. *Communiqué News Journal*. APA Office of Ethnic Minority Affairs.

García, Melinda A., and Melissa Tehee (eds). 2014. "Society of Indian Psychologists Commentary on the American Psychological Association's Ethical Principles of Psychologists and Code of Conduct." Society of Indian Psychologists. Retrieved from www.aiansip.org/commentary.html.

Gardner, Howard. 1999. *Intelligence Reframed: Multiple Intelligences for the 21st Century*. New York: Basic Books.

———. 2011. *Frames of Mind: The Theory of Multiple Intelligences*. 3rd ed. New York: Basic Books.

Gazzaniga, Michael, and Todd F. Heatherton. 2015. *Psychological Science*. 5th ed. New York: W. W. Norton.

Gergen, Kenneth J. 2009. *Relational Being: Beyond Self and Community*. New York: Oxford University Press.

———. 2015a. *An Invitation to Social Construction*. 3rd ed. Thousand Oaks, Calif.: Sage.

———. 2015b. "Multi-Being: Post-Structuralism, Psychodynamics, and Personal Identity." Paper in symposium, American Psychological Association Annual Convention, Toronto.

Gilligan, Carol. 1982. *In a Different Voice: Psychological Theory and Women's Development*. Cambridge, Mass.: Harvard University Press.

Giroux, Henry. 2011. *On Critical Pedagogy*. New York: Continuum Press.

Goleman, Daniel. 1995. *Emotional Intelligence: Why It Can Matter More Than IQ*. New York: Bantam Books.

———. 1996. *The Meditative Mind: The Varieties of Meditative Experience*, New York: Tarcher.

———. 2013. *Focus: The Hidden Driver of Excellence*. New York: Harper.

———. 2015. *A Force for Good: The Dalai Lama's Vision for Our World*. New York: Bantam.

Goleman, Daniel, and Richard Davidson. 2017. *Altered Traits: Science Reveals*

How Meditation Changes Your Mind, Brain and Body. New York: Avery.

Goleman, Daniel, and Kathleen Riordan Speeth, eds. 1982. *The Essential Psychotherapies: Theory and Practice by the Masters*. New York: New American Library.

Gone, Joseph P. 2008. "The Pisimweyapiy Counseling Centre: Paving the Red Road to Wellness in Northern Manitoba." In *Aboriginal Healing in Canada: Studies in Therapeutic Meaning and Practice,* edited by James B. Waldram. Ottawa: Aboriginal Healing Foundation.

———. 2009. "Psychotherapy and Traditional Healing for American Indians." *The Counseling Psychologist* 38 (2): 166–235.

Gonzales, Virginia. 1988. "Mexican Women and Migration: Implications for Mental Health." Doctoral dissertation, Harvard University, Cambridge, Mass.

Gonzalez Ortega, Carmen Ada. 1991. "Synergy in the Classroom: Explorations in 'Education as Transformation' with Puerto Rican Children and Their Teacher." Doctoral dissertation, Harvard University, Cambridge, Mass.

Grainger-Monsen, Maren, and Julia Haslett, producers/directors. 2005. *Hold Your Breath*. Film. Brooklyn, N.Y.: Icarus Films.

Grainger-Monsen, Maren, and Stephen Murphy-Shigematsu. 2011. "Worlds Apart in Explanatory Models of Illness and Health." In *The Picture of Health: Medical Ethics and the Movies*, edited by Henri Colt, Silvia Quadrelli, and Lester Friedman. New York: Oxford University Press.

Grande, Sandy. 2003. "Whitestream Feminism and the Colonialist Project: A Review of Contemporary Feminist Pedagogy and Praxis." *Educational Theory* 53 (3): 329–46.

Gray, Jacque, and Melinda García. 2011. Letter to David Kupfer, MD, chair, DSM 5 Task Force, on behalf of Society of Indian Psychologists, July 18.

Green, Elmer, and Alyce Green. 1977. *Beyond Biofeedback*. New York: Knoll Publishing.

Green, Joyce, ed. 2007. *Making Space for Indigenous Feminism*. Halifax, NS: Fernwood Press.

Griffiths, R., M. Johnson, W. Richards, B. Richards, U. McCann, and R. Jesse. 2011. "Psilocybin Occasioned Mystical-Type Experiences: Immediate and Persisting Dose-Related Effects." *Psychopharmacology* (Berl) 218 (4): 649–65.

Griffiths, Roland R., and Charles S. Grob. 2010. "Hallucinogens as Medicine." *Scientific American,* December, 77–79.

Gurdjieff, G. I. (1950). 1999. *Beelzebub's Tales to His Grandson: All and Everything*. New York: Penguin Books.

———. (1963). 2010. *Meetings with Remarkable Men.* New York: Penguin Books.

———. (1974). 1999. *Life Is Real Only Then, When "I Am."* New York: Penguin Books.

Guthrie, Robert V. 2003. *Even the Rat Was White: A Historical View of Psychology.* Boston: Allyn and Bacon.

Hampton, Eber. 1988. "Toward a Redefinition of American Indian/Alaska Native Education." Doctoral dissertation, Harvard University, Cambridge, Mass.

Hampton, Mary, Kim McKay-McNabb, Sherry Farrell-Racette, and Norma Jean Byrd. 2007. "Elders as Healers: Saskatchewan Elders Speak about Sexual Health." In *Cultural Healing and Belief Systems,* edited by James Pappas, William Smythe, and Angelina Baydala. Calgary, AB: Detselig Enterprises.

Hampton, Mary, Angelina Baydala, Carrie Bourassa, Kim McNabb, C. Placsko, Ken Goodwill, and Betty McKenna, producers. 2005. *Completing the Circle: Healing Words Spoken to Aboriginal Families about End of Life.* Video. Regina, SK: University of Regina, Luther College Community Psychology Research.

Harding, S. 2010. "The Hidden Curriculum in Medical Education." 7th Annual Public Lecture, sponsored by the University of Saskatchewan Process Philosophy Research Unit, Saskatoon, SK.

Harris, Benjamin. 1997. "Repoliticizing the History of Psychology." In Critical Psychology: An Introduction, edited by Dennis Fox and Isaac Prilleltensky. Thousand Oaks, Calif.: Sage.

Hart, Michael Anthony. 2002. *Seeking "Mino-Pimatisiwin": An Approach to Helping.* Halifax, NS: Fernwood Publishing.

Heavy Head, Ryan, and Narcisse Blood. 2011. "Kaahsinnooniksi: If the Land Could Speak" and "'Naamitapiikoan' Missed-Place: Blackfoot Influences on Abraham Maslow." Lectures sponsored by the Center for Cross-Cultural Research, Western Washington University, Bellingham, October 13–14.

Herman, Louis G. 2013. *Future Primal: How Our Wilderness Origins Show Us the Way Forward.* San Francisco: New World Library.

Hitchcock, Robert, Kazunobu Ikeya, Megan Biesele, and Richard B. Lee, eds. 2006. *Updating the San: Image and Reality of an African People in the 21st Century.* Senrie Ethnological Studies 70. Osaka, Japan: Senri Ethnological Studies.

Holloway, Wendy. 1989. *Subjectivity and Method in Psychology: Gender, Meaning and Science.* Newbury Park, Calif.: Sage.

hooks, bell. 1988. *Talking Back: Thinking Feminist, Thinking Black.* Toronto: Between the Lines.

———. 2000. *Feminism Is for Everybody: Passionate Politics*. Cambridge, Mass.: South End Press.

Humphreys, Keith, and Julian Rappaport. 1994. "Researching Self-Help/Mutual Aid Groups and Organizations: Many Roads, One Journey." *Applied and Preventative Psychology* 3: 217–31.

Huxley, Aldous. 1954. *The Doors of Perception*. New York: Harper.

Inman, A. 2008. "Race and Culture in Supervision: Challenges and Opportunities." Paper presented at 116th American Psychological Association Conference, Boston.

James, William. (1902) 1985. *The Varieties of Religious Experience*. Reprint, Cambridge, Mass.: Harvard University Press.

Johnson, Allan G. 1997. *The Gender Knot: Unraveling Our Patriarchal Legacy*. Philadelphia: Temple University Press.

Juarez, J. A., K. Marvel, K. L. Brezinski, C. Glazner, M. M. Towbin, and S. Lawton. 2006. "Bridging the Gap: A Curriculum to Teach Residents Cultural Humility." *Family Medicine* 38 (2): 97–102.

Jung, Carl Gustav 1965. *Memories, Dreams, Reflections*. New York: Vantage.

———. 2009. *The Red Book: Liber Novus*. Edited and with an introduction by Sonu Shamdasani. New York: W. W. Norton. (Note: a Reader's Edition of the *Red Book* was published in 2012 and contains the entire text but without the many striking illuminations enhancing the original edition.)

Kabat-Zinn, Jon. 2005. *Wherever You Go, There You Are*. Revised ed. New York: Hatchett Books.

———. 2013. *Full Catastrophic Living: Using the Wisdom of Your Body and Mind to Face Stress, Pain and Illness*. Revised ed. New York: Bantam.

Kamens, Sarah. 2010. "Controversial Issues for the Future DSM-V." *Society for Humanistic Psychology Newsletter,* January.

Katz, Alfred H. 1993. *Self-Help in America: A Social Movement Perspective*. New York: Twayne.

Katz, Richard. 1973. *Preludes to Growth: An Experiential Approach*. New York: Free Press.

———. 1981. "Education as Transformation: Becoming a Healer among the !Kung and Fijians." *Harvard Educational Review* 51 (1): 57–78.

———. 1982a. *Boiling Energy: Community Healing among the Kalahari Kung*. Cambridge, Mass.: Harvard University Press.

———. 1982b. "The Utilization of Traditional Healing Systems." *American Psychologist* 3716: 715–16.

———. 1983/84. Empowerment and Synergy: Towards Expanding Community Healing Resources." *Prevention in Human Services* 3 (2/3): 201–25.

———. 1999. *The Straight Path of the Spirit: Ancestral Wisdom and Healing Traditions in Fiji*. Rochester, Vt.: Inner Traditions.

———. 2009. "This Yuu'yaraq Project Is a Step Towards Healing": An Evaluation of the Yuu'yaraq project, Emmonak, Alaska." Research report prepared for Center for Native Health Research, University of Alaska, Fairbanks.

———. 2012a. "Breaking Psychology's Stranglehold over Therapeutic Services to Indigenous Peoples." Chapter ten in *Synergy, Healing, and Empowerment: Insights from Cultural Diversity,* edited by R. Katz and S. Murphy-Shigematsu. Calgary, AB: Brush Education.

———. 2012b. "Education as Transformation: An Approach to Training Healers." Chapter six in *Synergy, Healing, and Empowerment: Insights from Cultural Diversity,* edited by R. Katz and S. Murphy-Shigematsu.

———. 2012c. "Synergy and Empowerment: Renewing and Expanding the Community's Healing Resources." Chapter one in *Synergy, Healing, and Empowerment: Insights from Cultural Diversity,* edited by R. Katz and S. Murphy-Shigematsu. Calgary, AB: Brush Education.

Katz, Richard, Megan Biesele, and =Oma Djo. 2003. "Healing Makes Our Hearts Happy: Ju/'hoan Spirituality and the Struggle for Self-Determination." *Cultural Survival Quarterly.*

Katz, Richard, Megan Biesele, and Verna St. Denis. 1997. *Healing Makes Our Hearts Happy: Spirituality and Cultural Transformation among the Kalahari Ju/'hoansi*. Rochester, Vt.: Inner Traditions.

Katz, Richard, and Rachel Craig. 1987. "Community Healing: The Rich Resource of Tradition." *The Exchange* 8 (2). University of Alaska, Fairbanks.

———. 1988. "Health Is More Than Not Being Sick." *The Exchange* 9 (2). University of Alaska, Fairbanks.

Katz, Richard, and David Kolb. 1972. "Challenge to Grow: The Outward Bound Approach." In *Curriculum and the Cultural Revolution*, edited by D. Purpel and M. Belanger.

Katz, Richard, and Stephen Murphy-Shigematsu. 2012a. *Synergy, Healing, and Empowerment: Insights from Cultural Diversity*. Calgary, AB: Brush Education.

———. 2012b. "The Experience of Vulnerability: A Key to the Education of Health Professionals." Chapter seven in *Synergy, Healing, and Empowerment: Insights from Cultural Diversity,* edited by R. Katz and S. Murphy-Shigematsu gary, AB: Brush Education.

———. 2012c. "Will There Always Be Enough? Self-Help Groups as a Renewable Healing Resource." Chapter thirteen in *Synergy, Healing, and Empowerment: Insights from Cultural Diversity,* edited by R. Katz and S. Murphy-Shigematsu. Calgary, AB: Brush Education.

Katz, Richard, Danny Musqua, and Tania Lafontaine. 2012. "Training Culturally Sensitive Counsellors: A Case Study of the Masters of Aboriginal Social Work (MASW) Program." Chapter nine in *Synergy, Healing, and Empowerment: Insights from Cultural Diversity,* edited by Richard Katz and Stephen Murphy-Shigematsu. Calgary, AB: Brush Education.

Katz, Richard, and Edward Rolde. 1981. "Community Alternatives to Psychotherapy." *Psychotherapy: Theory, Research and Practice* 18(3): 365–74.

Katz, Richard, Niti Salloway, and Jack Salafia. 1983. "Education through Community Generated Interactive Video: A Contribution to Family Planning, Health Care and Rural Development in India." Unpublished manuscript.

Katz, Richard, and Niti Seth. 2012. "Synergy and Healing: A Perspective on Western Health Care." Chapter 2 in *Synergy, Healing, and Empowerment: Insights from Cultural Diversity,* edited by Richard Katz and Stephen Murphy-Shigematsu. Calgary, AB: Brush Education.

Katz, Richard, and Verna St. Denis. 1991. "Teacher as Healer." *Journal of Indigenous Studies* 2 (2).

Kawagley, Angayuqaq Oscar. 2006. *A Yupiaq Worldview: A Pathway to Ecology and Spirit.* 2nd ed. Long Grove, Ill.: Waveland Press.

Kegan, Robert. 1982. *The Evolving Self: Problem and Process in Human Development.* Cambridge, Mass.: Harvard University Press.

King, Jeff. 2012. "A Critique of Western Psychology from an American Indian Psychologist." In "Native American Culture and the Western Psyche: A Bridge Between," ed. Jerome Bernstein, special issue, *Spring: A Journal of Archetype and Culture* 87: 37–59.

King, Jeff, Jerome Bernstein, Gayle Morse, and Sidney Ann Stone Brown. 2016. "North American Indigenous Influences on Psychology: Yurok and Lakota Influences on Erikson; Taos Pueblo on Jung; The Robber's Cave Experiment; and Blackfoot Influences on Maslow." Presentation at the American Psychological Convention, Denver Colorado, USA, August 4–7.

King, Thomas. 2003. *The Truth about Stories: A Native Narrative.* Toronto: House of Anansi Press.

Kino-nda-niimi Collective, The, ed. 2014. *The Winter We Danced: Voices from the Past, the Future, and the Idle No More Movement.* Winnipeg, Manitoba: ARP Books.

Kirmayer, Laurence J., and Gail Valaskakis. 2008. *The Mental Health of Aboriginal People.* Vancouver: University of British Columbia Press.

Kluckhohn, Clyde, Henry Murray, and David M. Schneider, eds. 1953. *Personality: In Nature, Society, and Culture.* New York: Knopf.

Knight, Diane. 2001. *The Seven Fires: Teachings of the Bear Clan as Recounted by Dr. Danny Musqua.* Muskoday First Nations: Many Worlds Publishing.

Koss-Chioino, Joan D. 2006. "Spiritual Transformation, Ritual Healing and Altruism." *Journal of Religion and Science* 41 (4): 877–92. doi: 10.1111/j.1467-9744.2006.00785.x.

———. 2010. Introduction in *Special Issue: Do Spirits Exist? Ways to Know; Anthropology and Humanism* 35 (2): 131–41. Compiled and edited by J. Koss-Chioino.

Koss-Chioino, Joan D., and Philip Hefner, eds. 2006. *Spiritual Transformation and Healing: Anthropological, Theological, Neuroscience and Clinical Perspectives.* Lanham, Md.: Altamira Press.

Krippner, Stanley, Etzel Cardena, and Steven Jay Lynn. 2014. *Varieties of Anomalous Experience.* 2nd ed. Washington, D.C.: American Psychological Association.

Kuhn, Thomas S. 1970. *The Structure of Scientific Revolutions.* 2nd ed. Chicago: University of Chicago Press.

Kyrous, Elaina M., and Keith Humphreys. 2002. "Research on Self-Help and Mutual Aid Support Groups." *PsychCentral.* Retrieved from http://psychcentral.com/library/support_groups.htm.

Lafontaine, Tania. 2004. "Igniting the Warrior Spirit: A Search for Meaningful Work with Indigenous Youth." Master's thesis for Aboriginal social work degree, First Nations University of Canada, Saskatoon, SK.

LaRocque, Emma. 1996. "The Colonization of a Native Woman Scholar." In *Women of the First Nations: Power, Wisdom and Strength*, edited by Christine Miller and Patricia Marie Chuchryk, 11–18. Winnipeg: University of Manitoba Press.

———. 2010. *When the Other Is Me: Native Resistance Discourse 1850–1990.* Winnipeg: University of Manitoba Press.

Leary, Timothy. 1998. *Turn On, Tune In, Drop Out.* Berkeley, Calif.: Ronin.

———. 1999. *The Politics of Ecstasy.* Berkeley, Calif..: Ronin.

Leary, Timothy, Ralph Metzner, and Richard Alpert. (1964) 2000. *The*

Psychedelic Experience: A Manual Based on the Tibetan Book of the Dead. New York: Citadel.

Leary, Timothy, Ralph Metzner, Madison Presnell, Gunther Weil, Ralph Schwitzgebel, and Sarah Kinne. 1965. "A New Behavior Change Pattern Using Psilocybin." *Psychotherapy: Theory, Research and Practice* 2 (2): 61–72.

Lee, Eunjung. 2005. "Revisioning Cultural Competencies in Clinical Social Work Practice." *Families in Society* 91 (3): 272–79, 2010e.

Lee, Mary. 2006a. *Cree (Nehiyawak) Teaching Elder: Mary Lee.* Four Directions Teachings.com. Retrieved from www.fourdirectionsteachings.com /transcripts/cree.html.

———. 2006b. *Cree/biograhy, Mary Lee.* Four Directions Teachings.com. Retrieved from www.fourdirectionsteachings.com/cree_bio.html.

Lee, Richard B. 1967. "Trance Cure of the !Kung Bushmen." *Natural History,* November, 30–37.

———. 1979. *The !Kung San: Men, Women and Work in a Foraging Society.* Cambridge, UK: Cambridge University Press.

———. 2011. "The !Kung and I: Reflections on My Life and Times with the Ju/'hoansi." General Anthropology Division Keynote Address, November 18, 2011. Presented at the American Anthropological Association Annual Meeting, Montreal, Quebec.

———. 2012. *The Dobe Ju/'hoansi.* 4th ed. Belmont, Calif.: Wadsworth.

Lee, Richard B., and Irven DeVore, eds. 1968. *Man the Hunter.* Chicago: Aldine.

———. 1976. *Kalahari Hunter-Gatherers: Studies of the !Kung San and Their Neighbors.* Cambridge, Mass.: Harvard University Press.

Lightning, Walter C. 1992. "Compassionate Mind: Implications of a Text Written by Elder Louis Sunchild." *Canadian Journal of Native Education* 19 (2): 215–53.

Longden, Eleanor. 2013. "The Voices in My Head." TED talk video. Recorded August 8. www.youtube.com/watch?v=syjEN3peCJw.

Luke, Howard. 1998. *My Own Trail.* Edited by Jan Steinbright Jackson. Fairbanks: Alaska Native Knowledge Network.

Markus, Hazel Rose. 2015. "Psychology: Still Made in the USA." Paper presented in "Conversation Hour: Indigenous Culture and Scientific Psychology: Toward a Dialogue," co-chaired by L. Sundararajan and R. Shweder. American Psychological Association Annual Convention, Toronto.

Marshall, John. 1970. "*N!owa T'ama*": *The Melon Tossing Game.* Film. Watertown, Mass.: Documentary Educational Resources.

Marshall, Lorna. 1969. "The Medicine Dance of the !Kung Bushmen." *Africa* 39 (4): 347–81.

———. 1976. *The !Kung of Nyae Nyae*. Cambridge, Mass.: Harvard University Press.

Martin-Hill, D. 2003. "She No Speaks and Other Colonial Constructs of 'The traditional Woman.'" In *Strong Women Stories: Native Vision and Community Survival*, edited by Kim Anderson and Bonita Lawrence. Toronto: Sumach Press.

Maslow, Abraham. 1954. *Motivation and Personality*. New York: Harper and Row.

———. 1962. *Toward a Psychology of Being*. New York: Van Nostrand.

———. 1963. "The Need to Know and the Fear of Knowing." *Journal of General Psychology* 68 (1): 111–25.

———. 1971. *The Farther Reaches of Human Nature*. New York: Viking Press.

Maslow, Abraham, and John J. Honigmann. 1970. "Synergy: Some Notes of Ruth Benedict." *American Anthropologist* 72 (2): 320–33.

Maslow, Abraham, Richard Lowry, Bertha Maslow, and J. Freedman. 1982. *The Journals of Abraham Maslow*. New York: Penguin.

Mason, Randolph. 2000. "Healing of Aboriginal Offenders: A Comparison between Cognitive-Behavioral Treatment and the Traditional Aboriginal Sweat Lodge Ceremony." Master's thesis, Department of Psychology, University of Saskatchewan.

Master of Aboriginal Social Work. n.d. Program brochure. Saskatoon, SK: First Nations University of Canada.

Master of Aboriginal Social Work. n.d. Student guide. Saskatoon, SK: School of Indian Social Work/First Nations University of Canada.

Matsumoto, David, and Linda Juang. 2007. *Culture and Psychology*. 3rd ed. Belmont, Calif.: Wadsworth.

McCormick, Rod. 2005. "The Healing Path: What Can Counselors Learn from Aboriginal People about How to Heal." In *Integrating Traditional Healing Practices into Counseling and Psychotherapy*, edited by Roy Moodley and William West. Thousand Oaks, Calif.: Sage.

McHenry, Stacey. 2016. "Sliding between the 'World You Know and a World of My Own': The Lived Experiences of Women with Bipolar Disorders." Doctoral dissertation proposal, Psychology Department, University of Saskatchewan, Saskatoon.

McKay-McNabb, Kim. 2011. "Completing the Circle: Healing Words Spoken by Aboriginal Elders." Presentation to the Clinical Psychology Case Seminar,

Department of Psychology, University of Saskatchewan, Saskatoon, SK, February 1, 2011.

Meza, Albert. 1988. "Study of Acculturation of Chicano Students at Harvard College: Evidence for the Collectivist Ego." Doctoral dissertation, Harvard University, Cambridge, Mass.

Michell, Herman. 1999. "Pakitinasowin: Tobacco Offerings in Exchange for Stories and the Ethic of Reciprocity in First Nations Research." Retrieved from www .sifc.edu/Indian%20Studies/IndigenousThought/fall99/tobacco.htm.

———. 2012. "The Canoe Trip: A Northern Cree Metaphor for Conducting Research." *in education* 18 (1). http://ineducation.ca/ineducation/article /view/4/489.

Mihesuah, Devon A. 2003. *Indigenous American Women: Decolonization, Empowerment, Activism*. Lincoln: University of Nebraska Press.

Miller, Lisa. 2013. Lisa Miller talk at TEDx Teachers College. Video file. Recorded August 19. www.youtube.com/watch?v=mhu5rPf2FDI.

Miller, Lisa, ed. 2012. *The Oxford University Press Handbook of Psychology and Spirituality*. New York: Oxford University Press.

Misra, Girishwar, and Anand Prakash, eds. 2012. "Kenneth J. Gergen and Social Constructionism." *Psychological Studies* 57 (2): 121–25. www.researchgate .net/publication/257791974_Kenneth_J_Gergen_and_Social _Constructionism. doi: 10.1007/s12646-012-0151-0.

Moghaddam, Fathali. 2007. *Multiculturalism in Intergroup Relations: Psychological Implications for Democracy in Global Context*. Washington, DC: American Psychological Association.

Mohatt, Gerald, and Joseph Eagle Elk. 2000. *The Price of a Gift: A Lakota Healer's Story*. Lincoln: University of Nebraska Press.

Monkman, Lenard. 2015. "Indigenous Boys and Men at High Risk of Being Victims of Violence." CBC News, November 29. www.cbc.ca/news /indigenous/indigenous-boys-and-men-at-high-risk-of-being-victims-of -violence-1.3341222.

Moodley, Roy, and William West, eds. 2005. *Integrating Traditional Healing Practices into Counseling and Psychotherapies*. Thousand Oaks, Calif.: Sage.

Moos, Rudolf, and Christine Timko. 2008. "Outcome Research on Twelve-Step and Other Self-Help Programs." In *Textbook of Substance Abuse Treatment*, edited by M. Galanter and H. O. Kleber. Washington, DC: American Psychiatric Press.

Moraga, Cherríe, and Gloria E. Anzaldua, eds. 1983. *This Bridge Called My*

Back: Writings by Radical Women of Color. Latham, N.Y.: Kitchen Table, Women of Color Press.

Morimoto, Kiyo. 1993. "Notes on the Context for Learning." *Harvard Educational Review* 43 (2): 245–57.

Murphy-Shigematsu, Stephen. 1986. "The Voices of Amerasians: Ethnicity, Identity, and Empowerment in Interracial Japanese Americans." Doctoral dissertation, Harvard University, Cambridge, Mass.

———. 2002. *Multicultural Encounters: Case Narratives of a Counseling Practice*. New York: Teachers College Press.

———. 2009. "Teaching Cross-cultural Competence through Narrative." *Family Medicine* 41 (9): 622–24.

———. 2010a. "Microaggressions by Supervisors of Color." *Training and Education in Professional Psychology* 4 (1): 16–18.

———. 2010b. "Respect and Empathy in Teaching and Learning cultural Medicine." *Journal of General Internal Medicine* (Special Issue on Health Disparities Education) 25 (2): 194–95.

———. 2012. "A Narrative Approach to Transformational Education: Cultural Training for Health Care Providers." Chapter eight in *Synergy, Healing, and Empowerment: Insights from Cultural Diversity,* edited by R. Katz and S. Murphy-Shigematsu. *Calgary, AB: Brush Education.*

———. 2018. *From Mindfulness to Heartfulness: Transforming Self and Society with Compassion*. Oakland, Calif.: Barrett-Koehler.

Murray, Henry A. 1938. *Explorations in Personality: A Clinical and Experimental Study of Fifty Men of College Age*. New York: Oxford Press.

Murray, Henry A., and Edwin S. Shneidman. 1981. *Endeavors in Psychology: Selections from the Personology of Henry A. Murray*. New York: Harper & Row.

Musqua, Danny, Mary Lee, Richard Katz, and Tania Lafontaine. 2010. Remarks at a roundtable on Native American culture, gender, and healing, sponsored by the Institute for Research on Women and Gender, University of Michigan, Ann Arbor, October 14–15.

Nayacakalou, R. 1975. *Leadership in Fiji*. Oxford: Oxford University Press.

———. 1978. *Tradition and Change in the Fijian Village*. Suva, Fiji: University of the South Pacific.

Nolen-Hoeksama, Susan, Barbara Fredrickson, Geoffrey Loftus, and Willem Wagenaar. 2016. *Atkinson and Hilgard's Introduction to Psychology*. 16th ed. Boston: Cengage Learning.

Núñez-Molina, M. 1987. "Desarrollo del médium: The Process of Becoming a Healer in Puerto Rican Espiritismo." Doctoral dissertation, Harvard University, Cambridge, Mass.

Ondaatje, Michael. 2008. *Divisadero.* New York: Vintage.

Pahnke, Walter. 1963. "Drugs and Mysticism: An Analysis of the Relationship between Psychedelic Drugs and the Mystical Consciousness." Doctoral dissertation, Harvard University, Cambridge, Mass.

Paloutzian, Raymond, and Crystal L. Park, eds. 2005. *Handbook of the Psychology of Religion and Spirituality.* New York: Guilford Press.

Pappas, James D., William Smythe, and Angelina Baydala, eds. 2007. *Cultural Healing and Belief Systems.* Calgary, AB: Detselig Enterprises.

Pedersen, Paul. n.d. "Addressing Cultural Complexities in Practice: A Framework for Clinicians and Counselors." Forthcoming in *Contemporary Psychology.*

———. 1997. *Culture-Centered Counseling and Interviewing Skills.* Westport, Conn.: Greenwood/Praeger.

Pedersen, Paul, Walter Lonner, Juris Draguns, Joseph Trimble, and Maria Sharron-del Rio, eds. 2015. *Counseling across Cultures,* 7th ed. Los Angeles, Calif.: Sage.

Polanyi, Michael. 1958. *Personal Knowledge: Towards a Post-critical Philosophy.* Chicago: University of Chicago Press.

Poonwassie, A., and A. Charter. 2001. "An Aboriginal Worldview of Helping: Empowering Approaches." *Canadian Journal of Counselling* 35 (1): 63–73.

Price, M. 2011. "Searching for Meaning." *APA Monitor* (November 2011), Washington, D.C.: American Psychological Association.

Prilleltensky, Isaac, and Geoffrey Nelson. 2009. "Community Psychology: Reclaiming Social Justice." In *Critical Psychology: An Introduction,* 2nd ed., edited by Dennis Fox, Isaac Prilleltensky, and Stephanie Austin. Thousand Oaks, Calif.: Sage.

Ram Dass. 1971. *Be Here Now.* Sante Fe, N.M.: Lama Foundation.

Rappaport, Julian. 1981. "In Praise of Paradox: A Social Policy of Empowerment over Prevention." *American Journal of Community Psychology* 9 (1).

———. 1985. "The Power of Empowerment Language." *Social Policy.*

Rappaport, Julian, and Edward Seidman, eds. 2000. *Handbook of Community Psychology.* New York: Plenum/Kluwer.

Rappaport, Roy. 1978. "Adaptation and the Structure of Rituals." In *Human Behaviour and Adaptation,* edited by N. Blurton-Jones and V. Reynolds. New York: John Wiley and Sons.

Raskin, N., C. Rogers, and M. Witty. 2010. "Person-Centered Therapy." In

Current Psychotherapies, edited by Raymond Corsini and Danny Wedding. Belmont, Calif.: Brooks-Cole.

Ravuvu, Asesela. 1983. *Vaka i Taukei: The Fijian Way of Life.* Suva, Fiji: Institute of Pacific Studies, University of the South Pacific.

———. 1987. *The Fijian Ethos.* Suva, Fiji: Institute of Pacific Studies at the University of the South Pacific.

Reichmann, Rebecca. 1985. "'Consciencia' and Development: 'Tricicleros' Grassroots Labor Organization in the Dominican Republic." Doctoral dissertation, Harvard University, Cambridge, Mass.

Renee, L. 2011. "The Fast Track to Change." *Boston Globe,* July 30, 2011.

Rickel, Annette U. 1987. "The 1965 Swampscott Conference and Future Topics for Community Psychology." *American Journal of Community Psychology* 15 (5): 511–13.

Ring, David C., James H. Herndon, and Gregg S. Meyer. 2010. "A 65-Year-Old Woman with an Incorrect Operation in the Left Hand, Case 34-2010." *New England Journal of Medicine (Case records of the Massachusetts General Hospital)* 363: 1950–57. November 11, 2010,

Rizzuto, Ana-Maria. 1981. *The Birth of the Living God: A Psychoanalytic Study.* Chicago: University of Chicago Press.

Robbins, Brent. 2011. "Open Letter to the DSM-5." www.ipetitions.com/petition /dsm5.

Robinson, Forrest. 1992. *Love's Story Told: A Life of Henry A. Murray.* Cambridge, Mass.: Harvard University Press.

Rogers, Carl. 1951. *Client-Centered Therapy.* Boston: Houghton-Mifflin.

———. 1979. *On Personal Power.* New York: Delacorte.

———. 1982. "The Characteristics of a Helping Relationship." In *The Essential Psychotherapies: Theory and Practice by the Masters,* edited by D. Goleman and K. Speeth. New York: New American Library.

Ross, Stephen, Anthony Bossis, Jeffrey Guss, et al. 2016. "Rapid and Sustained Symptom Reduction Following Psilocybin Treatment for Anxiety and Depression in Patients with Life-Threatening Cancer: A Randomized Controlled Trial." *Journal of Psychopharmacology* 30 (12): 1165–1180.

Ryan, William. 1971. *Blaming the Victim.* New York: Vintage.

Salovey, Peter, and John D. Mayer. 1989. "Emotional intelligence." *Imagination, Cognition and Personality* 9 (3): 185–211.

Salsman, John M., Tamara L. Brown, Emily H. Brechting, and Charles R. Carlson. 2005. "The Link between Religion and Spirituality and

Psychological Adjustment: The Mediating Role of Optimism and Social Support. *Personality and Social Psychology Bulletin* 31(4): 522–35.

Sarason, Seymour. 1977. *The Psychological Sense of Community: Prospects for a Community Psychology.* San Francisco: Jossey-Bass.

Saskatchewan Indian Cultural College. 1981. "The Tipi Poster." Curriculum Studies and Research, Federation of Saskatchewan Indians, Saskatoon, SK.

Schick, Carol, JoAnn Jaffe, and Ailsa M. Watkinson, eds. 2004. *Contesting Fundamentalisms.* Halifax, NS: Fernwood.

Schneider, Kirk. 2011. www.saybrook.edu/newexistentialists/posts/11-01-11-0.

Seth, Niti. 1987. "'Baira ni Vato'—Women's Talk: A Psychological Context for Exploring Fertility Options in an Indian Village." Doctoral dissertation, Harvard University, Cambridge, Mass.

Shah, A. 2011. "Health Care around the World." Global Issues. www.globalissues .org/article/774/health-care-around-the-world. Last updated September 22, 2011.

Shah, Fernaz. 1987. "Cross-Cultural Program Implementation: Case Studies of the Original Fountain House Model in New York and Its Implementation in Lahore, Pakistan." Doctoral dissertation, Harvard University, Cambridge, Mass.

Shweder, Richard. 2015. "Universalism without the Uniformity." Paper presented at Conversation Hour: Indigenous Culture and Scientific Psychology; Toward a Dialogue, APA Annual Convention, Toronto. L. Sundararajan and R. Shweder, cochairs.

Simonis, Jacqueline. 1985. "Synergy and the Education of Helpers: A New Community Psychology Approach to Counselor Training." Doctoral dissertation, Harvard University, Cambridge, Mass.

Smith, Linda Tuhiwai. 1999. *Decolonizing Methodologies: Research and Indigenous Peoples.* London: Zed Books.

Solway, Jacqueline, and Richard B. Lee. 1990. "Foragers, Genuine or Spurious?: Situating the Kalahari San in History." *Current Anthropology* 32: 106–46.

St. Denis, Verna. 1992. "Community-Based Participatory Research: Aspects of the Concept Relevant for practice." *Native Studies Review* 8 (2): 51–74.

———. 2004. "Real Indians: Cultural Revitalization and Fundamentalism in Aboriginal Education." In *Contesting Fundamentalisms*, edited by C. Schick, J. Jaffe, and A. M. Watkinson. Halifax, NS: Fernwood.

———. 2007a. "Aboriginal Education and Anti-racist Education: Building Alliance across Cultural and Racial Identity." *Canadian Journal of Education* 30 (4): 1068–92.

————. 2007b. "Feminism Is for Everybody: Aboriginal Women, Feminism and Diversity." In *Making Space for Indigenous Feminism*, edited by J. Green.

————. 2011. "Silencing Aboriginal Curricular Content and Perspectives: 'There Are Other Children Here.'" *Review of Education, Pedagogy, and Cultural Studies* 33 (4): 306–17.

Sternberg, Robert. 1985. *Beyond IQ: A Triarchic Theory of Intelligence*. New York: Cambridge University Press.

————. 2007. *Wisdom, Intelligence and Creativity Synthesized*. New York: Cambridge University Press.

Stonechild, Blair. 2016. *The Knowledge Seeker: Embracing Indigenous Spirituality*. Regina, SK: University of Regina Press.

Straits, K. J. E., D. M. Bird, E. Tsinajinnie, J. Espinoza, J. Goodkind, O. Spencer, N. Tafoya, C. Willging, and the Guiding Principles Workgroup. 2012. "Guiding Principles for Engaging in Research with Native American Communities, Version 1." UNM Center for Rural and Community Behavioral Health and Albuquerque Area Southwest Tribal Epidemiology Center.

Sue, Derald Wing, and David Sue. 2015. *Counseling the Culturally Diverse: Theory and Practice*. 7th ed. New York: Wiley.

Sundararajan, Louise. 2005. "Happiness Donut: A Confucian Critique of Positive Psychology." *Journal of Theoretical and Philosophical Psychology* 25 (1): 35–60.

————. 2015. *Understanding Emotion in Chinese Culture: Thinking Through Emotion*. New York: Springer.

Suzuki, D. T. 1948. *An Introduction to Zen Buddhism*. London: Rider and Company.

Tart, Charles. 2009. *The End of Materialism: How Evidence of the Paranormal Is Bringing Science and Spirit Together*. Oakland, Calif.: New Harbinger.

Taylor, Eugene. 1999. *Shadow Culture: Psychology and Spirituality in America*. New York: Counterpoint.

————. 2011. *William James on Consciousness beyond the Margins*. Princeton, N.J.: Princeton University Press.

Tervalon, Melanie, and Jan Murray-Garcia. 1998. "Cultural Humility versus Cultural Competence: A Critical Distinction in Defining Physician-Training Outcomes in Multicultural Education." *Journal of Health Care for the Poor and Underserved* 9(2): 17–25.

Trimble, Joseph E. 2010. "Bear Spends Time in Our Dreams Now: Magical Thinking and Cultural Empathy in Multicultural Counselling Theory and Practice." *Counselling Psychology Quarterly* 23:241–253. http://dx.doi.org/10.1080/ 09515070.2010.505735

Trimble, Joseph E., Jeff King, Dennis Norman, Dolores Subia Bigfoot, and Teresa D. LaFromboise. 2014. "North American Indian Mental Health." In *The Massachusetts General Hospital Textbook on Cultural Sensitivity and Diversity in Mental Health,* edited by Ranna Parekh and D. Dominguez, 119–138. New York: Springer Science/Business Media. http://dx.doi .org/10.1007/978-1-4614-8918-4_5

Turner, Tara J. 2011. "Re-searching Métis Identity: My Métis Family Story." Doctoral dissertation, University of Saskatchewan, Saskatoon.

Turner, Victor. 1969. *The Ritual Process.* Chicago: Aldine.

Turtle Island Support Group, Coalition for a Public Inquiry into Ipperwash, Friends of the Lubicon, Skwelkwek'welt Protection Centre, Sutikalh Camp, House of Smayusta, and Nuxalk Nation. 2002. "Report on Racial Discrimination Against Indigenous Peoples in Canada: Summary." www .turtleisland.org/news/cerd.pdf.

United Nations Permanent Forum on Indigenous Issues. n.d. "Indigenous Peoples, Indigenous Voices Factsheet." www.un.org/esa/socdev/unpfii /documents/5session_factsheet1.pdf.

Van Gennep, Arnold. 1960. *The Rites of Passage.* Chicago: University of Chicago Press.

Villegas, Malia, Sabrina Rak Neugebauer, and Kerry R. Venegas, eds. 2008. *Indigenous Knowledge and Education: Sites of Struggle, Strength and Survivance.* Cambridge, Mass.: Harvard Educational Press.

Wade, Carole, Carol Tavris, Deborah Saucier, and Lorin Elias. 2017. 6th Canadian ed. *Psychology.* Upper Saddle River, N.J.: Pearson.

Waldram, James B., ed. 2008. *Aboriginal Healing in Canada: Studies in Therapeutic Meaning and Practice.* Ottawa: Aboriginal Healing Foundation.

Watkins, Mary, and Helene Shulman. 2010. *Towards Psychologies of Liberation.* New York: Palgrave Press.

Watson, John B. 1928. *Behaviourism.* London: Kegan and Paul.

Watts, Alan. 1957. *The Way of Zen.* New York: Pantheon.

Weber-Pillwax, Cora. 2001. "What Is Indigenous Research?" *Canadian Journal of Native Education.* 25 (2): 166–74.

Welwood, John. 1983. "Vulnerability and Power in the Therapeutic Process." In *Awakening the Heart: East/West Approaches to Psychotherapy and the Healing Relationship,* edited by John Welwood. Boulder, Colo.: New Science Library.

Wertz, Frederick J., Kathy Charmaz, Linda M. McMullen, and Ruthellen

Josselson. 2011. *Five Ways of Doing Qualitative Analysis: Phenomenological Psychology, Grounded Theory, Discourse Analysis, Narrative Research, and Intuitive Inquiry.* New York: Guilford Press.

Wise, Tim. 2011. "White Like Me." Public lecture, Saskatoon, SK, March 17, 2011.

Wolfe, Alexander. 1988. *Earth Elder Stories.* Calgary, AB: Fifth House.

Worthington, Roger L., Angela M. Soth-McNotl, and Matthew V. Moreno. 2007. "Multicultural Counseling Competencies Research: A 20-Year Content Analysis." *Journal of Counseling Psychology* 5 (4): 351–61.

Zimbardo, Philip, Robert A. Johnson, and Vivian McCann. 2016. *Psychology: Core Concepts.* 8th ed. Upper Saddle River, N.J.: Pearson.

Index

Page references from text in boxes are indicated in **bold**; maps in ***bold italic***